A HISTORY OF THE WORLD IN

100

MONUMENTS

Sylvain Grossenbacher

Disclaimer

Although every effort has been made to ensure the accuracy of the information contained in this book, it is subject to change at any time for a variety of reasons, including commercial, political, economic and climatic. The author, editors and publisher accept no responsibility for any losses, problems or accidents arising from changes in this information.

Printed by lulu.com

First Printing Edition, 2024
ISBN 978-1-4457-8655-1

From the origins of the universe in the entrails of the Large Hadron Collider where the Big Bang is being studied at the CERN to the birth of the internet at that very same place, the story of human progress is intricately woven. Starting from the city of Geneva, let us embark on a captivating journey around the world, traversing through the ages and eras to discover a curated selection of 100 monuments that have left an indelible mark on the history of humanity.

This book is divided in six sections covering the most common periods of human history: the prehistory, the ancient history, the middle ages, the early modern times, the 19th century, and the 20th century. Each selected monument is an invitation to remember a specific event or era it is linked to, in the long and fascinating chronicle of mankind. While focusing on the course of historical events in the central part of each even page, an insert on the left-hand side highlights the monument main characteristics illustrated on odd pages.

These monuments are not merely physical structures, but embodiments of our collective human experience. Some stand out for their unparalleled beauty and architectural ingenuity, while others hold immense historical and sentimental value, reflecting the full spectrum of our species' triumphs and tribulations.

It is now time to start.
Get ready, fasten your seatbelts, and let's...

TABLE OF CONTENTS

PREHISTORY

01 Large Hadron Collider   12
02 Smithsonian Museum Of Natural History   14
03 National Museum of Ethiopia   16
04 Lascaux Caves   18

ANCIENT HISTORY

05 Ziggurat of Ur   22
06 Great Pyramid of Giza   24
07 Minoan Palace of Knossos   26
08 Ishtar Gate   28
09 Trojan horse   30
10 The Capitoline Wolf   32
11 Winged bulls of Khorsabad   34
12 Temple of Mahabodhi   36
13 Temple of Confucius   38
14 Persepolis   40
15 Marathon Mound   42
16 The Acropolis   44
17 Statue of the warrior on horseback   46
18 Great Wall of China   48
19 Archaeological site of Carthage   50
20 Temple of Caesar   52
21 Petra   54
22 Mausol. of Augustus   56
23 Christ the Redeemer   58
24 Western Wall   60
25 Ruins of Pompei   62

26 Column of Marcus Aurelius   64
27 Diocletian's Palace   66
28 Column of Constantine   68
29 Colosseum   70

MIDDLE AGES

30 Sigiriya Rock   74
31 Basilica of Saint-Remi   76
32 Dome of the Rock   78
33 Chichén Itzá   80
34 Pillars of Hercules   82
35 Great Mosque of Cordoba   84
36 Aachen Cathedral   86
37 Church of Saints Cyril and Methodius   88
38 Viking World Museum   90
39 Sheikh Lotfollah Mosque   92
40 Hagia Sophia   94
41 Krak des Chevaliers   96
42 Angkor Wat   98
43 Kenchō-ji   100
44 Equestrian statue of Genghis Kahn   102
45 Registan Square   104
46 Grütli meadow   106
47 Palace of the Popes   108
48 Timbuktu   110
49 Kinkaku-ji   112
50 Go'ri Amir Mausoleum   114

51	Florence Cathedral	116
52	Gutenberg Museum	118
53	Walls of Constantinople	120
54	The Alhambra	122

EARLY MODERN

55	Archives of India	126
56	Belem Tower	128
57	Sistine Chapel	130
58	Chambord Castle	132
59	Wall of Reformers	134
60	Teotihuacan	136
61	Nao Victoria Museum	138
62	Machu Picchu	140
63	Collegium Maius	142
64	St. Basil's Cathedral	144
65	Fort St. Elmo	146
66	Amsterdam Stock Ex.	148
67	Jamestown Settlement	150
68	Prague Castle	152
69	Taj Mahal	154
70	Galileo Museum	156
71	Hofburg Palace	158
72	Westminster Abbey	160
73	Captain Cook's Landing Place	162
74	The Capitol	164
75	Royal Palace of Bangkok	166
76	Republic Monument	168
77	Tomb of Napoleon	170

19TH CENTURY

78	Lincoln Memorial	174
79	Mausoleum of Simón Bolívar	176
80	Swindon Steam Railway Museum	178
81	Hong Kong Bay	180
82	Galapagos Islands	182
83	Red Cross Museum	184
84	Himeji Castle	186
85	Victoria Falls	188

20TH CENTURY

86	Museum of Arts and Crafts	192
87	Sarajevo Museum 1878–1918	194
88	Mausoleum of Lenin	196
89	Palace of Versailles	198
90	Wall Street Stock Ex.	200
91	Muzeum II Wojny Światowej w Gdańsku	202
92	Normandy Cemetery	204
93	Palace of Nations	206
94	Forbidden City	208
95	Cu Chi Tunnels	210
96	Aeronautical Museum	212
97	Robben Island Museum	214
98	Neil Armstrong Museum of Air and Space	216
99	Checkpoint Charlie	218
100	Science Gateway	220

MONUMENTS IN EUROPE

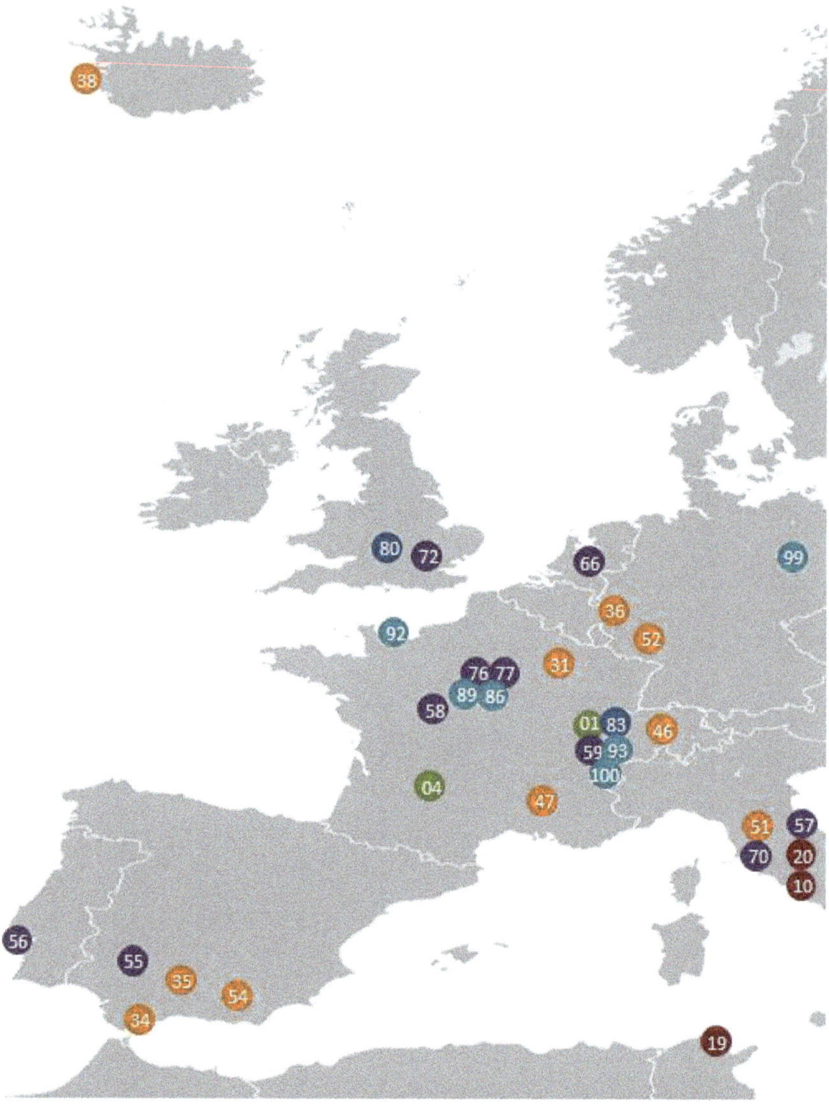
38
80
72
66
99
36
92
52
76
77
31
89
86
58
01
83
46
59
93
100
04
47
51
57
70
20
10
56
55
35
54
34
19

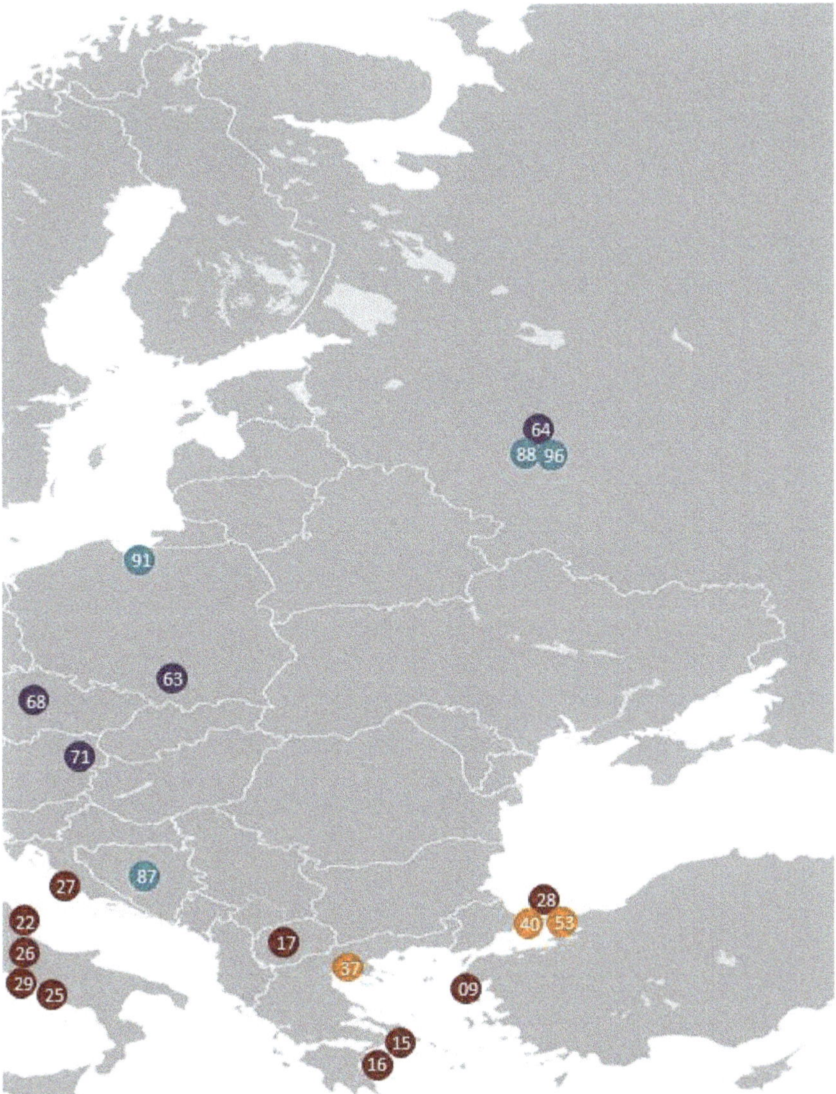
64
88
96
91
63
68
71
87
27
28
40
53
22
26
17
37
29
25
09
15
16
07
65

MONUMENTS IN THE REST OF THE

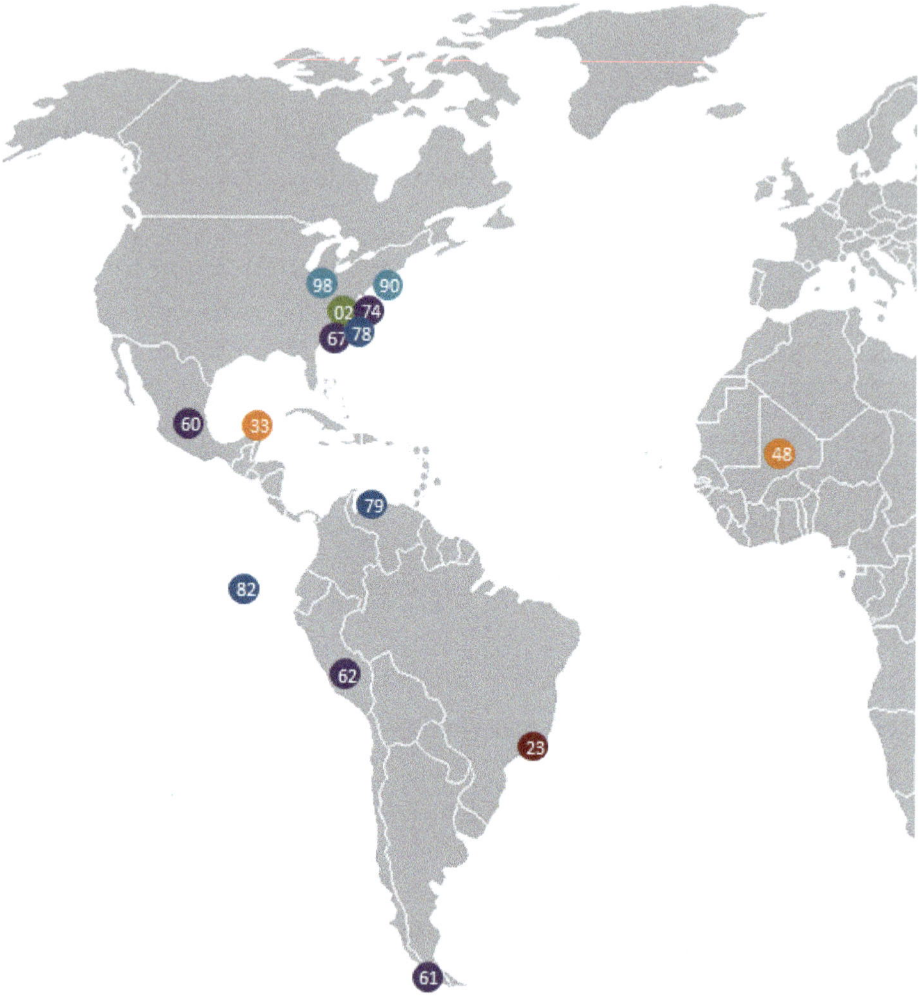
98
90
02
74
67
78
60
33
48
79
82
62
23
61

WORLD

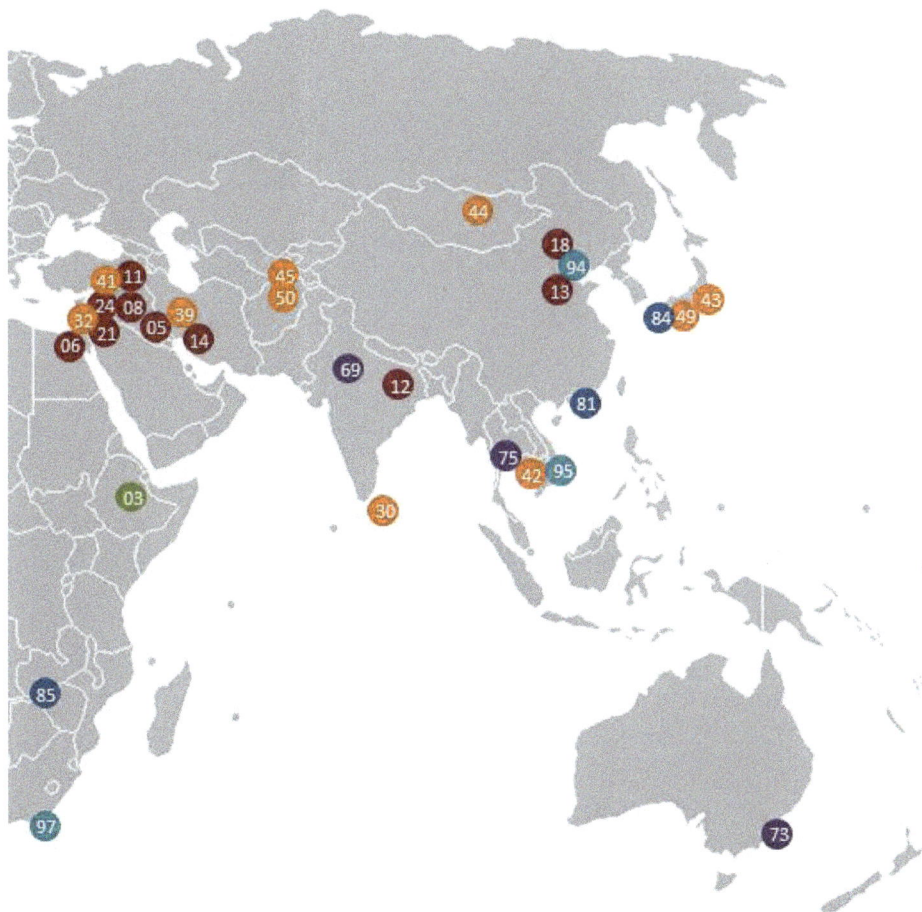

PREHISTORY

The Prehistory period spans from the first known use of stone tools by hominins around 3.3 million years ago to the beginning of recorded history with the invention of writing systems around 5,200 years ago. through key developments including the emergence of early human species, the development of tools and technology, and the rise of some of the earliest known civilizations.

Experience the Big Bang inside the

LARGE HADRON COLLIDER

#01 14bn BC

SWITZERLAND

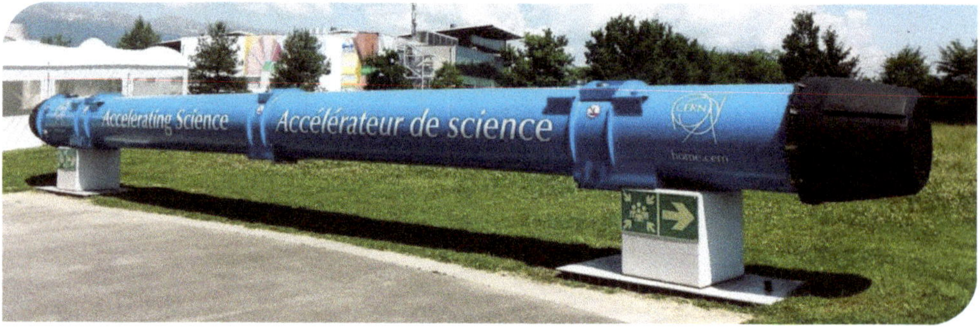
Accelerating Science
Accélérateur de science
CERN

The Large Hadron Collider (LHC) is a particle accelerator located at CERN (European Organization for Nuclear Research) in Switzerland. It was designed to enable scientists to discover new subatomic particles and better understand the fundamental laws of physics. The LHC is the largest and most powerful particle accelerator in the world. It is 27 km wide and 100 meters underground, which allows protons to collide at a speed close to that of light. The LHC was inaugurated in 2008 and has already led to many groundbreaking discoveries, including the discovery of the Higgs boson in 2012. It continues to be used for cutting-edge research in the field of particle physics and remains a vital tool for understanding the universe.

► The Big Bang, sometimes known as the "great explosion," is the term used to describe the original cosmological event that resulted in the creation of the universe. According to scientists, the cosmos was likely formed by a very small and extremely dense primordial atom that suddenly burst and expanded with tremendous force and speed. This atom was shattered into a million pieces by the immense heat that was produced. A hot, dense, incandescent gaseous combination that gave birth to our solar system and its galaxies proceeded to grow, cool, and change throughout time.

It was at this moment that the cosmic clock started ticking. In 1927, a Belgian priest and astronomer, Georges Lemaître, came up with the Big Bang Theory and the first proposition to explain how the universe works. While there are still some unsolved mysteries, the Big Bang theory provides the most comprehensive and well-supported explanation for the origin and evolution of the observable universe.

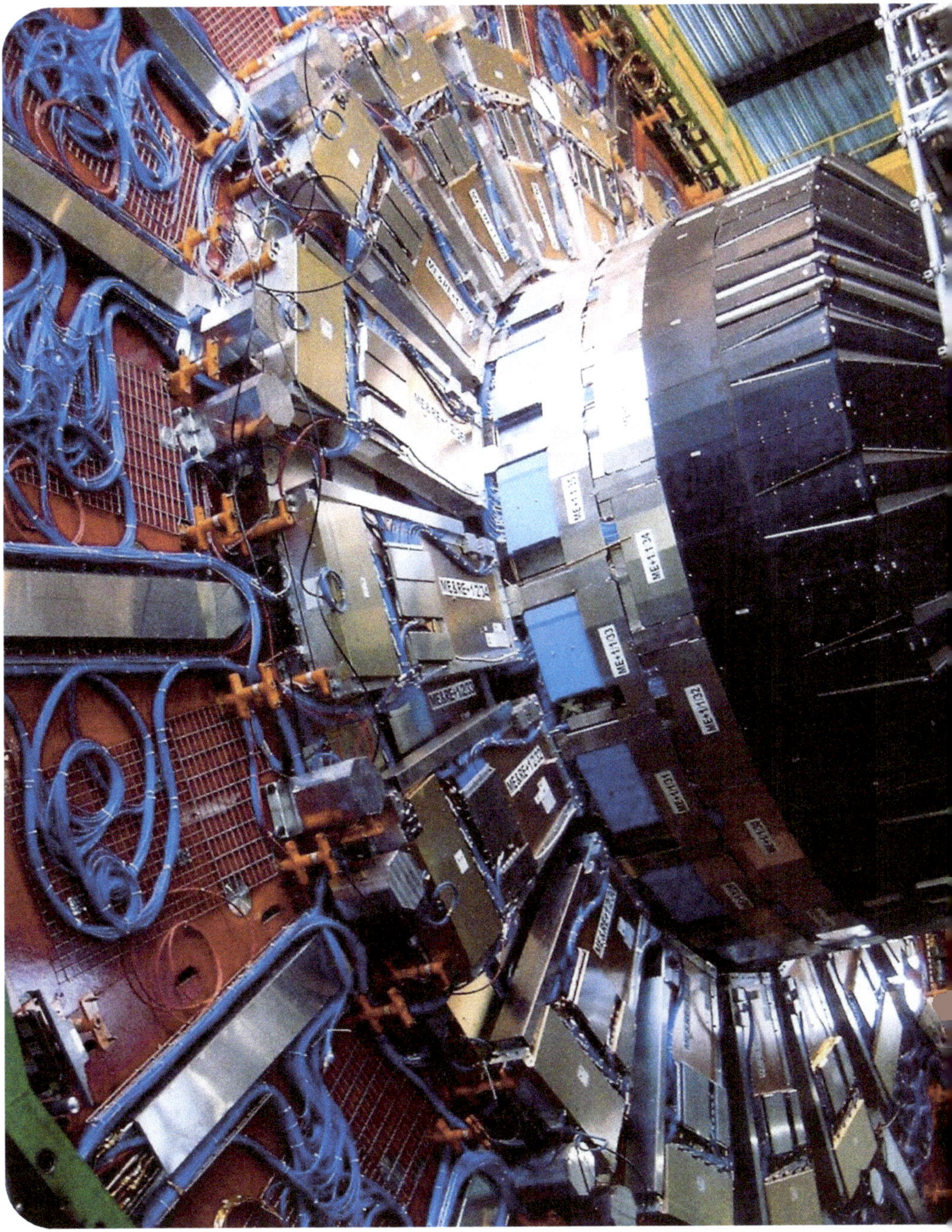

Meet the dinosaurs at the

SMITHSONIAN MUSEUM OF NATURAL HISTORY

#02

245m BC

USA

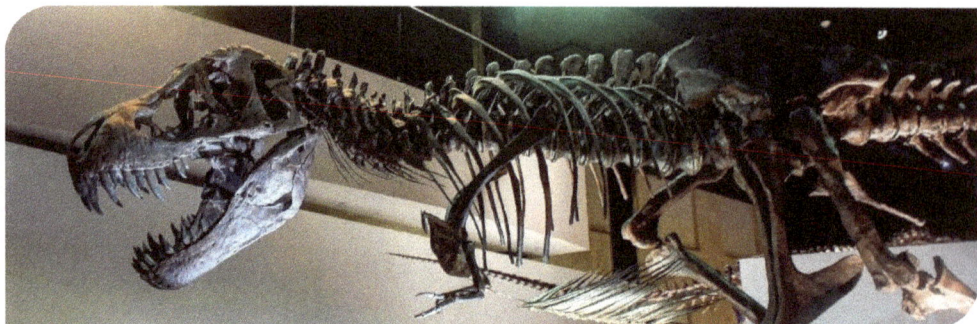

The Smithsonian Museum of Natural History is one of the most popular and famous museums in Washington D.C. This museum is dedicated to natural history. It houses an impressive collection of fossils, minerals and specimens of plants and animals. One of the museum's highlights is its Dinosaur Room, where visitors can see life-size replicas of these prehistoric creatures. The museum also has a variety of temporary exhibitions, which cover a wide range of topics from astronomy to anthropology. If you're interested in natural history or just looking for a fascinating and educational activity to do with your family, the Smithsonian Museum of Natural History is a must-see in Washington D.C.

► In the Mesozoic era, also known as the Secondary Era, dinosaurs were the first animals that came into existence. They are part of a family of organisms known as Sauropsids, whose current representatives are reptiles. They were either carnivorous or herbivorous creatures that could move on land or in the air on four legs or on their hind legs. Their bodies were decorated with crests, horns, and strange bony plates. According to fossils found around the world, they ruled the planet 245 million years ago. The most likely cause of their extinction was a meteorite impact several kilometers in diameter.

Several months following this impact, the earth was plunged into darkness and cold, causing a climate change to which humans were unable to adapt. Cold-blooded animals are affected by temperature when developing eggs and at birth. 65 million years ago, dinosaurs disappeared from the earth. Today, no animal can compare with the bite force of the T-Rex, which was 12,800 pounds per square inch.

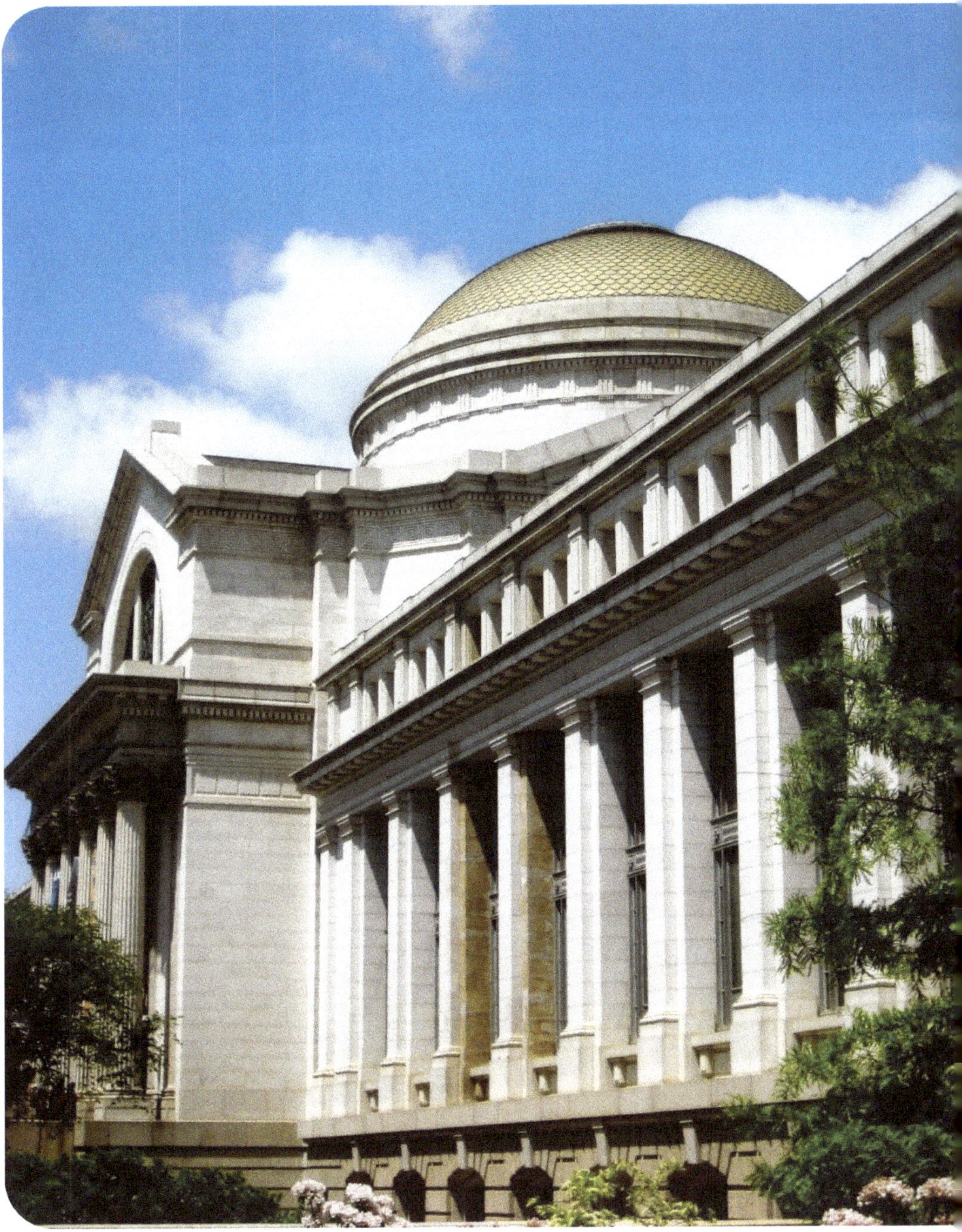

Learn about the *Australopithecus* at the

NATIONAL MUSEUM OF ETHIOPIA

#03 ⏱ **3m BC**

🗺 **ETHIOPIA**

The National Museum of Ethiopia in Addis Ababa is a must-see for lovers of Ethiopian history and culture. Located in the city of Addis Ababa, the museum houses an impressive collection of historical and cultural artifacts. These include illuminated manuscripts and ancient weapons to jewelry and traditional clothing. Among the museum's most notable pieces are the Arch of Emperor Haile Selassie, the Golden Throne of the Emperor, and the Skull of Lucy. This is a fossil over 3 million years old that is considered one of humanity's oldest specimens. The National Museum of Ethiopia is also known for its temporary exhibitions that highlight the cultures and traditions of different regions of Ethiopia.

▶ The presence of Australopithecus Afarensis, also known as Lucy, was discovered near Hadar in Ethiopia on November 24th, 1974 by a team of researchers of different nationalities. She lived about 3 million years ago and has long been considered the grandmother of humanity. Since her discovery, other older primates have been found, making Lucy a member of the primate species called Australopithecus afarensis.

Around 2.5 million years ago, Homo Habilis began to distinguish itself by developing the ability to make tools with animal teeth, bones, stones, and wood. Respiratory pathways also began to change to adapt to an increasingly dry environment, leading to the descent of the larynx and the first stuttering of articulated language. The Lucy specimen is considered the most complete skeleton of an early human ancestor, with 40% of the bones still intact.

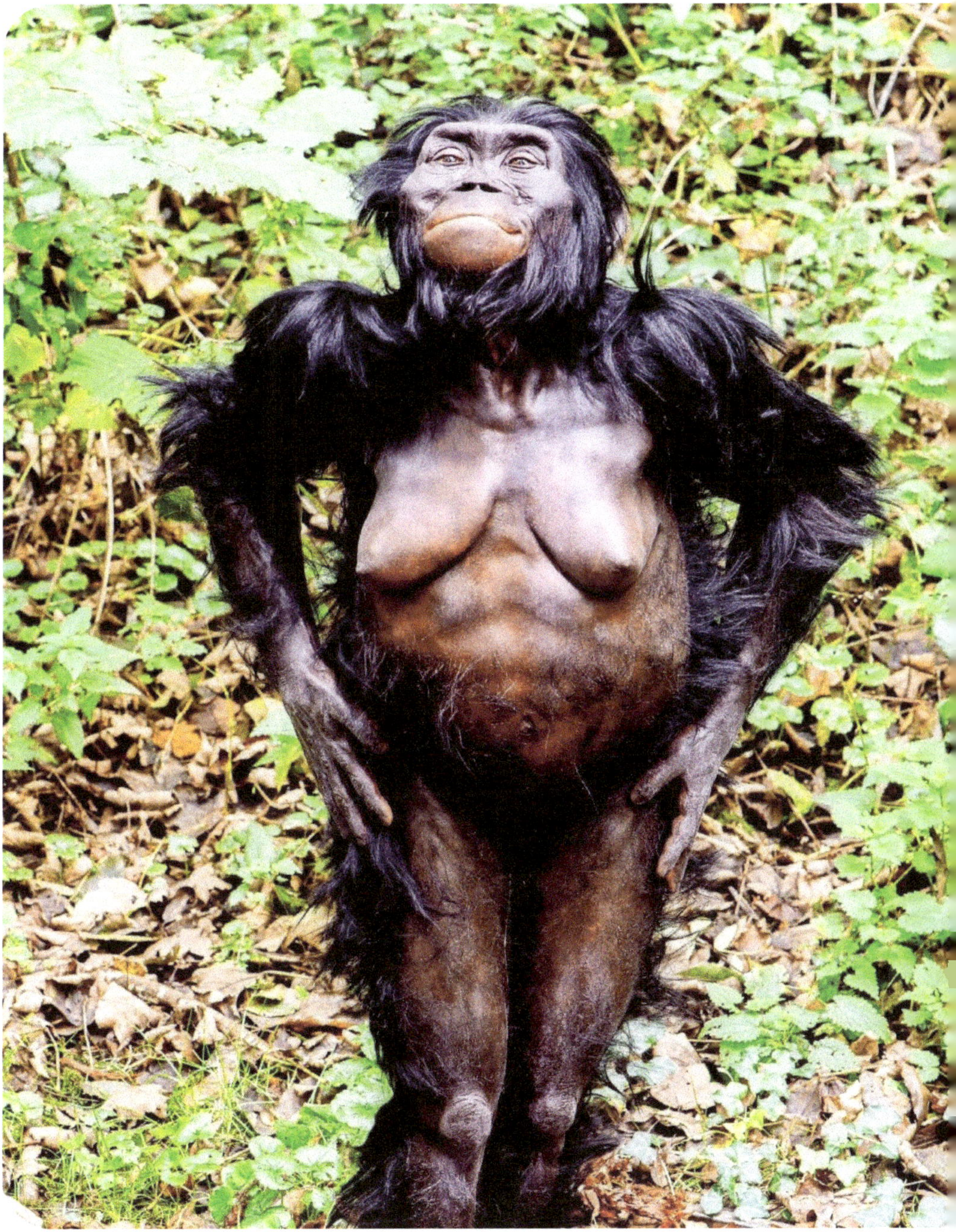

Discover primal art of Homo Sapiens at the

LASCAUX CAVES

#04 15k BC FRANCE

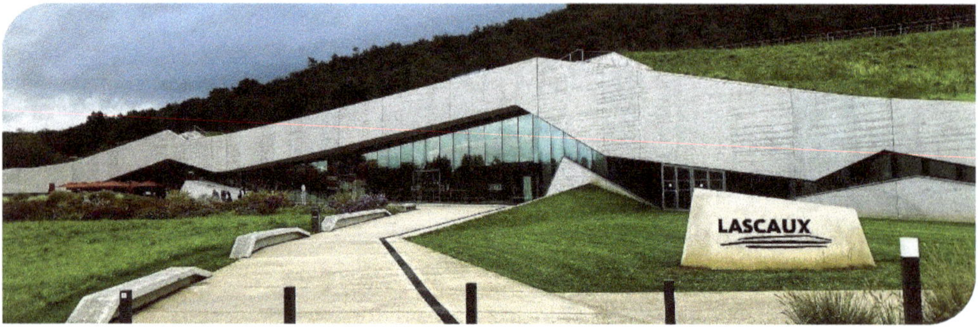
LASCAUX

The Lascaux Caves are a wonder of nature and a precious heritage for humanity. Located in southwestern France, these caves house one of the largest collections of prehistoric cave paintings in the world. The Lascaux Caves were discovered by chance in 1940 by a group of young people who were following their dog in the woods. Since then, they have been listed as a UNESCO World Heritage Site and have attracted millions of visitors from all over the world. The paintings that adorn the walls of the caves depict scenes of everyday life and religious ceremonies of the prehistoric peoples who created them. The Lascaux Caves are a fascinating testimony to the art and culture of our ancestors and they are really worth a visit.

► The arrival of Homo Sapiens, also known as Cro-Magnon man, in Europe marked the beginning of the Upper Paleolithic period, which took place between 35,000 and 10,000 years before our era and coincided with the end of the last ice age. Homo sapiens are from the East, possibly the Near East, Asia or Africa, and took advantage of a temporary improvement in the climate around -35,000 to colonize Europe. They invented the bone needle, which revolutionized their daily lives by allowing them to make water containers or heat them on hot stones. Cro-Magnon men coexisted with Neanderthals until their extinction around 30,000 years ago in Spain.

Humans gradually became aware of themselves, and the birth of consciousness coincided with that of the unconscious. This led to questions about the afterlife and superior powers, which gave rise to the first religions, burials and the first forms of artistic expression. The oldest known art in the world is a cave painting of a red disk, believed to be a depiction of the sun.

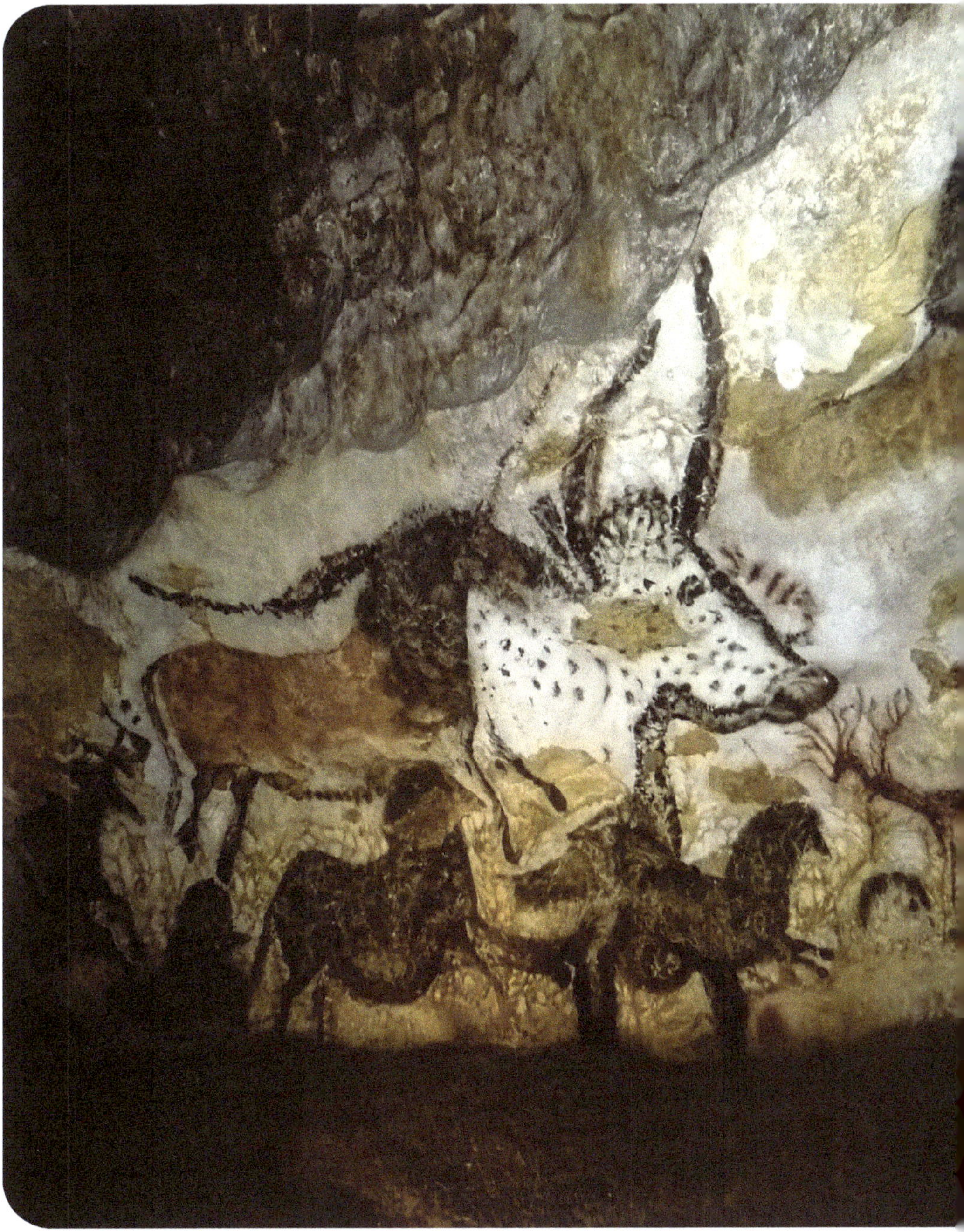

ANCIENT HISTORY

The Ancient history period spans from the rise of the earliest civilizations around 4000 BC to the fall of the Western Roman Empire in 476 AD, covering major developments like the emergence of writing, the growth of urban centers, the rise and fall of empires, and the advancement of technology, culture, and philosophy.

Learn about the first civilizations in Mesopotamia at the

ZIGGURAT OF UR

#05 3000 BC

IRAQ

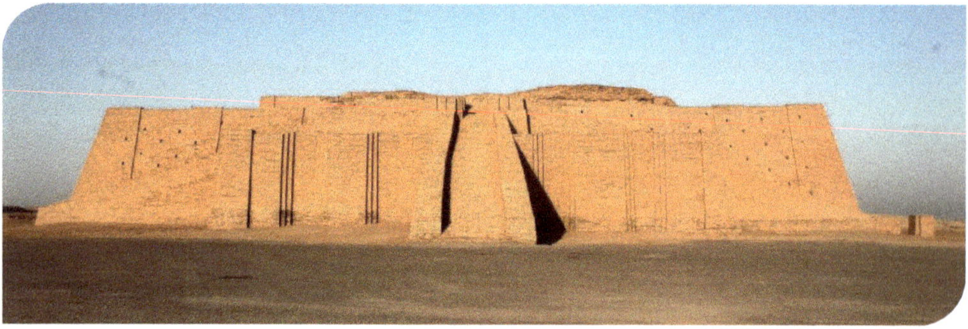

The Ziggurat of Ur is an archaeological site located in the southern region of modern-day Iraq. This massive brick pyramid structure dates back to the ancient Sumerian civilization, serving as the religious and political center of the city of Ur during its heyday. Ur was one of the earliest and most influential urban centers in the history of human civilization, and the Ziggurat stands as a testament to the architectural and engineering prowess of its inhabitants. Despite the ravages of time and the various conflicts that have plagued the region, the Ziggurat of Ur remains one of the most well-preserved and iconic structures from the ancient world. Visitors can still explore the site and marvel at the sheer scale and engineering feats that went into its construction.

► Around 5500 years ago, between the Tigris and Euphrates rivers, the seeds of what would become the first form of human writing were born. The Sumerians, who had become farmers, needed a sustainable system of accounting and inventory management to handle food surpluses. They used clay, an abundant material in this river region, to keep records of their crops and livestock. The pictograms represented objects and gradually, the need arose to expand the system.

The next step, which was the beginning of the establishment of a true written language, was to associate sounds with pictograms and finally to associate them only with sounds. The name cuneiform means in the shape of wedges, due to the shape of the stylus used. This marks the beginning of history, as a major contribution to the preservation and transmission of ideas was the emergence of writing. The Sumerians also used their writing system for some of the world's oldest known epic poems, such as the Epic of Gilgamesh.

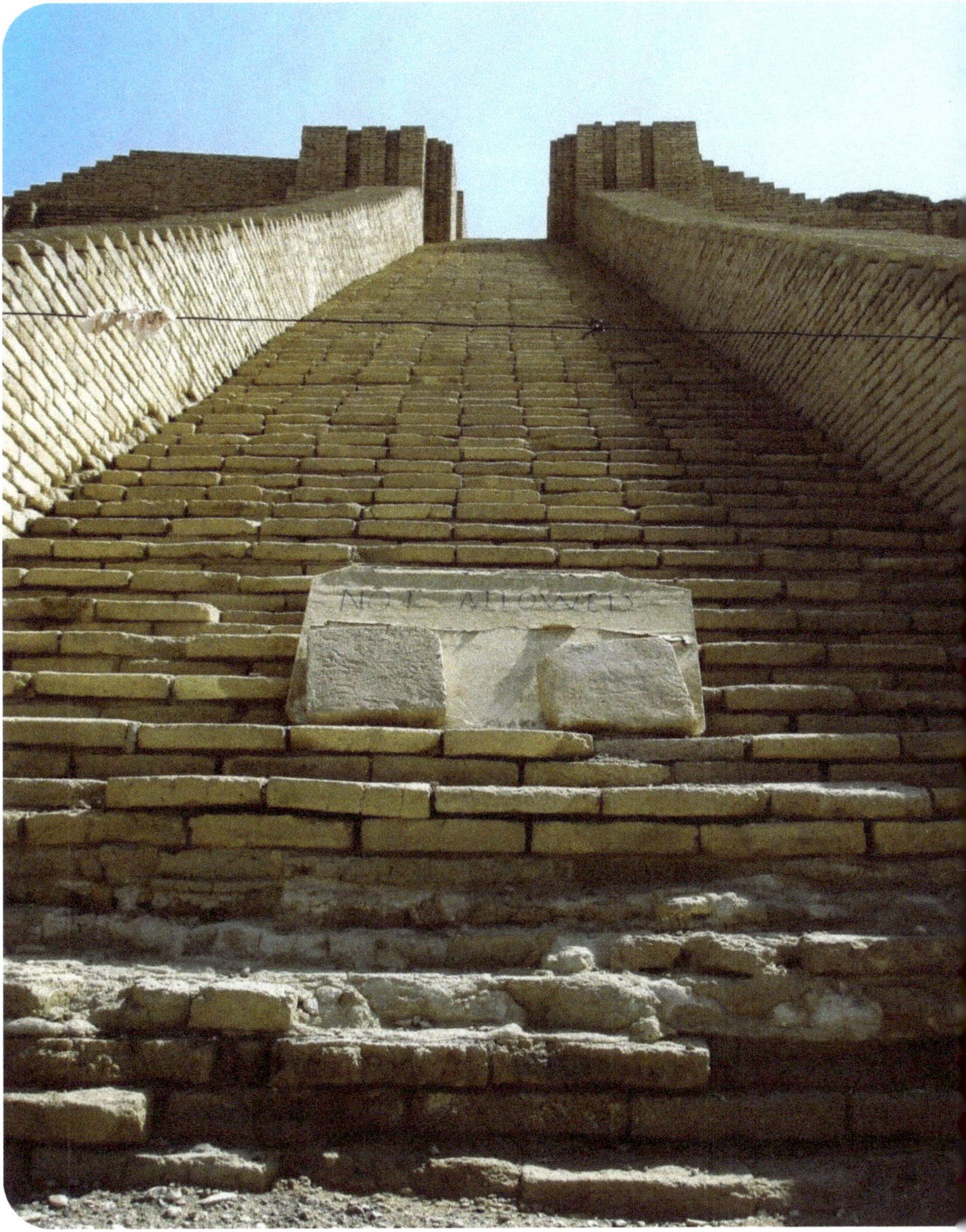
NOT ALLOWED

Get a sense of the greatness of egyptian's civilization at the

GREAT PYRAMID OF GIZA

#06 ⏱ **2550 BC**
🗺 **EGYPT**

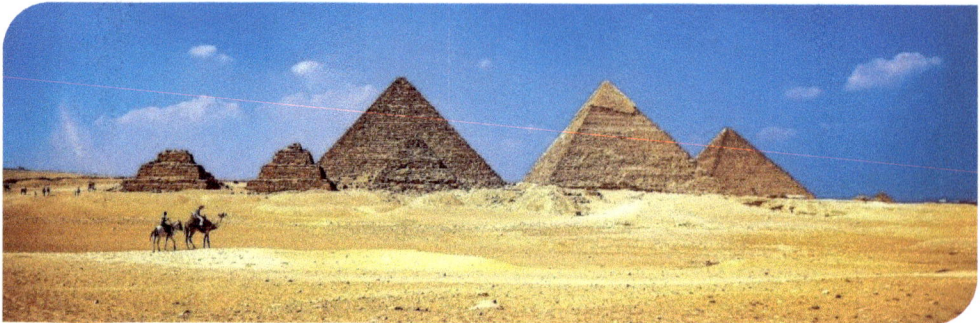

The Great Pyramid of Giza is a wonder of the ancient world that continues to captivate the imagination of people around the world. Located just outside of Cairo, Egypt, the pyramid is the largest of the three pyramids that make up the Giza Necropolis. It is the oldest and largest of the Seven Wonders of the Ancient World. It was built around 2550 BC as a tomb for Pharaoh Khufu. It is made up of over 2.3 million blocks of limestone, each weighing an average of 2.5 tons. The pyramid stands 147 meters (481 feet) tall, and is the only one of the Seven Wonders that still stands today. Despite being more than 4,500 years old, the pyramid is still a testament to the incredible engineering and construction skills of the ancient Egyptians, and is a must-see for anyone visiting Egypt.

▶ The beginning of the Ancient Egyptian Empire is considered the golden age of the pharaonic civilization. The centralization initiated under the Thinite dynasties allowed for artistic and architectural developments, notably the time of the first pyramids, such as the step pyramid at Saqqara under the rule of Djoser, and the three monumental pyramids of the Giza Plateau (Khufu, Khafre, and Menkaure). The pyramid of Khufu was considered the first of the seven wonders of the world for at least 2,000 years.

However, after the reign of the pharaoh Nitokris, a long period of decay led to the first intermediate period. This was followed by the invasion of the Delta by Asian people that marked the end of the Ancient Empire. The Great Pyramid of Giza was originally covered in white limestone casing stones, which reflected sunlight and made the pyramid shine like a jewel. These stones were later removed for building material, but some can still be seen at the base of the pyramid.

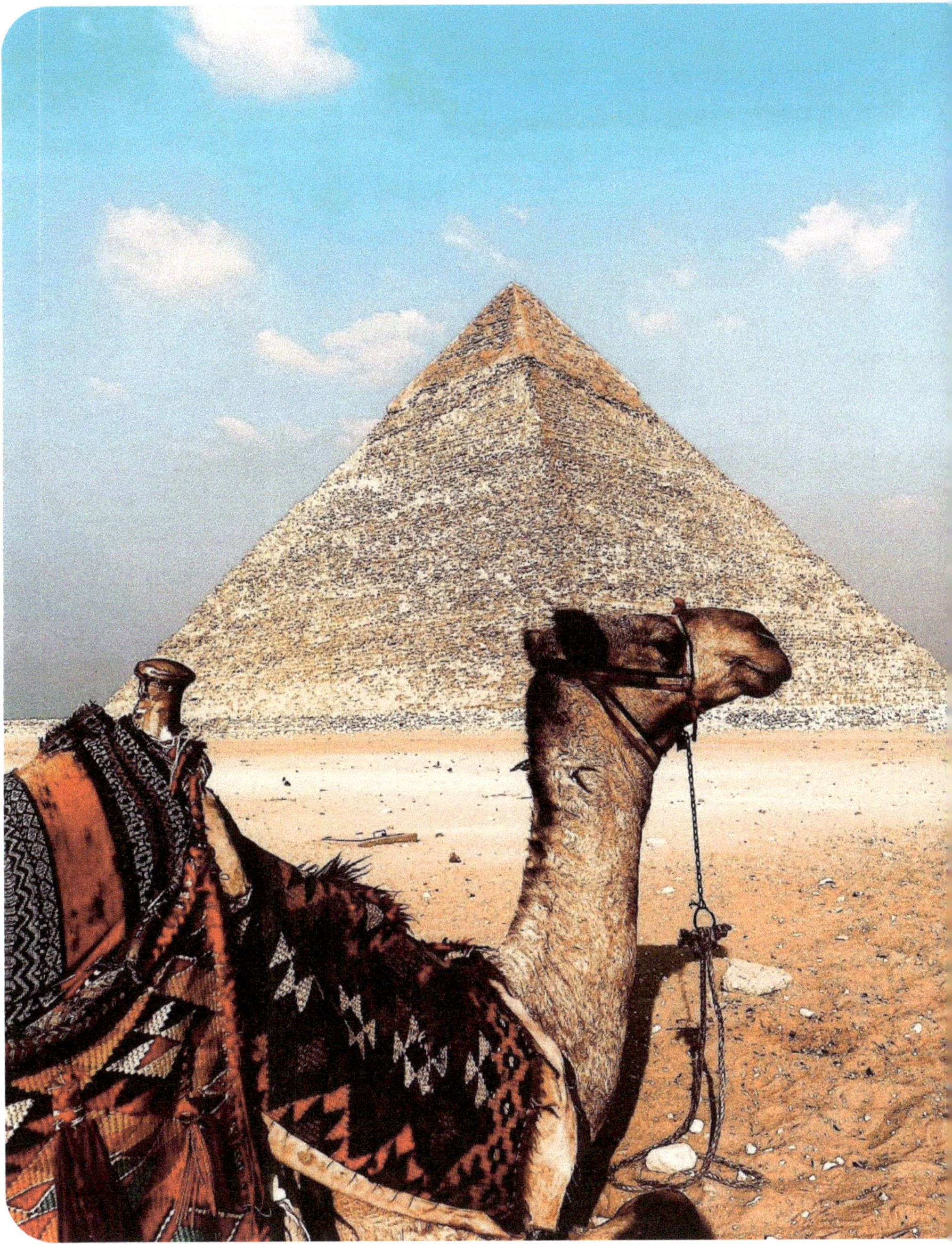

Watch the apogee of Cretan civilization at the

MINOAN PALACE OF KNOSSOS

#07 2000 BC

GREECE

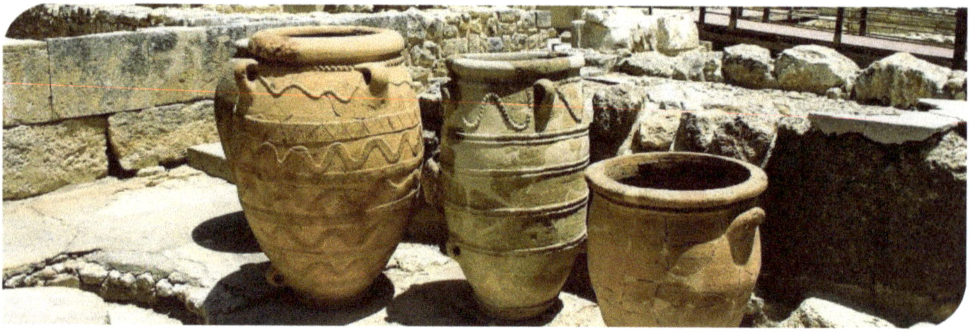

The Minoan Palace of Knossos is an archaeological site located on the island of Crete in Greece. It is one of the most prestigious sites of Greek antiquity. This is because it was the capital of the Minoan Empire, a prehistoric civilization that flourished between 2000 and 1100 BC. The Palace of Knossos was a veritable labyrinth of rooms and corridors, and it was decorated with colorful frescoes and ornamental motifs. There were also banquet halls, bedrooms and bathrooms. The Palace of Knossos was a place of life for royal figures and members of the Minoan nobility. However, it was also a place of worship for the gods and goddesses of Greek mythology. Today, the Palace of Knossos is open to the public and it has become one of the most popular sites in Crete for visitors from all over the world.

► The peak of the Cretan civilization, also known as the Minoan civilization, occurred between 2000 and 1100 BC. It was a period of remarkable prosperity and cultural flourishing on the island of Crete, located in the Aegean Sea. The Minoans, as they were called, developed a complex and sophisticated society with a robust economy based on trade and agriculture. They built impressive palaces, such as the Palace of Knossos, which served as centers of government and religion.

The Minoans also made significant advancements in the fields of art, architecture and engineering, as evidenced by the beautiful frescoes, pottery and jewelry discovered on the island. The peak of the Cretan civilization ended around 1100 BC with the mysterious collapse of the Minoan civilization, which remains a subject of debate among historians. It is believed to be the first civilization to have had a written language, known as Linear A. This language has not yet been deciphered.

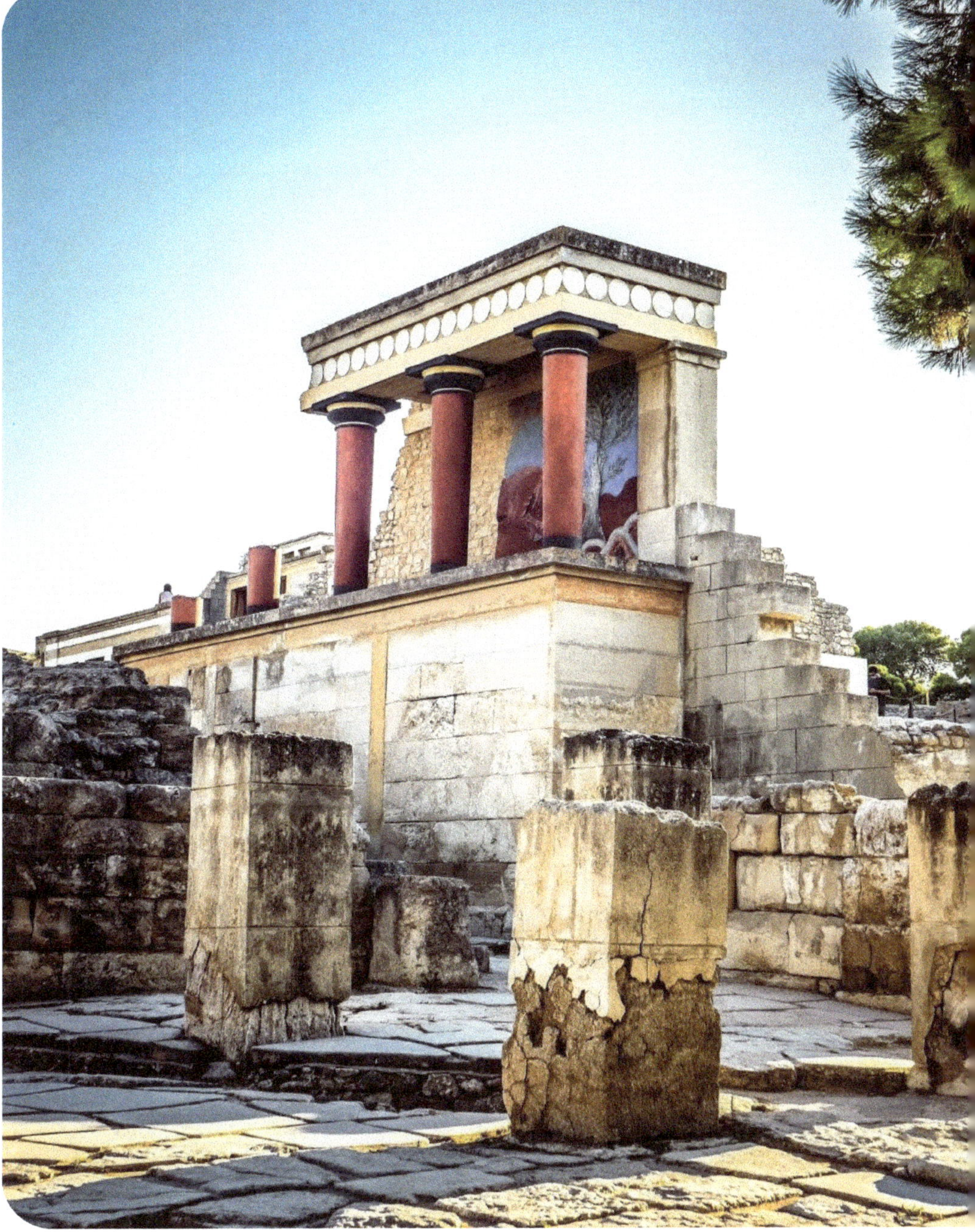

Delve into the first Babylonian empire at the

ISHTAR GATE

#08 1750 BC

IRAQ

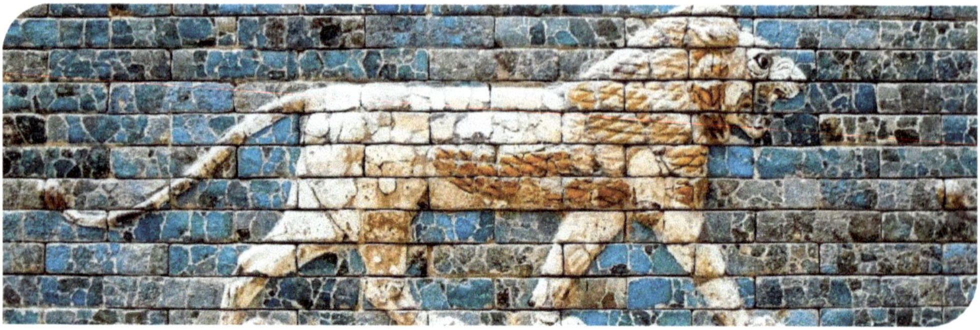

The Ishtar Gate is one of the most famous and iconic landmarks in the ancient city of Babylon, Iraq. Built by King Nebuchadnezzar II, the gate was dedicated to the Babylonian goddess Ishtar, the goddess of love and war. The original Ishtar Gate was an impressive structure, featuring vibrant blue bricks and intricate carvings of animals like bulls, lions, and dragons. The version of the Ishtar Gate that stands in Babylon today is actually a replica, built under the rule of Saddam Hussein in the 1980s. While not the original, seeing this iconic structure in person is still a breathtaking experience. The bright blue bricks and detailed carvings transport visitors back in time, allowing them to imagine the grandeur of the ancient Babylonian empire.

► The Babylonian empire reached its peak during the reign of Hammurabi, one of the longest rulers in ancient Near Eastern history. He completed the conquest of Sumer and Akkad, and put an end to the last Sumerian dynasty of Isin. He was the first king of the Babylonian empire and was the first to secure Babylon's hegemony throughout southern Mesopotamia. Babylon was the center of the Assyro-Babylonian civilization and was the most populous and wealthiest city in the ancient world before being invaded by the Hittites, Elamites, and Assyrians.

The city was destroyed and rebuilt by the Chaldeans, and it wasn't until the reign of Nebuchadnezzar II around -650 that it regained its former glory. The myth of the Tower of Babel may have originated from a ziggurat dedicated to the god Marduk in Babylon, built by the first Babylonian dynasty. It was believed to have been 90m in height, but it was not circular in shape. Hammurabi is best known for his law code which outlined 282 laws and punishments, many of which were based on the principle of an eye for an eye, a tooth for a tooth.

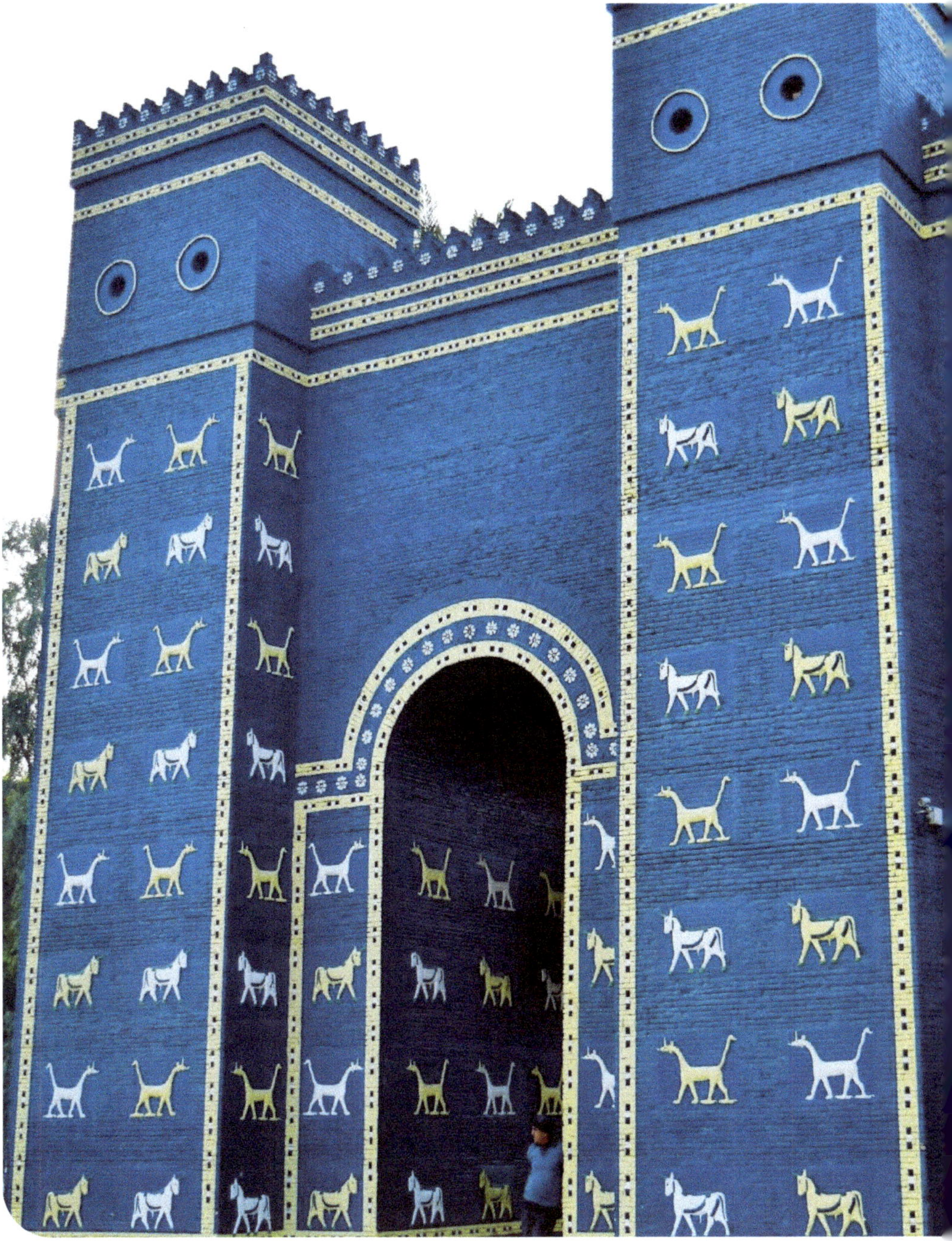

Learn about the Trojan War at the

TROJAN HORSE REPLICA

#09

1250 BC

TURKEY

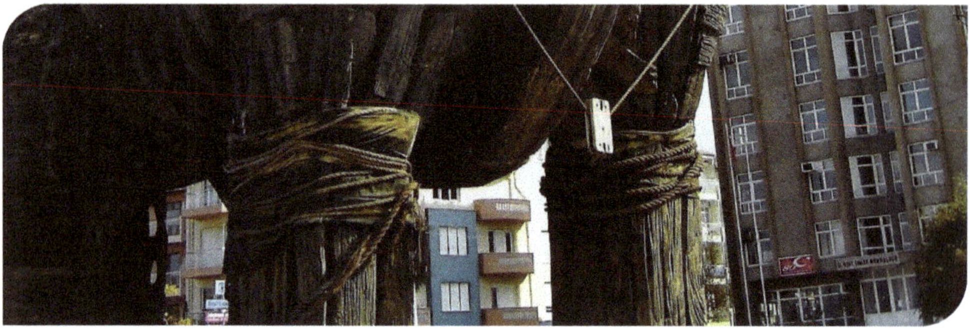

The Trojan horse is one of the most memorable elements of ancient Greek history, described in Homer's legend as a ruse to enter Troy. It was built in 1975 and attracts the attention of many visitors. According to legend, the Greeks used a wooden horse as a ploy to penetrate and conquer the city of Troy, making the Troians believe it was an offering to the goddess Athena. The Troians, believing that the horse was a gift of peace, carried it within their walls and celebrated their victory. However, this victory was short-lived, as the Greeks had hidden an army inside the horse and used this opportunity to attack and conquer Troy. Since then, the phrase 'Trojan horse' has become synonymous with deception or deception used to dupe someone.

► The Trojan War began as a result of the abduction of Helen, the wife of King Menelaus of Sparta, by the Trojan prince Paris. The Greeks continued to fight against the Trojans and launched raids on surrounding towns. Ulysses came up with the famous Trojan Horse plan, where Greek warriors hid inside a large wooden horse and pretended to lose the war. The Trojans brought the trap inside their walls as a sign of victory, celebrated and rejoiced. At night, the Greek warriors came out of the horse and opened the gates of the city.

Troy was sacked, members of the royal family were killed or taken into slavery, and Menelaus could finally bring Helen back to Sparta. During the battle, Achilles was finally struck and wounded in the heel by an arrow shot by Paris, and died. It is impossible to know if the war took place as described in Homer's Iliad, but the city of Troy in Asia Minor was destroyed by fire in 1250 BC. The Trojan Horse is nowadays a popular symbol of deceit and strategy.

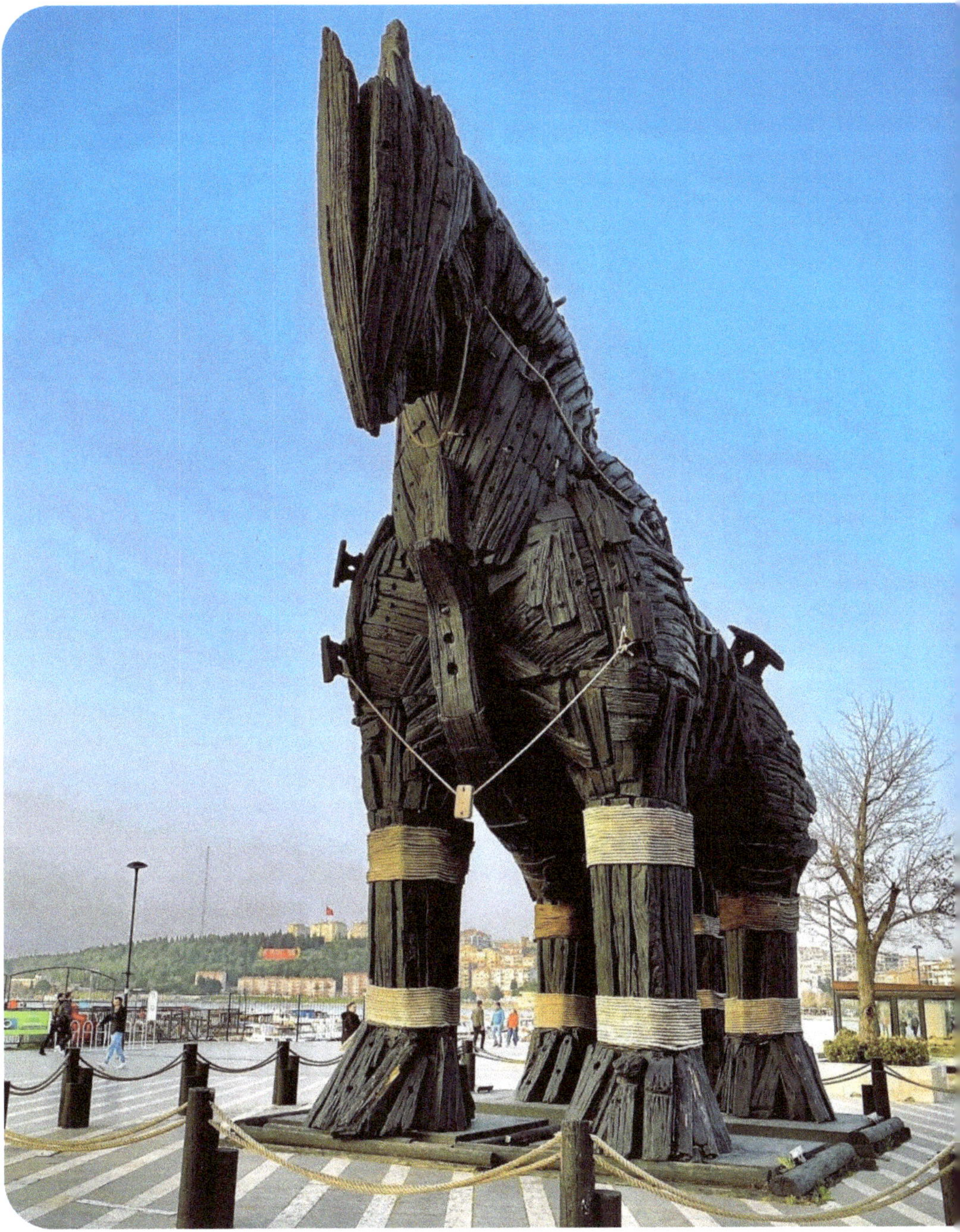

Recollect the legendary foundation of Rome with the

THE CAPITOLINE WOLF

#10 753 BC

ITALY

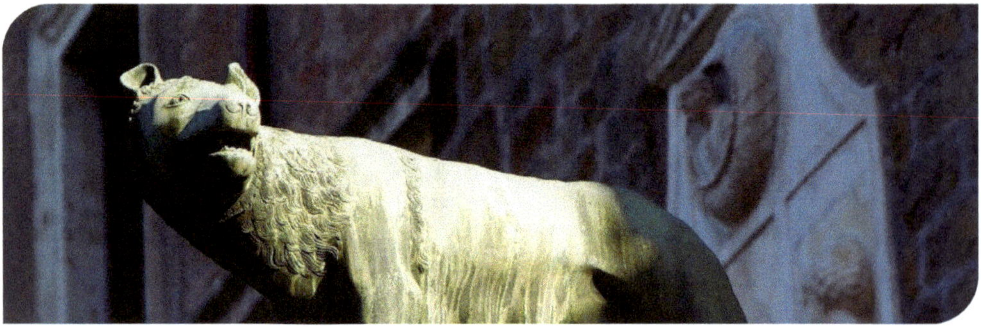

The Capitoline Wolf is one of the most iconic and recognizable statues in the city of Rome. Situated atop the historic Capitol Hill, which was once the political and religious heart of the ancient city, this remarkable sculpture has become a quintessential symbol of Rome. With its fierce yet maternal expression, it serves as a powerful reminder of Rome's mythical origins and the enduring strength and resilience of the city. Today, the statue remains one of the most popular tourist attractions in Rome, drawing visitors from around the world who come to marvel at its intricate details and bask in the aura of history and legend that surrounds it. As a testament to its enduring significance, the Capitoline Wolf has been widely reproduced and featured in various forms of art, literature, and popular culture.

► On April 21st, the legendary foundation of Rome took place between seven hills by the twin brothers Remus and Romulus. After the destruction of Troy, survivors set sail in search of a new land and were thrown into the Tiber River. They were raised by a she-wolf and a woodpecker, the bird of Mars, before being discovered by a shepherd and his wife. The twins decided to found a city and chose the place where they had been abandoned, leading to a fratricidal conflict. To settle the dispute, the twins consulted the auspices.

Remus was the first to see six vultures, but Romulus had observed twelve. Remus deliberately crossed the delimiting line that Romulus had just traced and was killed in a fit of anger. Romulus continued the construction of his city, which he named Rome after his own name. The famous she-wolf statue in Rome, known as the Lupa Capitolina, depicts the she-wolf who is said to have raised and nurtured the twin brothers.

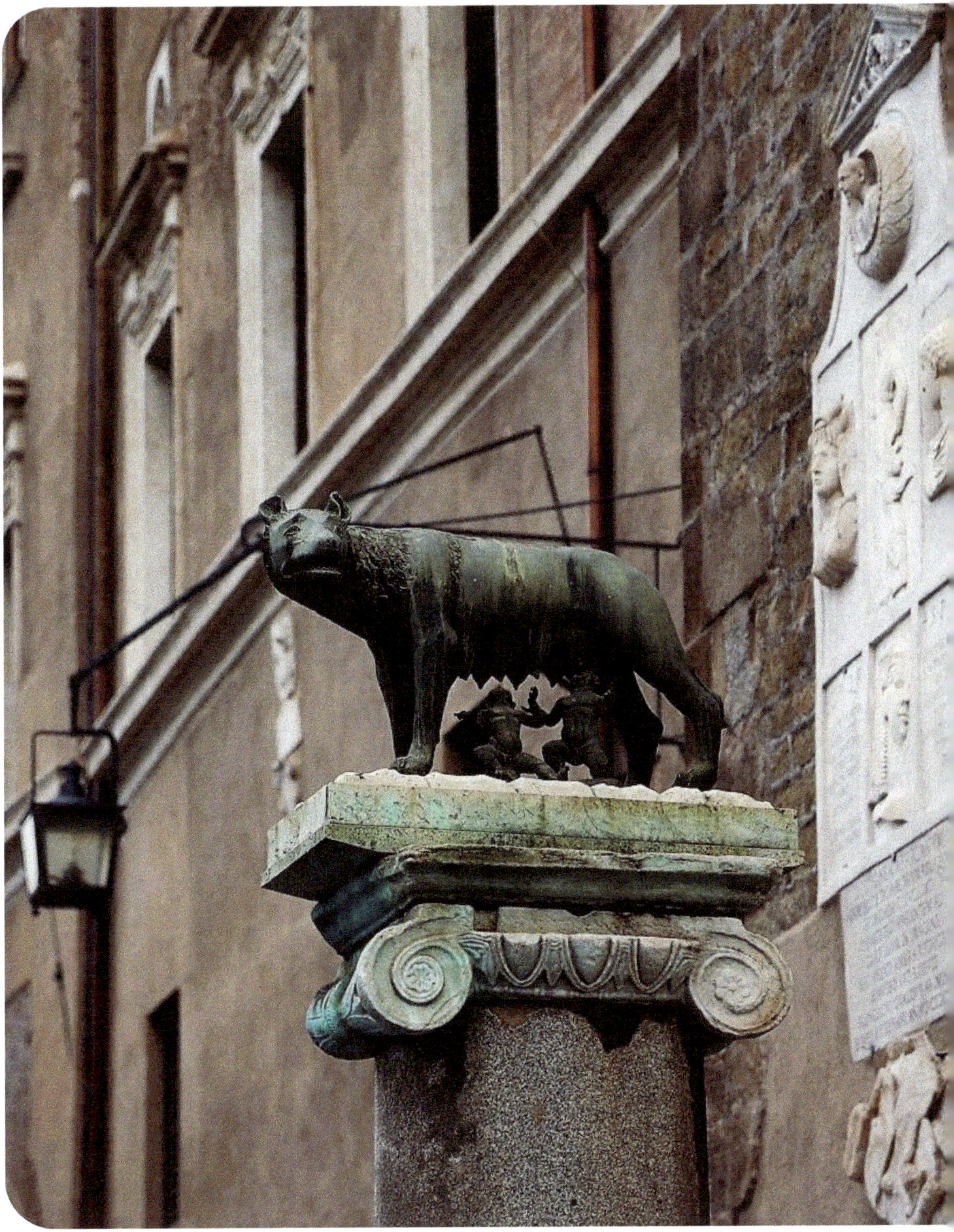

Grasp the apogee of Sargonid Assyria at the

WINGED BULLS OF KHORSABAD

#11

🕐 **722 BC**

📍 **IRAQ**

The Winged Bulls of Khorsabad are two monumental terracotta statues that were discovered in the ancient city of Khorsabad, Iraq. Dating from the ninth century BC, these statues are each about 4 meters high and they are considered one of the largest terracotta works of art of antiquity. Each bull is adorned with many intricate details and embossed patterns, and it is topped by a pair of outstretched wings. According to Sumerian mythology, these bulls were divine creatures that protected cities and kings. Today, the authentic Winged Bulls of Khorsabad are exhibited at the Louvre Museum in Paris. They attract thousands of visitors from all over the world every year who come to admire their beauty and majesty.

▶ Sargon II became king of Assyria from 722 to 705 BC. His name, Sharru-kīn, means the faithful king. In 722, he annexed the kingdom of Israel and deported its population. He crushed the rebellion of the Syrian provinces at Qarqar and Raphia, thus expanding the Assyrian kingdom. Assyria is one of the kingdoms of ancient Mesopotamia located in the north of present-day Iraq, in the triangle formed by the Tigris, Great Zab and Little Zab rivers.

It became an empire in the first millennium BC due to its many conquests. In the 8th and 7th centuries BC, Assyria controlled territories that stretched across the entirety or part of several present-day countries such as Iraq, Syria, Lebanon, Turkey and Iran. Sargon II then built vast palaces like that of Khorsabad, whose main gates were framed by large sculptures of winged bull protectors, the Lamassus. Sargon II was said to have been raised by a gardener and was originally a humble cupbearer to the king, before rising to power and becoming king himself.

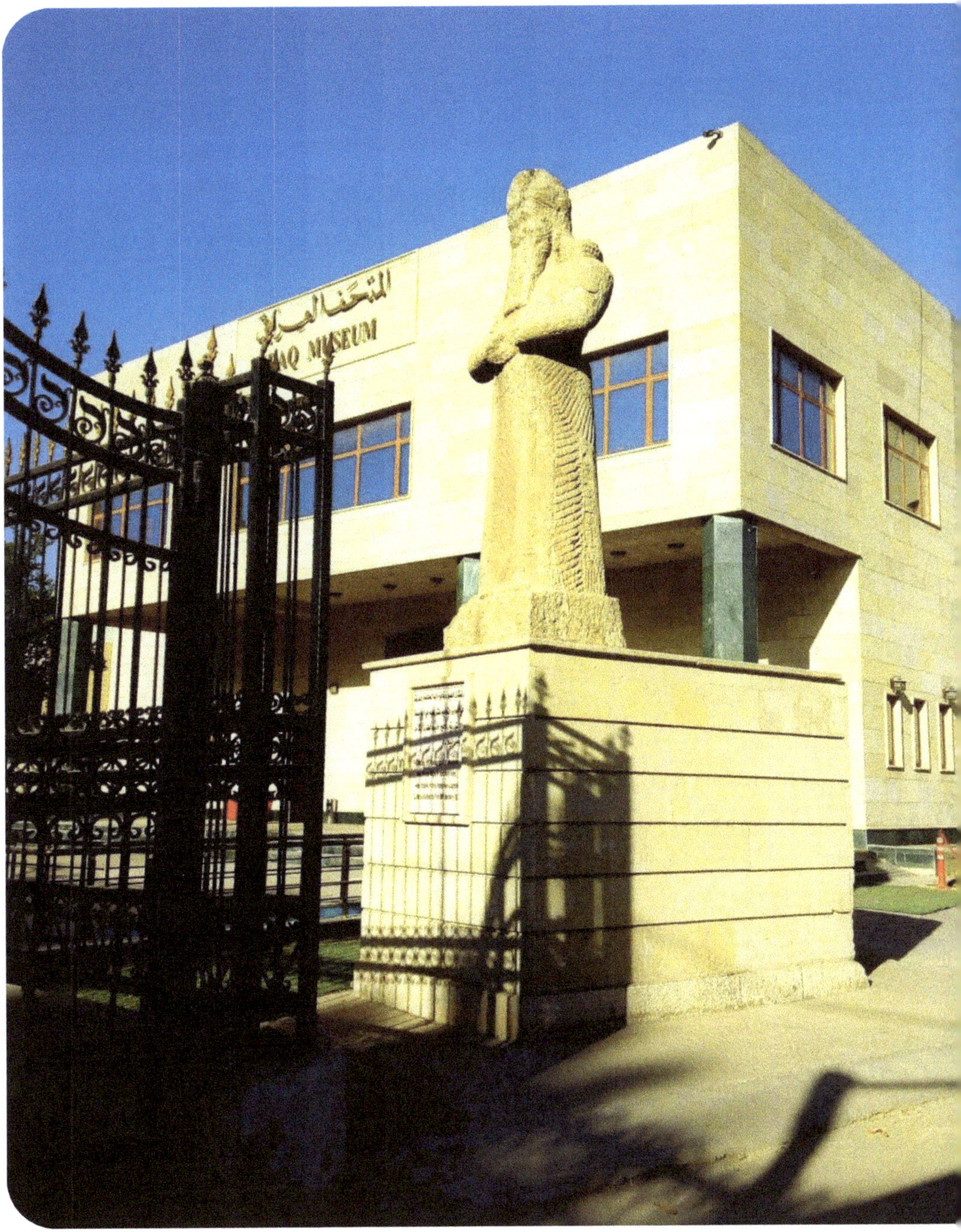
IRAQ MUSEUM

Reminisce Buddha's enlightenment at the
TEMPLE OF MAHABODHI

#12 ⏱ **563 BC**
📍 **INDIA**

The Mahabodhi Temple is a very revered Buddhist site located in Bodh Gaya, India. It was there that the Buddha attained spiritual awakening under the Bodhi tree, thus becoming the first human being to attain enlightenment. Since then, the temple has become a place of pilgrimage for Buddhists from all over the world. The Mahabodhi Temple is an imposing building, covered with gold leaf and Buddha statues. It is also home to a Bodhi bush believed to be a descendant of the original tree under which the Buddha attained enlightenment. The Mahabodhi Temple is a place of peace and contemplation for Buddhists around the world. It is a place where they can recharge their batteries and deepen their spiritual practice.

▶ The birth of Siddhartha Gautama, more commonly known as Buddha, the Enlightened One, took place in Lumbini, near the border of Nepal. Attracted by the idea of ultimate liberation of the individual soul (Moksha), Siddhartha settled on the banks of the Nairanjana river and practiced asceticism, constantly remaining in meditation. After six years of only consuming enough food and drink to stay alive, his body was emaciated and he was very weakened.

It was there that he attained enlightenment and became the Buddha (the Enlightened One). With desires and sufferings having disappeared, the Buddha reached Nirvana. Rather than rejecting his body and existence, he made a supreme sacrifice by returning to the world to share his enlightenment with others. This is so that all may end the cycle of suffering caused by the endless cycle of rebirths. The Buddha's teachings are known as "Dharma" and are considered one of the three jewels of Buddhism, along with the Sangha and the Buddha himself.

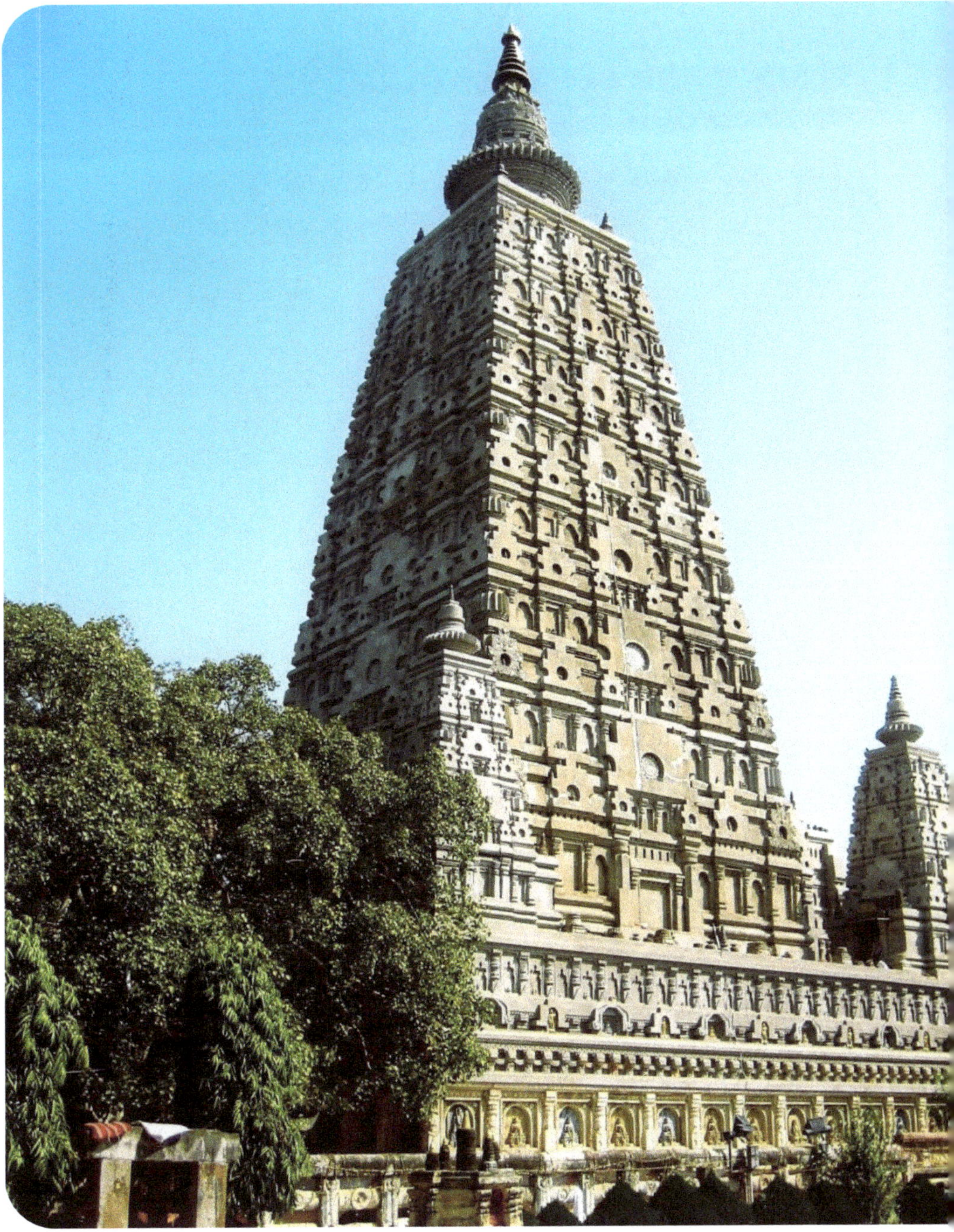

Comprehend Confucianism at the

TEMPLE AND CEMETERY OF CONFUCIUS

#13 551 BC

CHINA

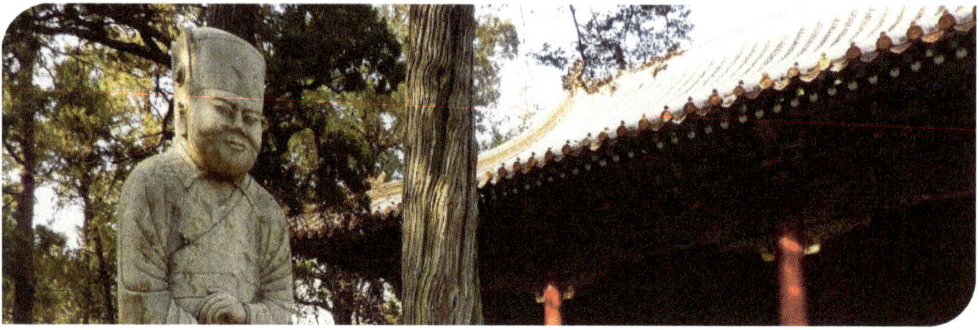

The Temple and Cemetery of Confucius are two must-see tourist sites located in Qufu, China. The Temple of Confucius is a temple complex that was built in honor of the Chinese philosopher of the same name. It was declared a UNESCO World Heritage Site in 1994 and is considered one of the most prestigious sites for Confucian culture. Confucius Cemetery, meanwhile, is the burial place of Confucius' family and has also been listed as a UNESCO World Heritage Site. The two sites are close to one another and are frequently visited together. If you are interested in the culture and history of China, the Temple and Cemetery of Confucius are places not to be missed on your trip to China.

► Confucius was born in the kingdom of Lu. Despite his immense influence, his life was remarkably simple. He was educated by his mother and distinguished himself by his insatiable thirst for learning. He became involved in politics, hoping to put his humanistic ideas into practice with governments. He became a magistrate and then Minister of Justice in the state of Lu.

However, he eventually realized that his superiors were not interested in his ideas and left the country for a twelve-year exile. During this time, his reputation as a visionary spread and his Analects and theories were widely popularized by his disciples. His doctrine can be summarized as follows: one must adopt right conduct by adopting the highest virtues, such as tolerance, kindness, benevolence, love for others, and respect for the elderly. Confucianism is a philosophical, moral and political school that has exerted significant influence on China and other countries in Asia, where it has been adapted to the local context.

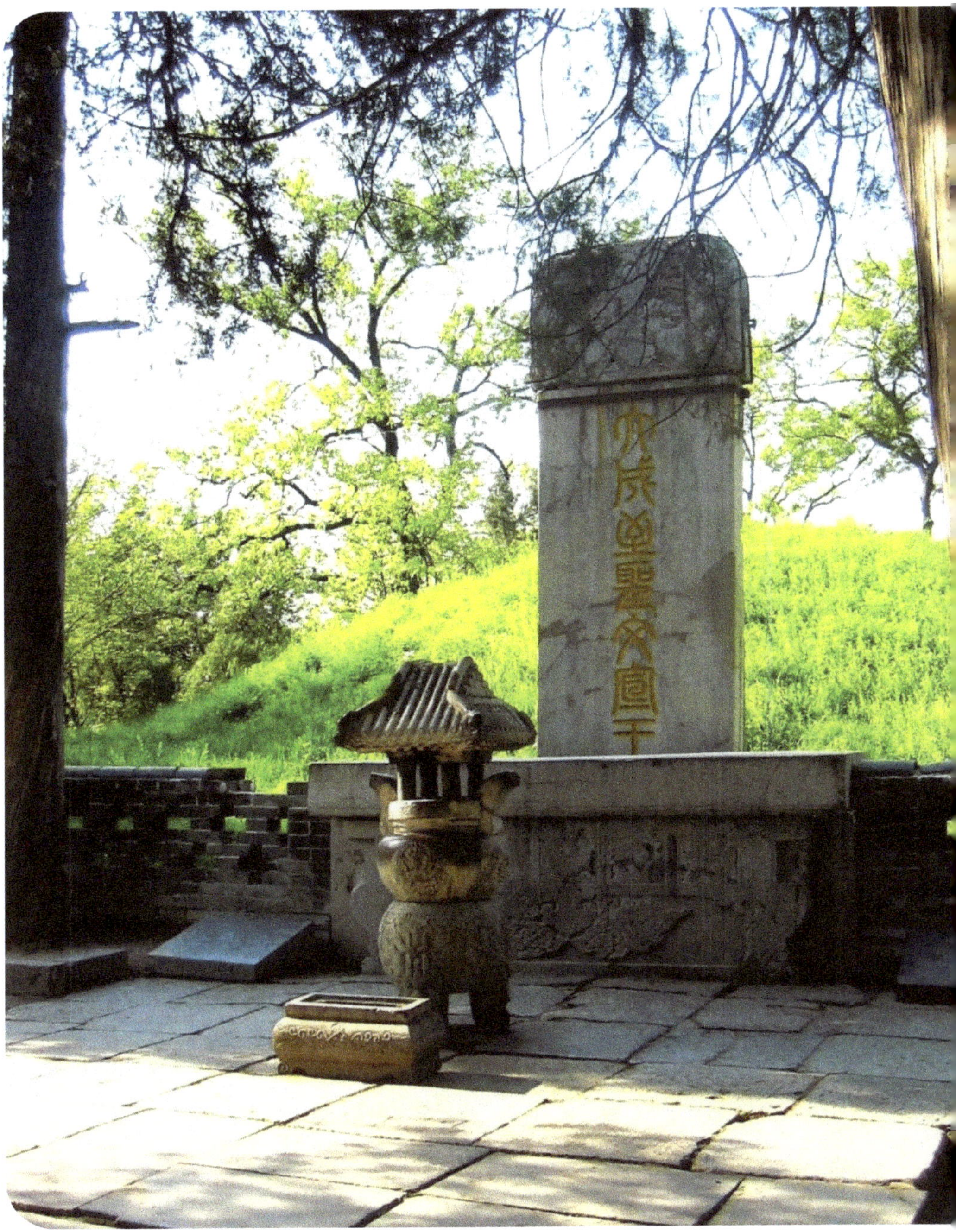

Feel Persian's empire dominance in

PERSEPOLIS

#14 🕐 **500 BC**
📖 **IRAN**

The archaeological site of Persepolis is one of the most prestigious in Iran. This place bears witness to the history of the Persian Empire and it offers visitors a fascinating insight into everyday life in antiquity. Located in the southern Iranian city of Shiraz, Persepolis was founded in 515 BC. by Emperor Darius I and was the capital of the Persian Empire until its fall in 330 BC. The site is composed of several magnificent buildings, such as the Palace of Apadana, the Palace of Tachara and the Palace of Hadish. Each of these buildings is richly decorated with motifs and epic sculptures, which tell the story of the Persian Empire and its culture. The archaeological site of Persepolis is now a UNESCO World Heritage Site.

▶ Persia became an independent kingdom under King Cyrus II before becoming an empire. Cyrus II, known as Cyrus the Great, was the founder of the Persian Empire, successor to the Medes Empire. The Achaemenid Empire was the first of the Persian Empires to rule over a large part of the Middle East.

The Persians conquered Babylon and reduced it to the status of a provincial capital. Biblical authors interpret the fall of Babylon as a divine punishment for punishing human pride manifested in the excess of the city. Cyrus then allowed the return of the Jews from Babylon in exile, who regained their freedom and returned to Jerusalem, bringing with them the official language of Babylon, Aramaic. In 500 BC, Darius I founded Persepolis, located 70 km northeast of Shiraz. Its construction, begun in 520 BC, lasted until 424 BC and was only intended to host the festivities of Norouz, the Persian New Year. This festival is still celebrated today and marks the beginning of spring, with traditional foods, music, and dancing. It was later destroyed by Alexander the Great in 323 BC.

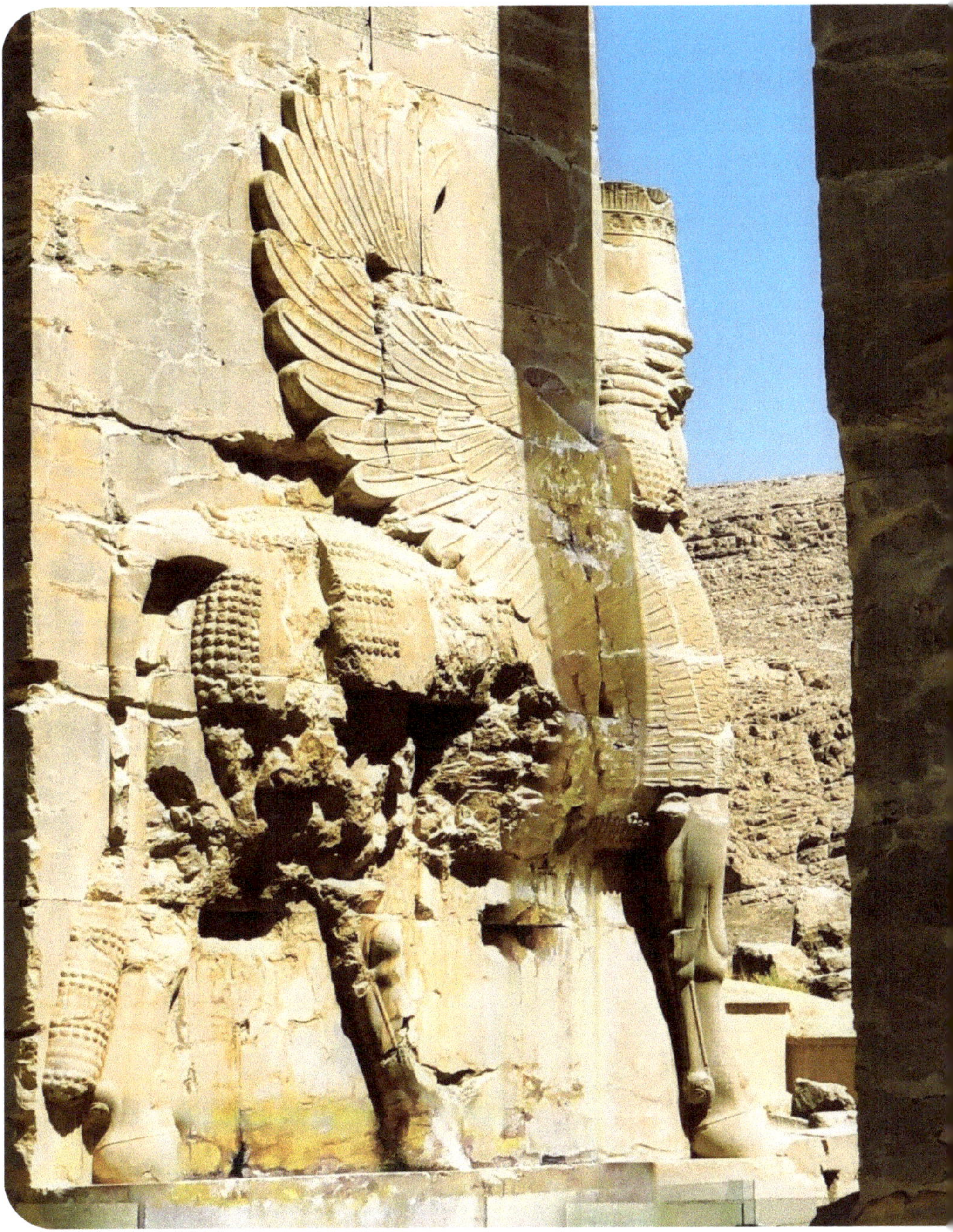

Revisit the Persian Wars at the

MARATHON MOUND

#15 ⏱ **490 BC**

🗺 **GREECE**

Marathon Mound is an archaeological site located in Greece, about 40 km from the city of Athens. This tumulus, also known as the Necropolis Mound, is the tomb of the Athenian soldiers who fought and died in the famous Battle of Marathon in 490 BC. According to legend, a soldier named Philippides ran to Athens to announce the victory of the Athenian army over the Persians, and died of exhaustion immediately after. The Marathon race honors this glorious 42-kilometer run.. The Marathon Mound is a popular pilgrimage site for Greeks and is considered a valuable historical place for the country. Nowadays, the tumulus is open to the public and it is possible to visit the tombs and immerse yourself in the history of ancient Greece.

▶ The first Persian War took place between the Persians and the Greeks in 490 BC. Thousands of Persians, led by the magnificent king Darius I, landed and invaded Greece on the plain of Marathon. Under the command of the strategist Miltiades, 10,000 Greek infantry soldiers charged and defeated the Persians, who were greatly outnumbered. According to legend, only 192 Greeks died compared to 6,400 Persians. The first Persian War ended on this plain.

Darius' reaction to this defeat was to prepare his revenge and launch an expedition, but he died in the year 486 BC, a few months later. Xerxes I succeeded him and landed in Greece in 480 BC where he was confronted by 300 Spartans led by King Leonidas. Xerxes still took Athens and burned the city, but the Athenian general Themistocles managed to sink the Persian fleet during the battle of Salamis. This Greek victory marked the beginning of the Athenian Golden Age and put an end to the expansion of the Persian Empire which then declined inevitably.

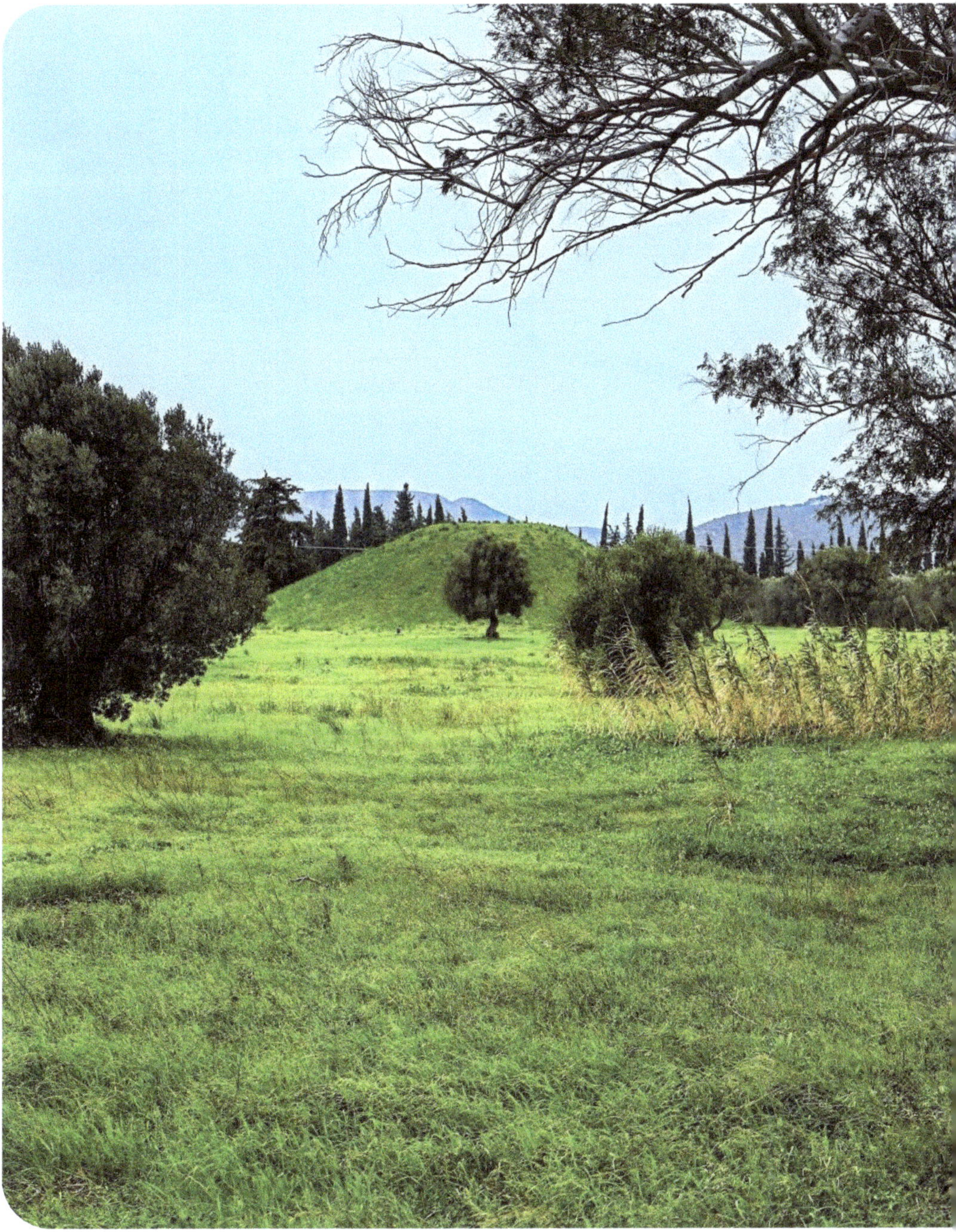

Witness the advent of the ancient Greek civilization at the

THE ACROPOLIS

#16 ⏱ **461 BC**

🗺 **GREECE**

The Acropolis is an emblematic place in the history of ancient Greece. Perched on a hill above the city of Athens, the Acropolis is home to many world-renowned archaeological sites, such as the Parthenon, the Temple of Athena Nikea and the Propylaea. This fortified citadel was built in the 5th century BC and it played a crucial role in the political, religious and cultural life of historical Greece. Today, the Acropolis is a very popular tourist site and is considered one of the most prominent symbols of ancient Greece. These monuments are certainly among the most aesthetically pleasing monuments in the world at this time. As for the Parthenon, it has been considered since ancient times as the finished model of the Doric temple.

▶ In Greece, Pericles rose to the highest magistracy of the city of Athens by becoming a *strategos*. This position is not unique, as there are ten *strategos*, but Pericles was consistently re-elected for fifteen years, an exceptional longevity. Pericles accompanied the peak of Athens and embellished the Acropolis of Athens. A group of artists implemented the development plans and transformed, under the direction of the sculptor Phidias, the rocky hill into an extraordinary architectural ensemble.

He began with the most iconic building in history: the Parthenon. Then there was the Erechtheion Temple, the sanctuary dedicated to Athena, goddess of war and wisdom. This temple was destroyed by the Persians during the second Persian war. The Temple of Nike, goddess of victory, and the Propylaea, vestibules leading to the sanctuaries. The Parthenon, which was built as a temple dedicated to Athena, was actually never used as a temple. Instead, it was used as a Treasury, a church, and even a mosque at different points in history.

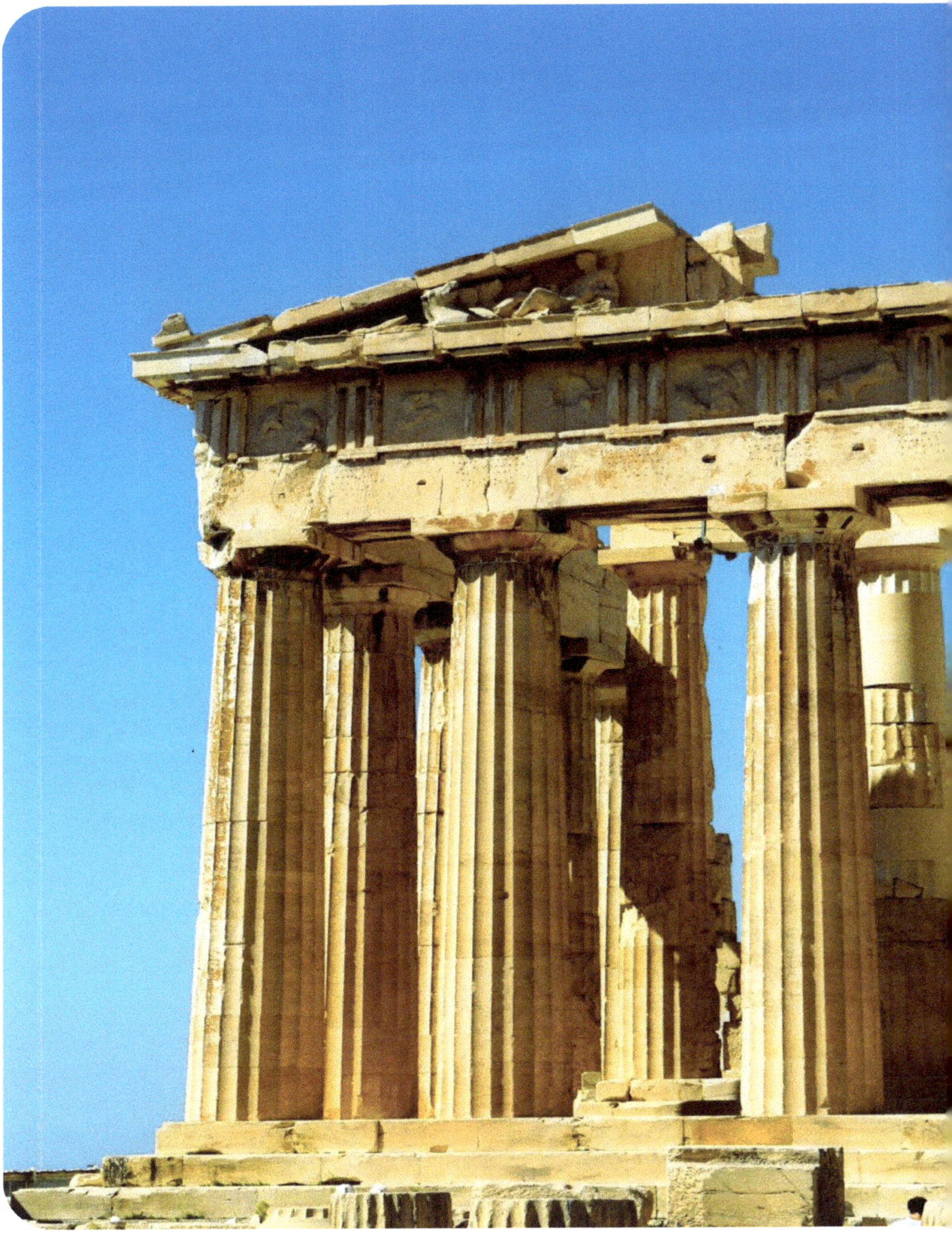

Feel Alexander the Great's huge Empire at the

STATUE OF THE WARRIOR ON HORSEBACK

#17

336 BC

N. MACEDONIA

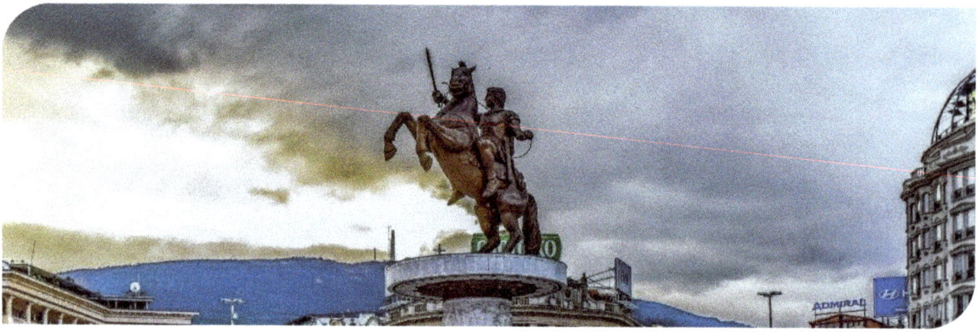
ADMIRAL

The Statue of the Warrior on Horseback of Skopje is an emblematic monument of the city of Skopje, located in Macedonia. It is located on Freedom Square, in the center of the city, and is a tribute to the Macedonian national hero, Alexander the Great. The statue, which is 22 meters high, is the work of Slovak artist Viktor Vasarely and was inaugurated in 2011. It has become one of the symbols of the city of Skopje and has become a gathering place for locals and visitors alike. Through his conquests, Alexander spread Greek culture across Asia as far as the Indus Valley. Tens of thousands of Greeks migrated to the dozens of newly established cities established in the conquered territories, often named in honor of Alexander.

► At the young age of twenty, Alexander the Great ascended to the throne of Macedonia in 336 BC. He picked up where his father left off by unifying Macedonia and Greek city-states in order to invade the Persian Empire led by Darius III, paving the way for the Macedonian period. He then continued on to conquer Phoenicia and marched all the way to Egypt where he was proclaimed Pharaoh. He founded Alexandria in 332 BC and its library, which was the most famous library of the ancient world and one of the main foundations of its fame. He would eventually advance to the edges of the Punjab and into the Indus Valley. There, he won the Battle of Hydaspes, briefly realizing the union between the East and the West.

A brilliant strategist but a poor administrator, his vast empire did not survive him, unlike the cultural legacy he spread to the East. In 326 BC, his soldiers refused to advance any further. He died in 323 BC in Babylon, likely of illness, at the age of thirty-two.

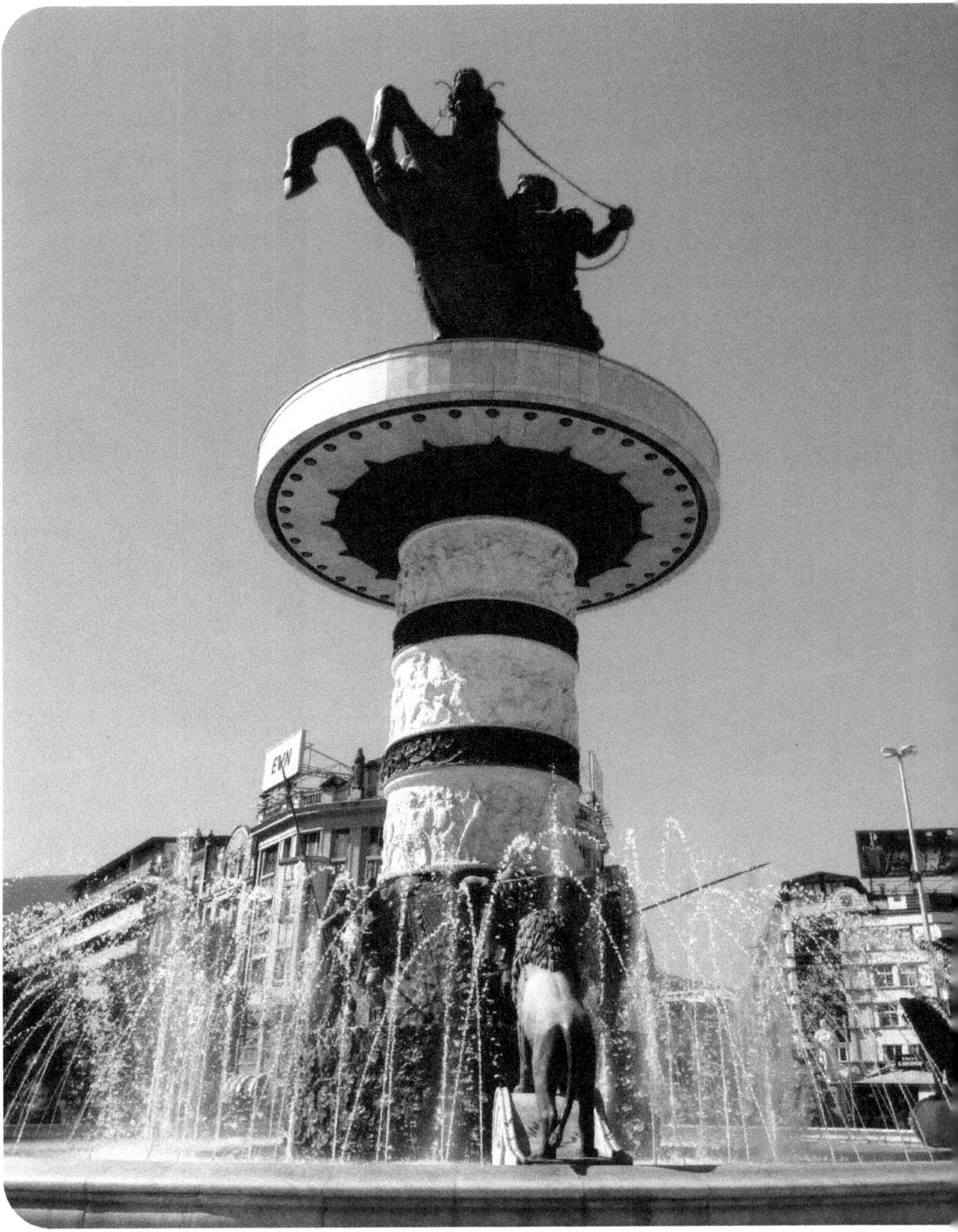
EVN

Study the birth of the Chinese Empire under Qin Shi Huang at the

GREAT WALL OF CHINA

#18 ⏱ **221 BC**
🗺 **CHINA**

The Great Wall of China is one of the wonders of the world and a must-see historical site for travelers. It stretches for more than 6,000 kilometers throughout China and was built more than 2,000 years ago to protect the country from barbarian invasions. Its grandeur and beauty are incredible and it is considered one of humanity's greatest building projects.

Many sections of the wall are now accessible to visitors and it is possible to walk on its walkways to enjoy breathtaking views of the surrounding mountains and plains. If you are a history lover or simply curious to discover this wonder of humanity, the Great Wall of China is a must-see trip.

► King Zheng of Qin became the first emperor of China under the name of Qin Shi Huang (literally, first emperor of Tsin). In 238 BC, he launched his armies against the 7 warring kingdoms of North China to create the Middle Empire. His minister Li Si advised him to divide his territories into 36 commanderies and increase central authority. The Qin dynasty, which ruled China from 221 BC to 207 BC, succeeded the Zhou dynasty and preceded the Han dynasty in China.

The Great Wall of China, the largest human construction in the world, was built to prevent the herds of neighboring tribes from mixing with those of the Chinese Empire. Satellite studies have shown that many segments (about 1000 km) are buried deep underground. The emperor Qin Shi Huang then built himself a mausoleum that covered an area of 56 km2 and buried 8,000 pottery statues of soldiers and horses. He ordered the burning of books and the execution of scholars in order to suppress dissenting voices and unify his empire under a single ideology.

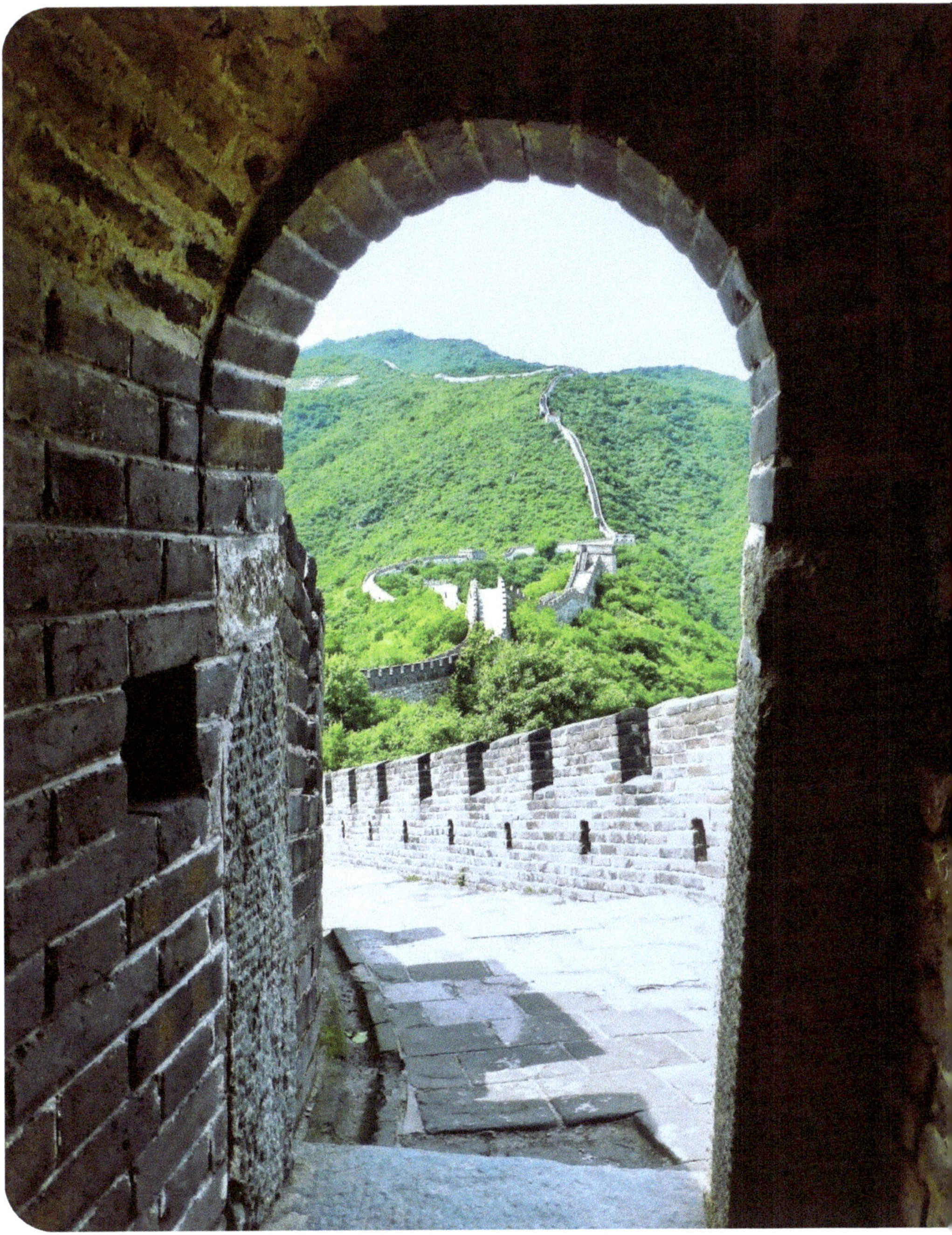

Study the destruction of Carthage during the Punic Wars at the

ARCHAEOLOGICAL SITE OF CARTHAGE

#19

⏱ **146 BC**

🗺 **TUNISIA**

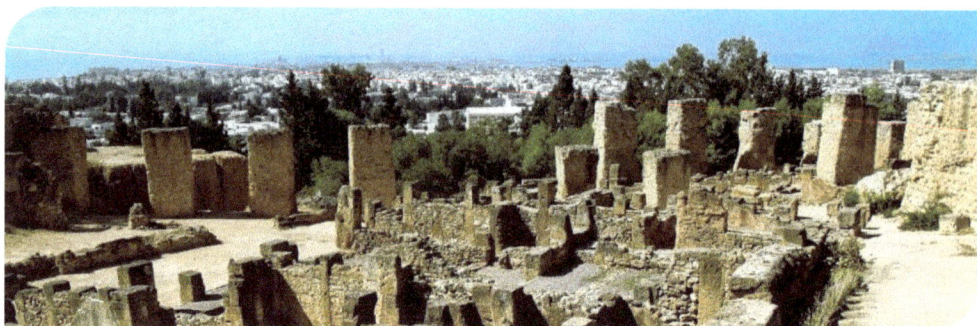

The Archaeological Site of Carthage is a fascinating place for history and culture lovers. Located near Tunis in Tunisia, it is the ancient city of Carthage, which was founded in the ninth century BC by Phoenician settlers. Founded by the Phoenicians on the shores of the Gulf of Tunis, the city of Carthage developed a remarkable civilization. It is the result of the convergence of the indigenous Berber culture with the Phoenicians' civilization The archaeological site of Carthage is full of historical treasures, with remains of Roman temples, houses, theaters and villas. In addition, there is a museum on site that offers mosaics, sculptures, and jewelry.

▶ The Punic Wars which took place between 264 BC and 146 BC were comparable to modern World Wars in terms of their scale. For the first time in history, we witnessed the confrontation and clashes between two imperialisms. The two cities were more competitors than fundamentally enemies. The Carthaginian Empire was first opposed to Greece before becoming the rival of Rome, their goal being identical : to conquer the entire Mediterranean basin.

The Carthaginian or Punic civilization was the origin of one of the greatest commercial and military powers of antiquity. In the spring of 146 BC, the Carthaginians, under the pressure of hunger and fatigue, are increasingly struggling to resist. Scipion launches the final assault and Carthage will be completely destroyed at the end of the Third Punic War. The Carthaginian general Hannibal is also famous for his daring crossing of the Alps with his army to attack Rome during the Second Punic War.

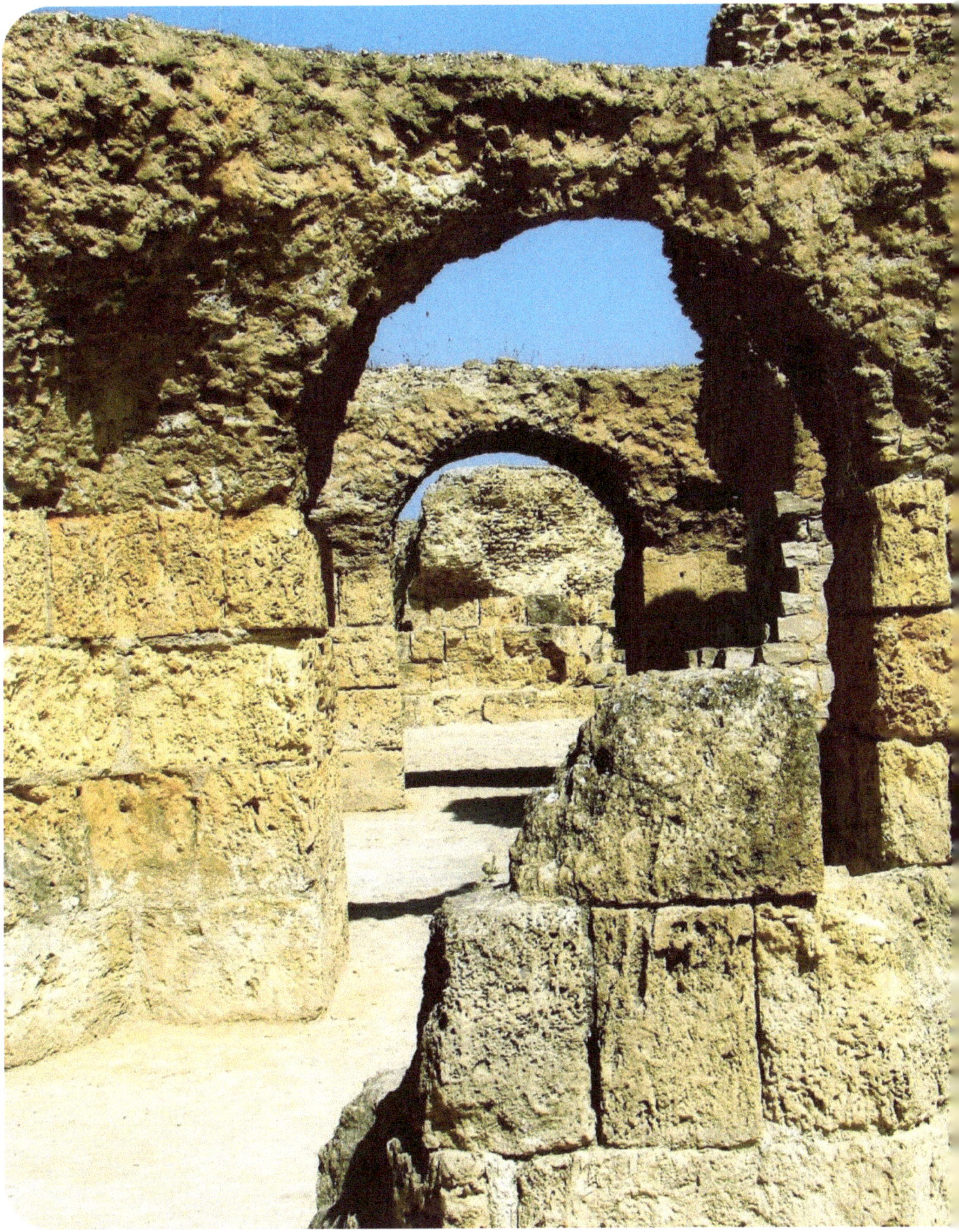

Reminisce the murder of Julius Caesar after crossing the Rubicon at the

TEMPLE OF CAESAR

#20 ⏱ **44 BC**

🗺 **ITALY**

The Temple of Caesar is an emblematic monument of ancient Rome. Erected in honor of Julius Caesar, this temple is considered one of the most prestigious in the city. Located in the Roman Forum, the Temple of Caesar was built shortly after the emperor's death in 44 BC. It was designed to celebrate the life and achievements of Caesar, who was considered one of the greatest rulers in Rome's history. The temple is adorned with marble columns and statues, which testify to the greatness of the emperor and the importance of his reign. Today, the Temple of Caesar is one of Rome's most popular sights for tourists, who come from all over the world to admire this iconic building.

▶ Julius Caesar, or Caius Julius Caesar, is the most famous character in Roman history. He fought Pompey in a struggle for absolute power at the head of what would become the Roman Empire. In 49 BC, the Senate ordered Caesar to return to Rome without his army. However, Caesar defied this order and crossed the Rubicon river with his army, sparking a civil war between him and Pompey. While doing so, he is attributed with the quote "*Alea jacta est*" (The die is cast), indicating that events have passed a point of no return.

The civil war between Caesar's supporters and Pompey's supporters ended with the latter's flight. Caesar managed to persuade the Senate to appoint him dictator, which gave him full powers. His adopted son, Brutus, nonetheless assassinated him with a fatal knife wound in the enclosure of the Roman Senate. Caesar's last words to him were "*Tu quoque, fili* (You too, my son). Julius Caesar wrote several books, including one about his conquests in Gaul and another about his time as governor of Spain.

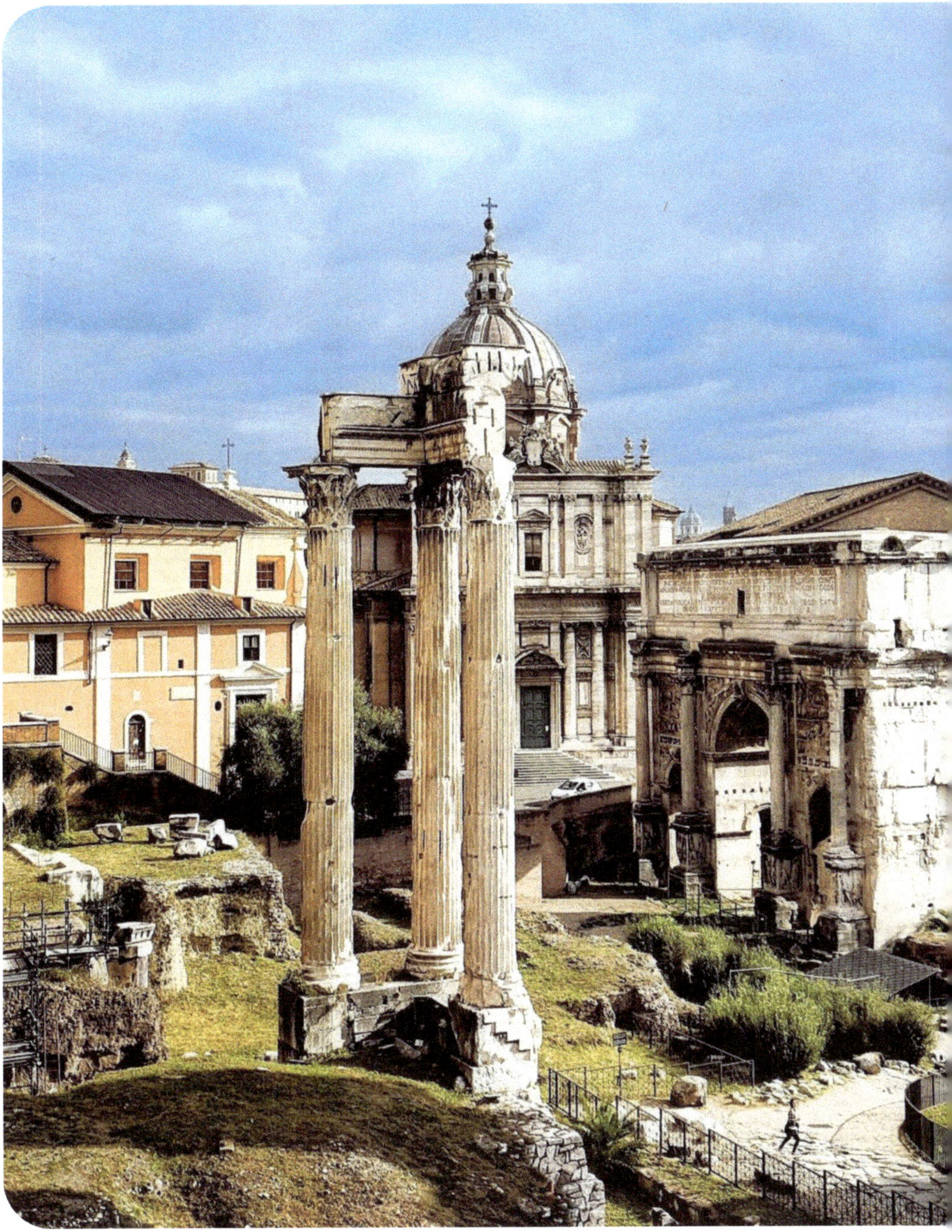

Contemplate the architectural skills of nomadic Nabataeans at

PETRA

#21

⏱ **32 BC**

🗺 **JORDAN**

Petra is an exceptional archaeological site located in Jordan, known for its magnificent temples and tombs carved into red sandstone. It is half built, half carved into the rock face, surrounded by mountains riddled with defiles and gorges. The universal value of Petra lies in the architecture of elaborate tombs and temples, the remaining religious highlights, canals, tunnels and diversionary dams that combine with an extensive network of cisterns and reservoirs that controlled and preserved seasonal rainwater, and numerous archaeological remains: copper mines, temples, churches and other public buildings. The fusion of Hellenistic architectural facades with traditional rock-cut Nabataean temples makes this place unique in the world.

▶ The Nabateans, a nomadic tribe, began settling in Petra. Most of their trade was conducted between oases without following a specific route. Petra is located 250 km south of Amman, the capital of Jordan. Its name comes from Greek and means rock. It was created by the Edomites who dominated the region between the 8th and 5th centuries BC. It then passed into the hands of the Nabateans who considered it protected by the god Duchara. Petra reached its peak between the 1st century BC and the 1st century AD, housing up to 30,000 inhabitants. It thrived due to its strategic position on trade routes between Arabia, the Red Sea, and the Mediterranean, as well as its shelter in a deep gorge.

Water was collected during floods through a ceramic water supply system that fed a significant network of underground cisterns. The opening of sea routes during the Roman era dealt a fatal blow to Petra and the Nabateans. It was occupied by the Romans, conquered by the Arabs and the crusaders, before being completely forgotten until its rediscovery in 1812 by Swiss traveler, Johann Ludwig Burckhardt.

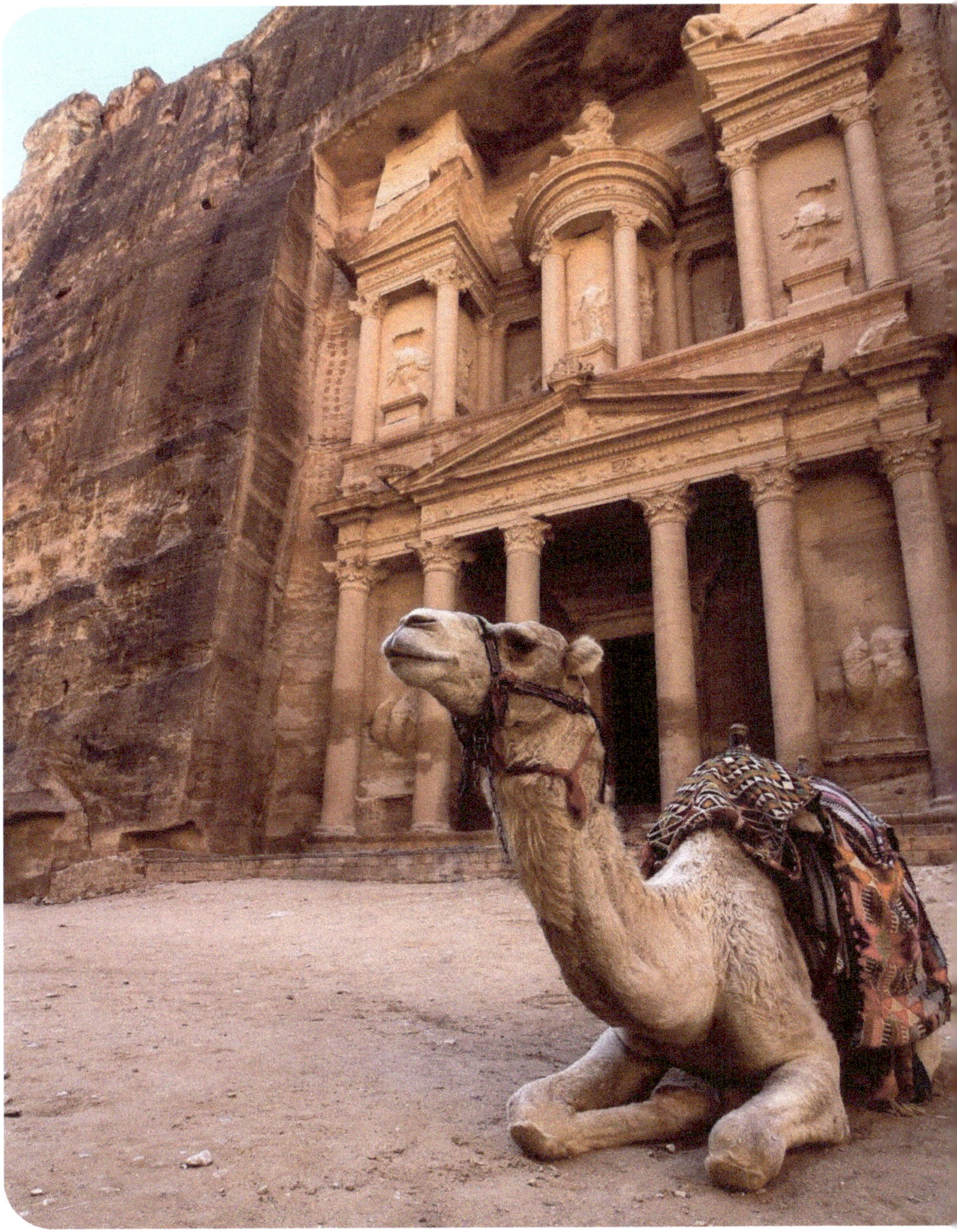

Apprehend the first Roman Emperor's appointment at the

MAUSOLEUM OF AUGUSTUS

#22 ⏱ **27 BC**
🗺 **ITALY**

The Mausoleum of Augustus is a remarkable monument located in the heart of Rome, Italy. This grand structure was built between 28 and 23 BC by the first Roman emperor, Augustus, to serve as his final resting place. The Mausoleum was designed to be an imposing and majestic structure, constructed from gleaming white marble and adorned with intricate statues and bas-reliefs depicting scenes from Roman mythology. The Mausoleum of Augustus stands as a testament to the power and legacy of the Roman Empire. As the final resting place of the first Roman emperor, who ruled for over four decades, the monument holds immense historical significance. In recognition of its cultural and historical value, the Mausoleum of Augustus was declared a UNESCO World Heritage Site in 1980.

▶ Augustus, also known as Gaius Julius Caesar Augustus, is considered the first Roman emperor. A military general and statesman, he came to power after the assassination of Julius Caesar in 44 BC. Augustus dominated his rivals and established himself as the undisputed leader of the Roman Republic. Augustus' legacy remains among the most remarkable of all Romans. He transformed Rome with the development of public transport and postal delivery, while maintaining peace in Rome by putting an end to the civil wars that had plagued the city for decades. This earned him a godlike status in the Roman pantheon, with the Senate even declaring him a living deity.

Beyond his political and military accomplishments, Augustus was also known as a passionate collector of art and literature. He created Rome's first public library, the Bibliotheca Palatina, which housed thousands of scrolls and became a hub of intellectual activity in the city. Augustus surrounded himself with poets, philosophers, and scholars, fostering a cultural renaissance that would define the Augustan Age.

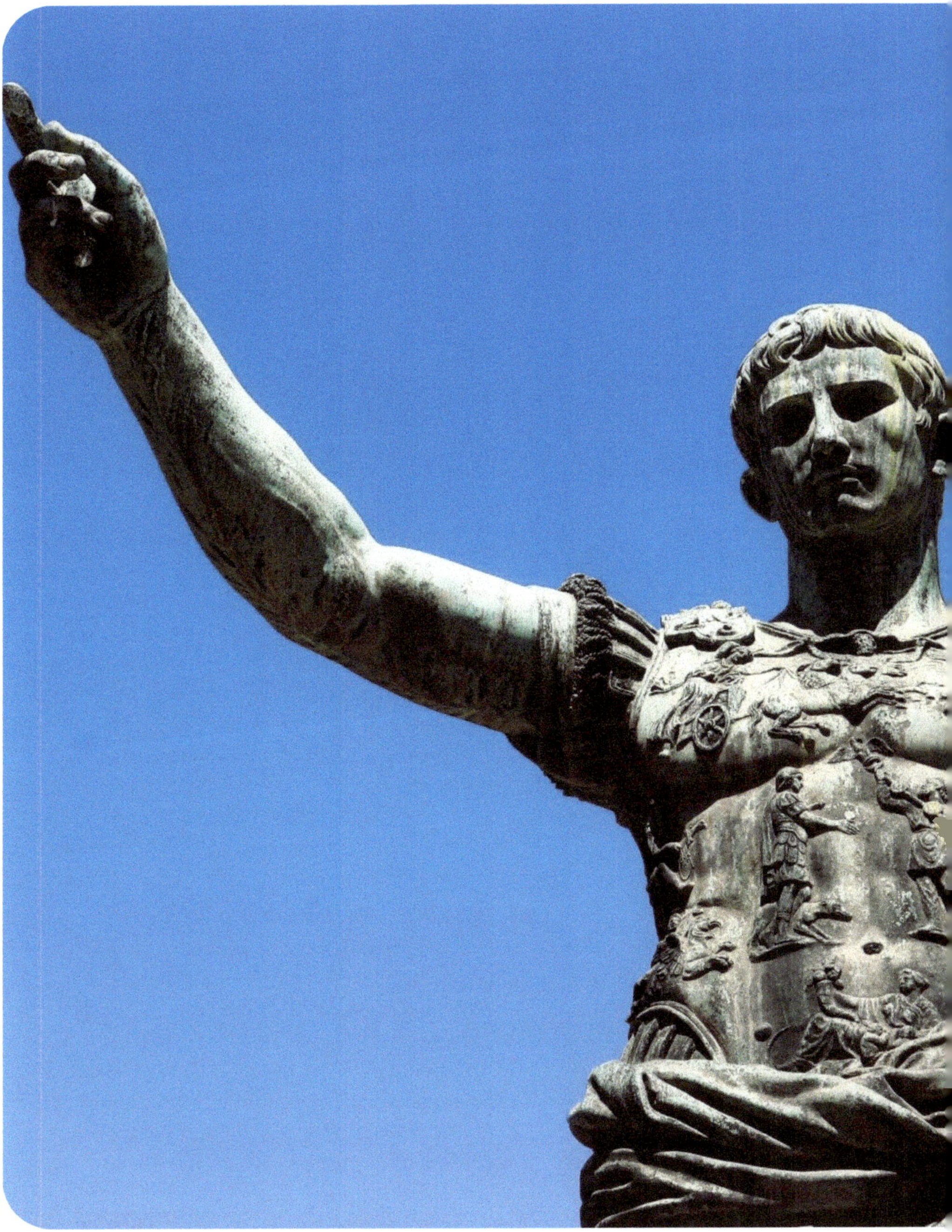

Recollect Jesus Christ's crucifixion watching

CHRIST THE REDEEMER STATUE

#23

⏱ **33 AD**

🗺 **BRAZIL**

The iconic Christ the Redeemer statue is an enduring symbol of Rio de Janeiro, Brazil. Perched atop the towering Mount Corcovado, this colossal bronze figure stands over 30 meters tall, its outstretched arms overlooking the stunning vistas of the city below. The statue's design, created by Brazilian engineer Heitor da Silva Costa and French sculptor Paul Landowski, is a striking representation of Jesus Christ in a pose of benediction. The name "Christ the Redeemer" is a reference to the Christian belief that Jesus, the Son of God, came to Earth to redeem humanity through his teachings and sacrifice. Despite its immense popularity as a tourist attraction, the statue remains a place of reverence and pilgrimage for the local Catholic community, who continue to find solace and inspiration in its towering presence.

▶ Jesus of Nazareth, known as Jesus Christ, was born in Judea during the reign of King Herod the Great. According to the gospels of Luke and Matthew, he was conceived in Bethlehem. However, some believe he was born elsewhere and that Bethlehem was chosen due to its prophetic significance as the city of King David. Jesus is the son of Joseph, a carpenter from the line of King David, and Mary, who conceived Jesus by the power of the Holy Spirit and is therefore known as "Virgin Mary." Jesus is considered by Christians as the Messiah and the Son of God, and is also considered a special prophet by Muslims.

When King Herod learned of the rumors of a « king of the Jews being born, he ordered the murder of all children under two years old in the Bethlehem region. Joseph is warned in a dream to flee to Egypt with Jesus and Mary. Jesus was later sentenced to death by the Sanhedrin for blasphemy and executed on a cross after being flogged and insulted by a crowd. His death is celebrated by Christians as the Passion of Jesus and his resurrection is celebrated as Easter.

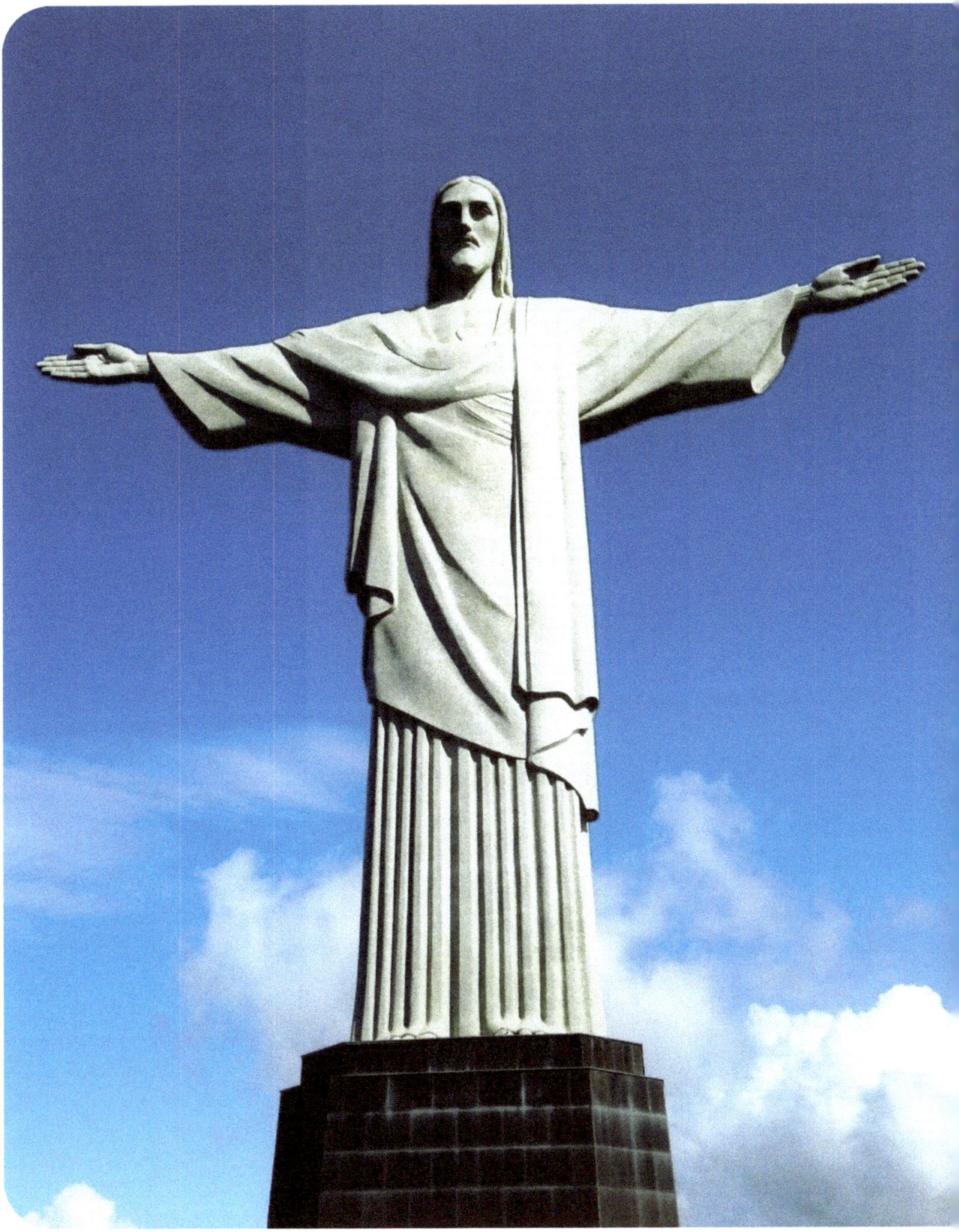

Grasp Solomon's Temple's destruction at the

WESTERN WALL

#24

70 AD

ISRAEL

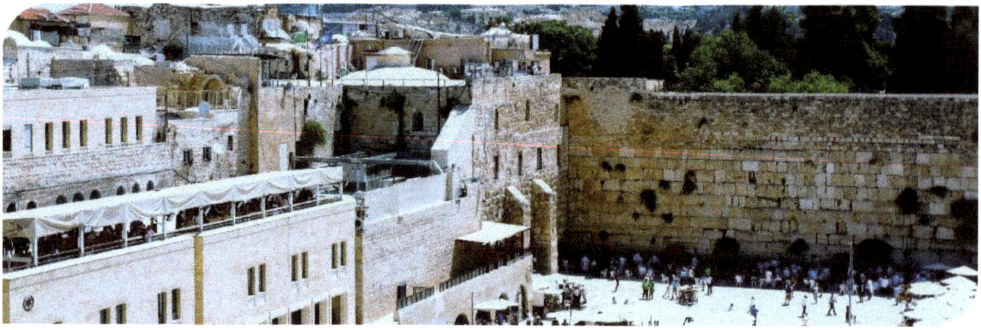

The Western Wall is a sacred site for Jews, located in Jerusalem. It is the place where they come to pray and express their prayers and wishes for the future. The Wall is also known as the Kotel and is considered one of the holiest sites of the Jewish religion. According to tradition, it is located near the place where the Temple of Jerusalem once stood, which was destroyed by the Romans in 70 AD. Since then, the Wall has been used as a place of prayer for Jews and has become a symbol of their faith and connection to God. People come from all over the world to visit the Western Wall and place their prayers there, in the hope that God will answer them. It is a place of peace and spirituality, where people can reconnect with their faith and history.

► On a Sabbath day in the year 66 AD, in Caesarea, a man sacrificed birds at the entrance of the synagogue, which caused anger among the Jews. This led to street battles between Jews and pagans. A team of Jews was sent to Sebaste to meet the Procurator Gessius Florus, but he refused to listen to them. The disturbances then reached Jerusalem. Florus chose this moment to take 17 talents from the Temple's treasury, which led to a chain reaction of revolts and reprisals. After trying to suppress the revolt in blood, Florus retreated to Caesarea while the insurgents gained control of the Temple's esplanade. Titus' troops then attacked Jerusalem.

Titus took control of Antonia and burned the outer gates of the Temple, then attacked the Temple which was completely burned. Jerusalem was razed, except for the three towers of Herod's palace and a part of the wall. The Romans created the province of Judea, distinct from Syria. The Sanhedrin was dissolved. The sacrificial cult was no longer celebrated. In the fall of 70 AD, hundreds of thousands of Jewish prisoners were killed in public spectacles in Caesarea.

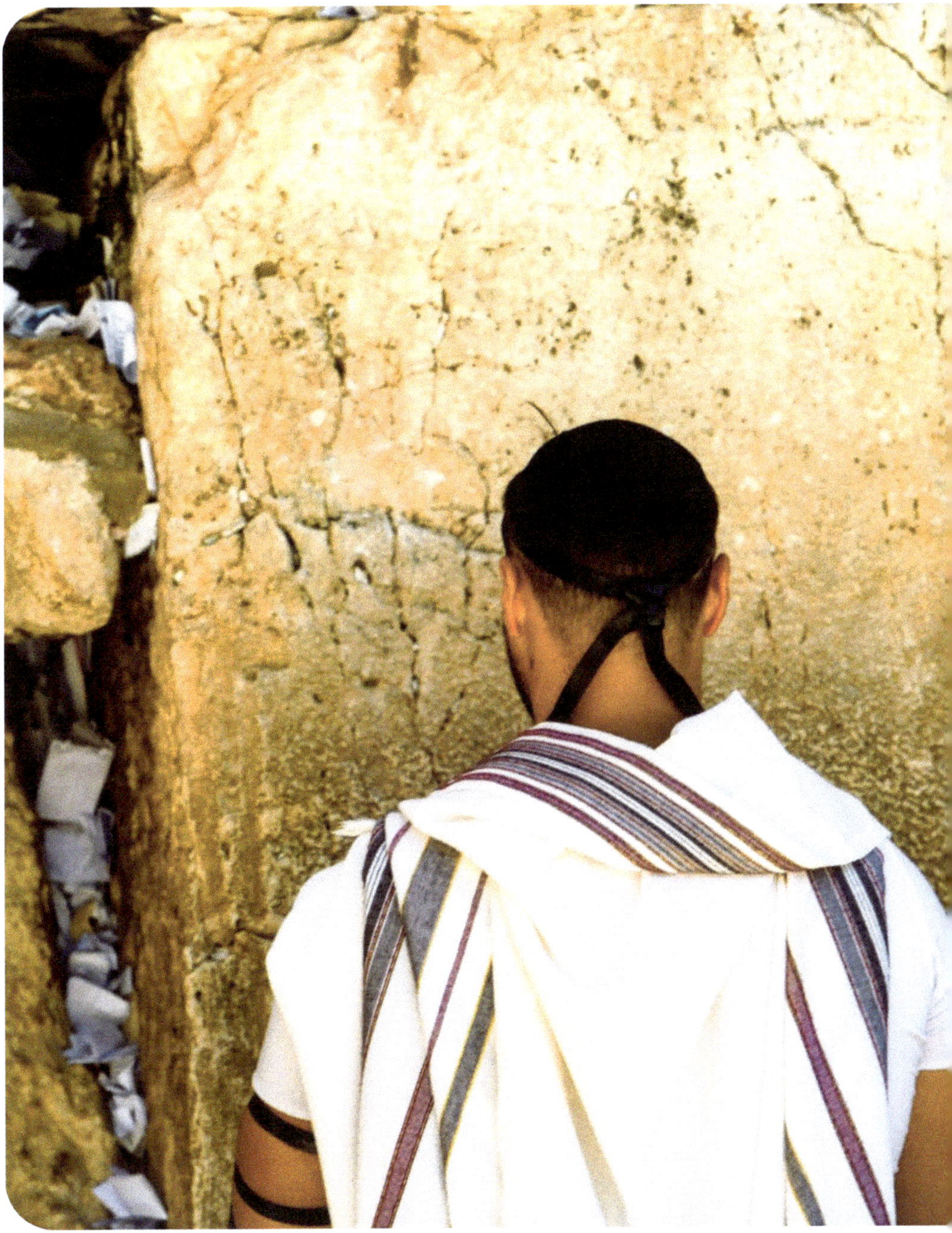

Witness Mount Vesuvius' eruption at the

RUINS OF POMPEI

#25 ⏱ **79 AD**
🗺 **ITALY**

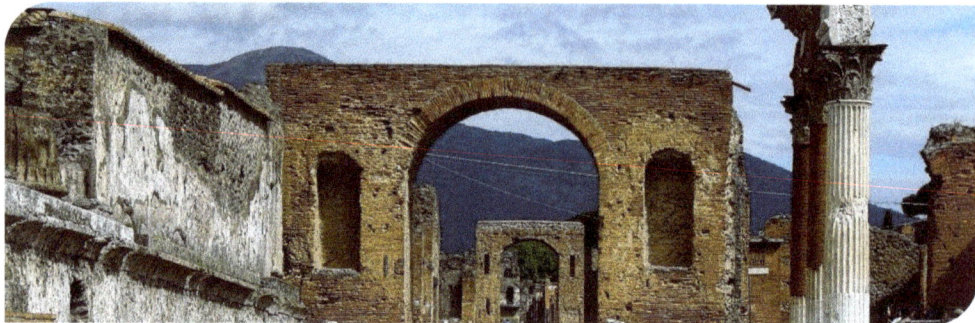

The Ruins of Pompeii are an extraordinary archaeological site located in Italy, near the bustling city of Naples. This ancient Roman city was once a thriving hub of activity, until it was tragically buried under a thick layer of ash and lava during the catastrophic eruption of Mount Vesuvius in the year 79 AD. For centuries, the remains of Pompeii lay hidden, forgotten beneath the volcanic debris, until they were rediscovered in 1748 by a team of curious explorers. Since then, the excavation and study of the Ruins of Pompeii have captivated historians, archaeologists, and visitors from around the world. As the layers of ash and debris were carefully removed, the city's well-preserved structures and artifacts were revealed, offering a remarkable glimpse into the daily lives of the Romans who once inhabited this vibrant metropolis.

▶ A volcano that was thought to be extinct for a long time swallowed the city of Pompeii under 7 meters of volcanic ash in 79 AD. A similar incident occurred to the nearby port of Herculaneum, which was covered by 16 meters of lava. These two locations in the Bay of Naples had already been destroyed in 62 AD by an earthquake, but had been rebuilt. The volcano, which was considered a simple mountain, erupted 10 years after reconstruction and killed thousands of people in just 24 hours.

Today, only 1400 traces of bodies have been found in the ruins of Pompeii, but most of the inhabitants were able to flee before the catastrophic eruption of Mount Vesuvius. This ancient Roman city, located in the Campania region of Italy, was completely buried under layers of volcanic ash and pumice, effectively preserving it for over 1600 years. Pompeii was forgotten and lost to the world until it was rediscovered by chance in the 18th century, and is now considered one of the most remarkable and well-preserved archaeological sites, offering a unique window into the daily life and culture of the Roman Empire.

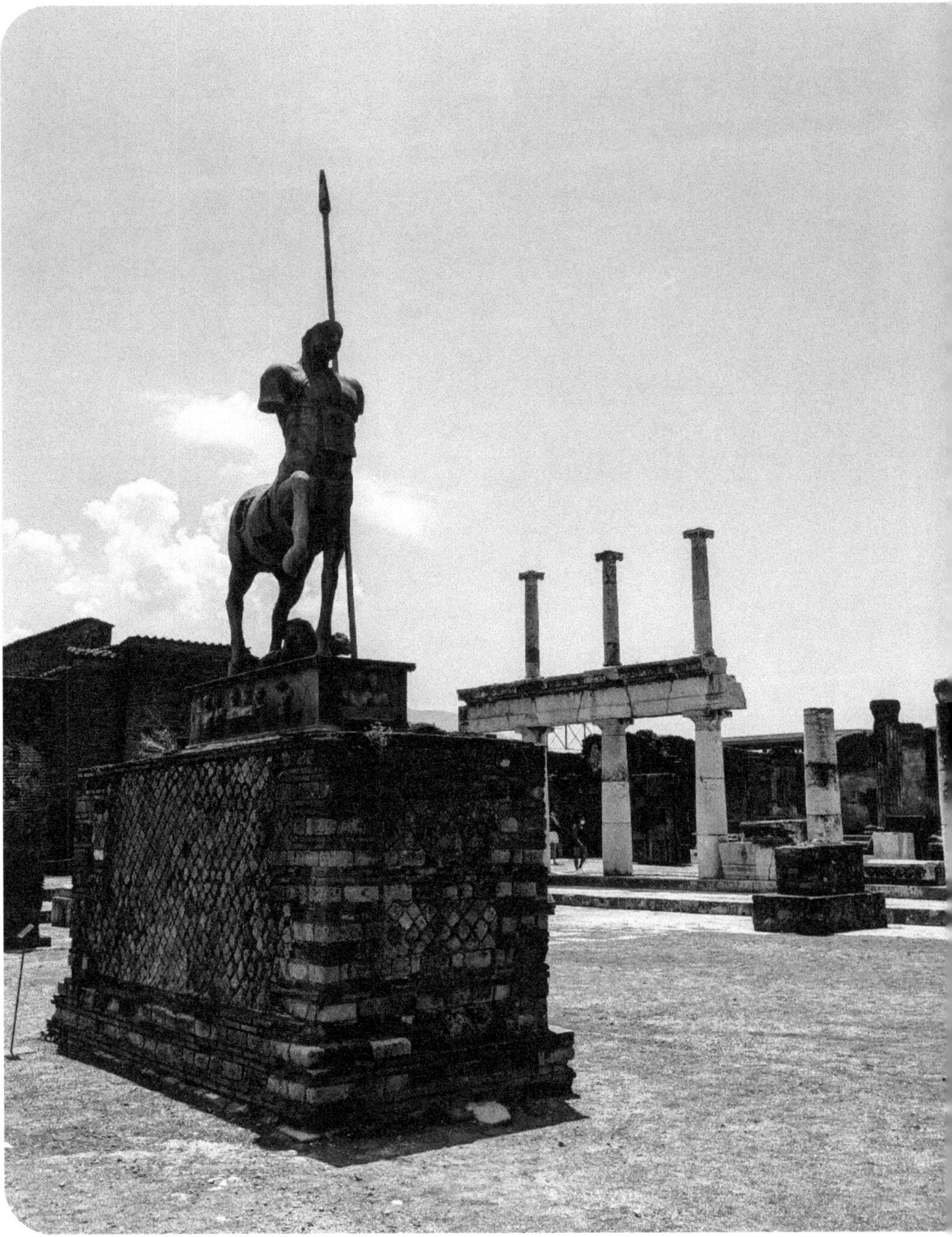

Study Marcus Aurelius' Stoicism at the

COLUMN OF MARCUS AURELIUS

#26 161 AD

ITALY

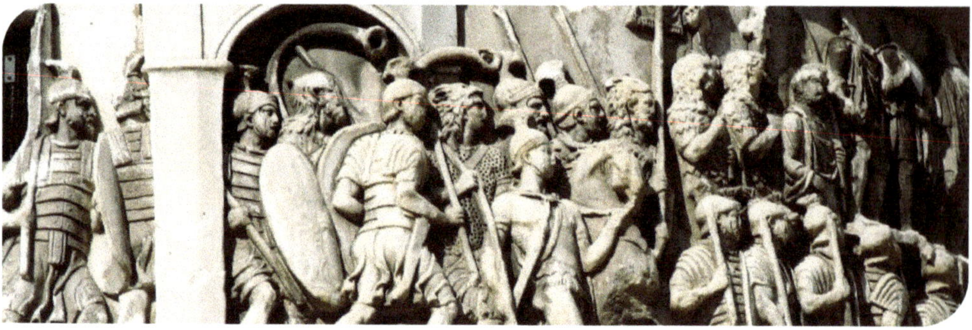

The Column of Marcus Aurelius is a remarkable monument located in the heart of Rome, Italy. Erected in honor of the emperor who reigned from 161 to 180 AD, this towering structure stands as a testament to the life and achievements of one of Rome's most influential rulers. Measuring an impressive 30 meters in height, the column is composed of 19 capitals, each representing a different military campaign undertaken by the emperor. The intricate relief sculptures adorning the column's surface depict the battles and triumphs of Marcus Aurelius, providing a vivid visual narrative of his reign. Its towering presence and intricate details serve as a powerful symbol of the grandeur and might of the Roman Empire at the height of its power.

► Marc-Aurelius was born in Rome in 121 AD to a noble Spanish family. After the death of his father, Hadrian entrusted the guardianship of Marc-Aurèle to his successor Antonin, who adopted and raised him, providing him with an excellent education. His reign was marked by numerous invasions that threatened the Empire from all sides. Upon his accession to the throne in 161 AD, the Parthians invaded the eastern provinces of the empire and the Roman army suffered a first setback. Shortly after the war against the Parthians, new threats emerged on the borders of the Empire. These included the barbarian peoples settled in the Danubian regions, the Quades and the Marcomans, who directly threatened northern Italy. Marc-Aurèle died in Vienna from the plague during a campaign to extend the borders of the Roman Empire to the north. Marc-Aurèle will remain in history as the man who realized Plato's dream of a "philosopher king. A prominent Stoic, he left a philosophical work imbued with the moral theories of the philosophers of the Portico and Epictetus.

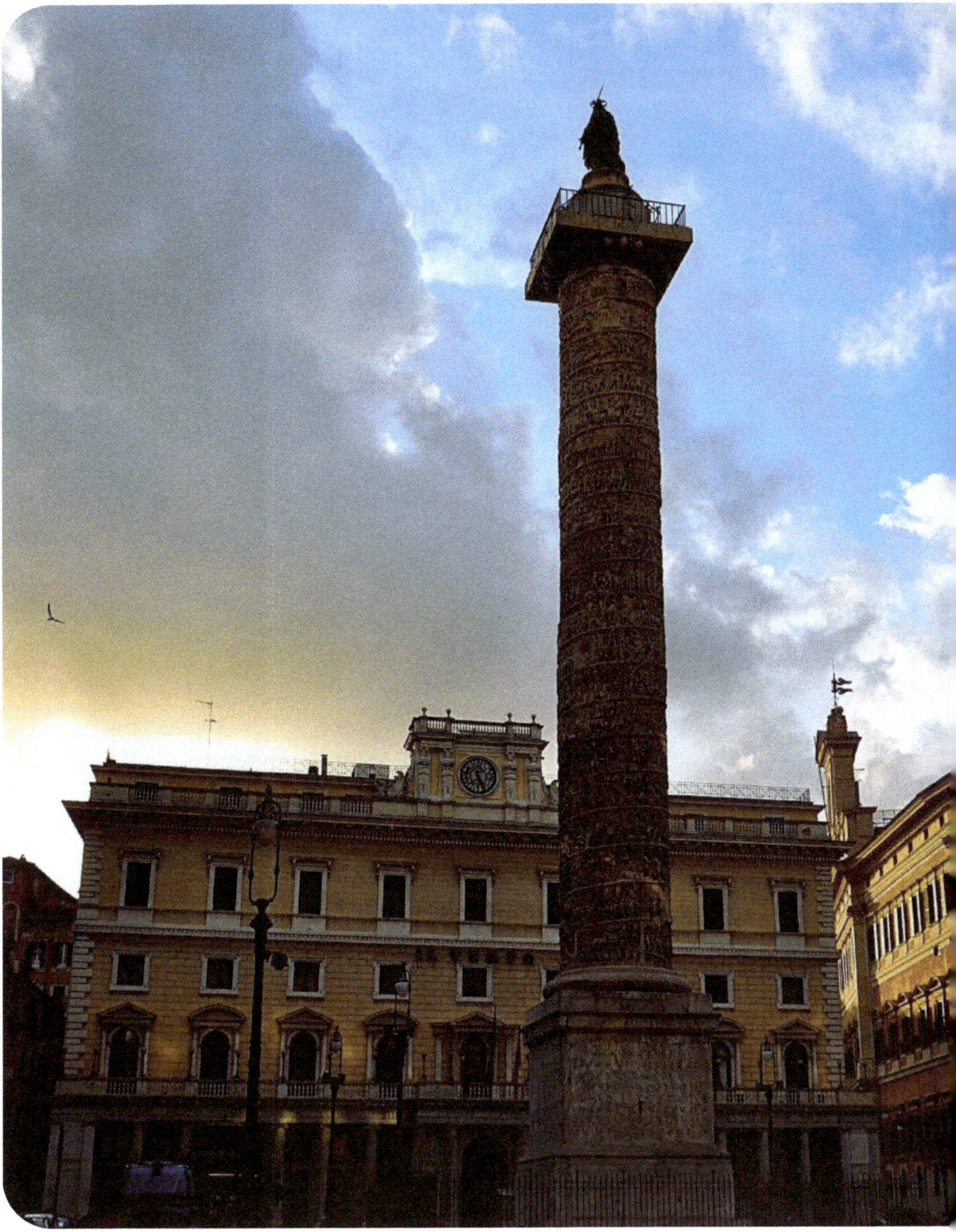

Delve into the tetrarchy of the Empire at the

DIOCLETIAN'S PALACE

#27 293 AD — CROATIA

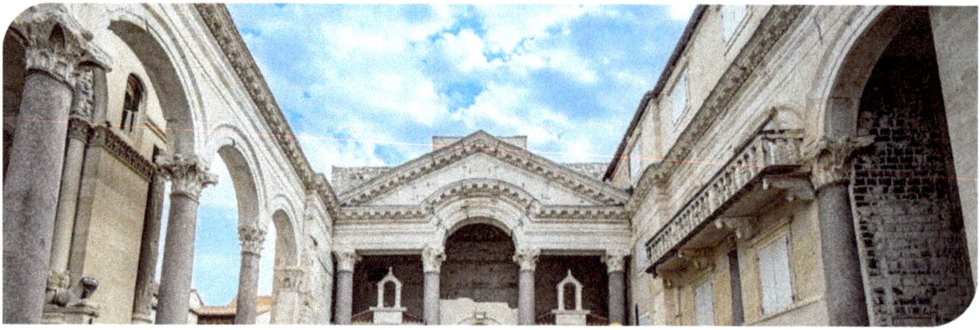

Diocletian's Palace is a historical site located in the Croatian city of Split, built in the 4th century as a summer residence for the Roman Emperor Diocletian. It is a UNESCO World Heritage Site and is known for its lush gardens and many buildings, including the Golden House, the Veterans House, and the Temple of Jupiter. It is also famous for its large throne room, which is considered one of the most beautiful throne rooms in the Roman Empire. The palace is open to the public and it is recommended to take a guide to learn more about the history and architecture of the palace. Around this palace, which features a 15th century BC sphinx that Diocletian brought from Egypt, the now Croatian city has developed. It is an enjoyable experience for anyone interested in Roman history and architecture.

► Diocletian introduced the tetrarchy, where each co-emperor would oversee a portion of the empire's borders. In September 284 AD, he was proclaimed emperor by his soldiers in the Chalcedon army. He immediately had to face several rebellions in his vast empire and called on Maximian to help him. He promoted him to the rank of Caesar in 285 AD, then to the rank of Augustus in 286 AD.

To ensure the defense and administration of the empire, Diocletian chose two additional collaborators in 293 AD, whom he promoted to the rank of Caesar. The empire, now a tetrarchy, was divided into 101 provinces grouped into 12 dioceses and 4 major regions, each of which was led by a Caesar or Augustus: Diocletian, the East, Maximian, Italy and Africa, Galerius, Illyria and the regions of the Danube, Constantius, Britain, Gaul and Spain. Each decree was jointly signed by the four rulers. This division of the Roman Empire into four parts facilitated the maintenance of order. As a result of the administrative reorganization, all its vast territories were centrally controlled, permanently ending Italy's dominance.

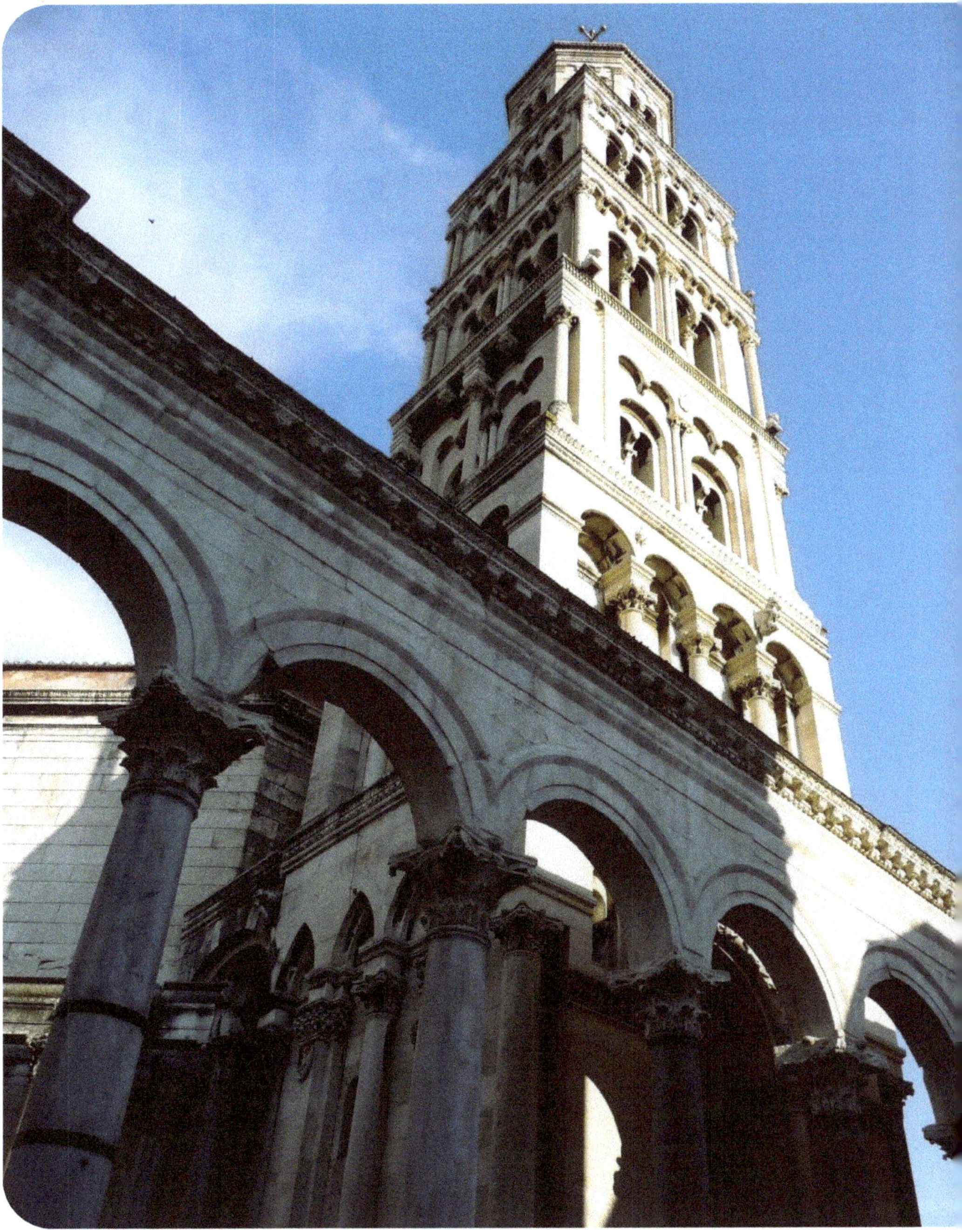

Study the conversion of Constantine at the

COLUMN OF CONSTANTINE

#28 313 AD

TURKEY

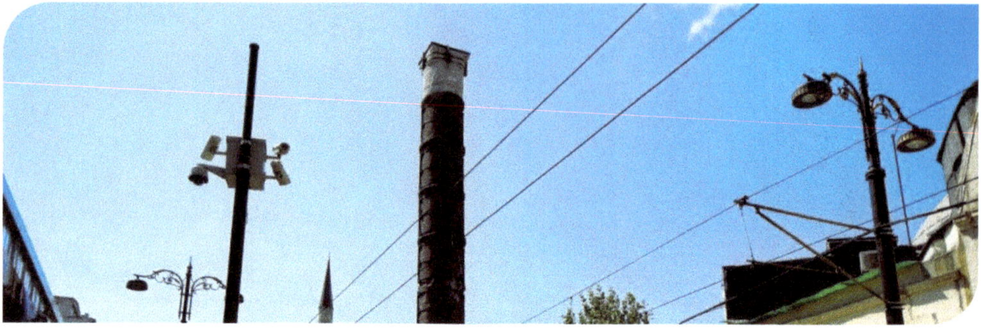

Constantine's Column in Istanbul is a historical monument that attracts many visitors every year. This column was built in honor of Roman Emperor Constantine I and is located in the Old City of Istanbul, next to the Byzantium Hippodrome. The column is made of red granite and is almost 40 meters high. It is surmounted by a bronze statue of Constantine I, which was added to the top of the column in the seventeenth century. At the bottom of the column, one can see many inscriptions in Latin and Greek that tell the story of the emperor and his life. Constantine's Column is a must-see for history and culture lovers in Istanbul and is a testament to the city's importance over the centuries.

► Flavius Valerius Constantine, also known as Constantine the Great, was born to Constance Chlore and Saint Helena and proclaimed emperor by the army in 306. He won a decisive victory against his Italian rival Maxentius and shared Roman territories with Licinius. Constantine claimed to have seen a bright sign in the sky later identified as the chi-rho symbol, which became an emblem of fighting Christianity, and converted to Christianism in 313 AD.

He issued the Edict of Milan which granted tolerance for Christians, and eventually defeated Licinius in 324. He summoned the ecumenical council of Nicaea and transformed the Greek city of Byzantium into a New Rome, which he named Constantinople. He moved the capital there and inaugurated it with dazzling pomp in 330. He was only baptized on his deathbed, on May 22, 337, and is considered a saint by Orthodox and Catholic Christians for making Christianity the official religion of the Empire. The city of Constantinople is built on seven hills, just like Rome, and was therefore named "New Rome".

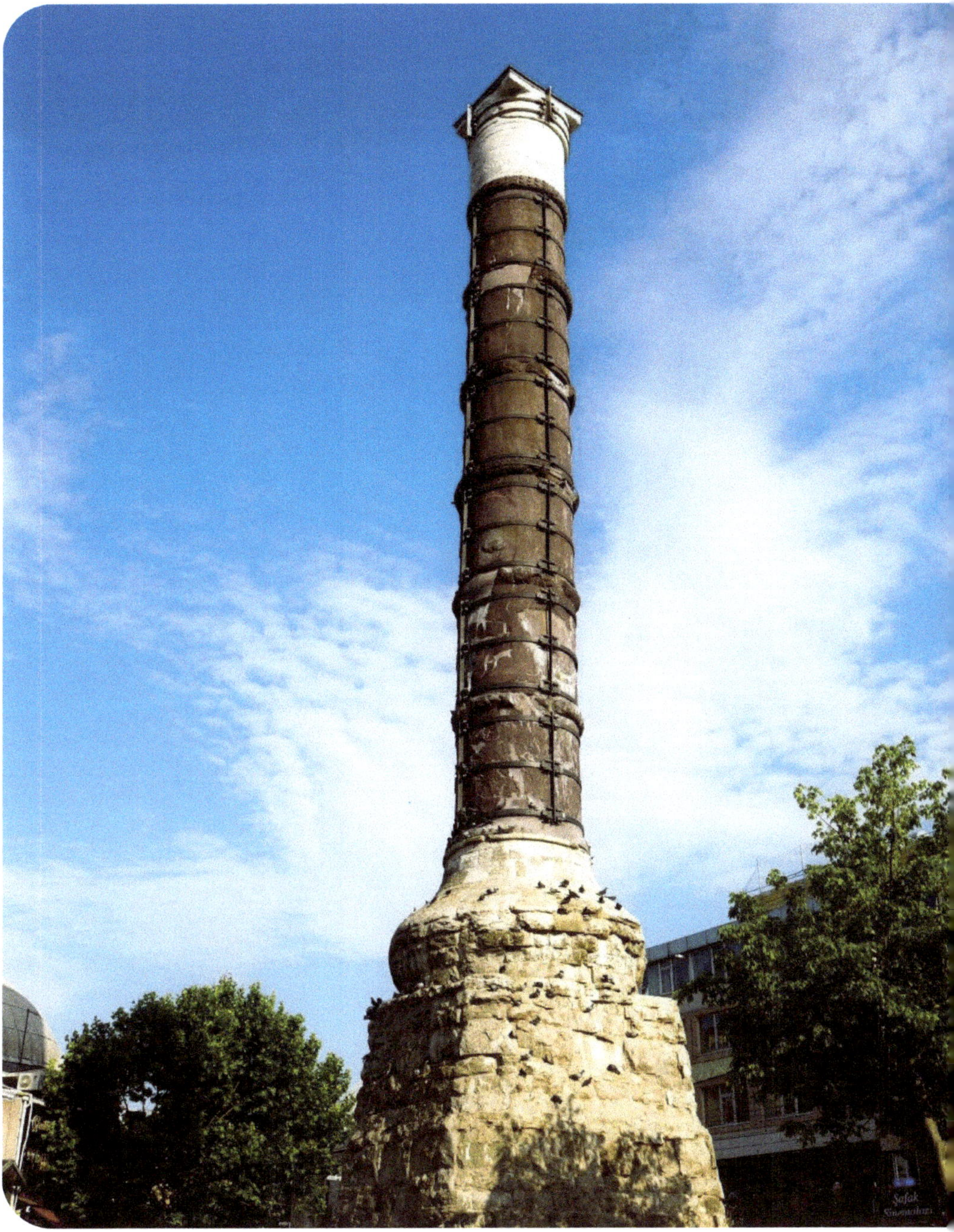

Witness the fall of the Western Roman Empire at the

COLOSSEUM

#29 ⏱ **476 AD**

🗺 **ITALY**

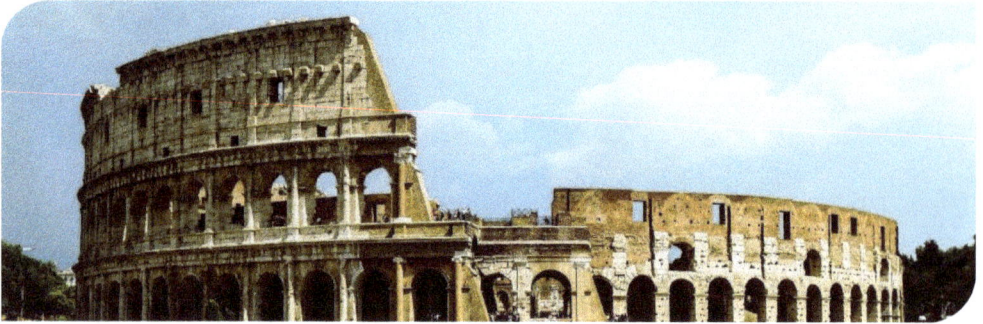

The Colosseum in Rome is undoubtedly one of the city's most famous and iconic landmarks. This magnificent amphitheater, built over 2,000 years ago, has a rich and captivating history that has captivated people from around the world for centuries. Constructed during the reign of the Roman Emperor Vespasian in the 1st century AD, the Colosseum was the largest amphitheater ever built and was the centerpiece of entertainment and spectacle in ancient Rome. Located in the heart of the Eternal City, the Colosseum serves as an ideal starting point for exploring Rome's rich cultural and historical heritage. From its stone tiers, visitors can gaze out over the city and catch glimpses of other iconic landmarks, such as the Pantheon and the Roman Forum.

▶ September 4th, 476 is considered the symbolic date of the fall of the Western Roman Empire. Barbarian peoples had long attempted to defeat Roman power, which was also weakened by corruption and a failing economy. Administrative difficulties related to the vastness of the Empire also contributed to its downfall. Enemies attacked on all fronts, with peoples such as the Vandals conquering North Africa and the Visigoths and Suebians gaining extensive territories in continental Europe. King Odoacer, leader of the Germanic Heruli, took Rome and dethroned the last Roman emperor of the West, Flavius Augustulus, in Ravenna.

This fall marked the end of the Pax Romana and the beginning of a period of wars and changes. This period saw the emergence of new Frankish kingdoms, the settlement of Germanic peoples, and the formation of Islamic territories. The phrase barbarian comes from the Greek word barbarous which was used to describe anyone who did not speak Greek or Latin.

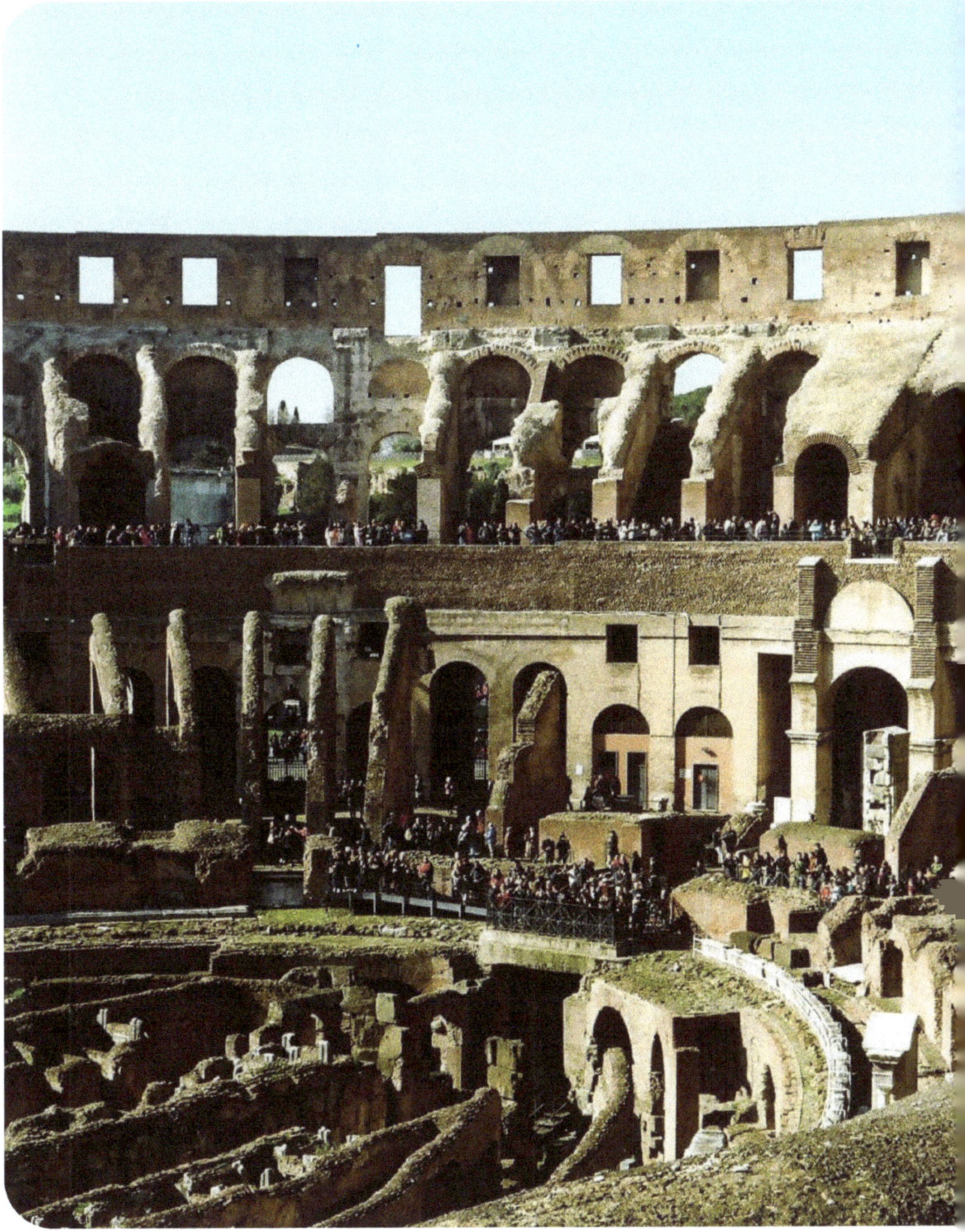

MIDDLE AGES

The Middle Ages in Europe spanned roughly 1,000 years, from the 5th to the 15th century. It was a long and complex period that saw the transformation of Europe from the fall of Rome to the dawn of the Renaissance, marked by the rise of Christianity, feudalism, the Crusades, universities, and the gradual emergence of modern nation-states.

Learn about Prince Kassapa's fortress history on the

SIGIRIYA ROCK

#30 477 AD

SRI LANKA

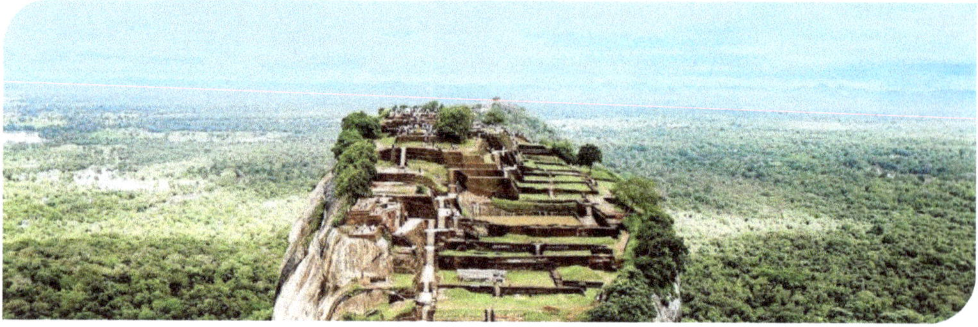

Sigiriya Rock is an exceptional historical and architectural site located in Sri Lanka. This gigantic rock rises to more than 200 meters in height and offers a breathtaking view of the surrounding valley. Once used as a royal fortress, the Rock of Sigiriya is now a must-visit for tourists who come to discover the many architectural treasures that are preserved there. Some of the most popular attractions include hanging gardens, rock frescoes and the remains of former royal dwellings. The Rock of Sigiriya is also famous for its fascinating history and many myths and legends. If you are interested in the history, architecture and culture of Sri Lanka, do not miss the opportunity to visit Sigiriya Rock on your next trip.

► The history of Sigiriya fortress is marked by violence. It was built by Prince Kassapa who, in his quest for power, killed his father and chased his brother out of the kingdom. Instead of remaining in Anuradhapura, the capital of the time, he decided in 477 AD to build an imposing fortress on the Sigiriya rock. Kasyapa feared the revenge of his half-brother Mogallana and settled on this impregnable site where he lived for 18 years. After a prolonged period of blockade, Kasyapa, the previous occupant of the Sigiriya fortress, ultimately surrendered. Kasyapa was subsequently executed, and the site of Sigiriya was abandoned in the year 495 AD.

Sigiriya, therefore, served as the royal capital for a relatively brief period of only 18 years, 8 of which were dedicated to the construction of the magnificent palace complex that once adorned the summit of the rock. The fortress of Sigiriya is also renowned for its iconic lion paw-shaped staircase, which provided access to the palace ruins perched atop the towering rock formation.

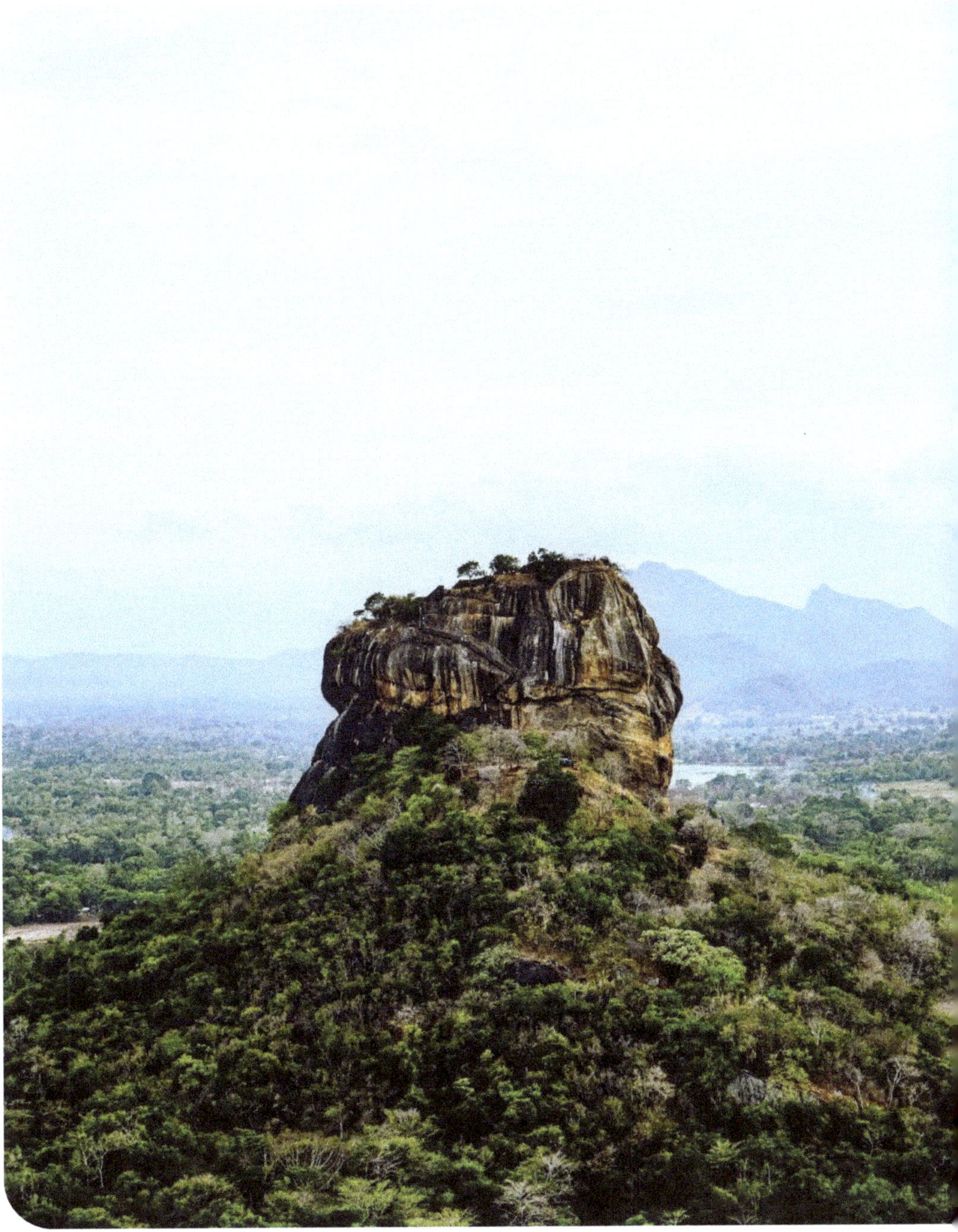

Reexperience the proclamation of Clovis as King of the Franks at the

BASILICA OF SAINT-REMI

#31 498 AD

FRANCE

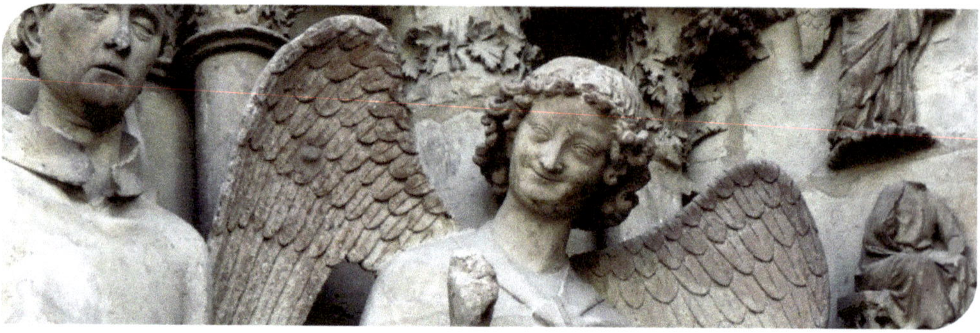

The Basilica of Saint-Remi in Reims is one of the most famous landmarks in the Champagne-Ardenne region. Located in the city center of Reims, it is a true jewel of Gothic art and is recognized as a leading historical and cultural site. The basilica is dedicated to Saint Remi, bishop of Reims in the fifth century, who baptized King Clovis and played a crucial role in Gaul's conversion to Christianity. The basilica was built in the early twelfth century and has undergone many renovations and restorations over the centuries. It is known for its stained-glass windows, frescoes and statues, which testify to the history and spirituality of this building.

► In 481 AD, Clovis succeeded Childéric and set his goal to unite all the Franks under his authority. His Catholic wife Clotilde converted him during the battle against the Alamans. On December 24th, 498 AD, he was baptized in Reims by Saint Rémi, which was the first conversion of a barbarian king and of paramount importance for the Church. At this time, Gaul was mainly pagan- The fact that a young conquering king adhered to the Catholic Church could only help spread its doctrine. For Clovis, this had advantages, as he made allies in all camps, all Catholics in enemy territory becoming his supporters.

After his victory over the Visigoths at Vouillé in 507 AD, he expanded the kingdom of the Franks to the Garonne and became master of all Gaul. The last significant act of his reign was the holding of a general council in Orléans in 511 AD, which reorganized the Church of the Gauls. Clovis is considered the founder of the French monarchy and his descendants, known as the Merovingians, ruled over France for over 200 years.

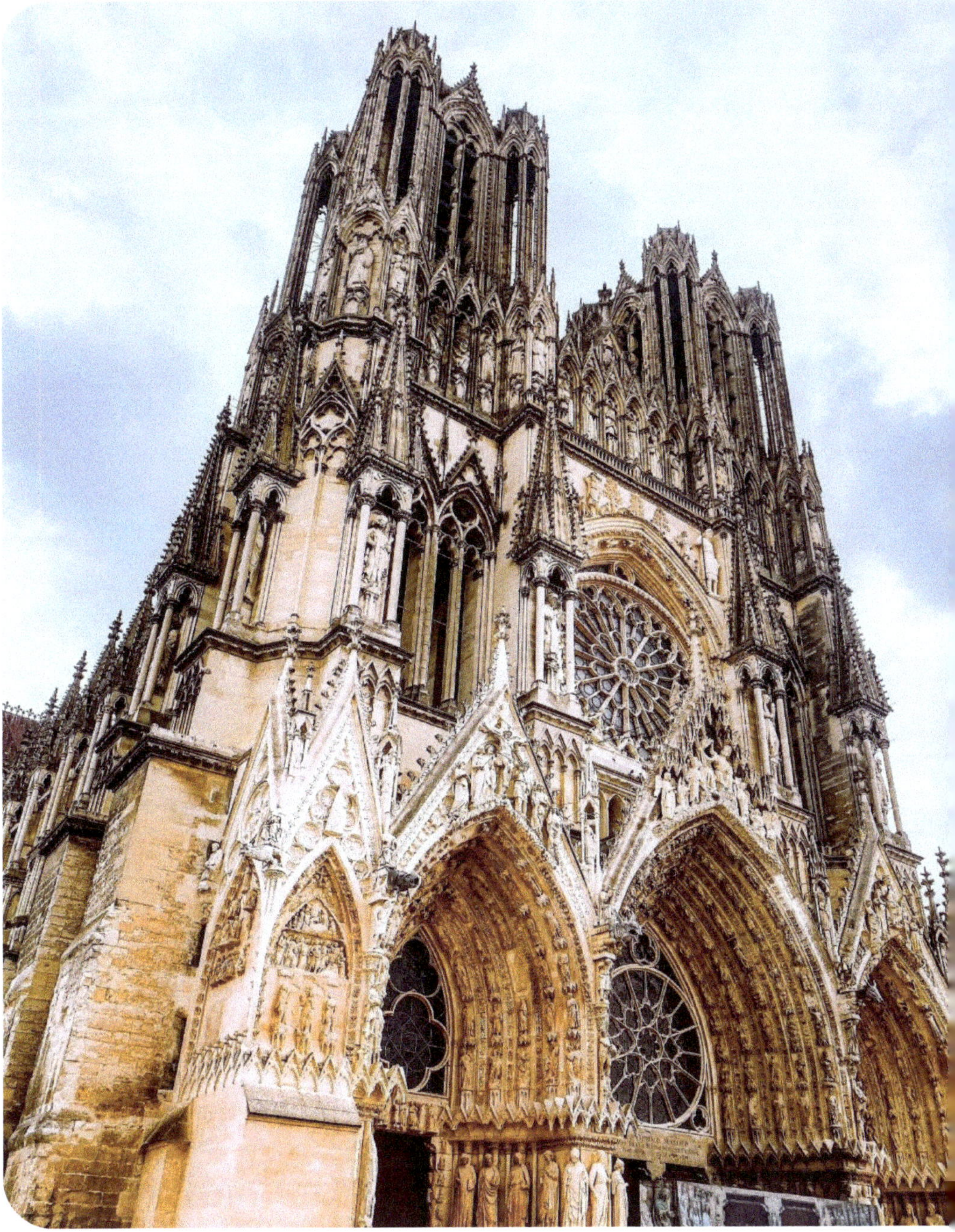

Visualize the rise of the Prophet Muhammad and the birth of Islam at the

DOME OF THE ROCK

#32 632 AD

PALESTINE

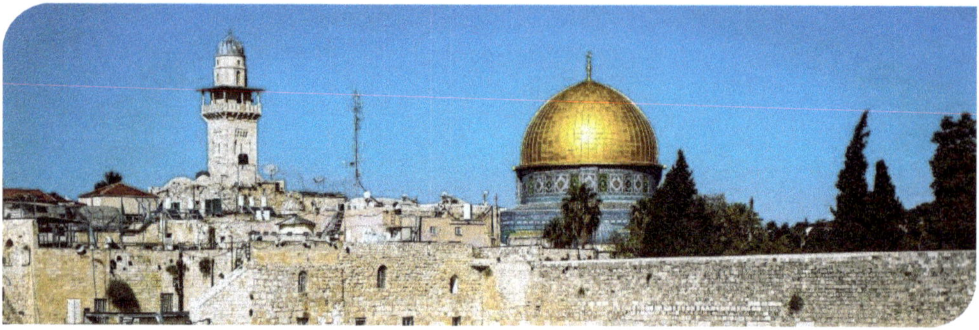

The Dome of the Rock is an absolute must-see destination for any visitor to the holy city of Jerusalem. As one of the most sacred sites for Jews, Christians, and Muslims alike, this iconic structure holds immense historical and spiritual significance. Built in the 7th century, the Dome of the Rock commemorates the spot where the Prophet Muhammad is believed to have ascended to heaven during his miraculous night journey. As you wander through the Dome's ornate interiors, you can't help but be struck by the profound sense of history and reverence that permeates the space. The Dome's enduring significance as a symbol of unity and interfaith harmony is a powerful reminder of the shared roots and values that underpin the Abrahamic faiths.

► In 570 AD, Mina gave birth to Muhammad, who was entrusted to a Bedouin tribe to be raised. During his early years, Muhammad had meditations that led to a revelation from the angel Gabriel. He was tasked with spreading a monotheistic message, in which the people of Mecca should submit to one god, Allah, and consider Muhammad his prophet.

However, due to the hostility of the important officials in Mecca, Muhammad had to flee. Upon arriving in Medina, he was recognized as a mediator and established a code of life. This led to the foundation of a theocratic monotheistic state, led by Muhammad who held both temporal and spiritual power. According to Muslim belief, after his death, the Prophet Muhammad rode on a mount called Bouraq from the al-Haram Mosque to the Al-Aqsa Mosque in Jerusalem, then traversed the seven heavens to be in the presence of the divine. He received the recommendation to pray fifty times daily which was lowered to five prayers, at his request.

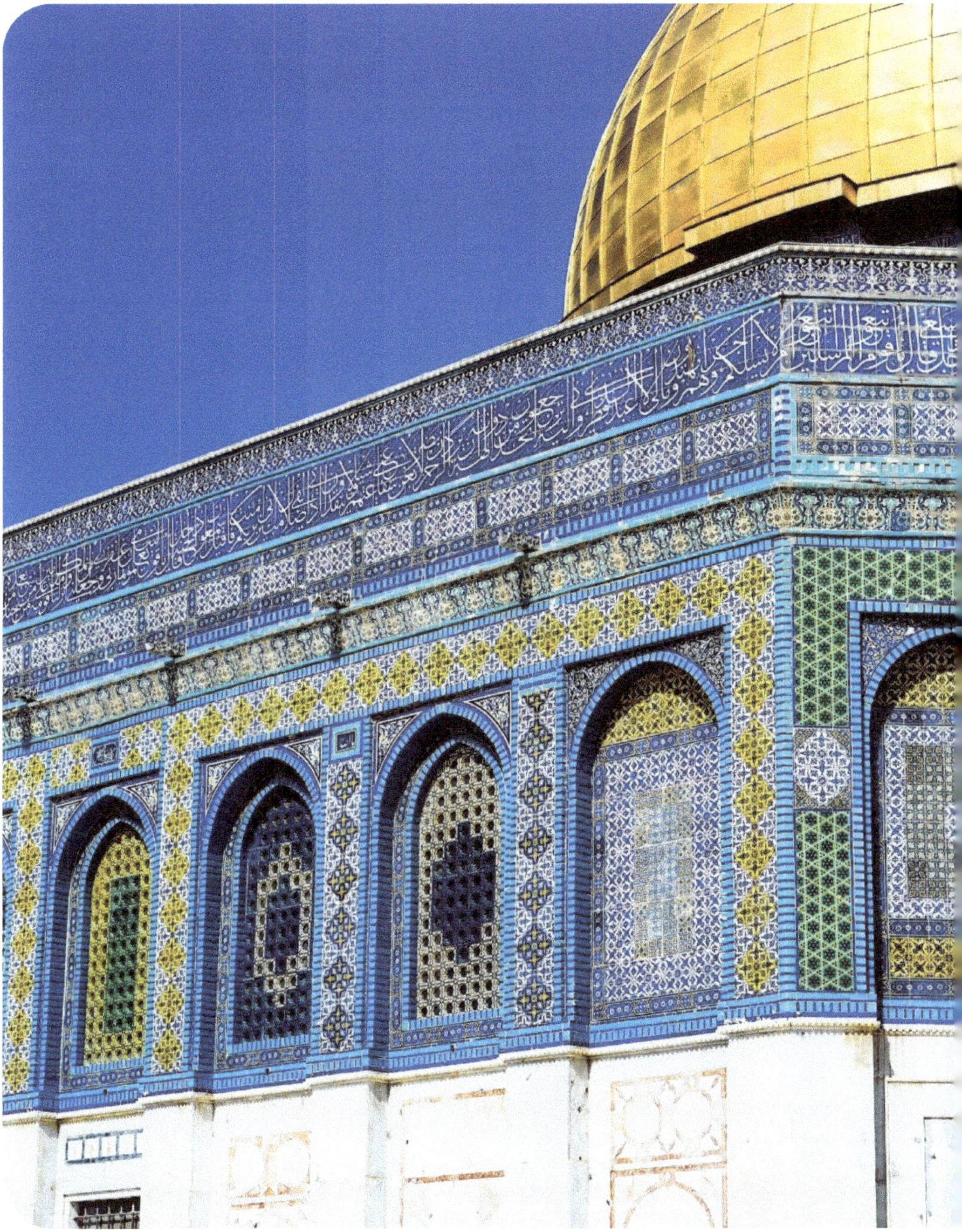

Envision the apogee of Mayan civilization at

CHICHÉN ITZÁ

#33 700 AD

MEXICO

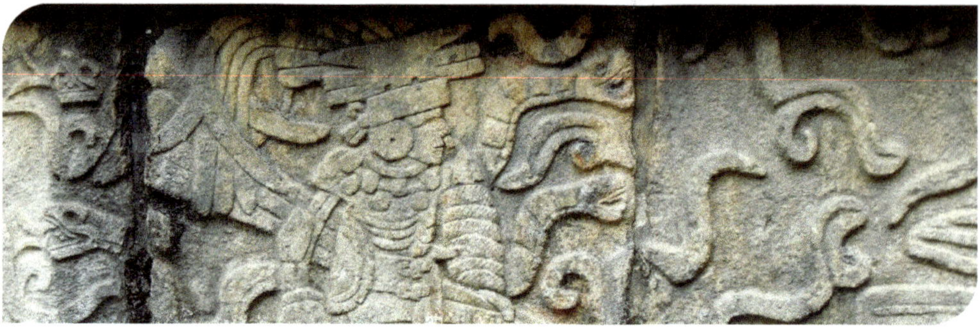

Chichén Itzá is a pre-Columbian archaeological site located in the state of Yucatán in Mexico. This Mayan city is considered one of the most influential religious and political centers in the region. The site includes many buildings and structures, including the famous Temple of Kukulcán, also known as "El Castillo", which is one of the most emblematic symbols of Mexico. Chichén Itzá is also known for its famous ball games and underground chambers, which were used for religious rituals. Today, the site is a UNESCO World Heritage Site and attracts millions of visitors each year. If you're passionate about pre-Columbian history and culture, Chichén Itzá is a must-see place to visit on your trip to Mexico.

► The Maya civilization is a pre-Columbian civilization that developed in Southeast Mexico, Western Honduras and El Salvador, Northern Belize, and Guatemala. It emerged in the early 3rd millennium BC and reached its peak between the 3rd and 18th centuries. This was before gradually declining and disappearing during the Spanish conquest in the 16th century. Its main achievements are architectural, with the construction of monumental temples and pyramids, and astronomical, as evidenced by the many cycles of the Maya calendar.

Chichén Itzá is an ancient Maya city located on the Yucatan peninsula. It developed during the classical period near two natural cavities (cenotes). The date of its foundation varies according to local sources, but it was built between the 6th and 10th centuries in the characteristic Maya style. During the spring and autumn equinoxes, the setting sun casts a shadow on the northern stairway of the Temple of Kukulkan. This shadow looks like a serpent, symbolizing the god Kukulkan, descending the pyramid.

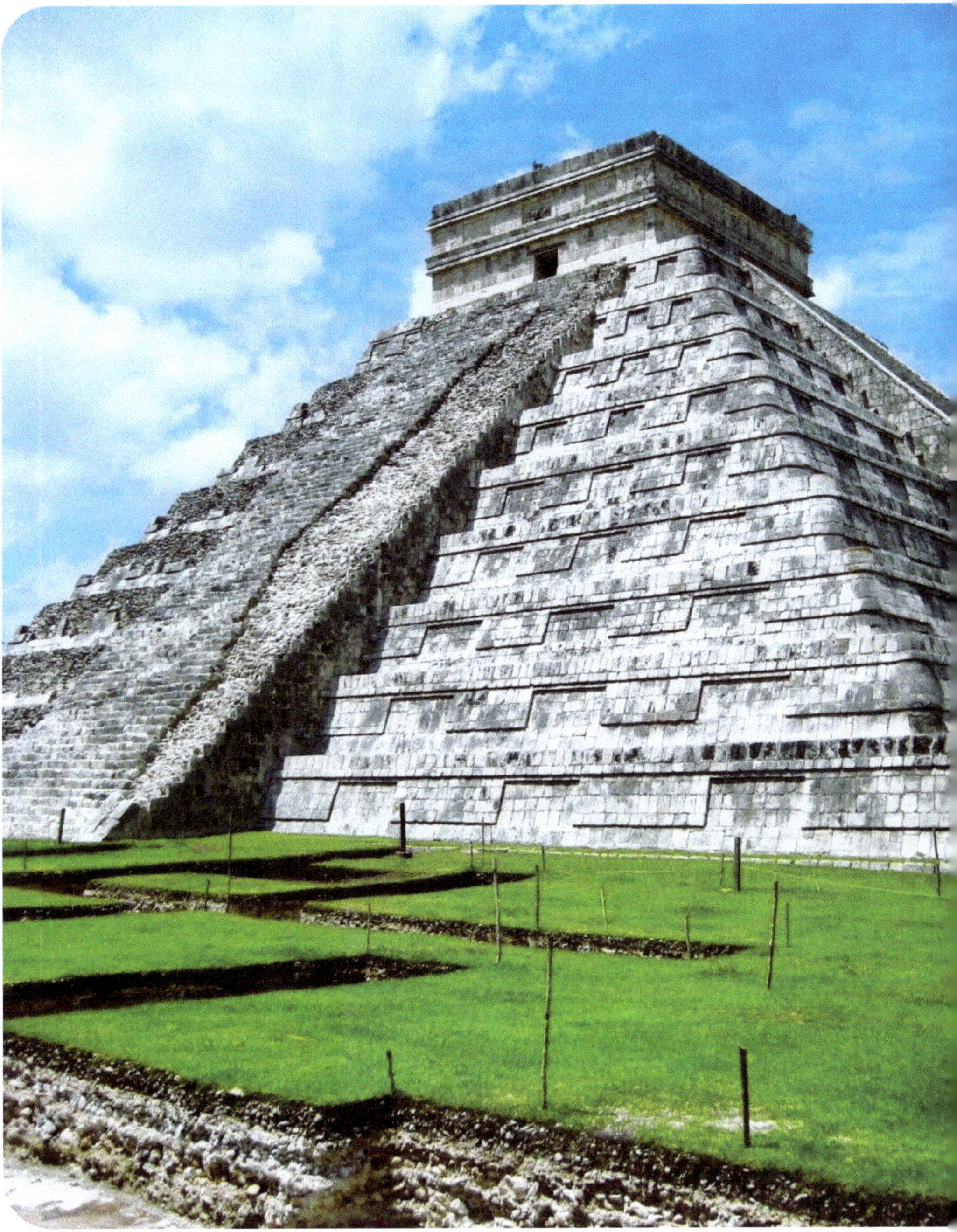

Revisit the invasion of Spain by Moorish troops through the

PILLARS OF HERCULES

#34 711 AD
GIBRALTAR

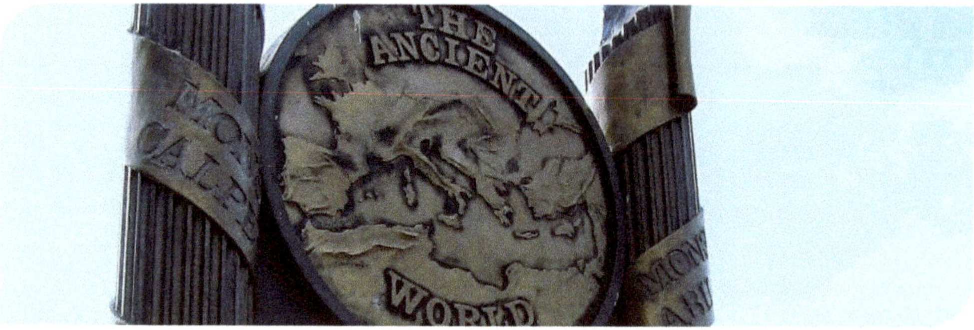
THE ANCIENT WORLD

The Pillars of Hercules are a famous natural site located at the southwestern tip of Spain and Morocco. These are two massive rocks that stand proudly on the Strait of Gibraltar and were named in honor of the mythical hero Hercules. According to Greek mythology, Hercules used these rocks to close the passage between the Atlantic Ocean and the Mediterranean. This was done in order to protect the inhabitants of the region from sea monsters. Today, the Pillars of Hercules are an iconic site and a place of pilgrimage for lovers of history and mythology. The site is also famous for its panoramic ocean views and for its many outdoor activities, such as hiking and biking.

► The Muslim conquest of the Iberian Peninsula was the initial expansion of the Umayyad Caliphate in Spain, which stretched from 711 AD to 726 AD. This conquest resulted in the destruction of the Visigothic Kingdom and the creation of Al-Andalus. It marked the greatest western advance of the Umayyad Caliphate and Islam's dominance in Europe. In April 711 AD, the Berber leader Tariq ibn Ziyad, governor of Tanger, landed on the cliffs of the Columns of Hercules at the head of 7,000 men.

He then occupied and fortified the Rock of Gibraltar, which he named after himself (Jabal-al-Tariq). The Visigoths of Roderic were defeated by the Muslims of Tariq ibn Ziyad, who succeeded in conquering Spain in three years. Tariq then took Cadiz, Ecija, Cordoba and Toledo. In May 756 AD, the Umayyad emir ‘Abd al-Rahman took Cordoba, which became the capital of Al-Andalus. The Spanish emirates then became independent after this, ending their dependence on Damascus.

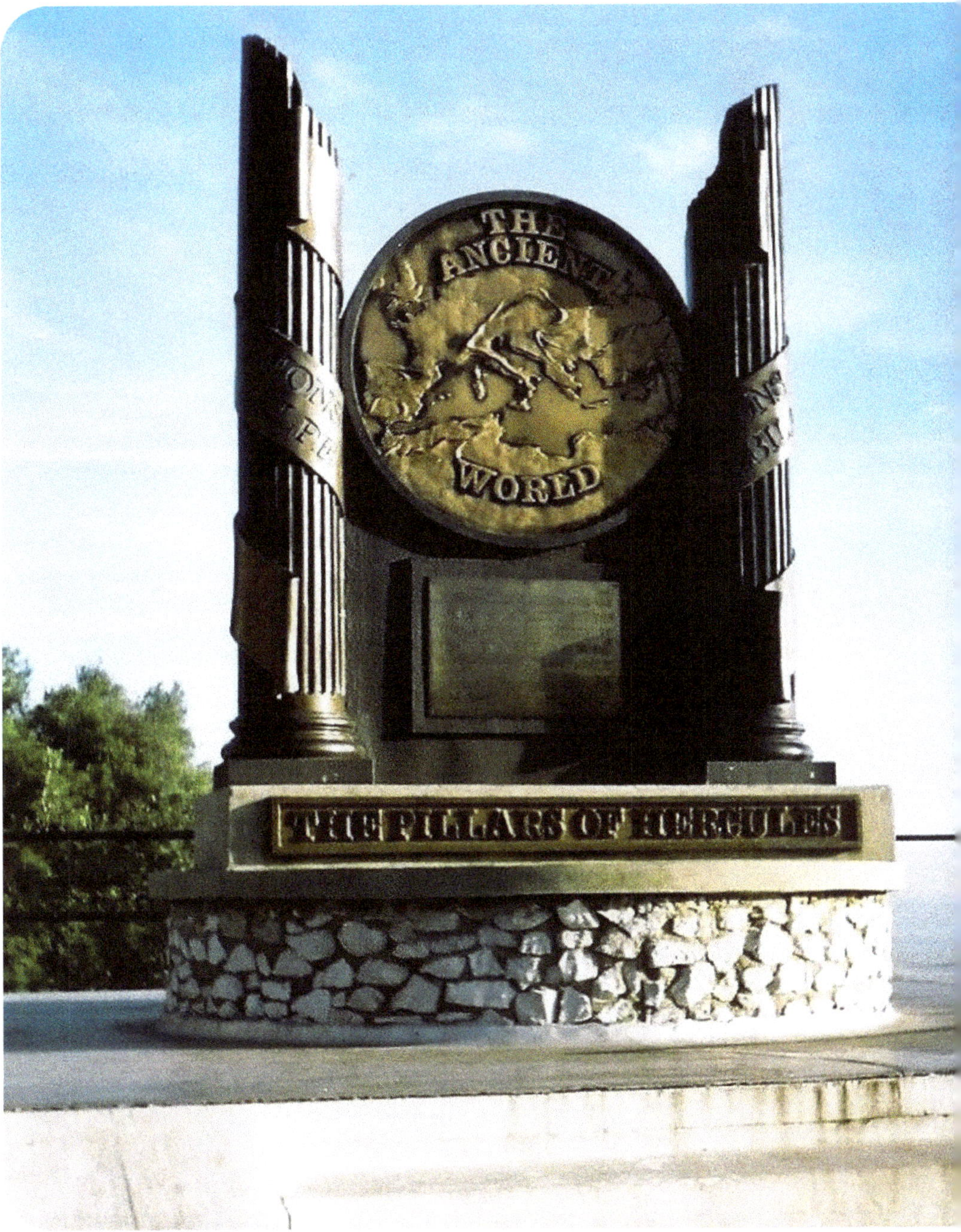
THE ANCIENT WORLD
THE PILLARS OF HERCULES

Watch the foundation of Al-Andalus around the

GREAT MOSQUE OF CORDOBA

#35 756 AD

SPAIN

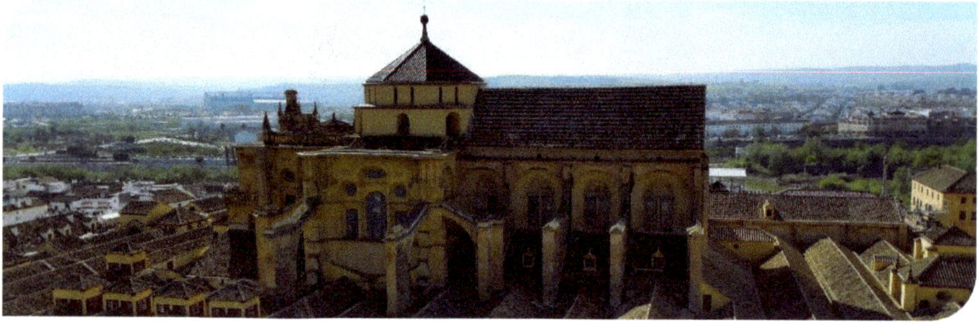

The Great Mosque of Cordoba is one of the finest and most striking examples of Islamic architecture in Spain. Built in the eighth century, this mosque is a real architectural and historical jewel. With its 800 marble and granite columns, cedar wood ceiling and mosaic-covered walls, the Great Mosque of Cordoba is a true ode to beauty and finesse. But what makes this mosque even more unique is its fusion of different architectural styles. Indeed, over the centuries, many artists and craftsmen have contributed to the decoration of the mosque, each bringing their personal touch and cultural heritage. Today, the Great Mosque of Cordoba is a must-see tourist site for anyone interested in the history of Spain and Islam.

► Abd er-Rahman el-Dachil, from the Omayyad dynasty, took power in Cordoba and named himself emir of Al-Andalus. Spain thus became the first independent Muslim state. During the reign of Abd er-Rahman I, the country had an exemplary administration. However, he was not able to subdue the mountainous regions in the north, which remained Christian. Abd Al-Rahman I, also known as Abdarrahman I, was born in Damascus in 731 AD and died in Cordoba in 788 AD.

He was the first independent Omayyad emir of the Emirate of Cordoba, founded in 756 AD. Miraculously surviving the massacre of his family, who were almost entirely exterminated by the Abbasids, he sought refuge in Spain. He was called by the Moors to settle in this country. He reduced almost the entire country under his power, established his residence in Cordoba and reigned peacefully for 31 years. Abd Al-Rahman I was a patron of the arts and literature, and Cordoba became a cultural center under his rule, known for its libraries, poets, and philosophers.

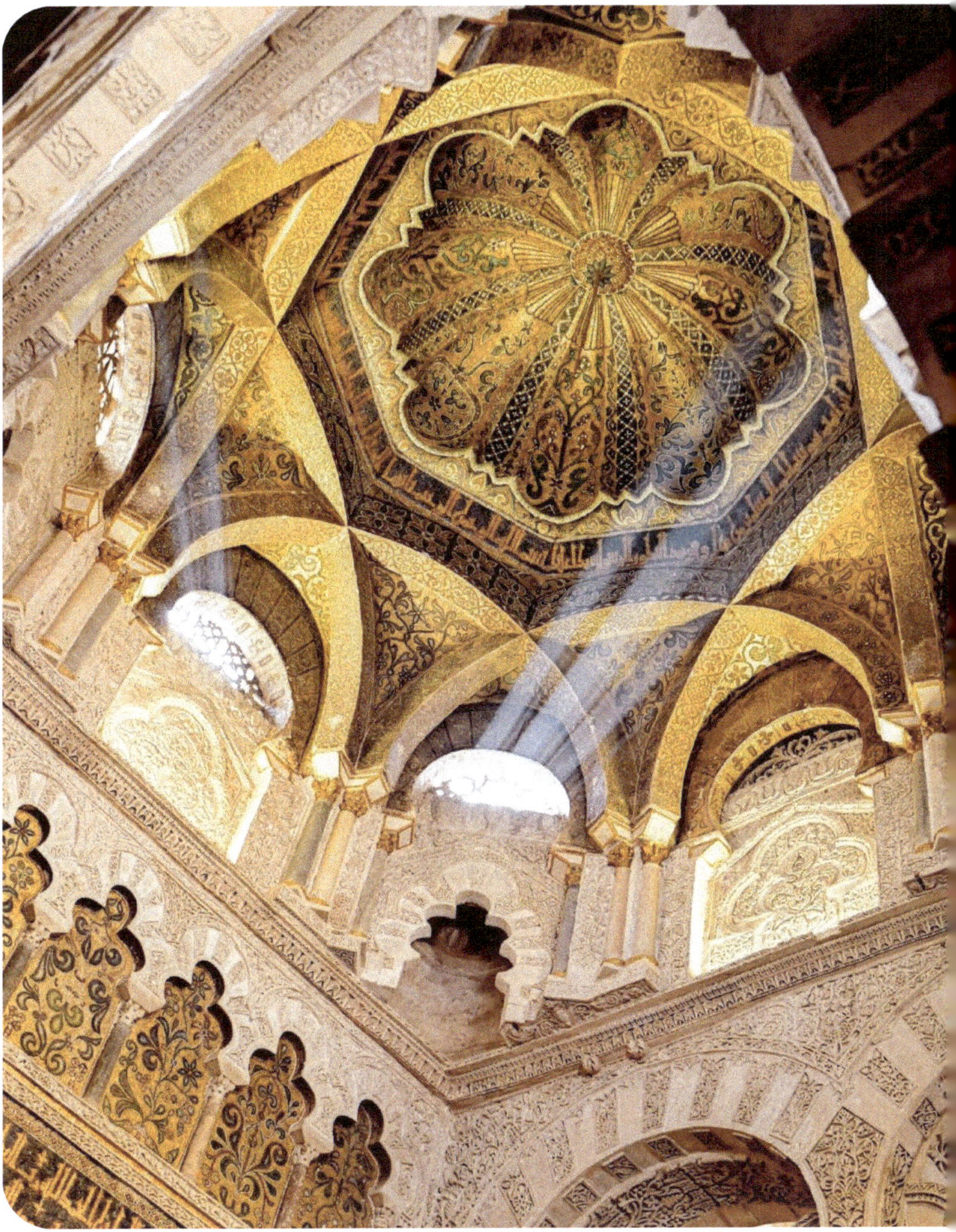

Understand Charlemagne's crowning as
Imperator Romanorum at the

AACHEN CATHEDRAL

#36 ⏱ **800 AD**

🗺 **GERMANY**

Aachen Cathedral is one of the most prestigious in Germany and has a fascinating history dating back more than 1,300 years. It was built on the site of the former Roman imperial palace and was consecrated in 936 by Emperor Otto I. Since then, it has been the coronation site of many German emperors and has become a symbol of the power and influence of the Holy Roman Empire. The cathedral is also famous for its sacred relics, including those of St. Peter and St. Mary Magdalene. Its façade is decorated with magnificent sculptures and frescoes, witnesses of the importance of art in the religious life of the time. Today, Aachen Cathedral continues to attract visitors from all walks of life and remains a sacred pilgrimage site for many faithful.

▶ Charlemagne, king of the Franks and Lombards, was crowned emperor of the West, *Imperator Romanorum*, by Pope Leo III in 800 AD. He sought to reclaim the legitimate heritage of the Roman Empire, in ancient Gaul and Germany. As a defender of the Christian faith, his conquests were accompanied by the voluntary or forced conversion of the defeated peoples. He also restored a unified government. Charlemagne embarked on major administrative reforms to better govern, such as replacing oral orders with written ones, founding monasteries and schools, and promoting the arts. He attempted to restore the civilization they had lost.

His civilizing influence and the renaissance of Latin letters paradoxically led to the emergence of a new written language, which would become French. Charlemagne is known for promoting education and the arts, and is credited with founding the first universities in Europe. He also had a love of music and even composed hymns himself.

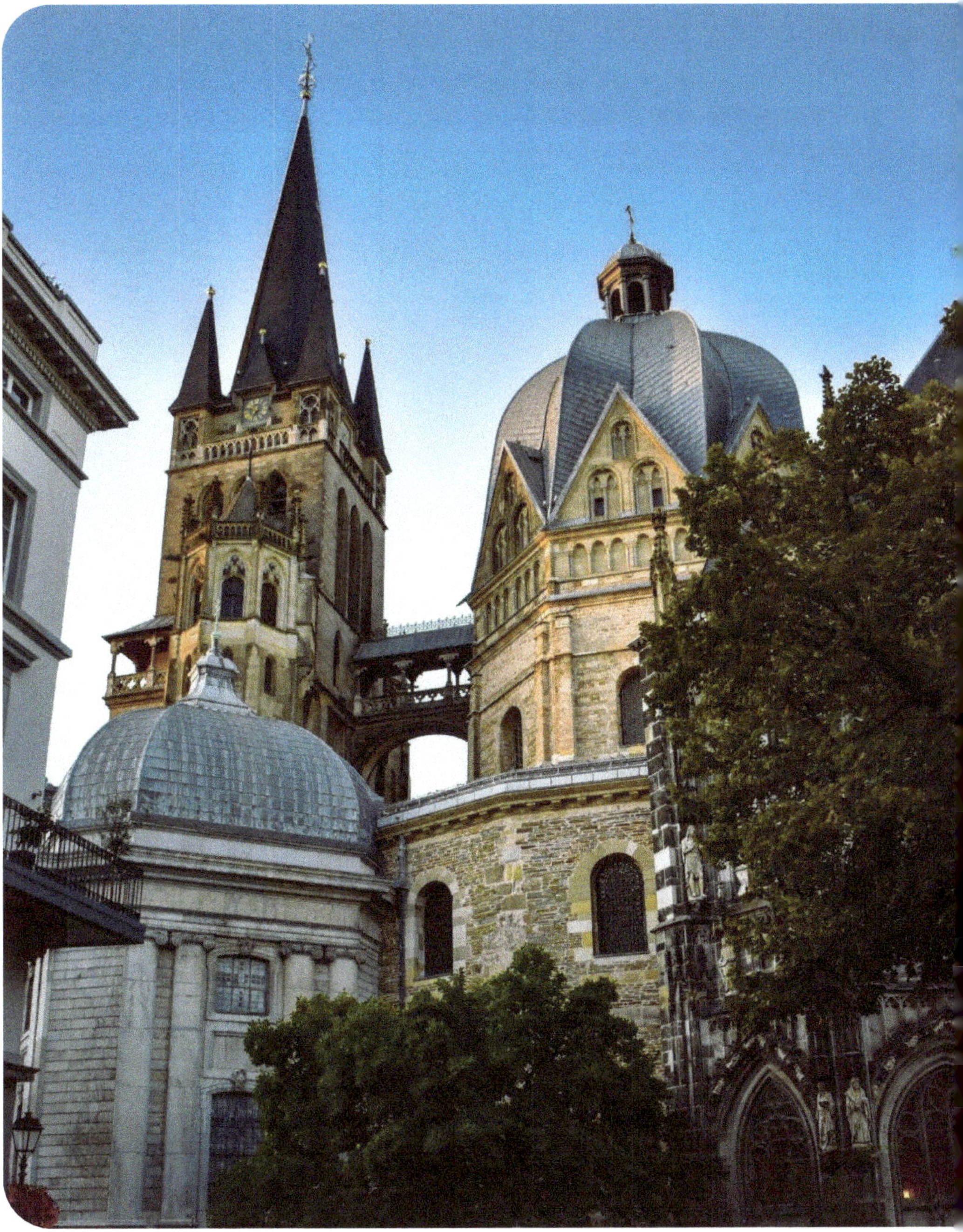

Recall Cyril and Methodius evangelization of the Slavic countries at the

CHURCH OF SAINTS CYRIL AND METHODIUS

#37 ⏱ **862 AD** 🗺 **GREECE**

The Church of Saints Cyril and Methodius is an Orthodox Christian church located in Thessaloniki, Greece. It is famous for its imposing Byzantine architecture and murals dating back to the fourteenth century. It is also known as the place of worship of two saints of the Orthodox Church, Saint Cyril and Saint Methodius, who are considered the "apostles of the Slavs" for their work translating and spreading the Gospel in the ninth century. This church is a major place of pilgrimage for Orthodox Christians from all over Eastern Europe and is worth visiting to discover its history and architectural beauty.

▶ Cyril or Constantine the Philosopher and Methodius, bishop of Sirmium, embarked on the evangelization of the Slavic peoples in their own language. This was at the request of Prince Rastislav of Great Moravia who wanted to reduce the influence of Bavarian ecclesiastics in the region. In 862 AD, Cyril developed the Slavic Glagolitic alphabet, which allowed them to translate the Bible into Slavic and continue the evangelization of Great Moravia in 863 AD. They established the liturgy which allowed the foundation of the Bulgarian Church in 865 AD.

Today, the Cyrillic alphabet is used not only by Bulgarians, but also by Serbs, Montenegrins, Macedonians, Russians, Ukrainians, Belarusians, and many other non-Slavic peoples of the former USSR, as well as the Mongols: it remains an integral part of the cultural and linguistic identity of hundreds of millions of people across Eastern Europe and Central Asia. The widespread use of the Cyrillic script is a testament to its versatility and the enduring influence of the Slavic cultural sphere.

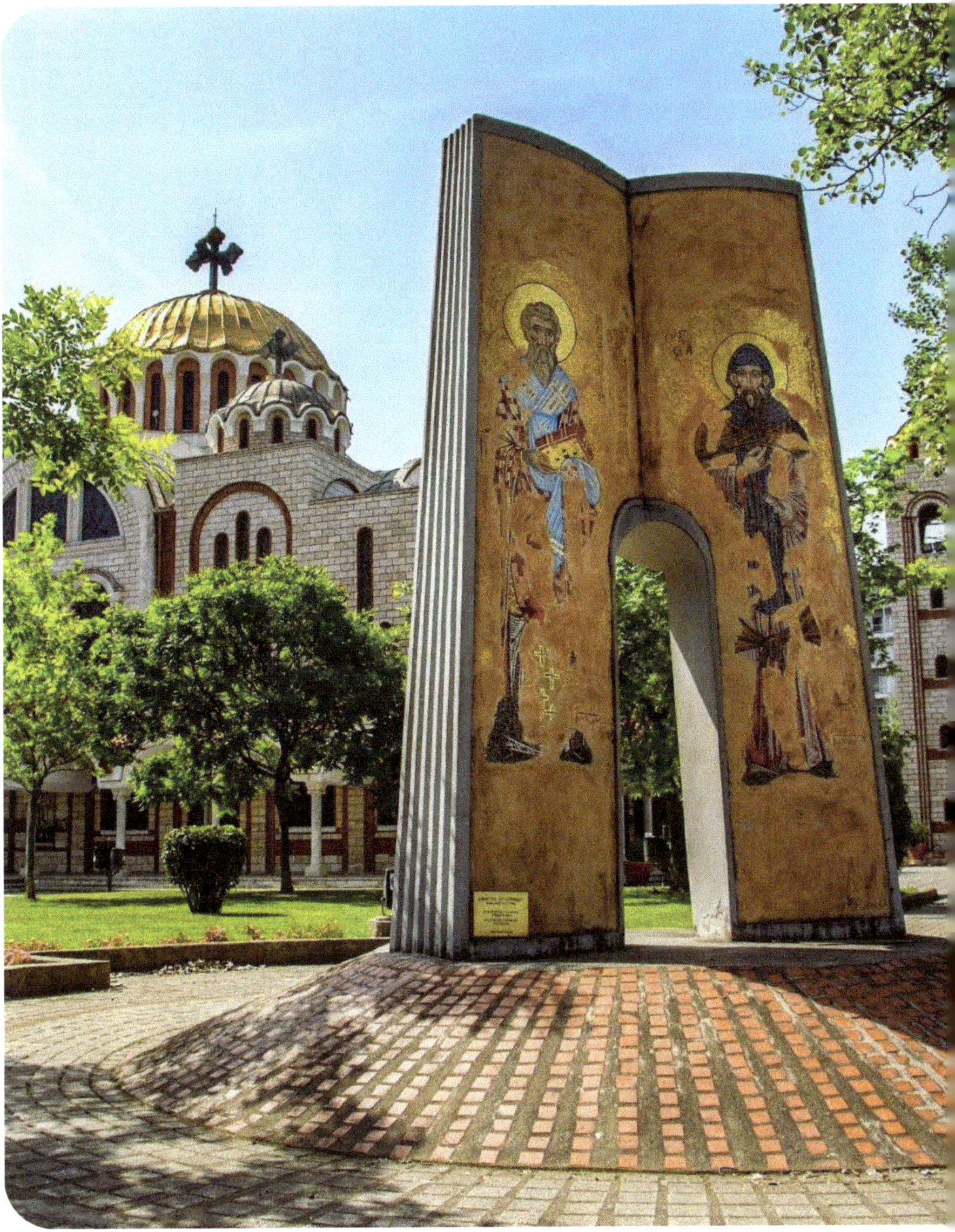

Venture into Vikings' raids throughout continental Europe at the

VIKING WORLD MUSEUM

#38 🕐 **1000 AD**

🗺 **ICELAND**

Viking World is a museum located in Reykjavik, Iceland that celebrates the culture and history of the Vikings. One of the museum's standout exhibits is "The Icelander," which focuses on the history of the Vikings in Iceland. Visitors can learn about the colonization of Iceland by the Vikings in the 9th and 10th centuries. In addition, they can learn about the unique culture and traditions that developed on the island over time. The exhibit features a range of artifacts, including weapons, jewelry, and household items, as well as interactive displays and educational videos. Whether you're a history buff or simply interested in discovering more about the Vikings, a visit to Viking World and the "The Icelander" exhibit is a must-see for any trip to Iceland.

▶ Viking raids were common in medieval Europe from the late 8th century until the early 11th century. These raids were led by Scandinavian warriors called Vikings, who navigated the seas in their ships called drakkars, in search of loot and conquest. The Vikings targeted a wide range of areas including monasteries, towns and even cities, and they were known for their brutal and violent tactics. These raids had a significant impact on European history as they disrupted trade and contributed to the spread of Scandinavian culture and language across the continent.

Despite the fear and destruction they caused, the Vikings were also skilled farmers, merchants and artisans. Their raids often led to the exchange of ideas and cultural exchange between the Vikings and the people they met. Some of the Vikings were also known as traders and explorers. They had traveled as far as North America and some even established settlements on the continent.

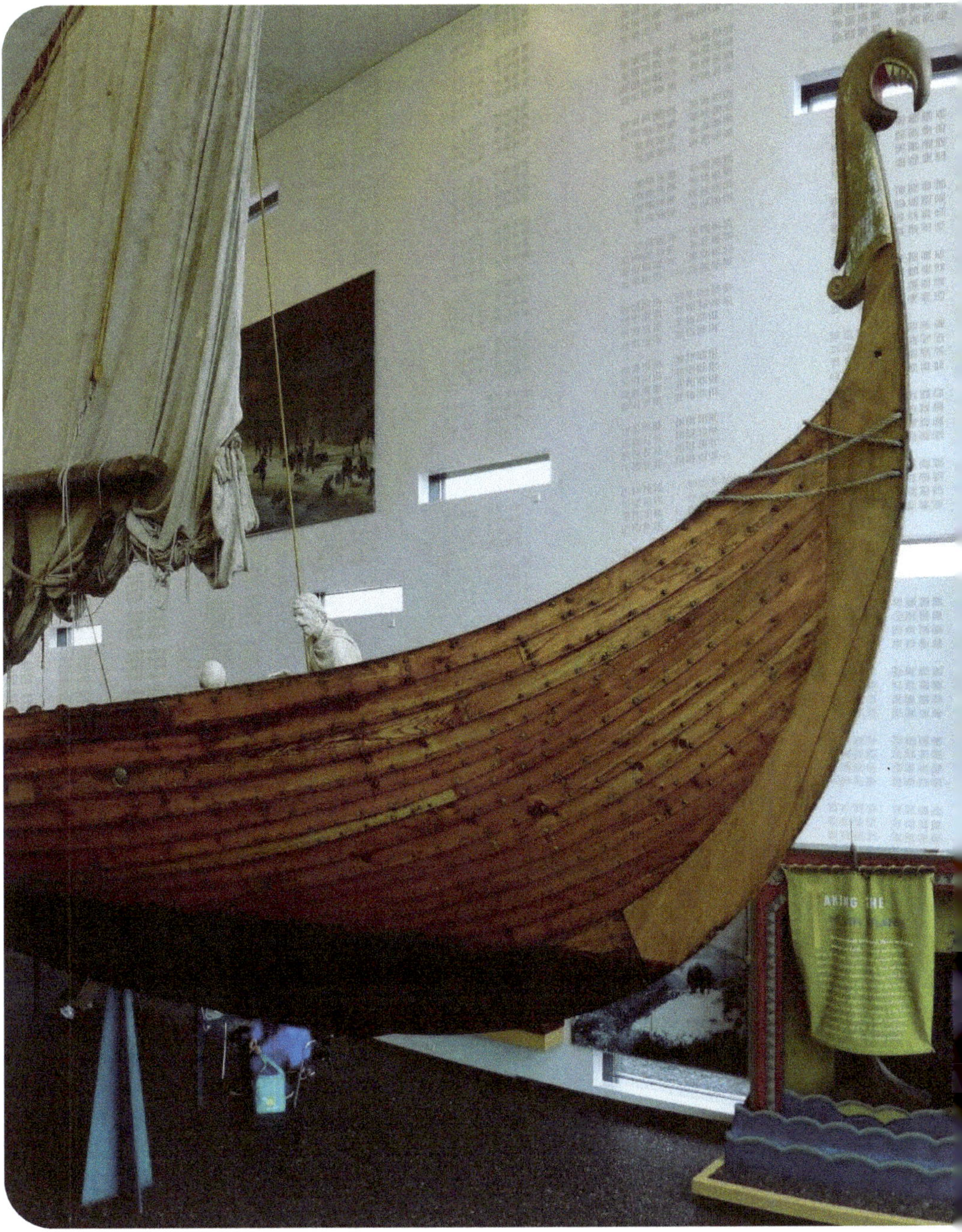

Discern the taking of Isfahan by Seljuk Turks at

SHEIKH LOTFOLLAH MOSQUE

#39

🕐 **1051 AD**

🗺 **IRAN**

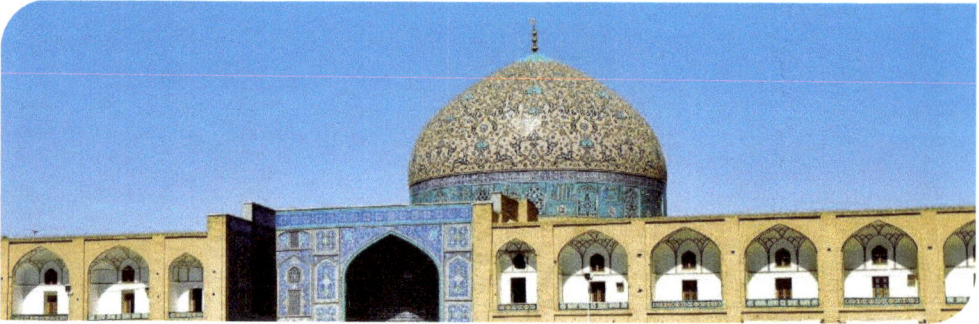

The Sheikh Lutfullah Mosque is an architectural gem located in Isfahan, Iran. It was built in the 17th century and is known for its outstanding beauty and lavish interior decoration. The mosque is mainly used for prayer and is a place of worship for Muslims. It is also open to the public for tours and is a popular tourist site. What makes the Sheikh Lutfullah Mosque so unique is its semicircle-shaped design, with a central dome and a minaret that rises high into the sky. Its glossy white marble façade and intricate and detailed patterns are stunning to behold. The interior of the mosque is equally impressive, with stucco ceilings decorated with geometric patterns and polished marble floors. If you are traveling in Iran, do not miss the opportunity to visit the Sheikh Lutfullah Mosque, a real architectural gem.

▶ The capture of Isfahan by the Seljuk Turks was a major event that took place in the 11th century. The Seljuks, coming from the steppes of Central Asia, were Sunni Muslims who swept through Persia, Iraq, Syria and Palestine. They presented themselves as defenders of the Abbasid caliphate threatened by the Fatimids of Egypt. Isfahan was then a prominent city in Persia, located in the southwest of the country. The Seljuks managed to take control of the city in 1051 AD, after a prolonged siege, ending the reign of the Abbasid caliphs in the region.

This capture was a decisive turning point in the history of Islam. It allowed the Seljuks to become the new masters of the region and to rule the Middle East for nearly a century. This victory also paved the way for a period of Turkification in the history of Islam. Isfahan is also known as the "half of the world," as it was considered the center of the world and the capital of the Seljuk Empire.

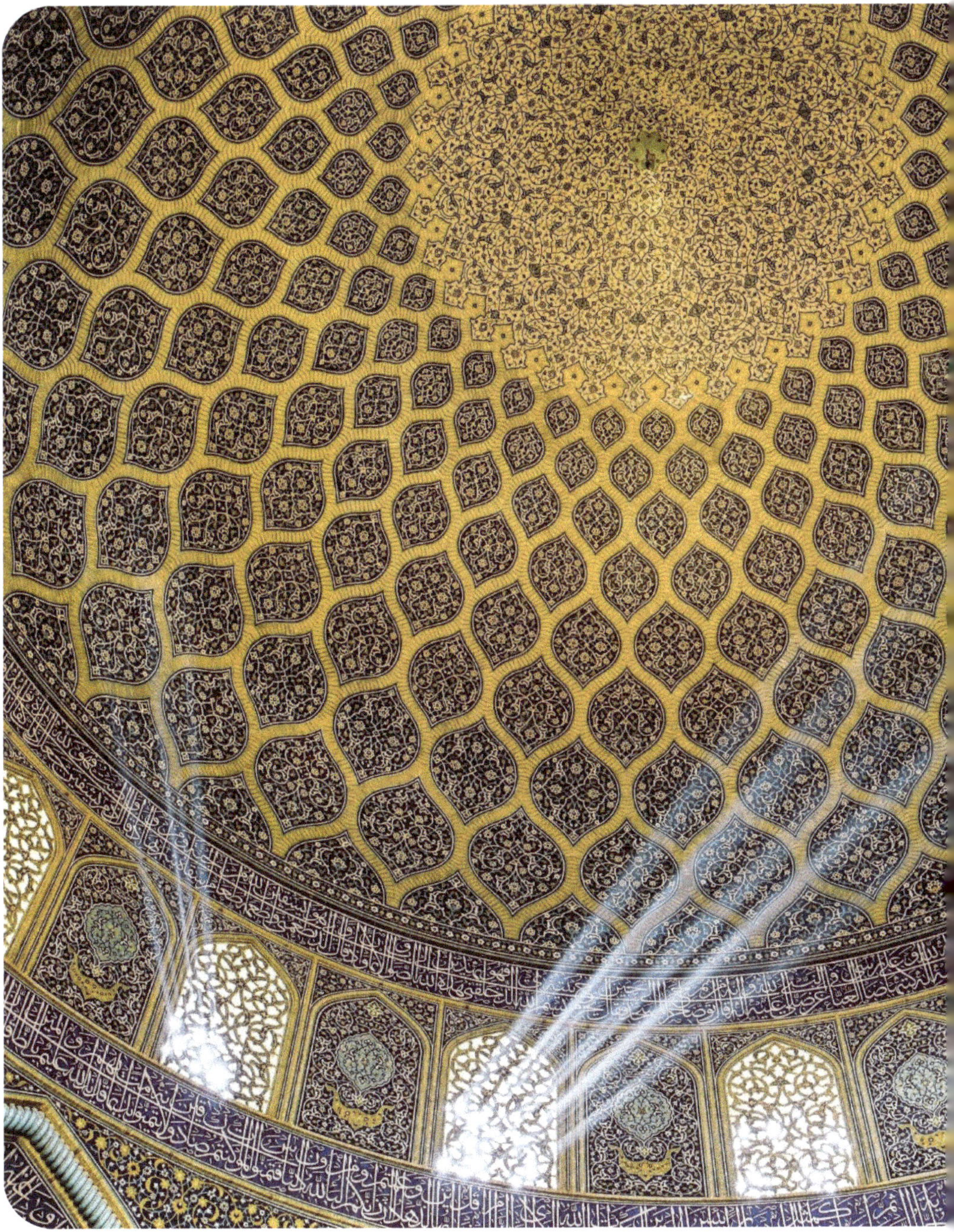

Conceive the schism of Rome and the birth of Byzantine Orthodoxy inside

HAGIA SOPHIA

#40   ⏱ **1054 AD**

🗺 **TURKEY**

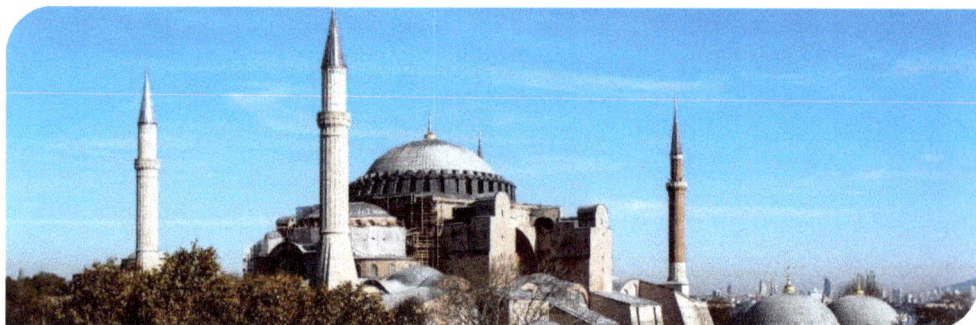

The Hagia Sophia cathedral is one of the most emblematic monuments of Constantinople, the former capital of the Byzantine Empire. This church, which was erected in the sixth century, is a true masterpiece of Byzantine architecture, recognized as one of the most aesthetically pleasing buildings of Christendom. Hagia Sophia is also considered a place of worship for Orthodox Christians, who still hold religious services there. The cathedral is also a popular tourist site, attracting millions of visitors from all corners of the world every year. If you are passing through Constantinople, do not miss the opportunity to discover this incredible building, which will certainly leave you with an unforgettable memory.

▶ On July 14th, Pope Leo IX was excommunicated by the Patriarch of Constantinople, Michel Cérulaire, who himself was excommunicated at Saint Sophia by the legate of the Pope. These reciprocal excommunications thus consecrated the Great Schism of the East, a rupture between the Catholic Church and the Orthodox Church. The reasons for this rupture are to be found in the doctrinal and liturgical differences that had been brewing between the two Churches since the 8th century, as well as in the political rivalries between Rome and Constantinople, the Byzantine Empire having become the first power of the medieval world.

To this day, each of the two churches claims to be the true Catholic Church, denying this title to the other. A movement toward ecumenism loosened relations in the 20th century. The Roman Catholic Church is the main religion of the world and the most influential branch of Christianity.

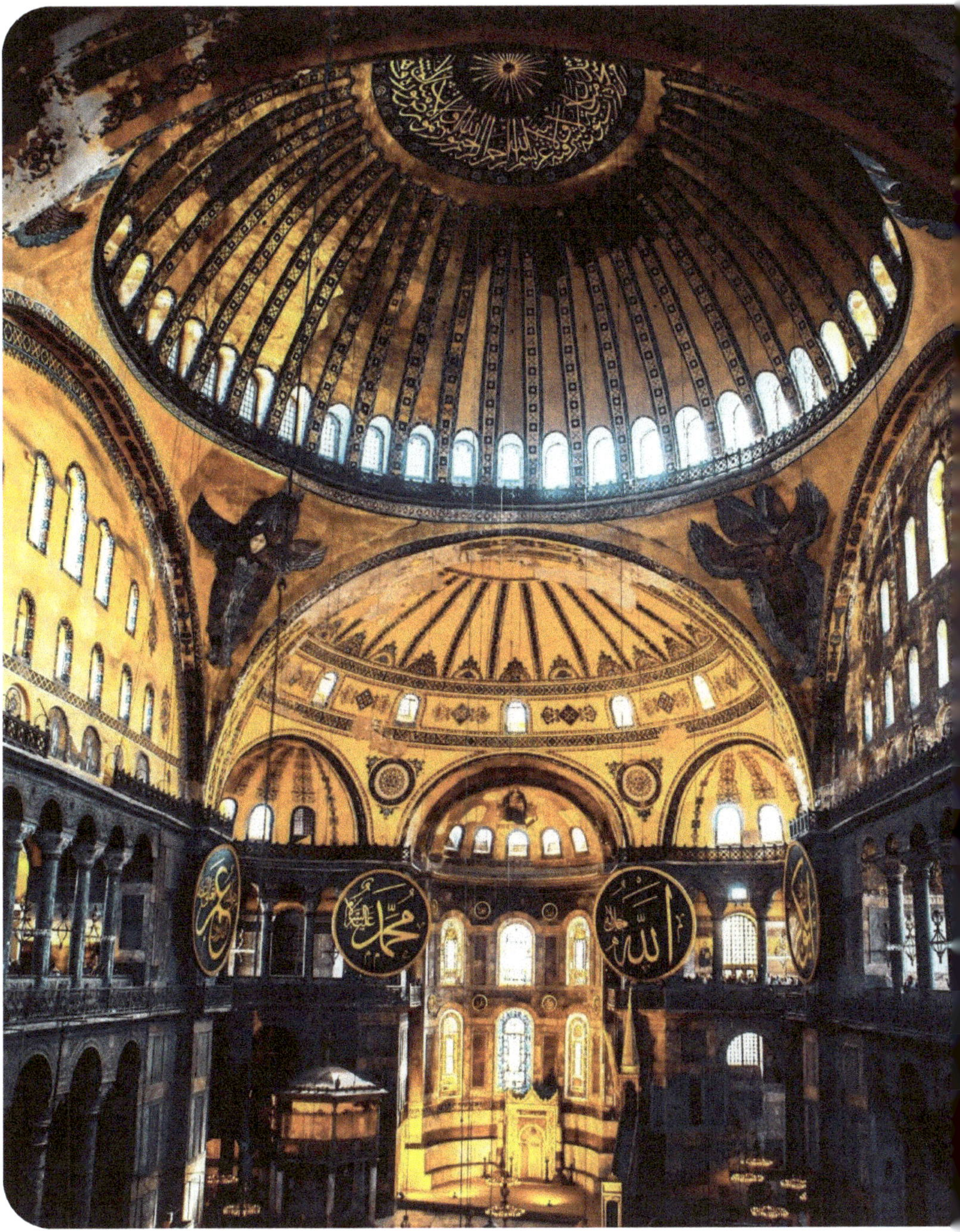

Comprehend the crusaders' seizure of Jerusalem at the

KRAK DES CHEVALIERS

#41 ⏱ **1099 AD**
🗺 **SYRIA**

Krak des Chevaliers is a castle located in Syria, near the city of Homs. This fortress was built in the eleventh century by the Crusaders. It was used as a military base and as a refuge for local populations during the wars between the Crusaders and the Muslims. Krak des Chevaliers is considered one of the best-preserved castles of medieval times in the East, and has been a UNESCO World Heritage Site since 2006. The fortress is surrounded by imposing ramparts and moats, and it includes several buildings, such as a chapel, banquet halls and rooms for soldiers. Krak des Chevaliers is now a very popular place to visit for tourists visiting Syria, and it offers a fascinating insight into Crusader life during medieval times.

▶ The crusaders captured Jerusalem in 1099 AD and committed looting and massacres of the population. The heavily armed Frankish knights developed the technique of the cavalry charge with a lance. All the Muslims in Jerusalem were killed. The conquered lands were given to one of the leaders of the crusade, Godefroy de Bouillon. The crusader leaders created the first Christian states in the East.

These states established Western hegemony in the Mediterranean and favored the commercial interests of the French, Normans and Italians, to the detriment of those of the Byzantines. There was no mixing of populations as in previous invasions of Syria. These states remained isolated islands. The term "crusade" itself, with its roots in the Latin word "crux," underscores the religious fervor and sense of divine purpose that drove the expansion of these Western powers. The cross worn by the crusaders symbolized their unwavering commitment to the cause, whether it was the reclamation of the Holy Land or the defense of Christendom.

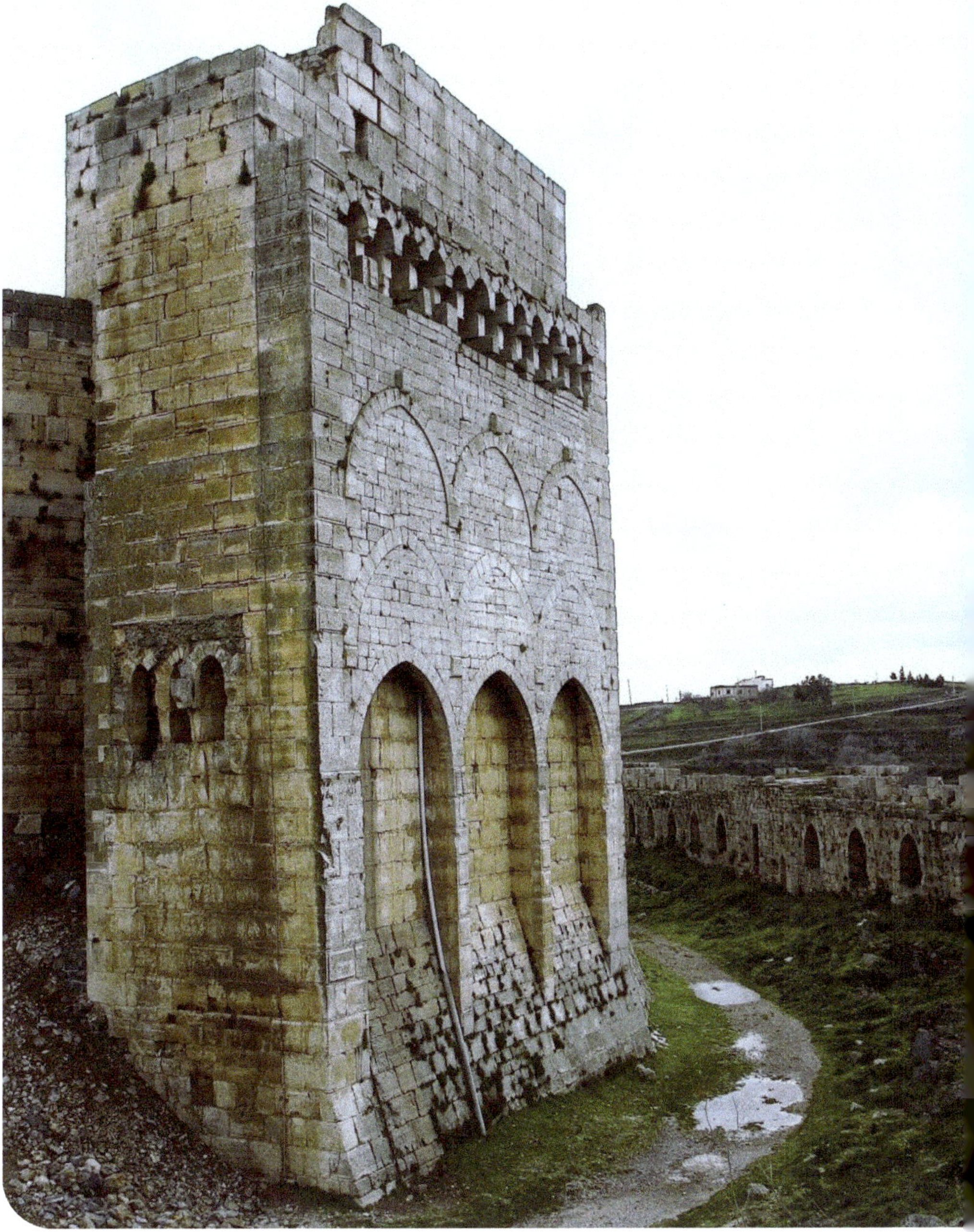

Witness Khmer king Suryavarman II architectural masterpiece at

ANGKOR WAT

#42 1147 AD

CAMBODIA

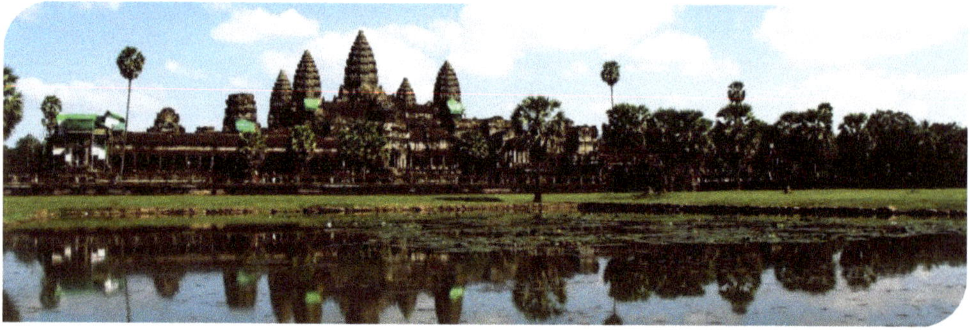

Angkor Wat is a magnificent Cambodian temple located near the city of Siem Reap. This architectural marvel is widely regarded as one of the most prestigious and spectacular archaeological sites in the world. Built in the 12th century, this temple is not only the largest Hindu temple ever constructed, but it is also one of the oldest surviving religious structures on the planet. What makes Angkor Wat truly unique is its sheer size and remarkable complexity. The temple complex consists of several main buildings, as well as a vast array of other structures, including ornate palaces, intricate terraces, and sacred basins. The attention to detail and the scale of this ancient site are truly breathtaking, with every corner revealing new architectural wonders and hidden treasures.

► Yasovarman I, the Khmer emperor, established his capital at Angkor in 1147 AD. At the top of Phnom Bakheng, a hill that overlooks the Angkor plain by 60 meters, he had a temple-mountain built in the shape of a five-tiered pyramid and with 109 towers representing Mount Meru, the center of the universe according to Indian cosmology. He also covered his kingdom with Ashramas which served as both stopovers for travelers and monasteries, all built according to the same model. From the 14th century, the Khmer empire experienced a long decline.

Historians have proposed various causes for this decline such as religious conversion from Hinduism to Buddhism, internal power struggles, vassal rebellions, foreign invasions, plague and ecological collapse. The Angkor Wat temple is considered the largest religious monument in the world and was originally built as a Hindu temple, but later converted to Buddhism.

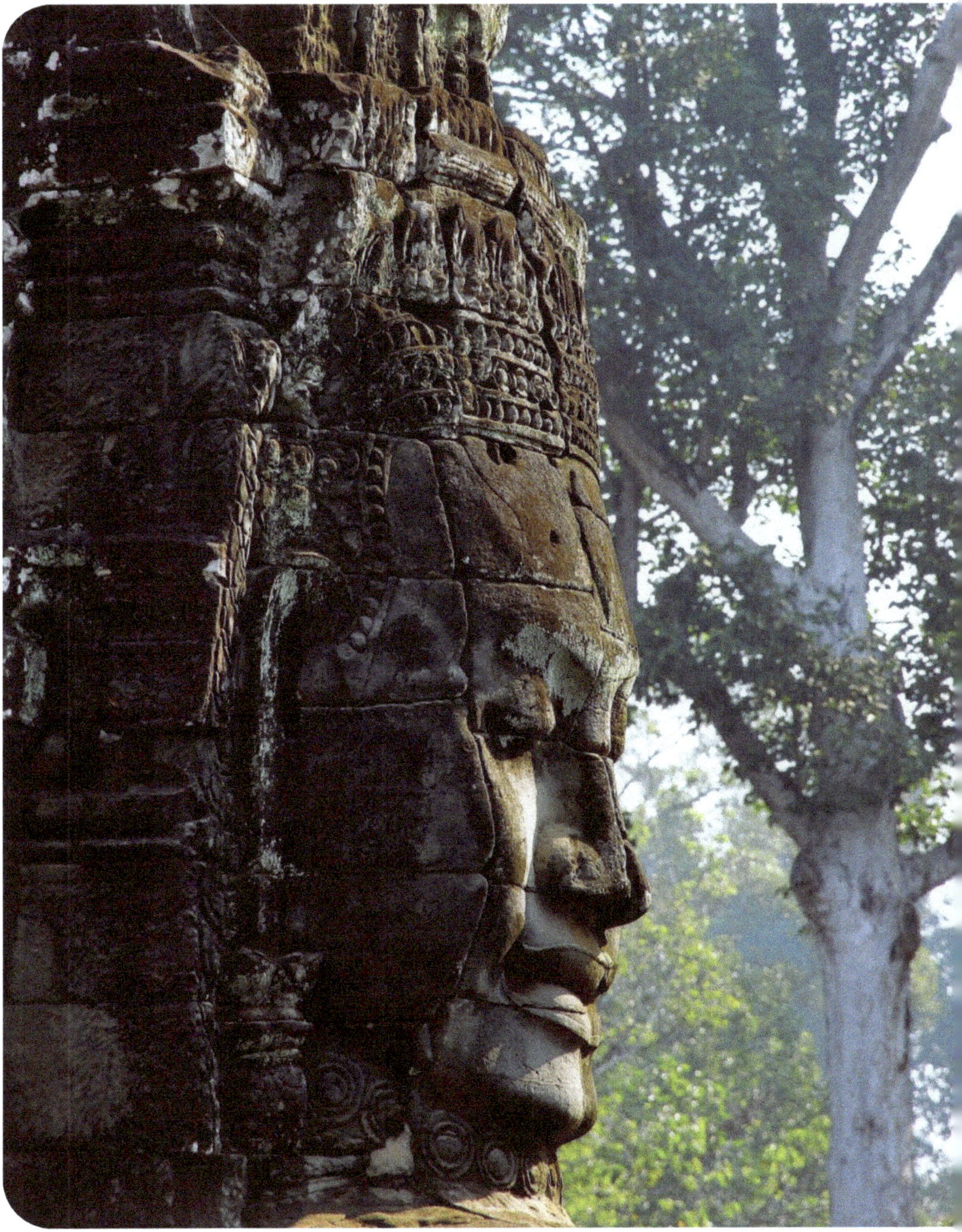

43

Recollect the first Shogunate set up by
Minamoto no Yoritomo at the

KENCHŌ-JI

🕐 **1192 AD**

🗺 **JAPAN**

*The Gozan, or five Kamakura
temples of the Rinzai school, were
built in the thirteenth century in the
city of Kamakura in Japan to rival
the five temples in Kyoto in terms of
wealth and power. They are all
located in northern Kamakura,
near Kita-Kamakura Station and
the slopes of Gionyama, and are
classified according to their
importance. The first and oldest of
these temples is Kenchoji, founded
in 1253 by the Hojo regents to
show their piety and wealth.
Kenchō-ji is the oldest Zen temple
in Kamakura, Japan, and was
built on the orders of Emperor
Kameyama to promote the Zen
religion. It has the largest Hatto
(Dharma Hall) in eastern Japan
and is adorned with a garden
designed by Zen master Muso
Kokushi. It is also known for its Zen
gardens and peaceful parks.*

▶ After winning the long civil war between the
Minamoto and Taira clans, the samurai Minamoto-
no-Yoritomo recognized the emperor's inability to
govern the country. He therefore adopted the title of
shogun (general in Japanese) and created the first
military government of the country in 1192 AD,
called *bakufu*, without replacing the imperial
government which remained in place in Kyoto. He
established this military government in Kamakura
(south of present-day Tokyo) and allowed the
Samurai to control Japan. The Shogunate remained
the official regime of Japan during the long feudal
period of the archipelago, which did not end until the
mid-19th century.

During this time period, Zen Buddhism also deeply
impacted the former capital. Today, Kamakura is
dotted with 65 Buddhist temples. The largest and one
of the oldest temples in the area is the Kenchō-ji
temple with its many secondary buildings. Kamakura
is known as The Kyoto of Eastern Japan due to the
many ancient temples and historical sites found in
the area.

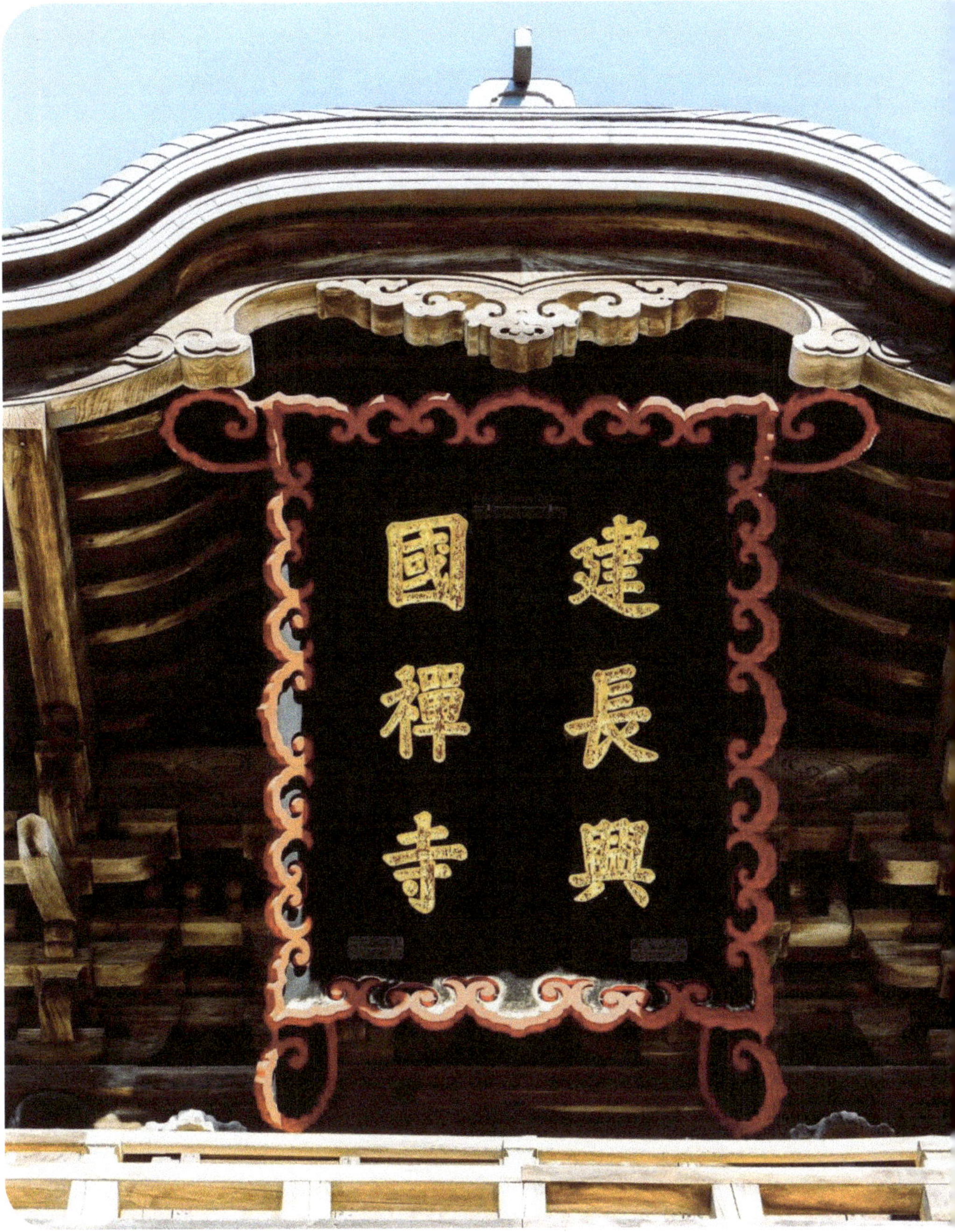
建長興國禪寺

Visualize Genghis Khan's Mongol Empire at the

EQUESTRIAN STATUE OF GENGHIS KAHN

#44

1206 AD

MONGOLIA

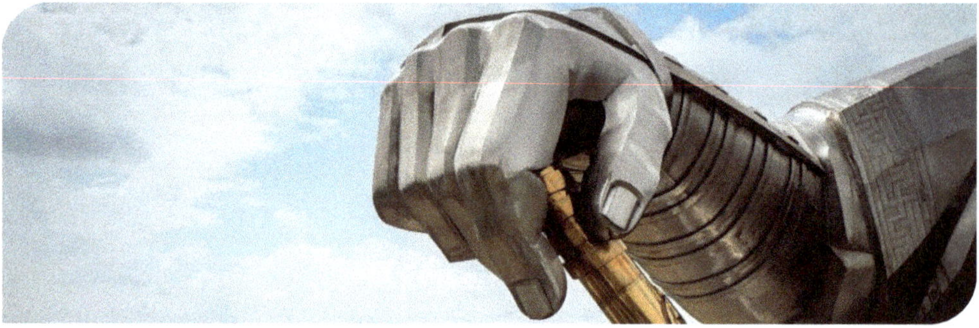

The Equestrian Statue of Genghis Khan is a must-see attraction for anyone visiting Mongolia. This impressive statue is over 40 meters high and depicts the famous conqueror on his war horse. It is located in Tsonjin Boldog, about 50 km east of Mongolia's capital, Ulaanbaatar. The statue is surrounded by an amusement park that includes a museum about the life and conquests of Genghis Khan. In addition, there is a zipline course and other outdoor activities. The equestrian statue of Genghis Khan is a true symbol of Mongolia and attracts thousands of visitors from all over the world every year to admire it. If you are passing through Mongolia, do not miss the opportunity to visit this unique attraction.

► The Mongol armies united under Genghis Khan and spread across Asia and Eastern Europe. Genghis Khan, whose real name is Temutchin, was born in the steppes of Central Asia around 1155 AD. He was in his forties when he succeeded in gaining recognition as a sovereign by all the tribes and received the name Genghis Khan (universal king in Mongolian) in 1206 AD. In 1219 AD, he crossed the Syr-Darya, entered Transoxiana (modern Uzbekistan) and marched on Bukhara. The prestigious city, rich in Islamic-Persian artistic treasures, was occupied in February 1220 AD and its garrison was massacred, but Genghis Khan refrained from looting the city. He showed the same indulgence for Samarkand the following month.

Genghis Khan died at around 60 years old, after his victory against the kingdom of the Tanguts (northwest China). The Mongol Empire was divided among his three sons. Genghis Khan is considered to be one of the most successful military leaders in history, and his empire was the largest contiguous empire in history.

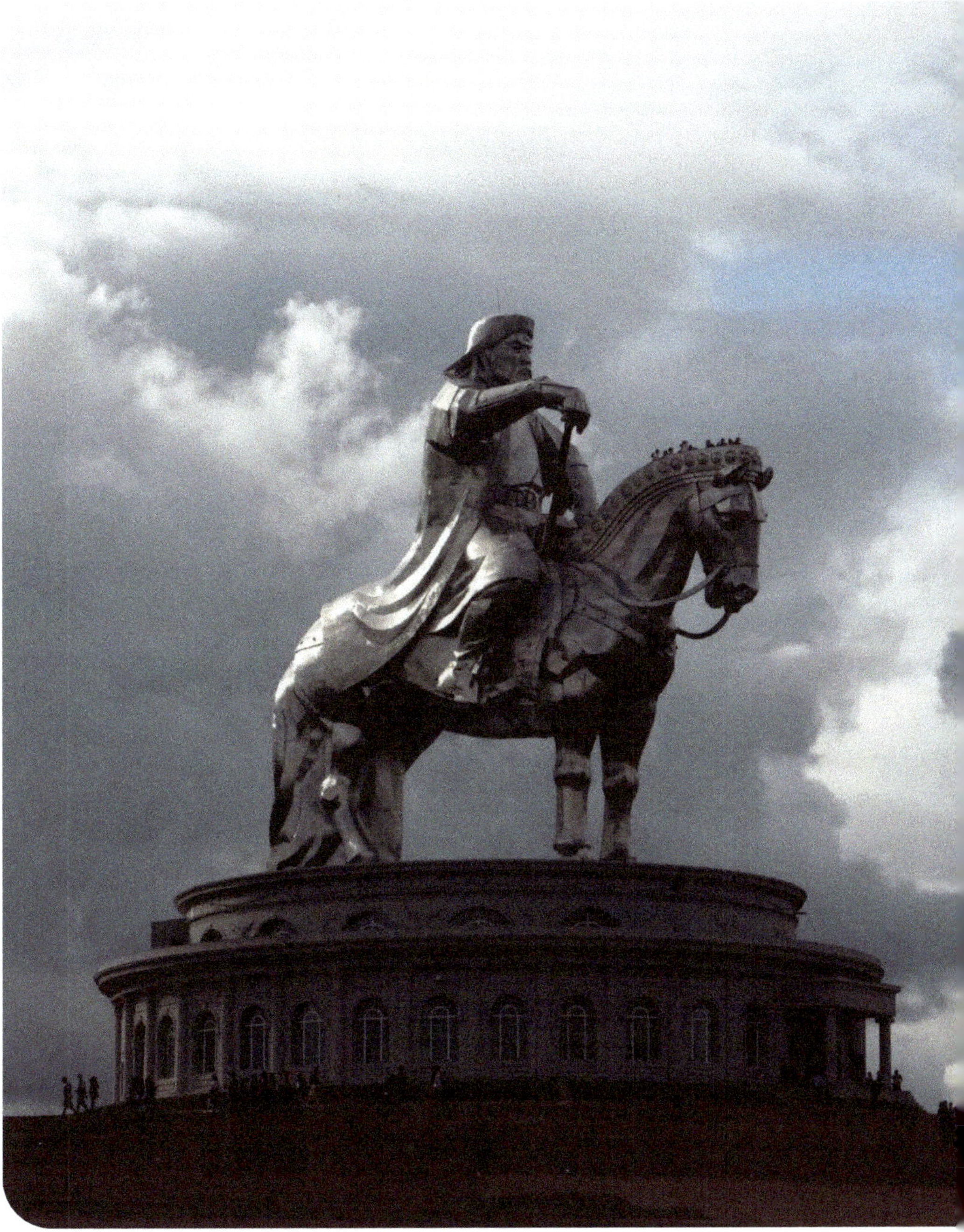

Re-experience Marco Polo's travels to the depths of the Far East at

REGISTAN SQUARE

#45 ⏱ **1275 AD**
🗺 **UZBEKISTAN**

Registan Square is one of the most famous and iconic places in Samarkand, Uzbekistan. This large square is surrounded by three Islamic-style buildings, each with its own courtyard and arcades. The most famous building is Madrasah Ulugh Beg, which was built in the fifteenth century and is known for its minarets and golden domes. Registan Square has been the heart of Samarkand for many centuries and has been the center of the city's cultural, religious and political life. Today, it remains a must-see for visitors to Samarkand and is considered one of the finest examples of Islamic architecture in Central Asia. If you are visiting Samarkand, do not miss the opportunity to stroll through Registan Square and discover all the beauty and history of this unique place.

▶ The Romans discovered a mysterious fabric from the distant Orient in the first century BC. Silk, a symbol of luxury and wealth, was the first traded product between the East and the West. During the Middle Ages, Arab sailors and merchants dominated trade with the Middle Empire by bringing back porcelain and spices from Canton. The capture of Constantinople in 1204 AD allowed the crusaders to access Eastern ports and caravan routes, through which Marco Polo, a Venetian merchant, passed.

He returned to Venice 24 years after his departure and later participated in a war against Genoa where he was captured. He narrated his long odyssey that led him to the court of Kubilaï Khan to Rusticello of Pisa, a fellow prisoner. They helped him to write the Book of Wonders of the World, written in French, a work that later inspired Christopher Columbus. The silk road was not only a trade route for silk, but also for other luxury goods such as gold, ivory, and precious stones.

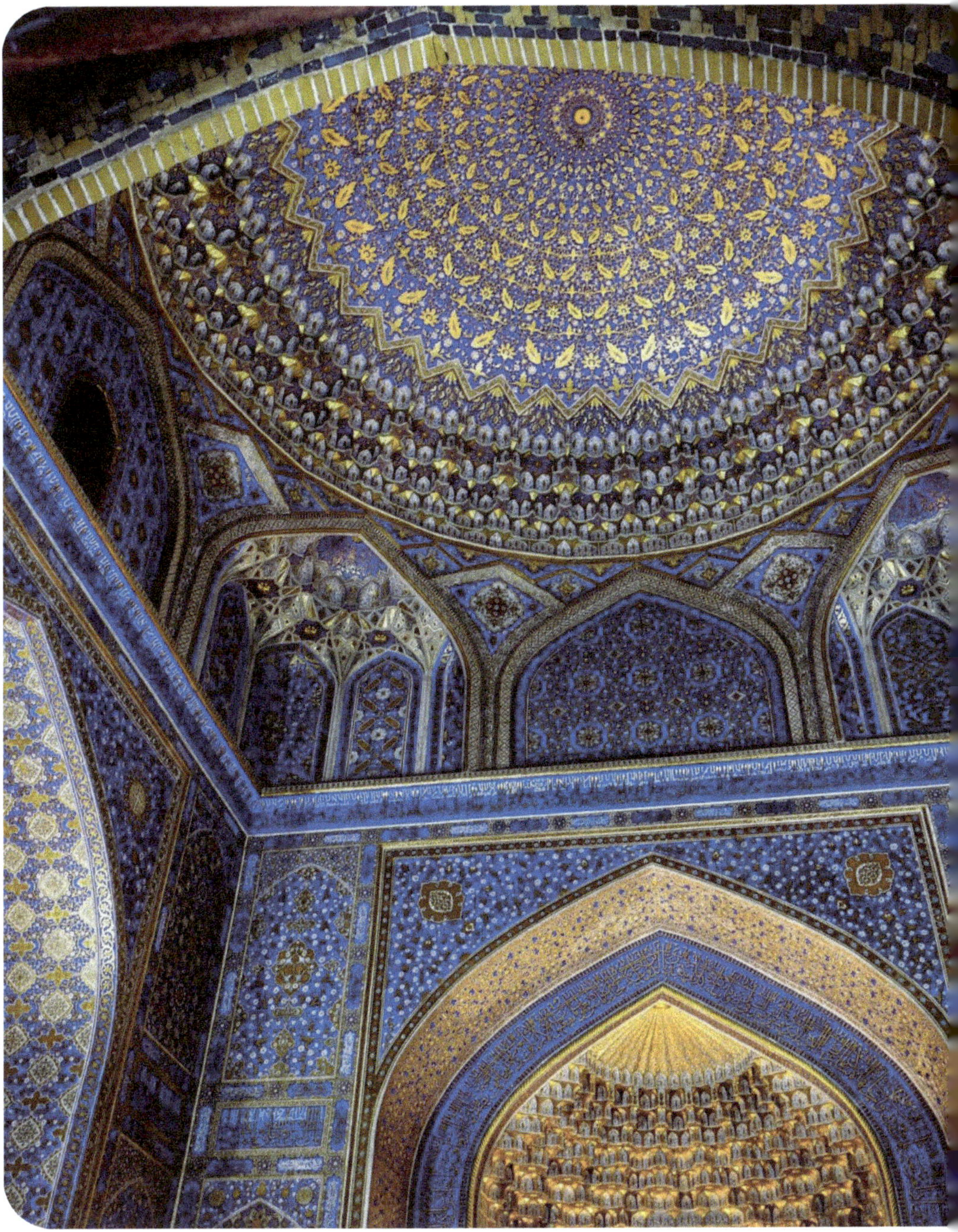

Comprehend the foundation of Switzerland at the

GRÜTLI MEADOW

#46 1291 AD

SWITZERLAND

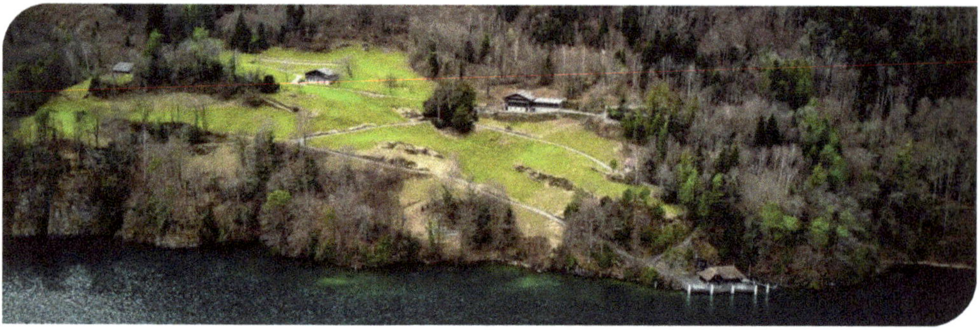

The Grütli is a historically significant site that is closely tied to the founding of Switzerland in 1291. Since that fateful day, the Grütli has become a revered symbol of Swiss freedom and national pride. The site has been transformed into a public park, open to all who wish to walk in the footsteps of the Confederation's founders. Today, the Grütli remains a place of patriotism, where Swiss citizens and tourists alike can connect with the nation's origins and the enduring spirit of unity that has sustained it through the ages. The meadow's significance as the birthplace of Switzerland is a source of immense pride and inspiration, serving as a constant reminder of the courage, determination, and shared vision that laid the foundation for one of Europe's most stable and prosperous democracies.

► The Federal Charter of August 1291 AD is considered the oldest constitutional text in Switzerland. It is the result of an agreement between the communities of the valleys of Uri, Schwyz and Nidwald. These communities pledged to defend each other against the Habsburgs and to support any outsider likely to attack or harm them. This text also provides for the maintenance of feudal ties and the impossibility of a foreigner claiming the position of judge. It also defines elements of criminal and civil procedures, as well as arbitration practices between valleys.

The Oath of Grütli is a founding myth of Switzerland that takes place on the Grütli meadow overlooking Lake Lucerne. Founded in the late 19th century, this agreement between three communities in central Switzerland is considered the foundation of the Swiss Confederation. The Swiss flag is based on the flag of Schwyz, one of the three communities that signed the pact in 1291 AD.

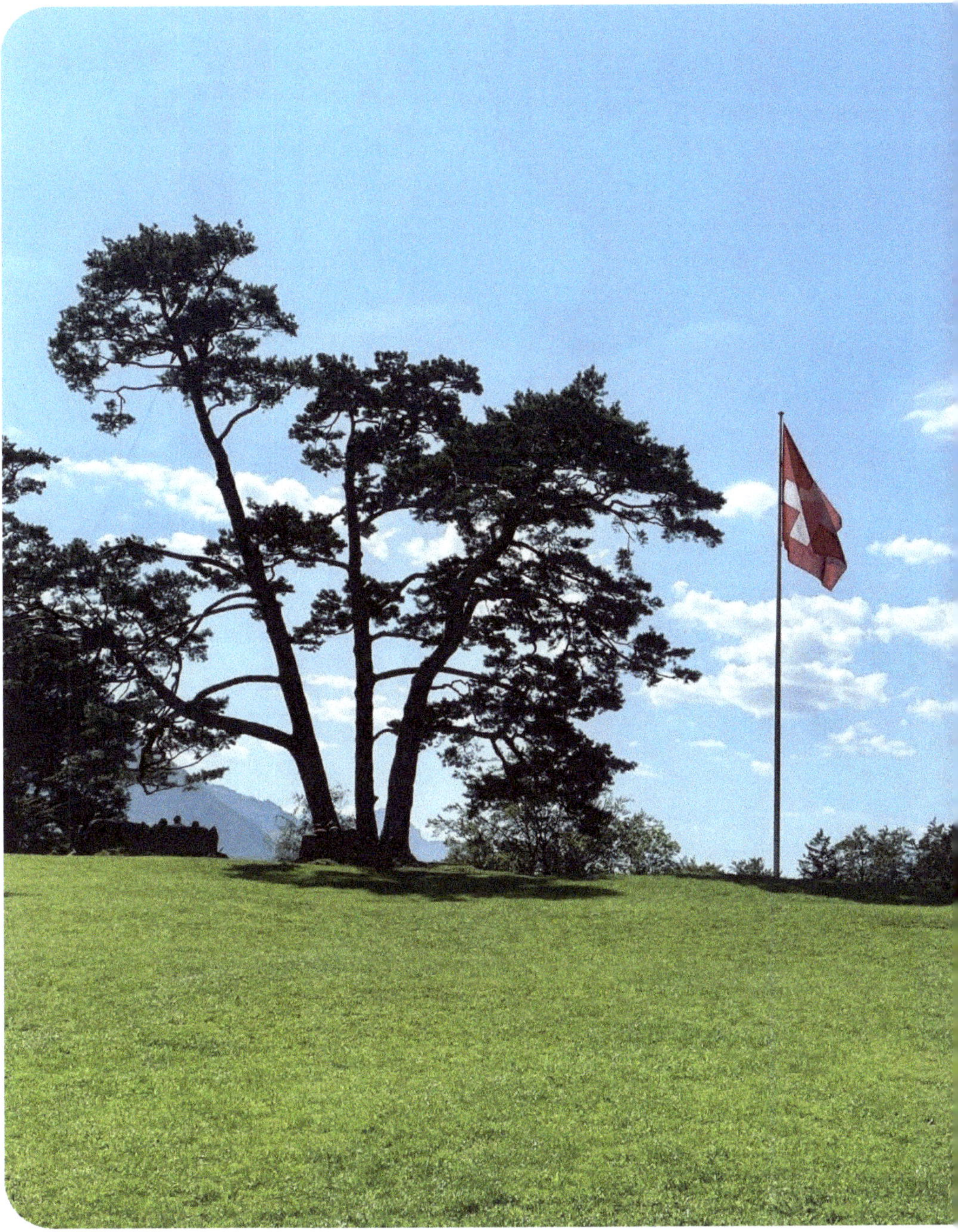

Understand the leave of papacy to Avignon due to the chaotic situation in Italy at the

PALACE OF THE POPES

#47 🕐 **1309 AD**

🗺 **FRANCE**

The Palais des Papes is one of the most emblematic sites of the city of Avignon, built in the 14th century and was the seat of the papacy for more than a hundred years and home to 7 popes. It is considered one of the largest Gothic palaces in Europe and is composed of several rooms, each with its own history and charm. Visitors can discover the Throne Room, where popes received ambassadors and dignitaries, or the Saint-Jean-Baptiste Chapel, where religious ceremonies took place. The inner courtyard of the palace is also a pleasant place to walk and admire the architecture. It is possible to visit it solo or in a group, with a guide who will make you discover the history and secrets of this emblematic place.

▶ In 1309 AD, French Pope Clement V decided to move the papacy's seat from Rome to Avignon due to civil war. This began a period of prosperity for the city as the papal court attracted European poets, princes, scholars, and artists. As a result, the papacy permanently settled in Avignon, making it the European capital of Christianity. The population of Avignon grew from 6,000 in 1309 AD to 40,000 in 1376 AD, becoming the second-largest city in France behind Paris. Most cardinals appointed by the Pope and his successors were French or Spanish. Pope Urban V attempted to return to Rome, but the chaotic situation there prevented him from remaining.

Pope Gregory XI eventually returned to Rome and defeated the rebels in 1377 AD. The Papal Enclave was demarcated by papal markers and was part of the Papal States for sixty years. In 1791 AD, after the French Revolution, the Papal Enclave was reclaimed by France and its inhabitants voted to be annexed to Vaucluse. Avignon was the capital of the Christian world for more than 70 years.

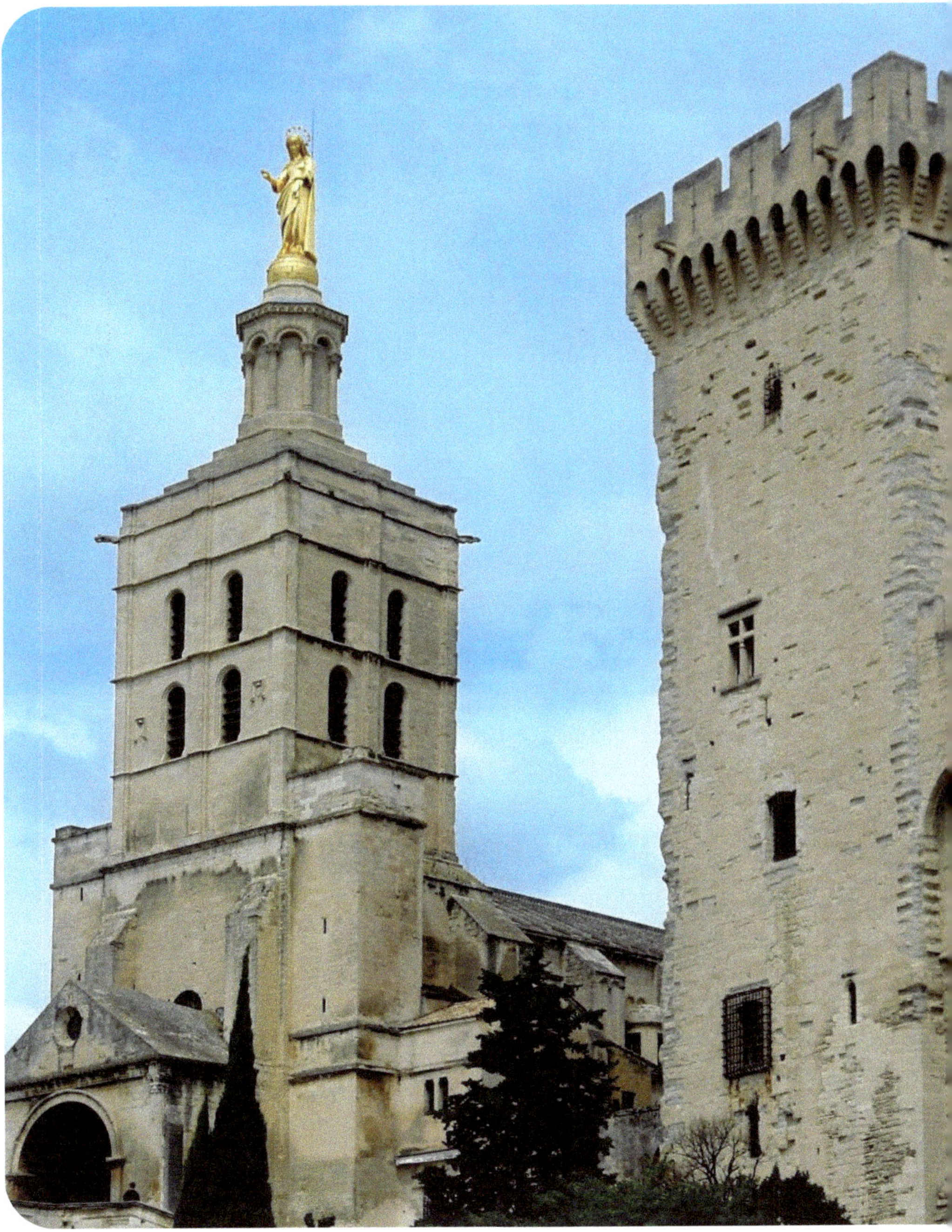

Imagine the apogee of the Kingdom of Mali in

TIMBUKTU

#48 1327 AD

MALI

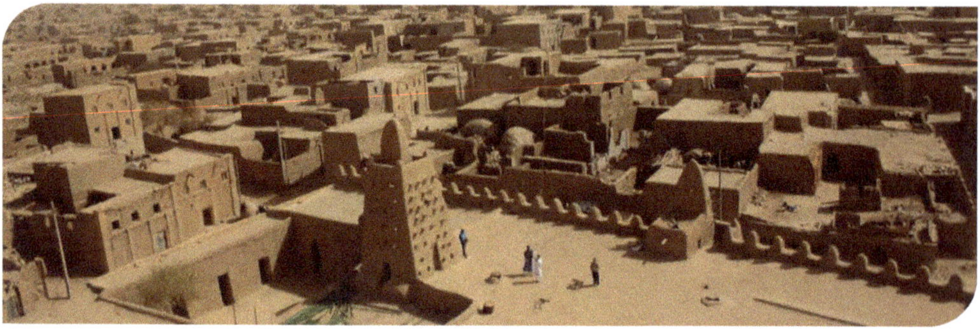

Timbuktu, a city with a captivating history, is nestled in the northern reaches of Mali. In its heyday, Timbuktu was a center of learning, boasting numerous schools, libraries, and centers of scholarship. The city's reputation as a seat of knowledge and culture attracted scholars, scribes, and intellectuals from across the region and beyond. The Djingareyber Mosque, a stunning 14th-century architectural marvel, stands as a testament to the city's rich heritage and the devotion of its people. Despite the challenges it has faced in recent years, Timbuktu remains a captivating and resilient city, a living embodiment of the enduring power of human ingenuity, creativity, and the pursuit of knowledge. As travelers venture to this remarkable destination, they are sure to be enchanted by the city's timeless allure and the enduring legacy of its storied past.

► The golden age of the Kingdom of Mali was a period of exemplary prosperity and cultural flourishing. Located in West Africa, the Kingdom emerged in the 13th century and quickly became a major power in the region. Under the rule of Emperor Sundiata Keita, the Kingdom expanded its territory and wealth through trade and diplomacy. The main city of Mali, Timbuktu, became a center of learning and scholarship, attracting researchers and students from all over the world. The Kingdom also had a thriving artistic and cultural scene, with poets, musicians and artisans all contributing to its dynamic society.

Overall, the golden age of the Kingdom of Mali was a period of remarkable prosperity and cultural achievements that left a lasting impact on the history of West Africa. The Kingdom of Mali was one of the wealthiest and most powerful empires in West Africa during its golden age, and it was known for its impressive architecture and its prosperous trade routes, particularly its gold trade.

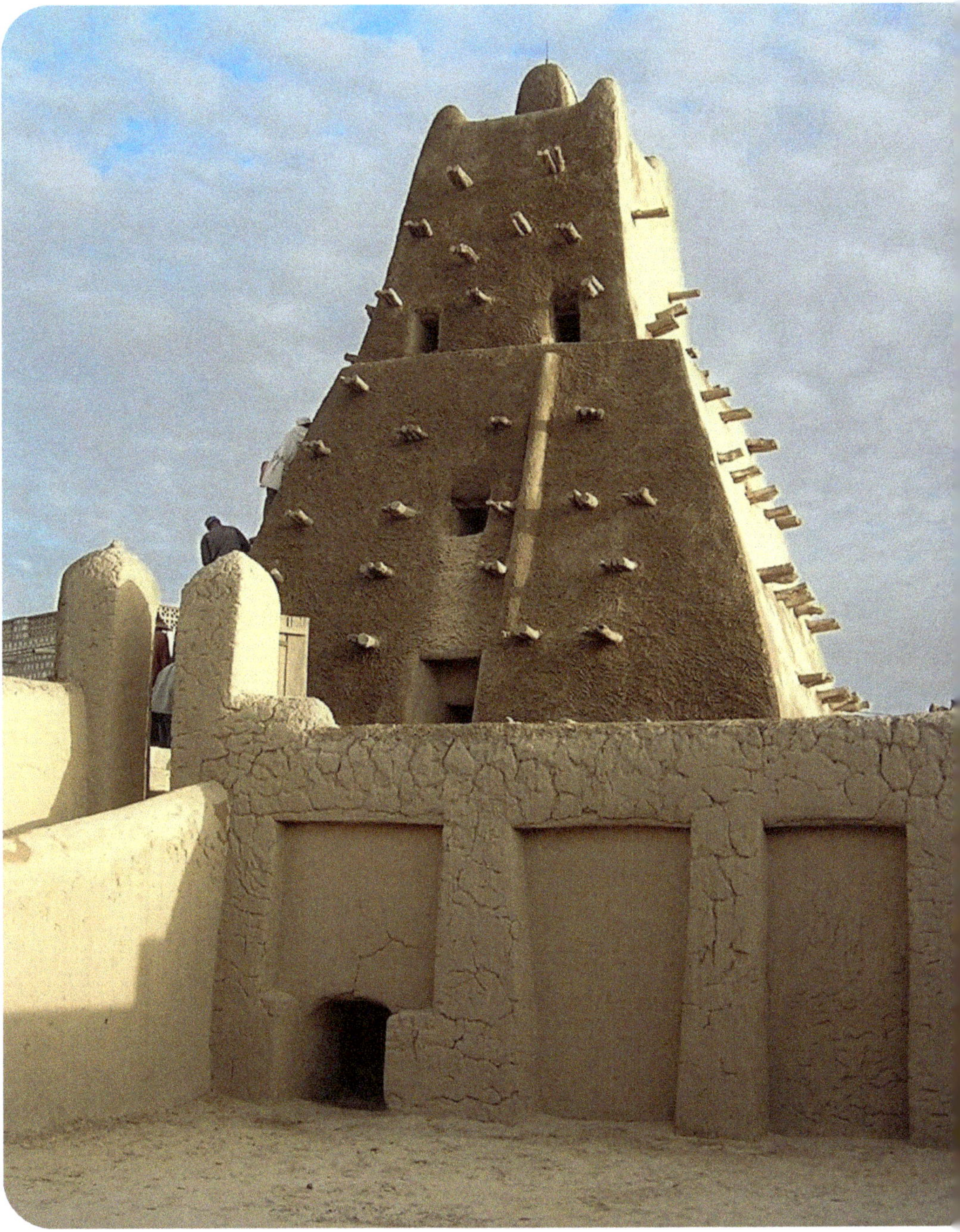

Grasp the overthrow of the Kamakura Shogun by Ashikaga Takauji at

KINKAKU-JI

#49 ⏱ **1336 AD**
🗺 **JAPAN**

The Temple of the Golden Pavilion or Kinkaku-ji is one of the most iconic and popular sites in Kyoto, Japan. This Zen Buddhist temple fascinates visitors with its sparkling golden structure reflected in the peaceful pond just below. The temple was built in 1397 and it has been restored several times over the centuries. The main building, which is covered in pure gold, is dedicated to the memory of the emperor and contains many precious relics. In addition to its architectural beauty, the Temple of the Golden Pavilion is famous for its landscaped Zen garden, which is considered one of the most picturesque in Japan. Visitors can stroll along the winding paths and admire the carefully arranged waterfalls, rocks and trees.

▶ Ashikaga Takauji overthrew the Kamakura shoguns and founded the second shogunate by restoring power to Kyoto in 1336 AD. He distinguished himself from his predecessors by supporting the emperor in his fight against the Kamakura *bakufu*. The Ashikagas were therefore closer to imperial authority than their predecessors who sought to distance themselves from it. This led to the establishment of Japanese feudalism, the fusion of samurai and court culture, and a flourishing of the arts.

The tea ceremony developed during this time and it was during this era that the most famous temples of Kyoto were built. This feudal system eventually broke down into a long period of internal wars known as the Sengoku period. The Ashikaga shogunate was abolished a century later in 1573 AD, when Oda Nobunaga expelled the fifteenth and last Ashikaga shogun, Yoshiaki, out of Kyoto.

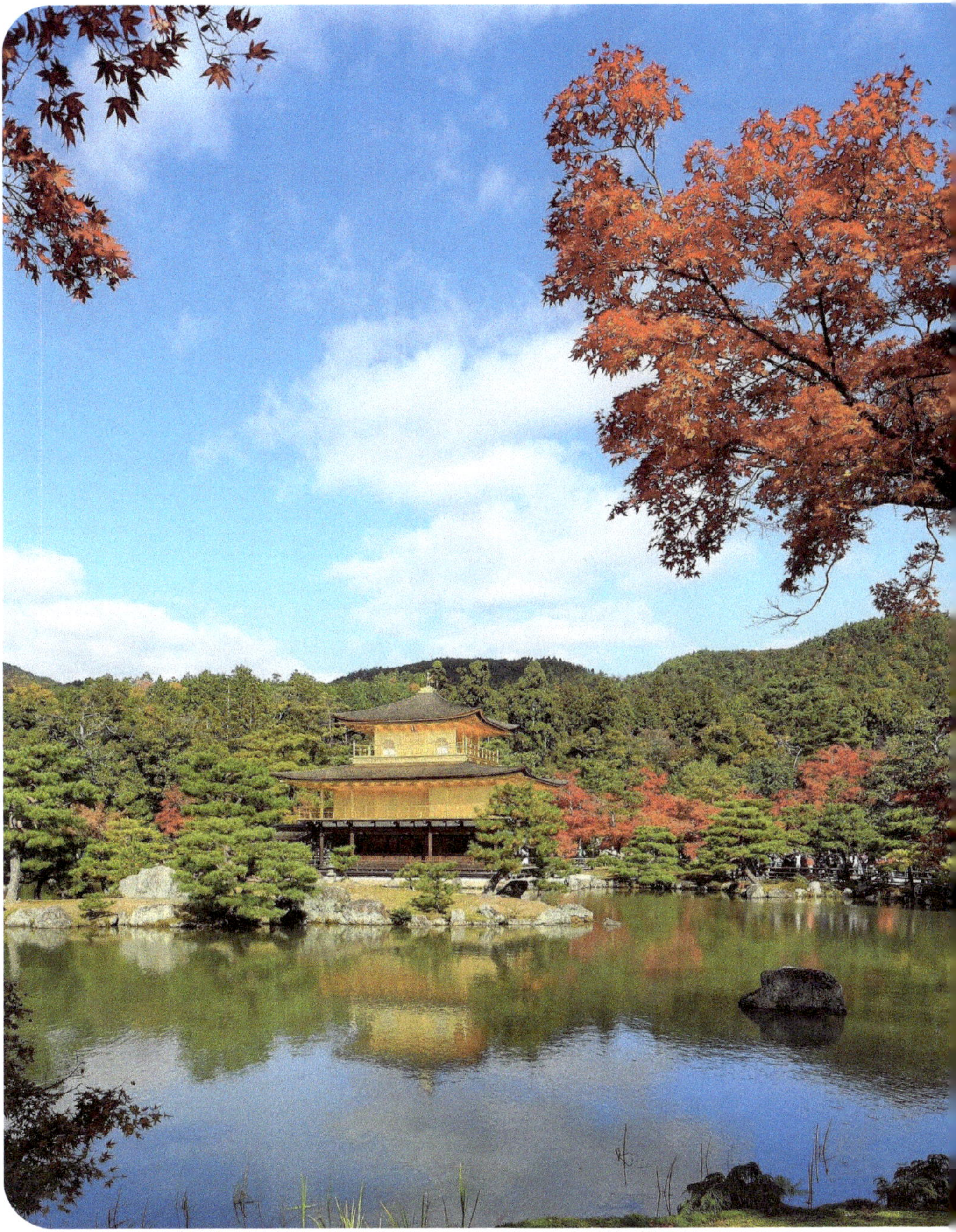

Sense Tamerlane's empire's legacy in Samarkand at the

GO'RI AMIR MAUSOLEUM

#50 1370 AD

UZBEKISTAN

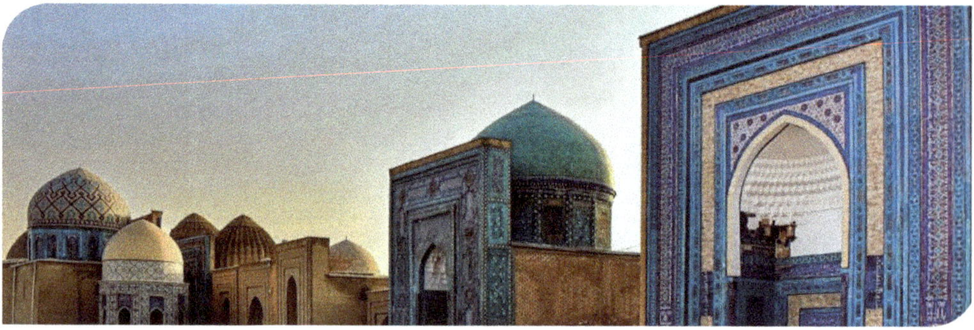

The Go'ri Amir Mausoleum is a must-see historical site in the city of Samarkand, Uzbekistan. This imposing white marble structure is the mausoleum of Emperor Timur, also known as Tamerlane. Built in the early fifteenth century, the Go'ri Amir Mausoleum is a stunning example of Islamic architecture of the time. It has golden domes and minarets that rise proudly to the sky. The mausoleum is also known for its turquoise and marble mosaics, which decorate the interior walls and ceilings. Although the Go'ri Amir Mausoleum has suffered a lot of damage over the centuries, it has been carefully restored. It is now considered one of the most remarkable architectural wonders of Uzbekistan.

► On April 8th, 1336 AD, a boy was born near Samarkand, who would leave a lasting mark on history, Amir Timur also known as Tamerlan. In 1352 AD, at the age of 16, he offered his talents to the emir Kazghan of Transoxiane. Kazghan quickly offered him the command of a battalion and even the hand of his daughter, the lovable Aldjaï. It was during one of these military expeditions, mixing exploits and pillages, that Timur was wounded in one leg and became Timourleng. This is pronounced Tamerlan in the West. At the end of the Middle Ages, nearly two centuries after the Mongol expansion, Tamerlan had created an empire more limited and ephemeral than that of Genghis Khan.

Tamerlan was also a protector of the arts and letters, contributing to Samarkand's greatness. His descendants, the Timurids, continued his patronage and his memory is carefully maintained around his tomb. After his death in 1405 AD, his empire, governed by his descendants was dismantled by neighboring powers until the final assault of the Uzbeks of the Chaybanid dynasty.

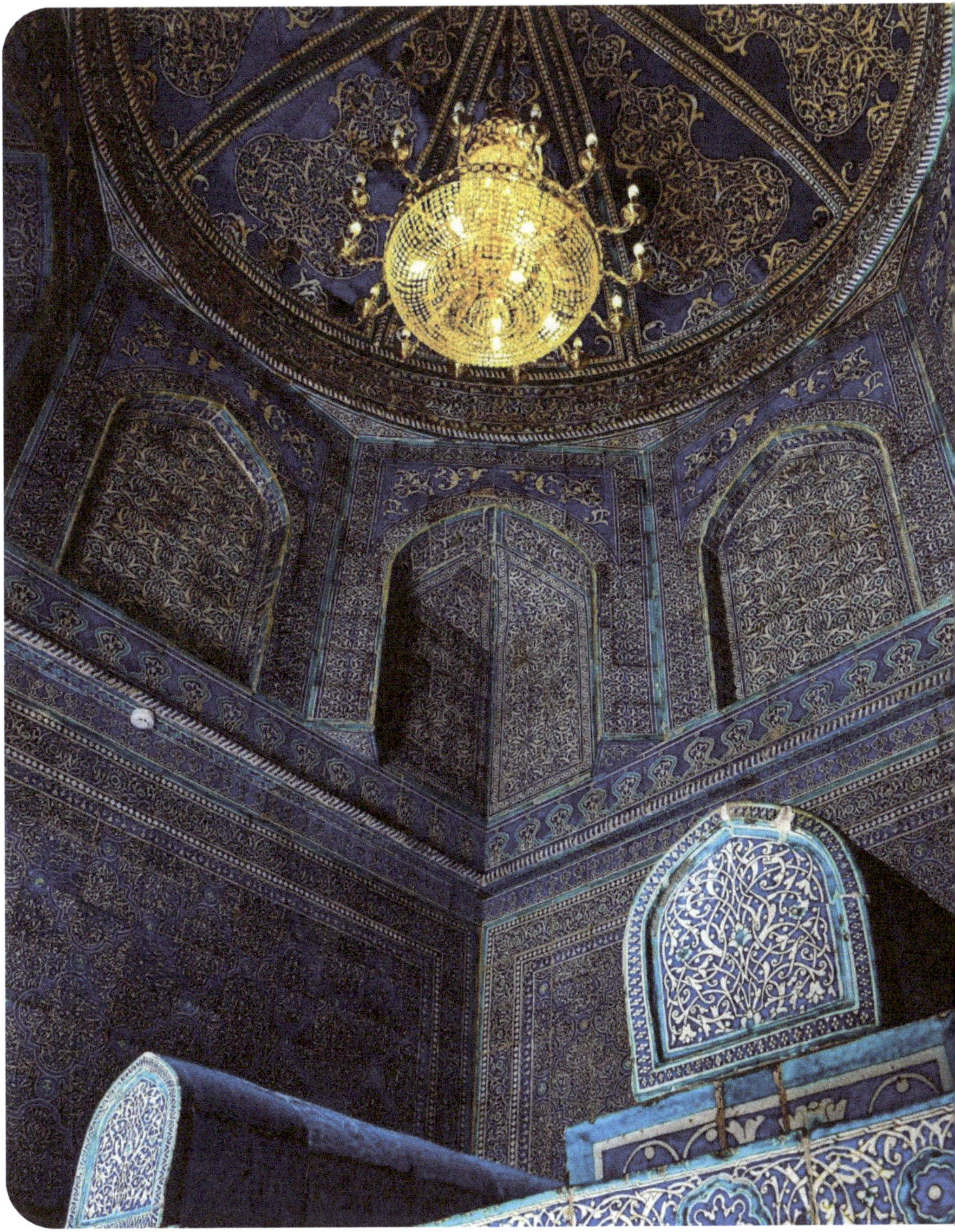

Perceive the birth of Italian Renaissance inside

CATHEDRAL OF FLORENCE

#51

1420 AD

ITALY

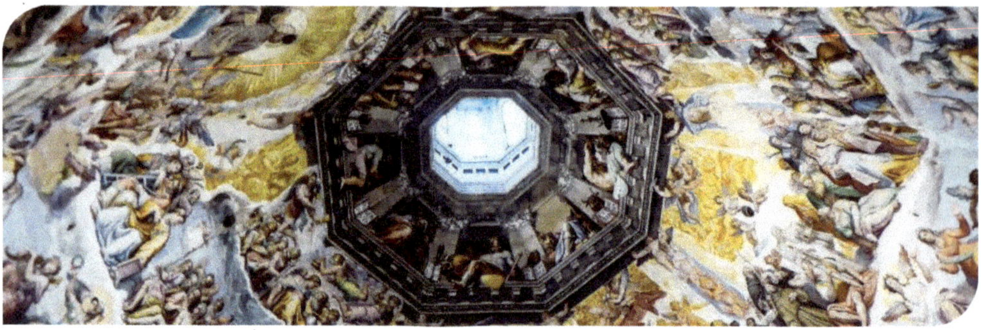

Florence Cathedral, also known as the Basilica di Santa Maria del Fiore, is a true architectural masterpiece that stands as a testament to the city's rich cultural heritage. Located in the heart of Florence, this imposing structure is a prime example of Gothic art and architecture, showcasing the ingenuity and craftsmanship of the city's master builders. The cathedral's most iconic feature is its massive dome, designed by the renowned architect Filippo Brunelleschi, which is one of the largest domes in the world and has become a symbol of the city of Florence. Inside, the cathedral's vast interior is a study in Gothic grandeur, with soaring arches, intricate stained-glass windows, and ornate decorations that captivate visitors from around the world.

► During the 15th century, European societies underwent significant transformations. The Renaissance was both a historical period and an artistic movement. It saw Italian artists rediscover the heritage of ancient Greece and Rome, which is why this period is literally called "Rebirth". Florence, in Italy, played a similar role to Athens in classical antiquity. It was one of the most influential cities in the history of art, literature, political organization, and economy of the peninsula between the 13th and 16th centuries. It was the city of the Médicis, Dante, Machiavelli, Amerigo Vespucci, Brunelleschi and many other painters who formed the Florentine school.

The Renaissance brought about a radical change in the way the world was represented. This change put the emphasis on man rather than God, thus marking the end of the Middle Ages and the beginning of Modern Times.

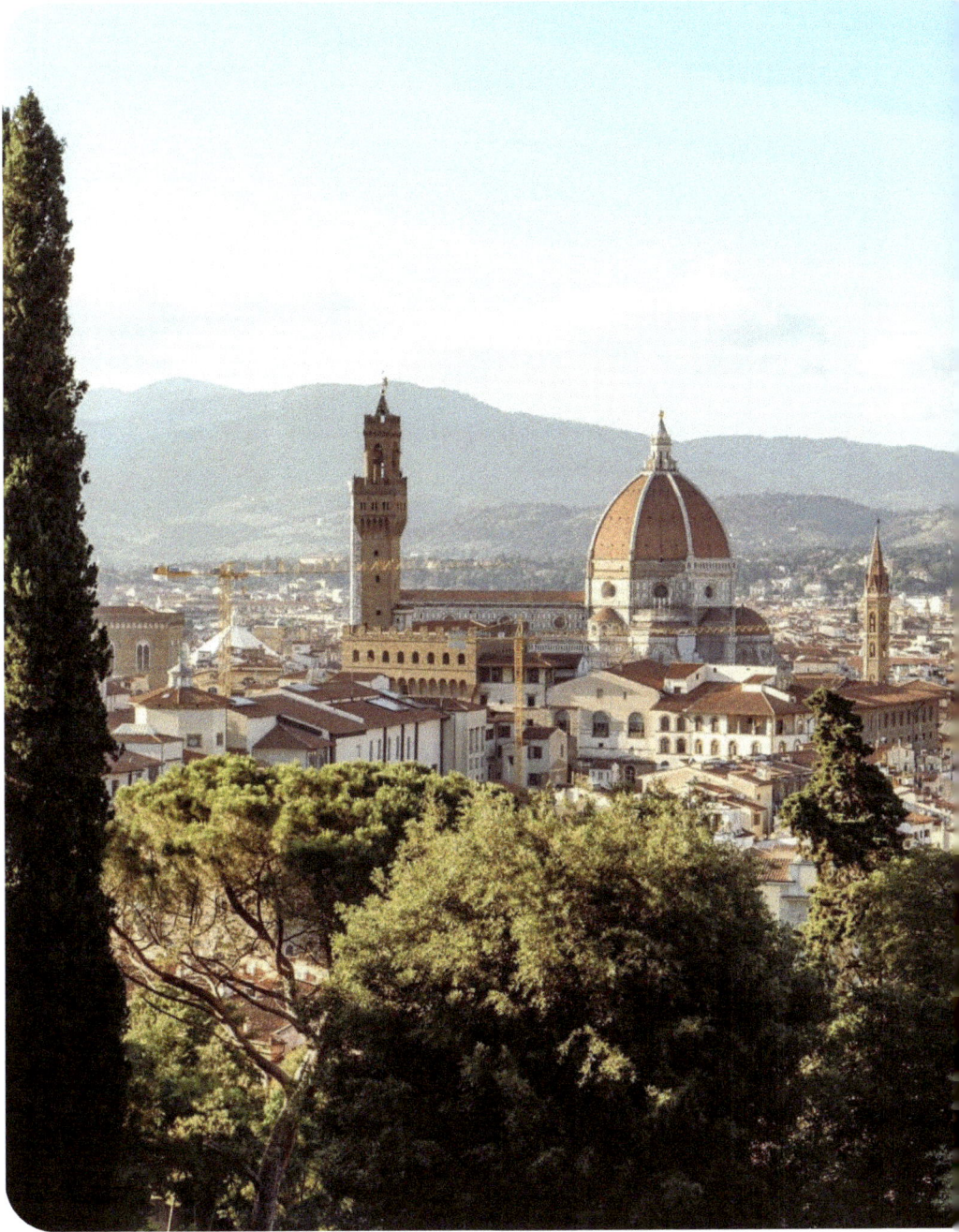

Imagine Gutenberg printing the first book in the

GUTENBERG MUSEUM

#52 ⏱ **1450 AD**

🗺 **GERMANY**

The Gutenberg Museum is a must-see for history and printing enthusiasts. Located in Mainz, Germany, this museum pays tribute to the famous inventor Johann Gutenberg and his revolutionary invention of the printing hand press. The museum has a collection of more than 200,000 objects, including the first copies of the Bible printed by Gutenberg, as well as other rare and valuable works. Visitors can also see the original hand presses and movable type used for printing. The Gutenberg Museum is a fascinating place to learn more about the history of printing and the impact of Gutenberg's invention on the publishing world. If you are in Mainz, do not miss the opportunity to visit this exciting museum.

▶ In 1454 AD, Johannes Gutenberg developed the basics of printing. He replaced wooden characters with lead and antimony alloy characters that could be reused infinitely. He also invented a printing press that allowed a sheet of paper to be applied to the inked characters using a lever. He created thick and shiny printing ink that did not penetrate the paper unlike Chinese ink. With these revolutionary tools, Gutenberg began printing books, and after improving his press, he embarked on printing the Bible.

Johannes Gutenberg's pioneering work marked a pivotal turning point in the history of printing during the Renaissance era. Prior to the advent of Gutenberg's revolutionary printing press, knowledge and information were largely confined to the realm of monasteries, where monks carefully handwrote and meticulously copied manuscripts. However, Gutenberg's groundbreaking invention of movable type printing transformed this landscape, enabling the widespread dissemination of knowledge and ideas like never before.

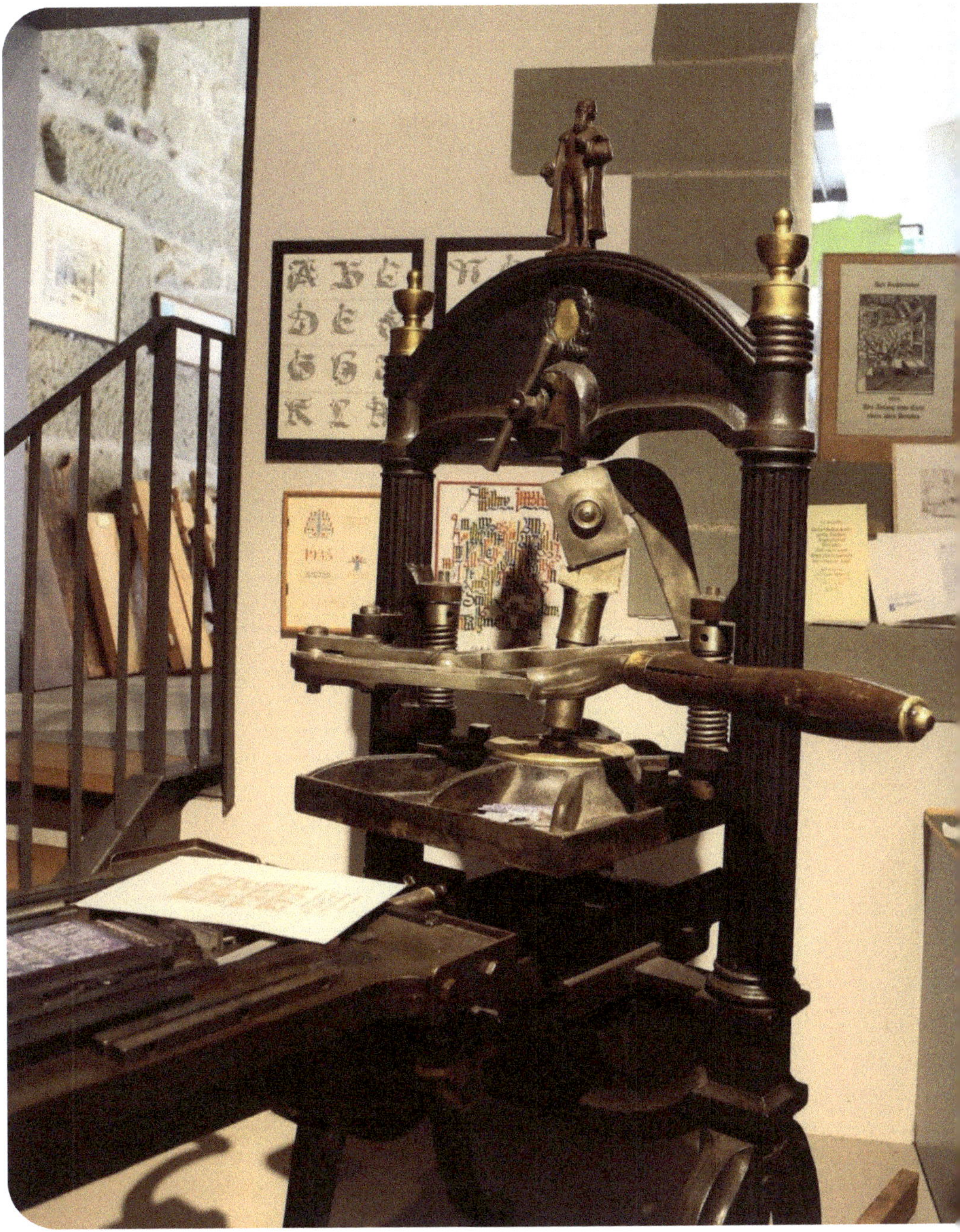

Picture the Ottoman Turks penetrating into the

WALL OF CONSTANTINOPLE

#53 ⏱ **1453 AD**
🗺 **TURKEY**

The Wall of Constantinople is a remarkable defensive edifice that was erected over the centuries to protect the city of Constantinople, the capital of the Eastern Roman Empire. It was built by Emperor Constantine I in the 4th century and has been constantly improved and strengthened over the years. It is nearly 20 km long and includes towers, bastions and fortified gates. Despite repeated attacks by the Byzantine Empire and Turkish invaders, the Walls of Constantinople managed to resist and were a determining factor in protecting the city over the centuries. Today it is still standing and is a fascinating historical site to visit for anyone interested in the history of the Roman Empire.

▶ The Byzantine Empire, which had been a shield against Arab invasions, thus protecting most of Christian Europe, had resisted for over a thousand years the assaults of twenty different peoples and suffered no less than thirty sieges. Constantinople was for centuries one of the wealthiest and most populous cities in the world. Furthermore, the city was strategically located at the crossroads between East and West, Asia and Europe. However, the Byzantine Empire, which had begun to decline in the 13th century, controlled only a small territory around the city founded by Constantine, when Sultan Mehmet II launched the siege in 1453 AD. The city fell seven weeks later and became the capital of the Ottoman Empire. Saint Sophia's Basilica became a mosque and caused a migration of Greek scholars to Italy, where they contributed to the development of Hellenism and the Renaissance. The fall of Constantinople is considered to be the end of the Middle Ages and the start of the early Modern Period.

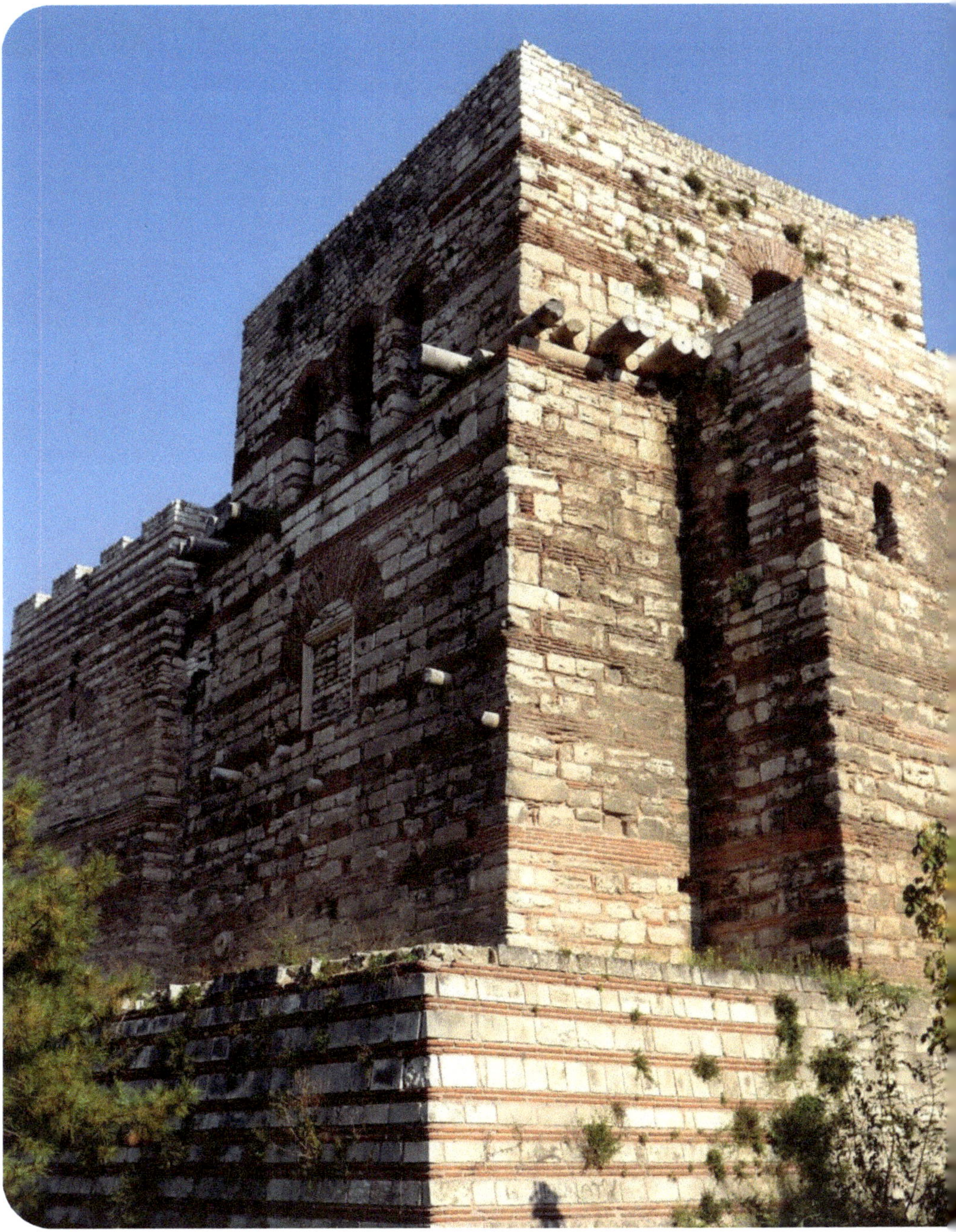

Visualize the success of the Spanish Reconquista inside the

ALHAMBRA CASTLE

#54 1492 AD

SPAIN

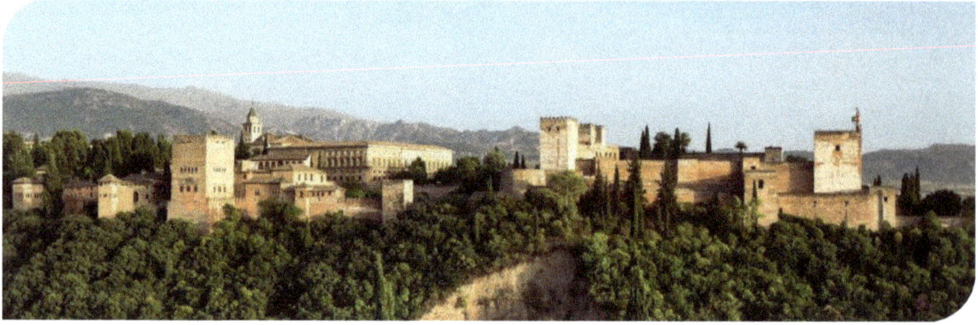

The Alhambra is a castle and palace located in Granada, Spain. This marvel of Moorish architecture is considered one of Spain's most iconic sites and was declared a UNESCO World Heritage Site in 1984. The Alhambra palace complex is known for its intricate tile work and water features, including the Court of Lions, its lush gardens, fountains adorned with mosaics and sumptuous reception rooms. There are also magnificent prayer halls, numerous bathrooms and sumptuous rooms for distinguished guests. The beauty of the Alhambra is further enhanced by its location on a hill overlooking Granada, offering stunning views of the city and the surrounding mountains.

► After receiving a revelation, Muhammad gave the Arabs a common religion, Islam, and imposed political and religious unity. Following the death of the Prophet, the Arabs embarked on conquests and within ten years, they conquered Syria, Chaldea, Assyria, Egypt and finally Persia. They also conquered Spain, where they maintained their presence for almost eight centuries, and founded Al-Andalus. The emirate of Granada was the last territory controlled by the Moors before being pushed out of the Iberian Peninsula during the Reconquista.

Between 1238 AD and 1492 AD, the Nasrid dynasty obtained relative peace in exchange for vassal agreements with the kings of Castile. The Nasrids took advantage of this to beautify the fortress of the Alhambra and establish a sumptuous palace. The palaces of the Alhambra, with their exuberant decoration, are representative of the last Hispano-Moorish style, that of the Nasrid dynasty which created the Kingdom of Granada in 1238 AD.

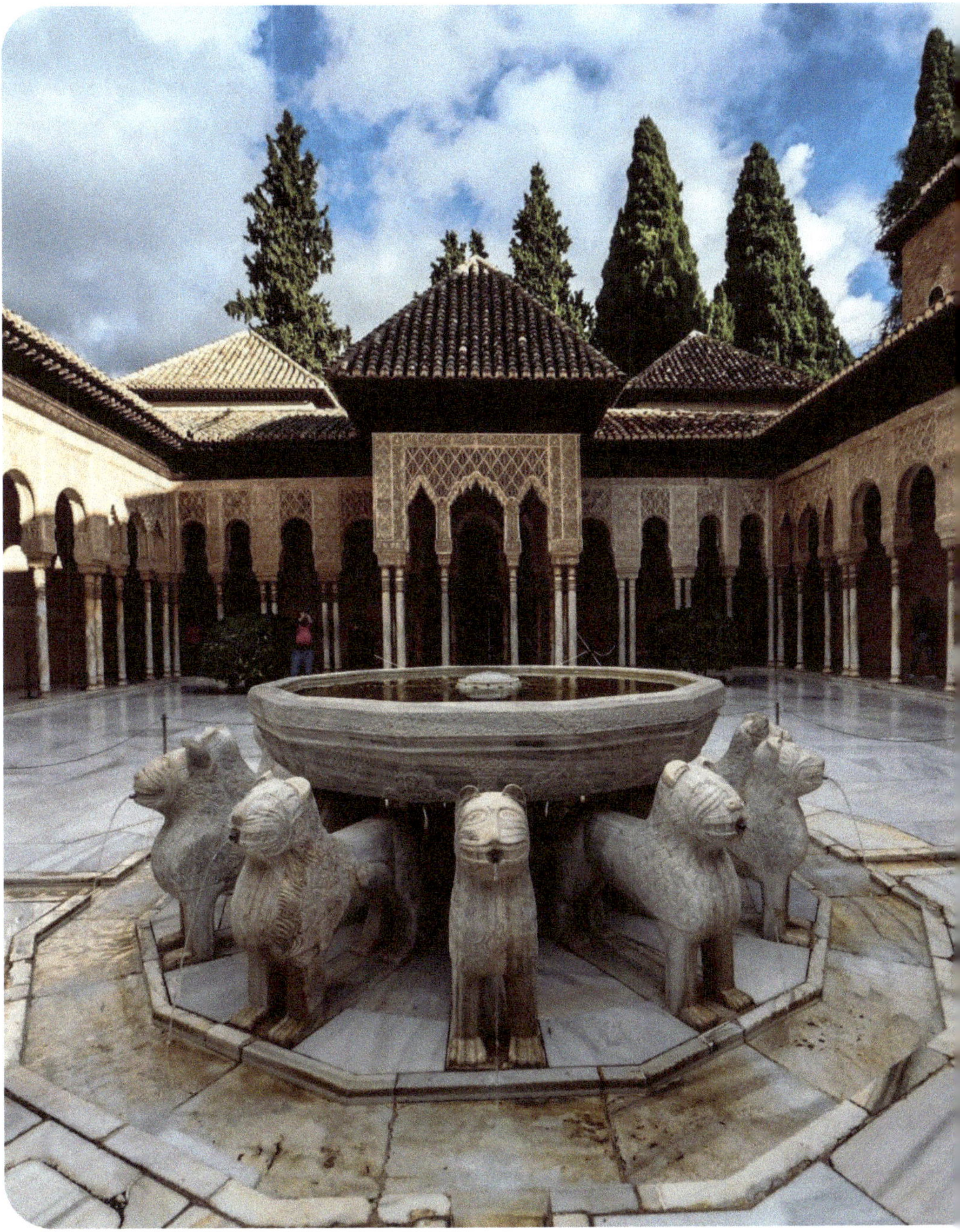

EARLY MODERN

The Early Modern period is the period in European history spanning from the late 15th century to the late 18th century, marked by major events like the Reformation, the colonization of the Americas, the Scientific Revolution, and the Enlightenment.

Conceive Christopher Columbus successful journey to the Americas at the

ARCHIVES OF INDIA

#55 1492 AD

SPAIN

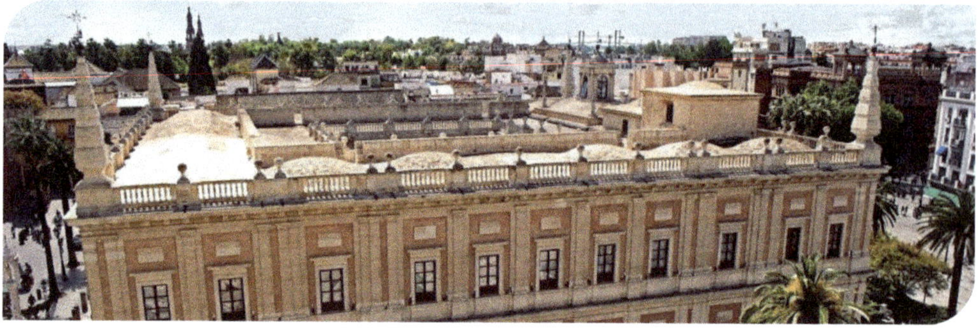

The Archives of the Indies, located in the historic city of Seville, Spain, are a veritable treasure trove of Spain's rich colonial past. This imposing and stately building houses millions of priceless documents and maps, meticulously chronicling the voyages of discovery, the relations between Spain and the Americas, Africa, and Asia. These archives represent one of the most comprehensive and invaluable documentation centers for scholars and researchers seeking to unravel the complexities of Spain's colonial history. Historians, anthropologists, and other academics from around the globe flock to the Archives of the Indies each year, eager to delve into the vast repository of primary sources that offer unparalleled insights into the triumphs, challenges, and legacies of Spain's colonial endeavors.

► In the early 1480s, Columbus began to envision a way to navigate across the Atlantic to reach the East Indies. He knew since antiquity that the Earth was round, and he was inspired by the tales of Marco Polo. His project was rejected by a group of experts in Portugal, but he decided to present it to other leaders who wanted to compete with Portugal. In 1486 AD, he was finally received by Ferdinand of Aragon and Isabella of Castille, and set off with three ships and 90 crew members from Palos on August 3rd, 1492 AD.

He reached the island of Guanahani (Bahamas) after 65 days of navigation, and believed he had arrived in the East Indies. He discovered San Salvador, Cuba and Haiti, which he called Hispaniola, and returned to Spain in March 1493 AD. He left a garrison of 39 men in Haiti to build a fort and hunt for gold. Columbus actually made four voyages across the Atlantic, not just the first one in 1492 AD. On his fourth and final voyage, he believed he had discovered the mainland of Asia, but in reality it was Central America.

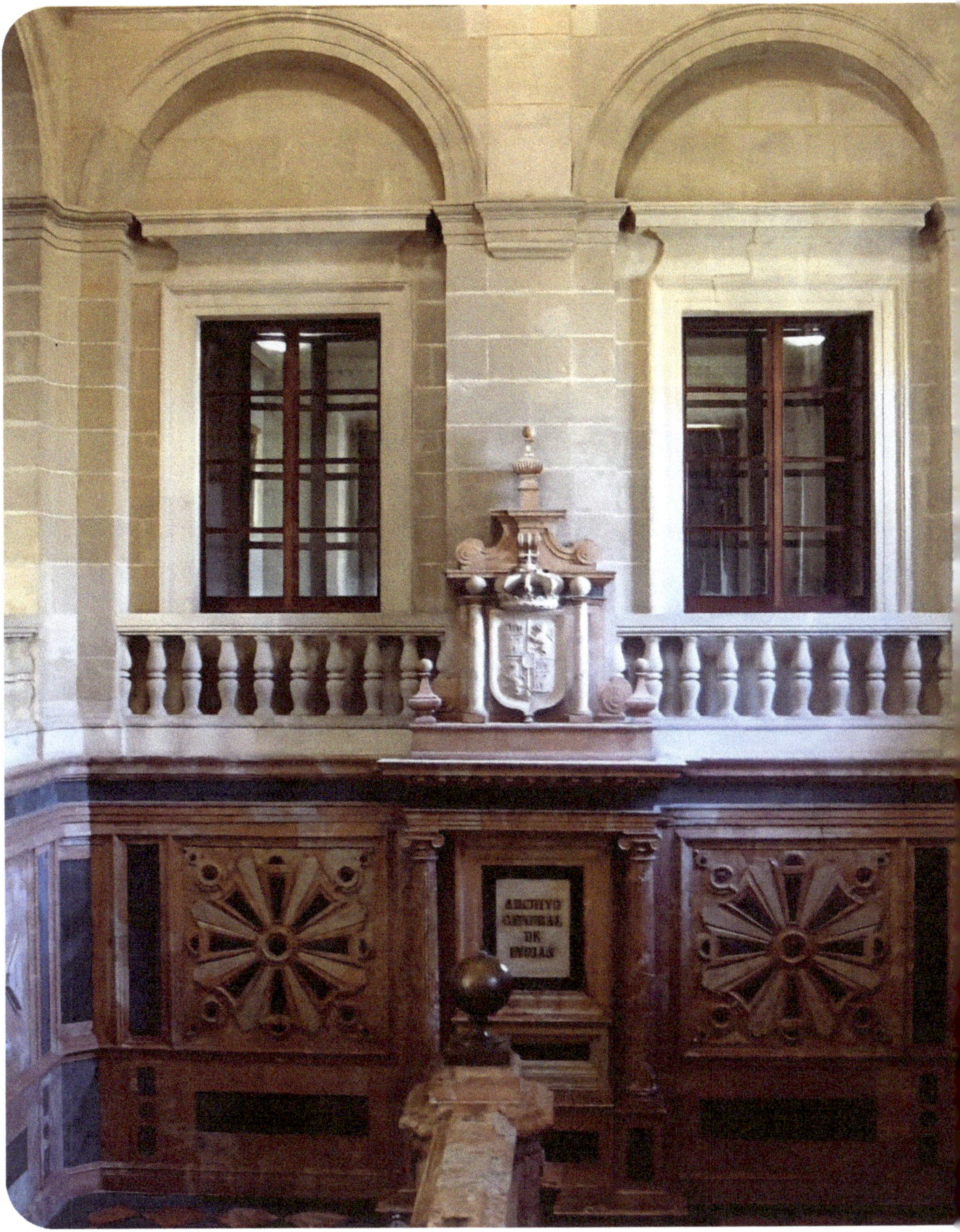

Witness Vasco da Gama's sea route to India starting from the

BELEM TOWER

#56

1498 AD

PORTUGAL

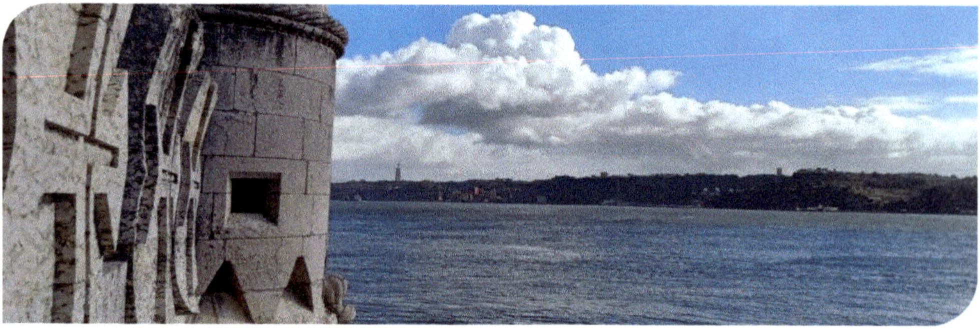

The Tower of Belém is an iconic and captivating landmark that has stood tall in Lisbon for centuries. Constructed in the early 16th century, this towering structure was originally built to serve as a fortified gateway, protecting the city from potential enemy invasions during a time of great maritime exploration and expansion. Today, the Belém Tower stands as a testament to Portugal's rich history and architectural prowess. Situated on the picturesque banks of the Tagus River, this magnificent structure boasts a striking Gothic-style design, complete with intricate arches, ornate carvings, and thick, sturdy walls that have withstood the test of time. The tower's strategic location offers visitors breathtaking panoramic views of the river, the city skyline, and the surrounding landscape.

► During the time when Vasco de Gama embarked on his expedition in 1497 AD, the Portuguese were already familiar with the West African coast, they had been exploring since the 14th century. They were however still searching for a sea route to reach the Indies. Bartolomeu Dias, had already attempted to find this route in 1488 AD but turned back before reaching the southernmost point, the Cape of Good Hope. Gama followed in his footsteps by leaving Portugal in July 1497 AD with four ships and 200 men. He made a stop at Cape Verde, then made it to the island of Saint Helena and rounded the Cape of Good Hope in November 1497 AD. He made several stops along the African coast before arriving in Mozambique, stopping in Mombasa, and eventually crossed the Indian Ocean to reach Calicut in May 1498 AD. This expedition opened the way for the development of maritime trade between Europe and Asia. Vasco de Gama is considered as the first person to have completed a voyage to India by sea, opening up a route for the spice trade and transforming the economic and political landscape of the world.

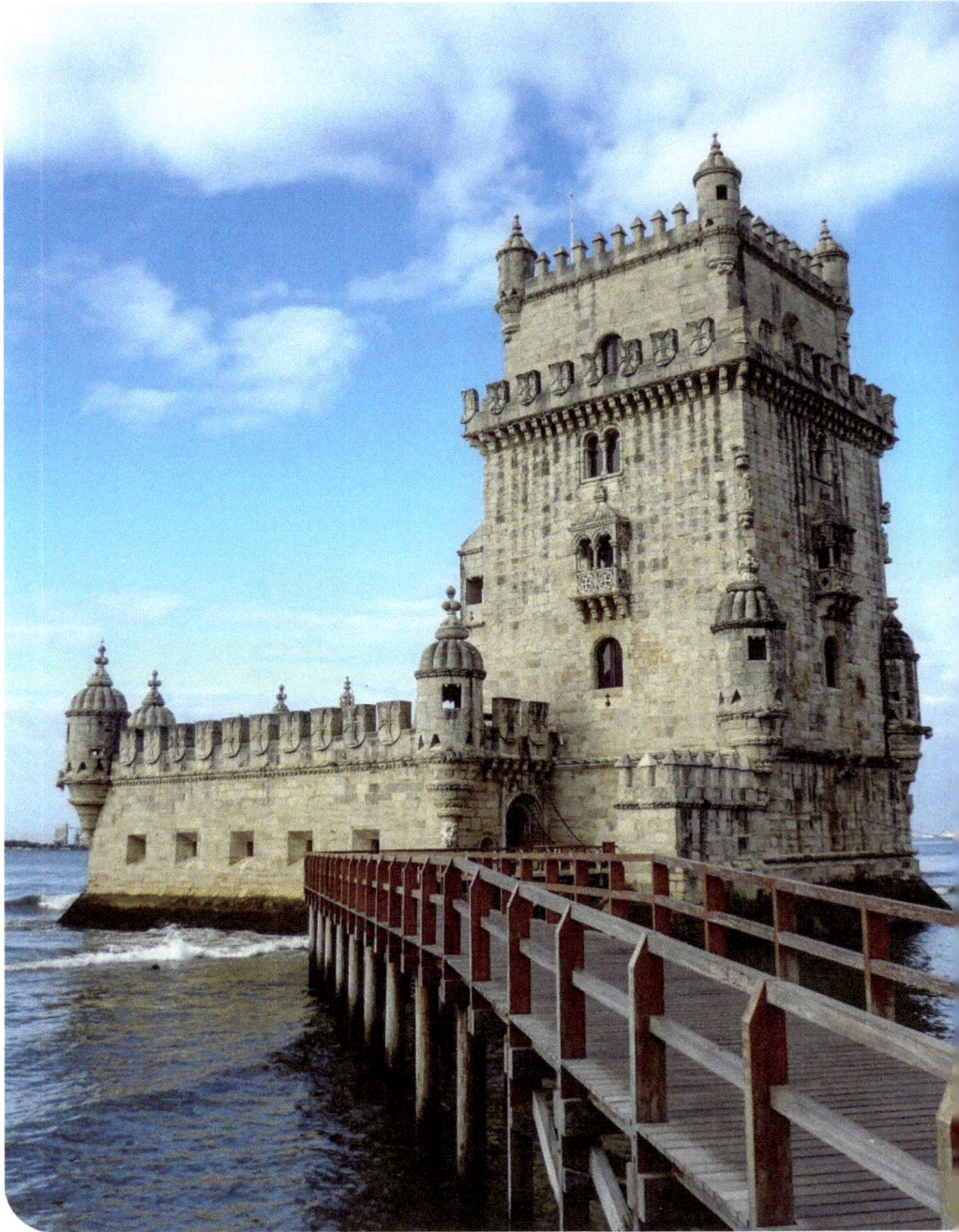

57

Be in awe watching Michael-Ange's masterpiece on the ceiling of

SISTINE CHAPEL

🕐 1512 AD

📖 **VATICAN**

The Sistine Chapel is arguably one of the most famous and visited sites in Rome. Located in the Apostolic Palace of the Vatican, it is considered one of the jewels of Renaissance art. Commissioned by Pope Julius II in 1508, the chapel was made by the greatest artists of the time, such as Michelangelo, Raphael and Botticelli. Its interior decoration is a real treasure, with its monumental frescoes, painted ceilings and mosaics. The Sistine Chapel is also the place where popes are elected and where the most meaningful religious ceremonies take place. If you visit Rome, do not miss the opportunity to discover this exceptional place, which will immerse you in the history of art and religion.

▶ The Renaissance is both a period of history and an artistic movement. It gradually emerged in Italy during the late 14th centuries before spreading throughout Europe. This era marked the end of the Middle Ages and the beginning of modern times. Italian artists brought to light the heritage of Greek and Roman antiquity. This change began with Giotto, an Italian artist who greatly influenced painters of the 15th century. A few years later, Michelangelo painted the ceiling of the Sistine Chapel in Rome.

It is in this room that the cardinals, gathered in conclave, elect each new pope. The vault was originally painted blue and dotted with stars, but in 1508 AD, Julius II asked Michelangelo, who at the time did not practice fresco painting, to cover it. The vault is now divided into 9 panels representing the creation of the world. The center is dedicated to scenes from Genesis, including the famous "creation of man," where God touches the outstretched hand of Adam to give him life.

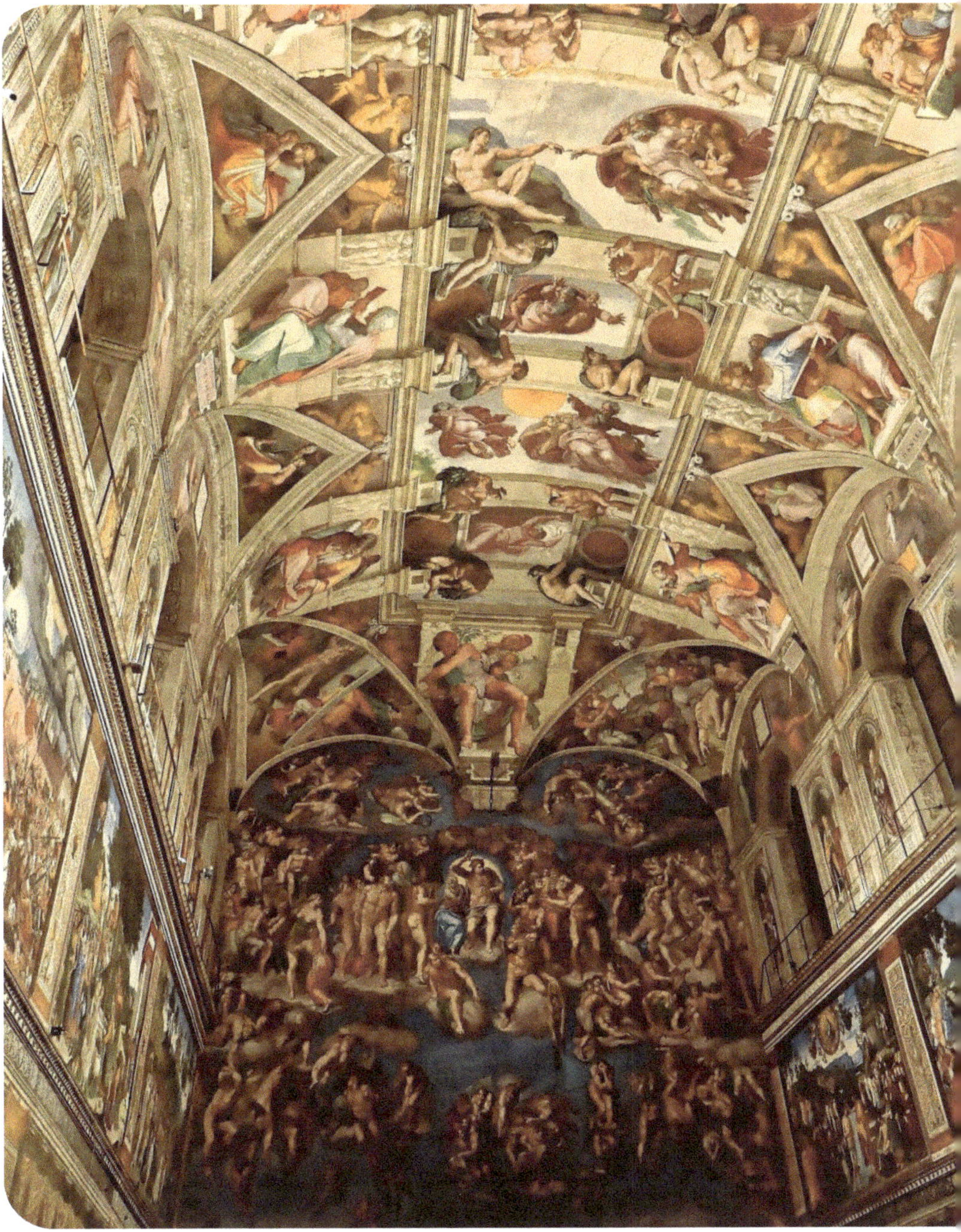

Relive the Italian War and competition for the imperial crown at the

CHAMBORD CASTLE

#58

1515 AD

France

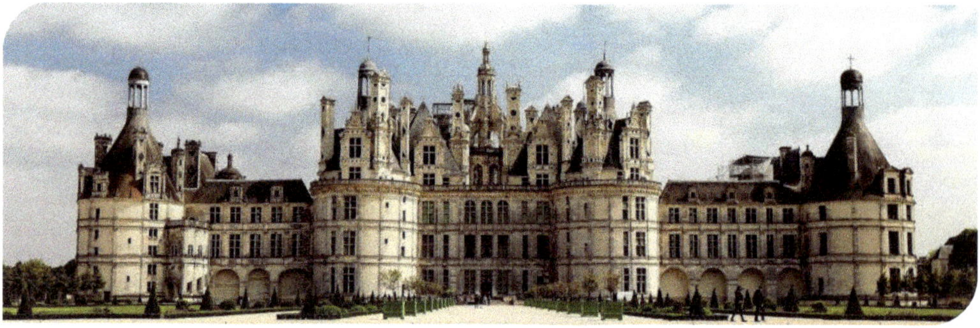

The Château de Chambord is a real architectural jewel located in the Loir-et-Cher, in France. Designed by Francis I in the 16th century, this castle is a stunning blend of Renaissance and Gothic style, with its tiled roofs, octagonal towers and pointed windows. With its 440 rooms, 282 fireplaces and 13 hectares of parks and gardens, the Château de Chambord is a true royal palace. But what really makes this castle unique is its central double staircase, which allows visitors to climb to the second floor without ever crossing paths. It is said that Francis I asked his architect, Leonardo da Vinci, to design this staircase so that he could escape discreetly during his visits to the castle. Anyway, this staircase is a true marvel of engineering and a real tourist attraction."

► The Italian War was a series of conflicts that took place between 1494 AD and 1559 AD, mainly in Italy. These conflicts were motivated by the desire for power and territory among the major European powers, particularly France, Spain and the Holy Roman Empire. The imperial crown was also a central issue in these conflicts, with each power seeking to gain control of the Holy Roman Empire and its vast territories.

The competition for the imperial crown was fierce, with each side trying to outmaneuver the other for the advantage. Finally, the Italian War ended with the Treaty of Cateau-Cambrésis in 1559 AD, which put an end to the fighting and established a new balance of power in Europe. One of the most famous battles of the Italian War was the Battle of Pavia in 1525 AD, in which the French army was decisively defeated by the Spanish. During the battle, King Francis I of France was captured and held prisoner by the Spanish for over a year- He was forced to accept harsh terms before he could finally return to his kingdom.

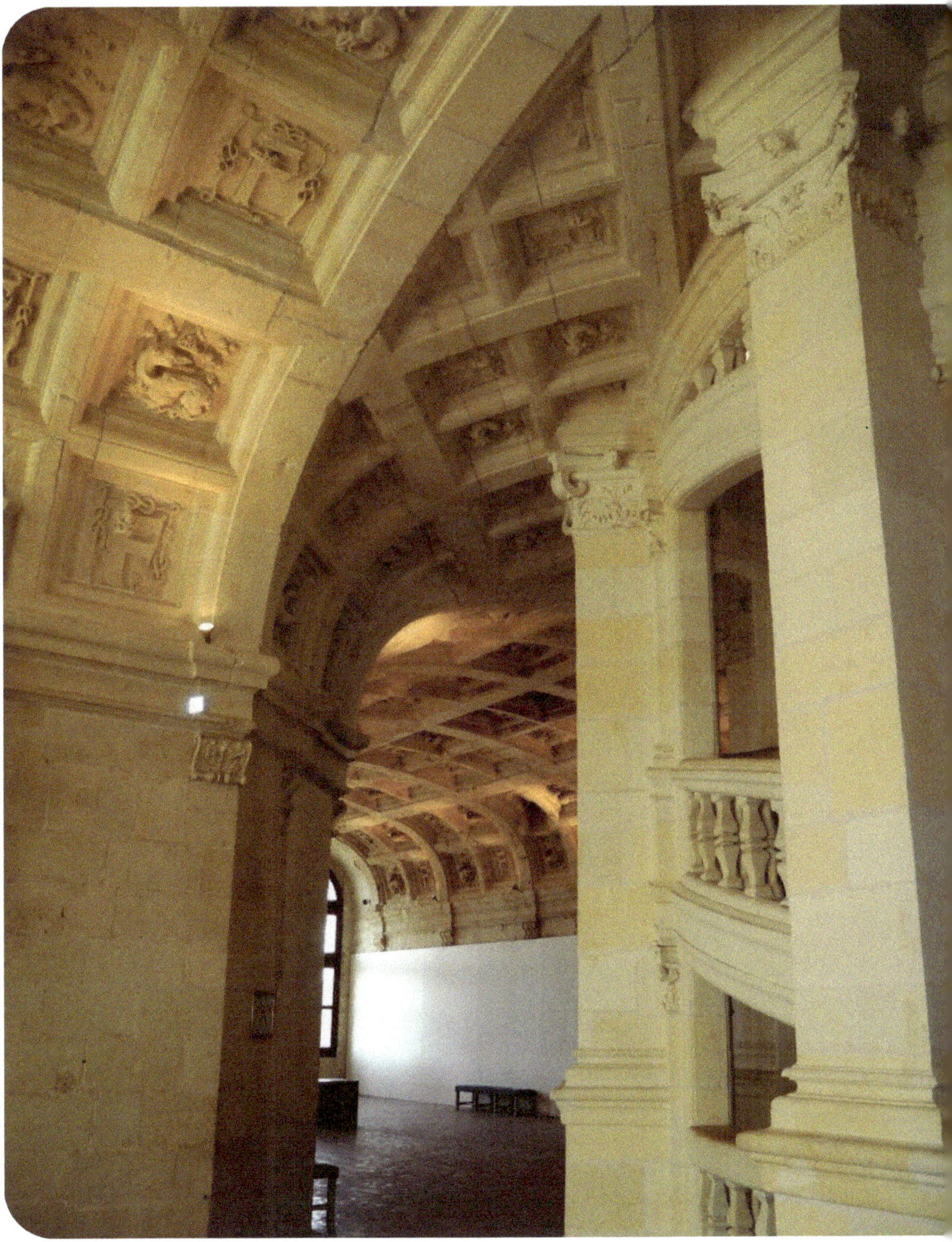

Study the Protestant Reformation in front of the

WALL OF REFORMERS

#59 1517 AD

SWITZERLAND

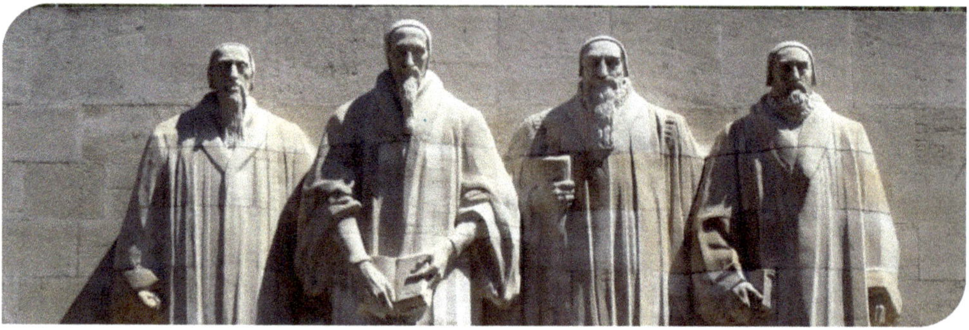

The Reformation Wall is a monumental tribute to the Protestant Reformation movement. Located in the heart of the city, this impressive structure stands as a testament to the pivotal figures and events that shaped the course of European history. Constructed between 1909 and 1917, the wall was built to commemorate the 400th anniversary of the Reformation. Designed by architect Alphonse Laverrière, the wall features statues of four key Reformers - John Calvin, Theodore Beza, William Farel, and John Knox - who played a crucial role in the Reformation. These larger-than-life sculptures are flanked by bas-relief panels depicting significant moments from the 16th century religious revolution.

► In the early 16th century, the Catholic Church was criticized for its wealth and excesses. German monk Martin Luther proposed a reform that resulted in a new Christian movement: Protestantism. He specifically criticized the sale of indulgences by the Church to finance the construction of Saint Peter's Basilica in Rome. These letters were supposed to guarantee access to paradise for the faithful. Martin Luther posted 95 theses on the door of the church of the Wittenberg castle to inform Christians about the abuses of the Church. His persistent opposition led to his excommunication by the Pope in 1521 AD.

He stated that virtuous actions do not allow access to paradise, only grace can allow it. In 1541 AD, Frenchman John Calvin founded the Reformed Church in Geneva. The 95 theses that Martin Luther posted on the church door in Wittenberg were not only a criticism of the Church but also a call for a public debate on the issues he raised. This act is considered the beginning of the Protestant Reformation.

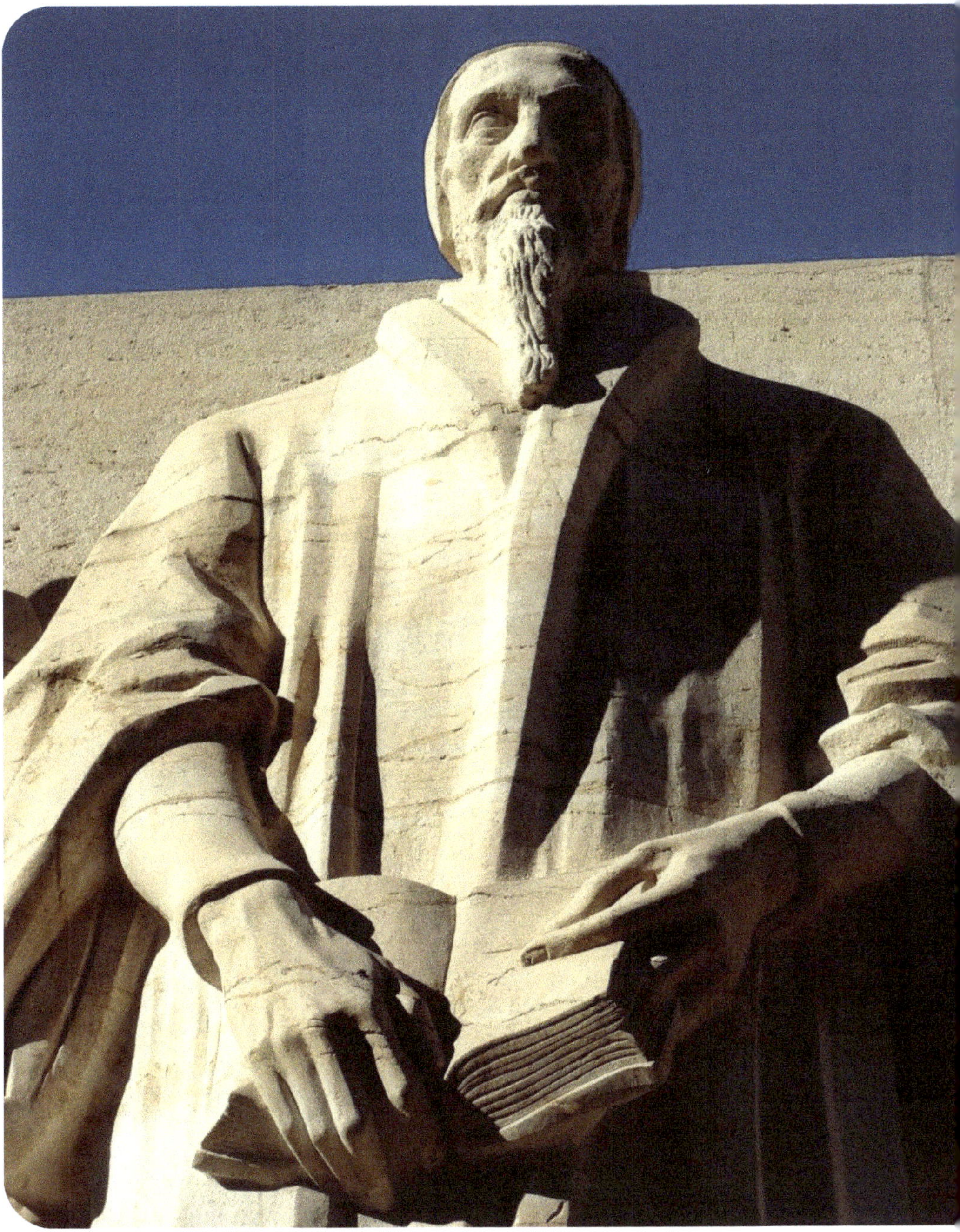

Apprehend the fall of the Aztec Empire wandering around

TEOTIHUACAN

#60   ⏱ **1521 AD**
🗺 **MEXICO**

Teotihuacan is one of the most famous and prominent archaeological sites in North America. Located about 50 km east of Mexico City, this historic site is known for its imposing pyramids, vast avenues and numerous temples and palaces. Teotihuacan was founded about 2,000 years ago and has become one of the most prosperous and influential cities of its time. Its population reached 125,000 at its peak, making it one of the most populous cities in the world at the time. Today, Teotihuacan is considered one of the most eloquent witnesses to the pre-Columbian civilization of North America and is a UNESCO World Heritage Site. If you are interested in history and archaeology, do not miss the opportunity to visit this incredible site during your trip to Mexico.

► In 1521 AD, Cortés besieged the city of Tenochtitlán (now Mexico City) for 75 days with an army of 200,000 men composed of Spanish and indigenous soldiers. The siege resulted in the destruction of the majestic capital of Mexico, ordered by Cortés, who became the master of the city. Additionally, the population of Mexico City was decimated by a smallpox outbreak that spared the Spanish. Cortés starved the city and is said to have executed 67,000 men (over 50,000 had already died from starvation or disease).

On August 13th, 1521 AD, the last Aztec fighters and their families were massacred by the troops of Hernán Cortés and their indigenous allies in Tlatelolco. It was built on an island in the middle of a lake and was connected to the mainland by three causeways. It was considered one of the most advanced cities in the world at the time. It had a complex system of canals and causeways that were used for transportation and trade.

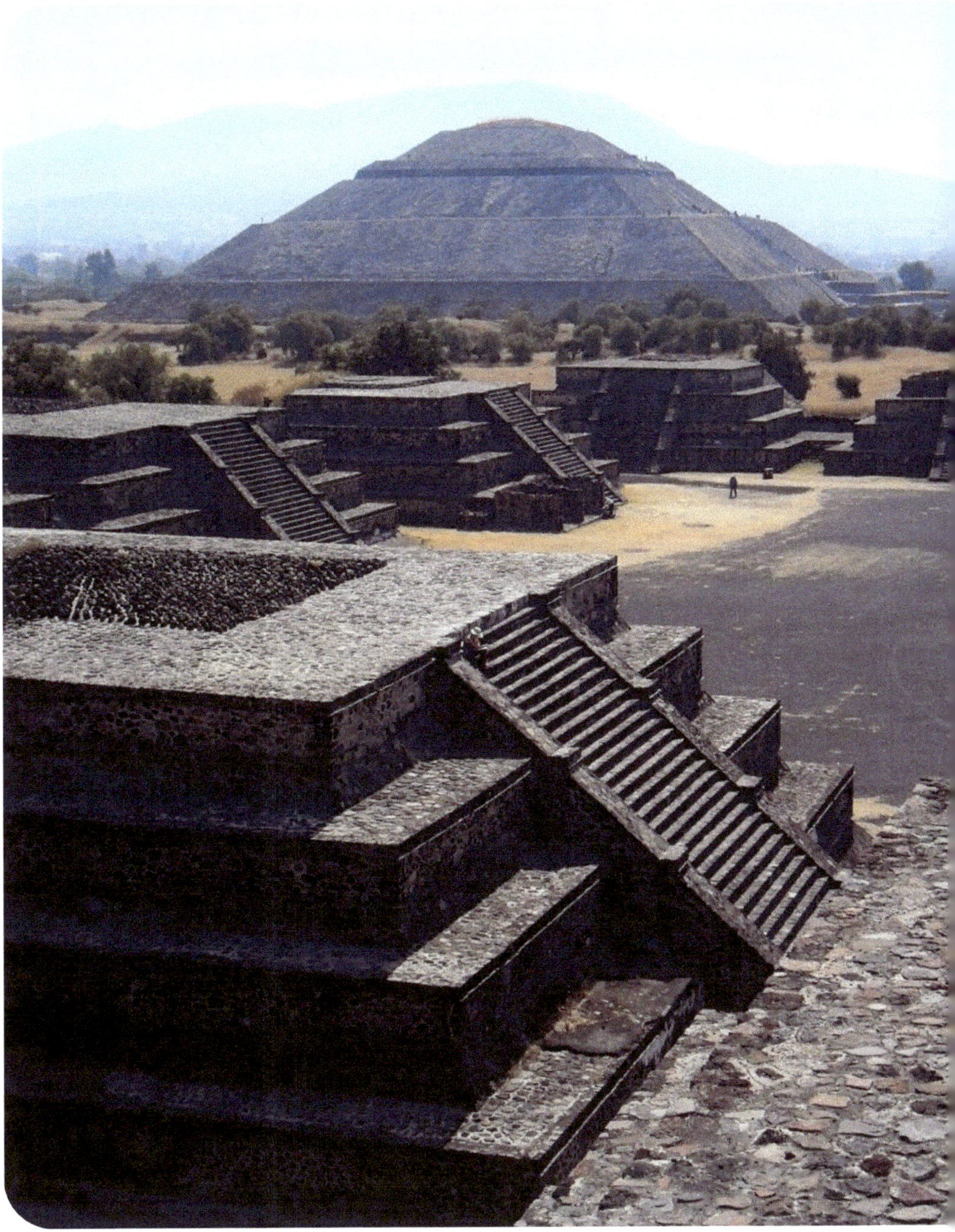

Conceive Ferdinand Magellan's immense
achievement at the

NAO VICTORIA MUSEUM

#61 🕐 **1522 AD**
🗺 **CHILE**

The Nao Victoria Museum is a museum located in Punta Arenas, Chile, which is dedicated to the history of navigation and discovery of South America. The museum is named after the ship Nao Victoria, which was the first ship to circumnavigate the world in 1519. The museum is a fascinating place for history and navigation enthusiasts. It displays a collection of ship models, old maps and historical documents that trace the history of navigation in the area. By visiting the Nao Victoria Museum, you can learn about the adventures and challenges explorers and sailors have faced throughout history. This is an exciting place to discover on your next visit to Punta Arenas.

▶ The primary goal of Magellan's expedition was to reach the Moluccas by sailing west in order to extend the spice route, not to circumnavigate the world. Funded by Spain, the expedition consisted of five ships and 237 men. They departed from Seville on August 10th, 1519 AD, navigated southwest, stopped at the Canary Islands, and sailed along the east coast of South America. On December 13th, 1519 AD, the fleet anchored in the bay now known as Rio de Janeiro before continuing south to circumnavigate the continent. After suppressing a mutiny in March 1520 AD, Magellan reached the Strait that now bears his name. He then crossed the Pacific for three months and 20 days and arrived in the Philippines in March 1521 AD. During an expedition to convert the king of the island of Mactan, Lapu-Lapu, Magellan was killed on April 27th by a poisoned arrow. Juan Sebastián Elcano then took command On December 21st, 1521, the last remaining ship, the Victoria, left Tidore, crossed the Indian Ocean, and arrived in Sanlúcar de Barrameda on September 6th, 1522 with 18 survivors.

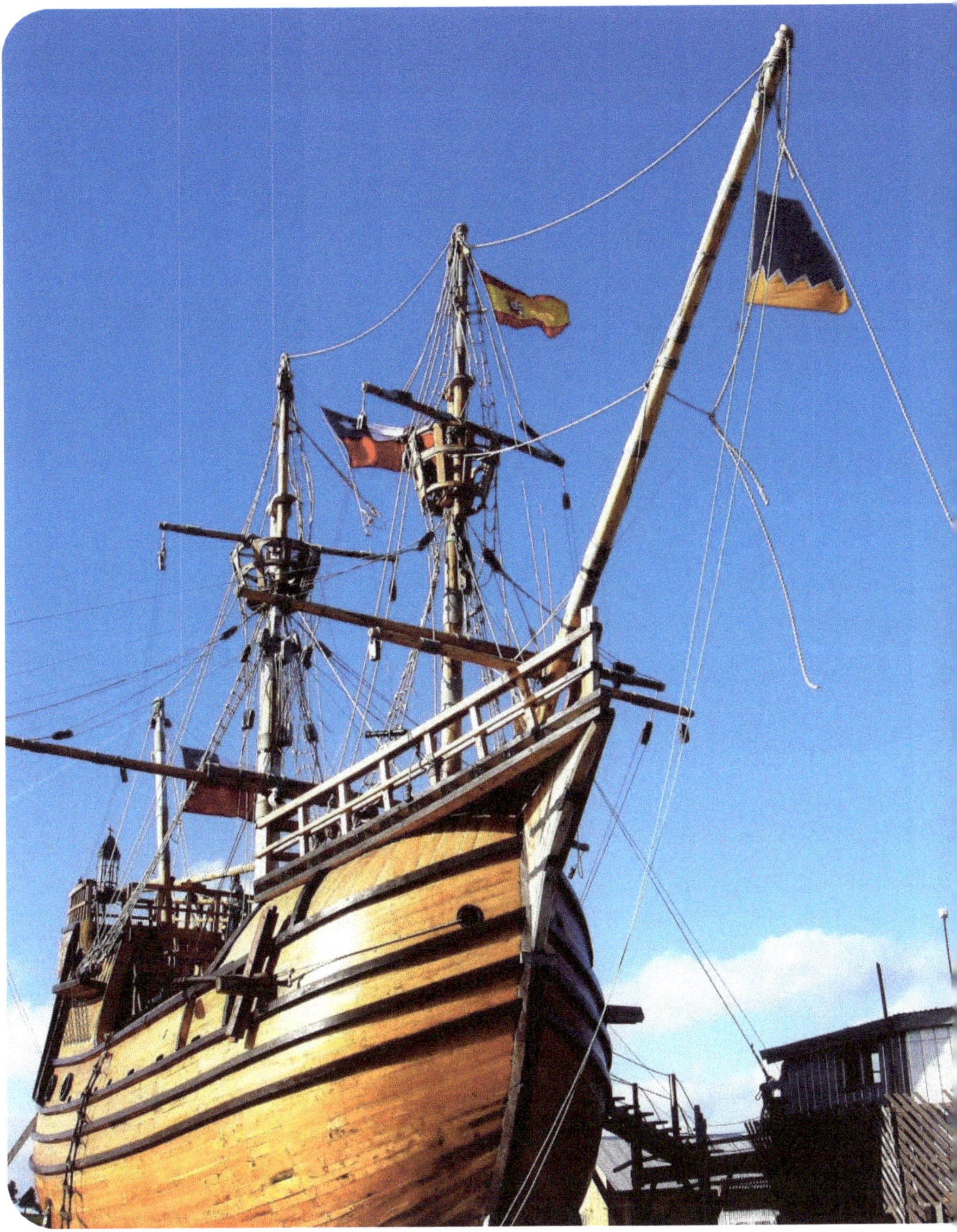

Comprehend the fall of the Inca Empire at the

MACHU PICCHU

#62 1533 AD

PERU

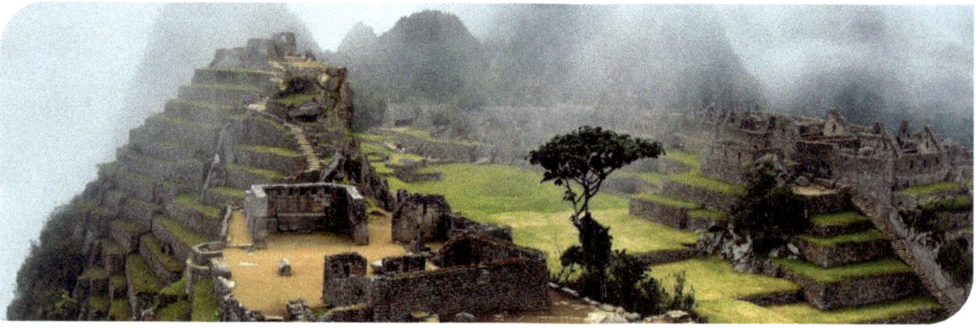

Machu Picchu is undoubtedly one of the most renowned and captivating archaeological sites in the world. This remarkable Inca citadel, nestled high in the Peruvian Andes, was constructed in the 15th century and is widely regarded as a masterpiece of Inca architecture. The site itself is a testament to the ingenuity, skill, and determination of the Inca people. What makes Machu Picchu remarkable is its relative inaccessibility. Unlike many other ancient sites, this Inca citadel can only be reached by undertaking a multi-day hike through the rugged Andes or by taking the famous Andes train, a journey that adds to the sense of exclusivity and adventure. This remote location, combined with the site's well-preserved state and stunning natural setting, has made Machu Picchu a true bucket-list destination for travelers.

► The Spanish conquest of America was marked by significant episodes, such as the fall of the Aztec Empire in 1521 AD. In addition, the submission of the Incas by Francisco Pizarro between 1532 AD and 1533 AD symbolized the end of pre-Columbian civilizations in the face of the arrival of Europeans. Pizarro landed in Peru in 1531 AD with only 200 men, captured coastal towns, and fortified himself on the Pacific shores before crossing the Andes to meet the Inca emperor Atahualpa. He captured him by surprise on November 16th, 1532 AD in Cajamarca, obtained a huge ransom and then had the emperor executed. In November 1533 AD, Pizarro triumphantly entered Cuzco, sealing the fate of the Inca Empire despite Indian rebellions to retake the imperial capital in 1536 and 1537. The years that followed saw rivalries between conquistadors to control Peru, such as the one that opposed Cortés and Velázquez in Mexico. The sacred city of Machu Picchu, a masterpiece of Inca architecture, remained hidden for centuries until it was discovered by American archaeologist Hiram Bingham in 1911 AD.

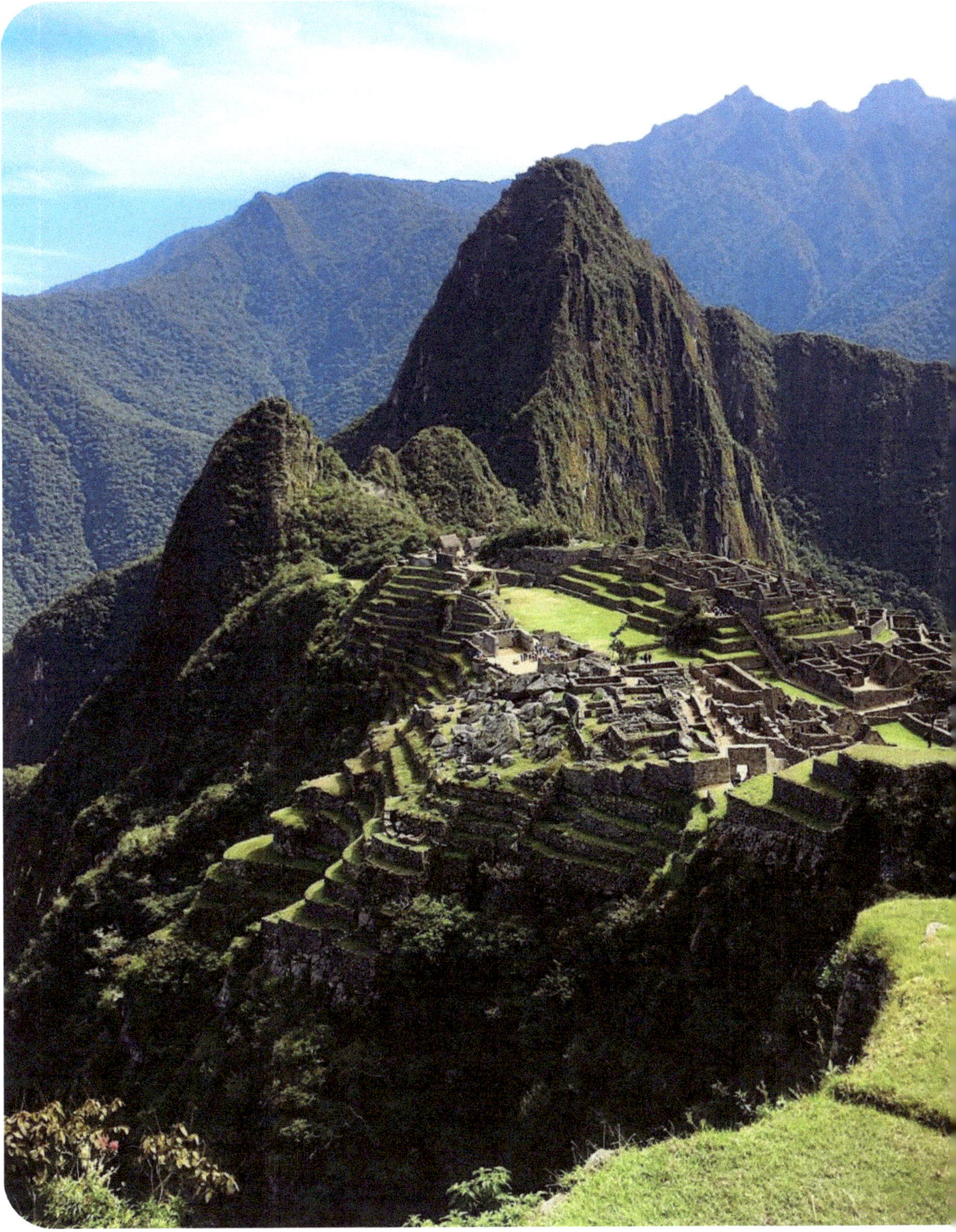

Witness Copernicus' probe of the heliocentric model's veracity at the

COLLEGIUM MAIUS

#63 1543 AD

POLAND

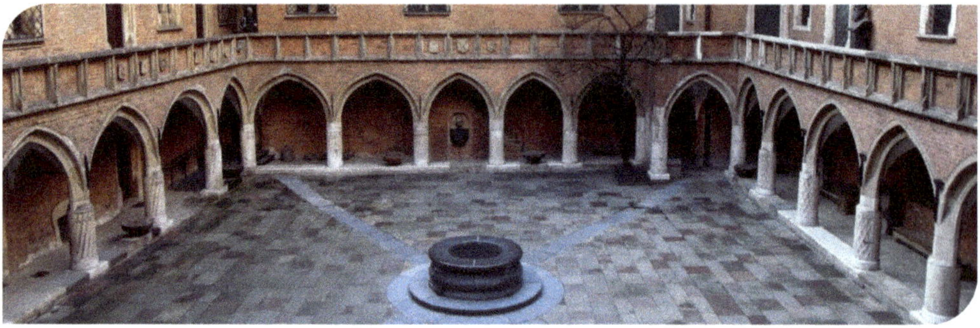

Collegium Maius is one of the oldest universities in Kraków, Poland. Founded in 1364 AD, this university was the city's first institution of higher education and has played a crucial role in the history of education in Poland. The Collegium Maius is also known for its magnificent historic buildings, which are now used as a museum. If you are interested in the history of education and Gothic architecture, the Collegium Maius is a must-see on your trip to Krakow. Visit the historic classrooms and discover the treasures of the library, which has more than 300,000 ancient volumes. You can also visit the university chapel, which is adorned with magnificent frescoes dating back to the fourteenth century.

► In the mid-16th century, in a world in full intellectual ferment, Nicolas Copernicus stated the unthinkable: the Earth is not at the center of the Universe. By stepping against the tradition of Greek scholars and the authority of the Church, he dethroned Man from his pedestal and established himself as a precursor of modern science. Copernicus criticized the Ancient Egyptian belief, adopted by the Church, that the Earth, immobile, is at the center of the Universe, which revolves around it (geocentrism, Ptolemaic system).

In his book, On the Revolutions of the Celestial Spheres, he defended the theory of heliocentrism: like other planets, the Earth revolves around itself and around the sun. His theory was not accepted until the late 17th century. Copernicus' brilliant discovery was suppressed, in the aftermath of his death, by the conspiracy of silence fomented by the Catholics and the Lutherans. These enemies united this time in the struggle against the truth of the Universe. His hypotheses were only confirmed by Kepler and Galileo in 1609 AD and 1610 AD.

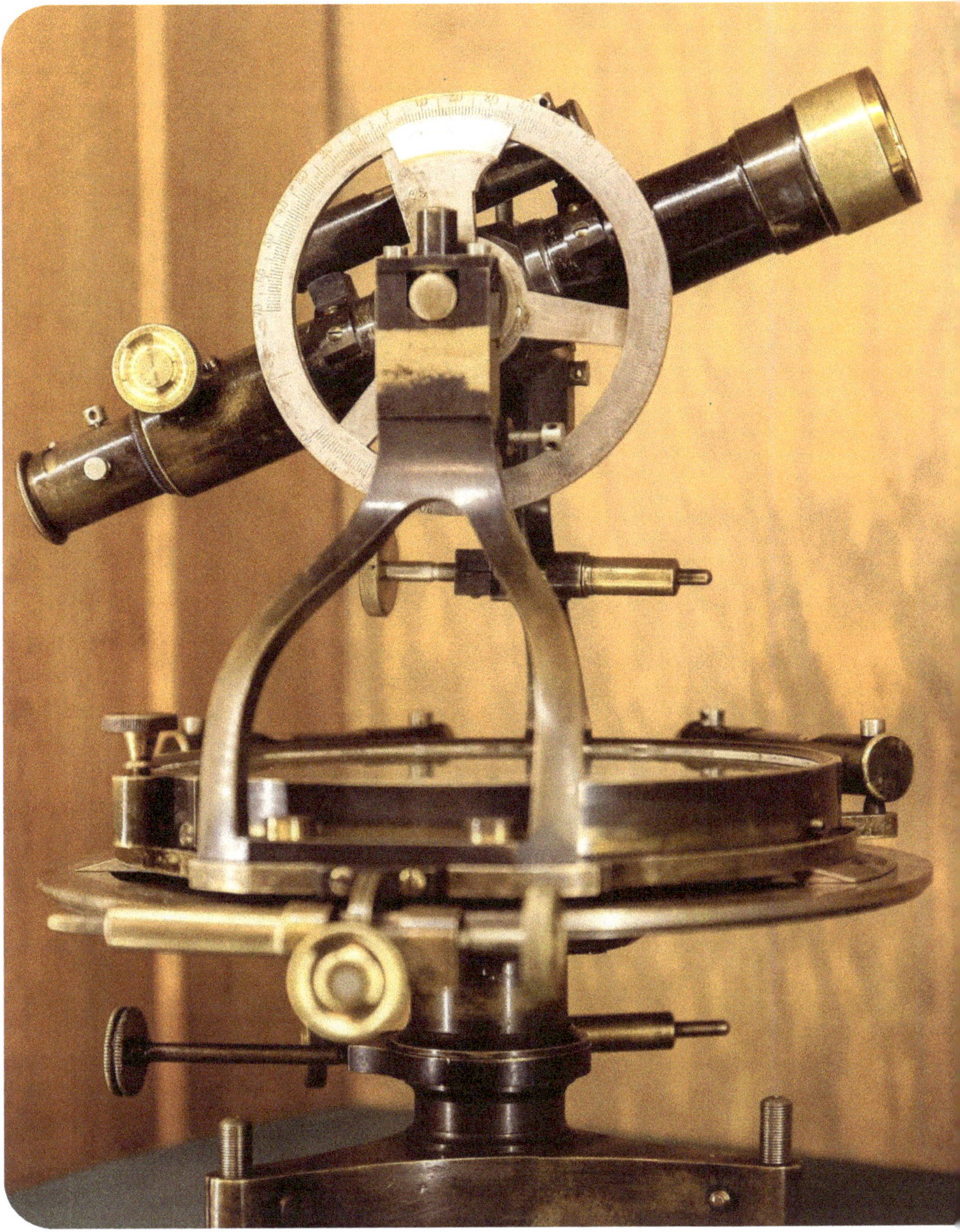

Recall Ivan the Terrible as the first tsar of Russia at the

ST. BASIL'S CATHEDRAL

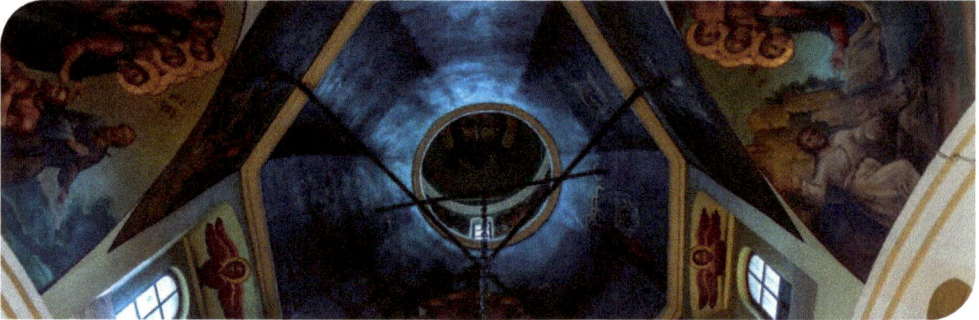

St. Basil's Cathedral is one of the jewels of the city of Moscow and one of the most famous monuments in Russia. This Orthodox cathedral was built between 1555 AD and 1561 AD and has become a symbol of Russia's power and glory. It was designed by Italian architect Barma and is considered a marvel of Russian art. The cathedral is known for its beauty and architectural richness, with its many golden domes, frescoes and icons. It is also the final resting place of many famous Russian rulers, including Ivan the Terrible and Peter the Great. St. Basil's Cathedral is a must-see for anyone visiting Moscow and a testament to the importance of the Orthodox Church in Russia.

▶ Ivan IV, also known as Ivan the Terrible, was born in 1530 AD. He ruled as Grand Prince of Vladimir and Moscow from 1533 AD to 1584 AD, serving as the first Tsar of Russia. He was crowned by the head of the Russian Church in 1547 AD, and took the title of Tsar. This title was previously reserved for Byzantine emperors and the khans of the Golden Horde. He ruled in a brutal manner, taking direct control of parts of Russia, exiling and killing thousands of nobles. To enforce his authority, Ivan IV maintained a personal army of 1,500 elite guards known as the Oprichnina, further solidifying his grip on power during his tumultuous reign.

He also led violent campaigns against the Tatars and the Teutonic Order. Ivan IV wanted to make Moscow the third Rome, but his reign was followed by a long stretch of political turmoil and anarchy that lasted until 1613 AD. His reign inspired many poets and novelists, including Tolstoy, who made him the hero of a remarkable novel and play.

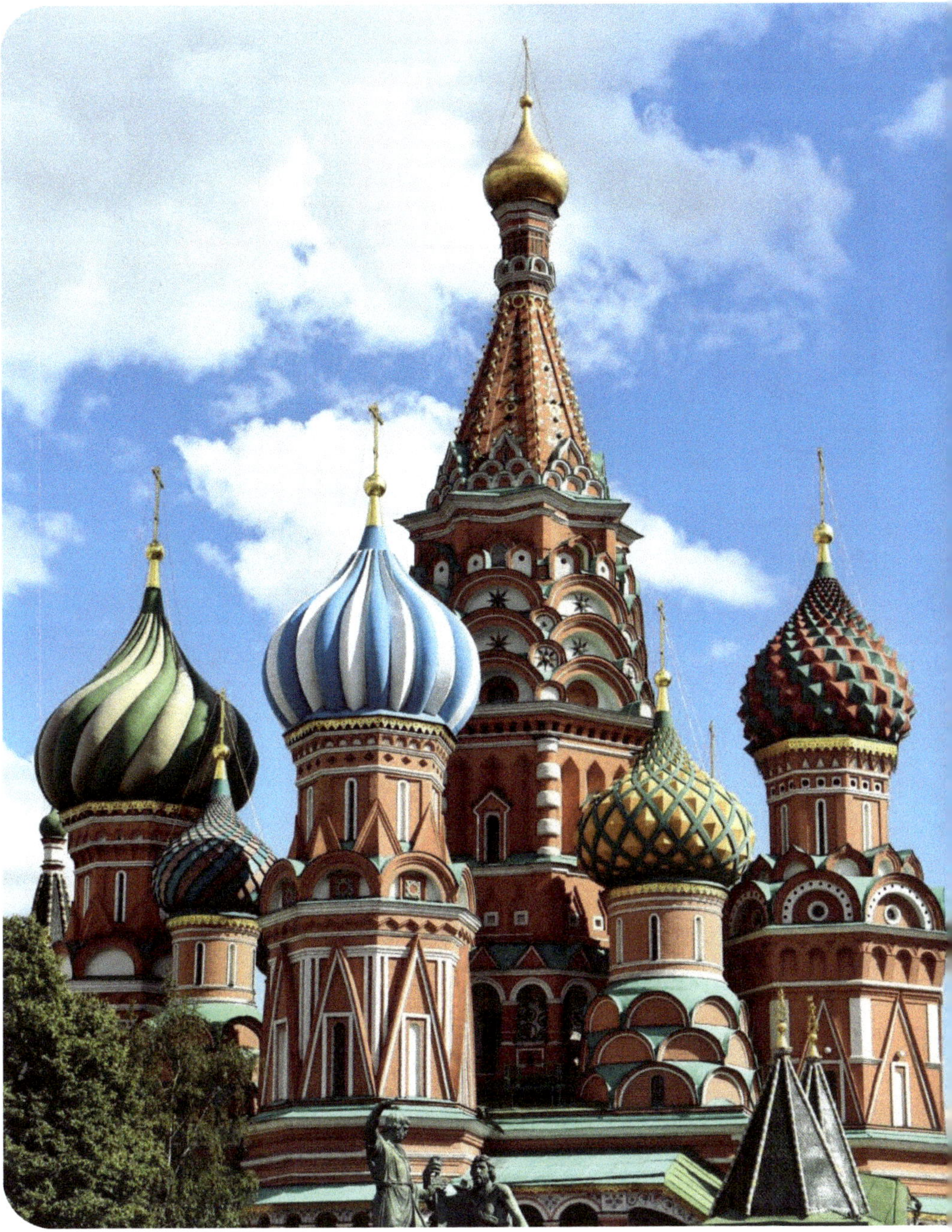

Apprehend the Great Siege of Malta inside the

FORT OF ST. ELMO

#65 ⏱ **1565 AD**

📖 **MALTA**

Fort Saint-Elmo is a historic fort on the island of Malta, built by the Knights of St. John in the late 16th century to protect the southern part of the island from Ottoman attacks. It is situated on the highest point of the peninsula of Marsaskala, offering breathtaking views of the sea and the surrounding landscape. It has played an important role in Maltese history, serving as a strategic military outpost for centuries. Today, it is a popular tourist destination, offering visitors the opportunity to explore its impressive architecture and learn about Malta's rich history. The fort features a museum showcasing artifacts from its past, including military uniforms and weapons used during the Ottoman siege. It is worth a visit on your trip to Malta.

▶ The history of La Vallette begins with the arrival of the Knights of St. John of Jerusalem, who were driven out of Rhodes by Soliman in 1522 AD. Charles Quint ceded to them this territory located between modern-day Sicily and Tunisia, making it an ideal location to contain the Ottoman threat. The construction of a fortification on the Xiberras peninsula was considered soon after the Order's arrival, and Fort Saint-Elme was built before the Ottoman attack of 1565 AD. Following the resistance during the Great Siege, the Knights reinforced the islands and built many churches.

Jean Parisot de La Vallette, the victorious Grand Master of the Ottomans, decided to construct a powerful fortification. The Knights of Malta are also known as the Knights Hospitaller, and they were originally founded in the 11th century as a monastic order to provide care for the sick and injured during the Crusades. Their symbol, a white eight-pointed cross, is still used today as a symbol of the island of Malta.

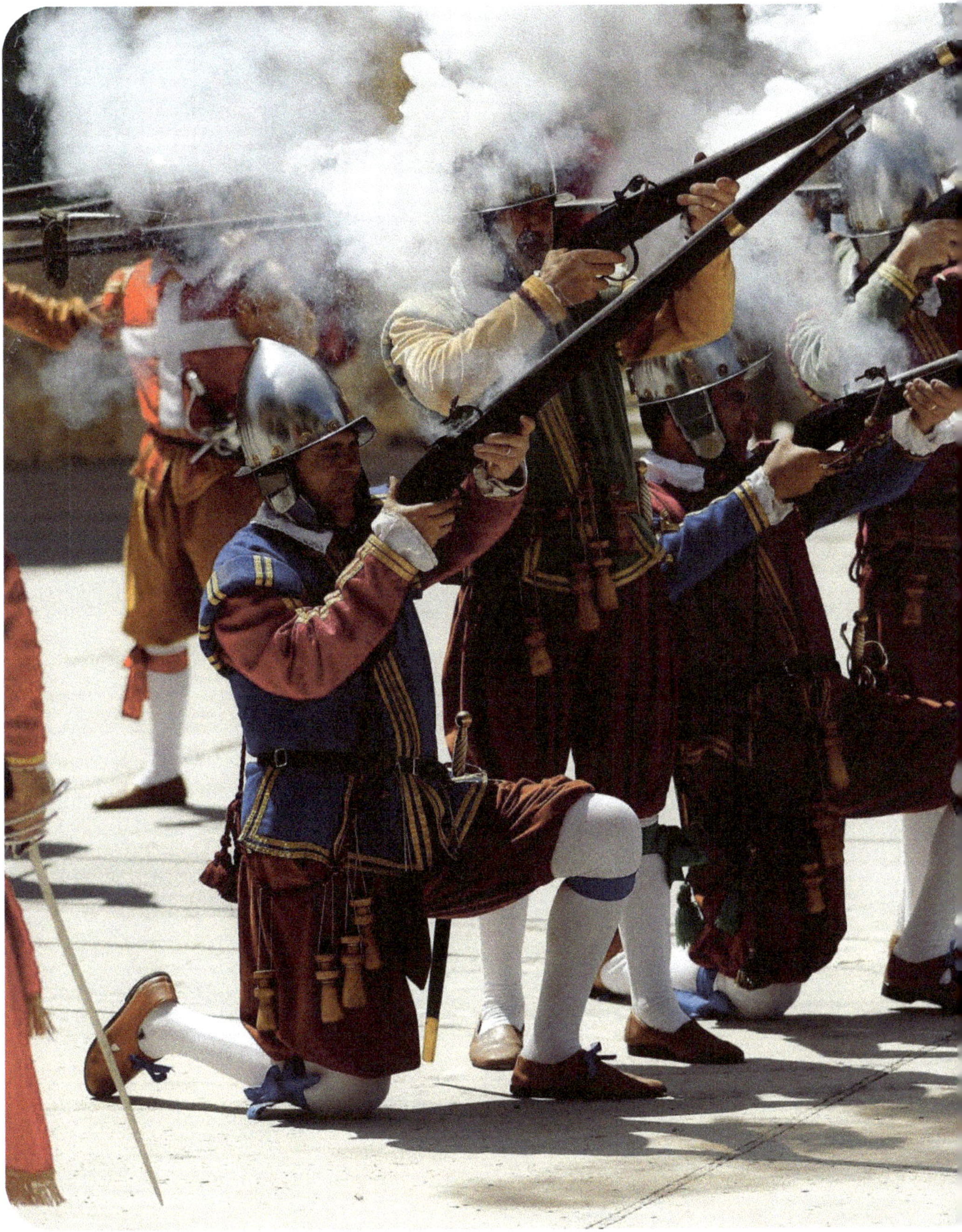

Visualize the foundation of the East India Company (VOC) at the

AMSTERDAM STOCK EXCHANGE

#66 1602 AD

NETHERLANDS

CONFERENCES
EVENTS
EXHIBITIONS

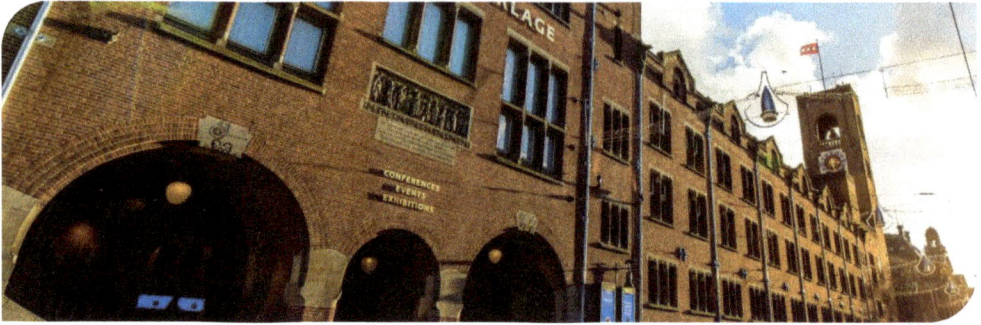

The Amsterdam Stock Exchange building, also known as Beurs van Berlage, is an iconic building located in downtown Amsterdam. It was designed by architect Henry van de Velde and was inaugurated in 1903. Since then, it has been the seat of the Amsterdam Stock Exchange and has become one of the city's best-known symbols. The building is a perfect example of Dutch Art Nouveau, with its sinuous lines and ornamental floral motifs. Its red brick façade and tall towers are easily recognizable and have become a popular attraction for visitors to the city. Today, the Amsterdam Stock Exchange building is still used for stock market trading, but it is also open to the public for tours and cultural events.

► In the 17th century, the Dutch Provinces emerged as a major maritime and commercial power. The Dutch East India Company (VOC) was founded in 1602 AD and became one of the most prosperous and powerful European trade companies. Its mission was to economically and commercially exploit Southeast Asia, particularly present-day Indonesia, on behalf of the Dutch Provinces. Permanent employees were stationed in Asian ports and many ships were grouped into a dedicated fleet. They imported spices, fabrics, and porcelain. In 1619 AD, they settled on the island of Java and founded the city of Batavia (present-day Jakarta), which became the center of this commercial empire. The revenues generated by this activity were very lucrative and merchants became very wealthy. The Dutch Golden Age owes part of its flourishing economy to this activity, which made Amsterdam one of the first financial and commercial centers in Europe. The Dutch East India Company was the first company to issue stocks and bonds, making it the first listed public company.

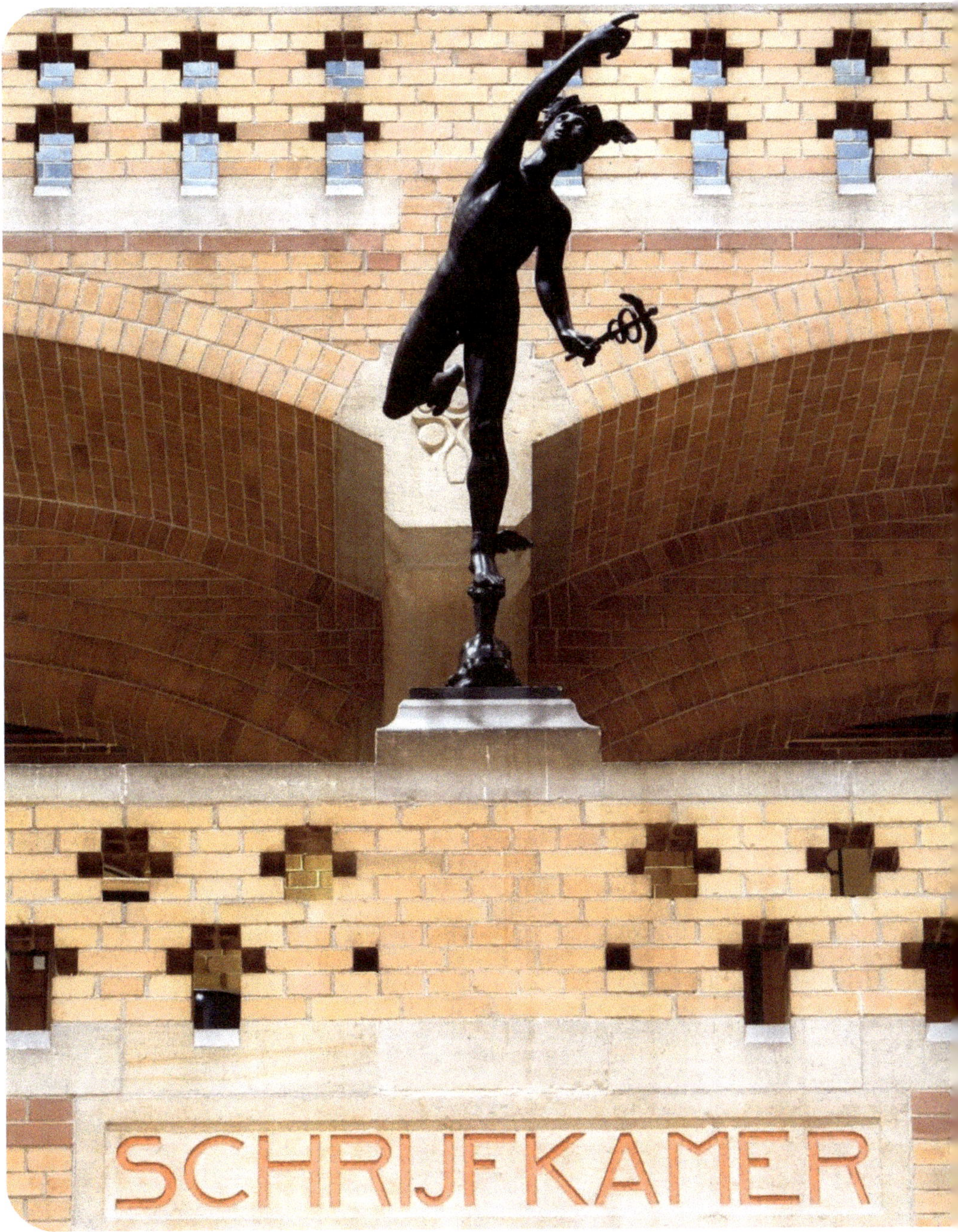
SCHRIJFKAMER

Spot English settler's establishment of their first permanent encampment on the New World in

JAMESTOWN SETTLEMENT

#67 ⏱ **1607 AD**
🗺 **USA**

The Jamestown Settlement is a historic site located in Virginia, United States. It was established in 1607 and is considered the first permanent settlement of Europeans in North America. Today, the Jamestown Settlement is an interactive museum that allows visitors to learn about the history of North American colonization. This allows visitors to gain a better understanding of the daily lives of early European settlers. There are reconstructions of villages, houses and ships, as well as exhibits on the culture and technology of the time. The Jamestown Settlement is a fascinating place to visit for anyone interested in the history of America and its first inhabitants.

▶ Fleeing from the religious and political repression imposed by King James I of England, a group of Puritans (radical Protestants) made the arduous journey across the Atlantic Ocean to seek a new life in the untamed lands of North America. In April of 1620 AD, three English ships, including the famous Mayflower, set sail from the shores of England, carrying these determined Puritan settlers and their crews. They were driven by a deep desire for religious freedom and the opportunity to build a society that aligned with their strict Calvinist beliefs.

These pilgrims signed a pact, the Mayflower Compact, where they committed to creating a society based on fair and just laws. This agreement laid the groundwork for the development of democratic principles and the concept of a social contract, which would later influence the formation of the United States government. The pilgrim fathers are now considered the ancestors of Americans. However, the first true English colony in America was founded in 1630 AD by puritans settled in Massachusetts Bay.

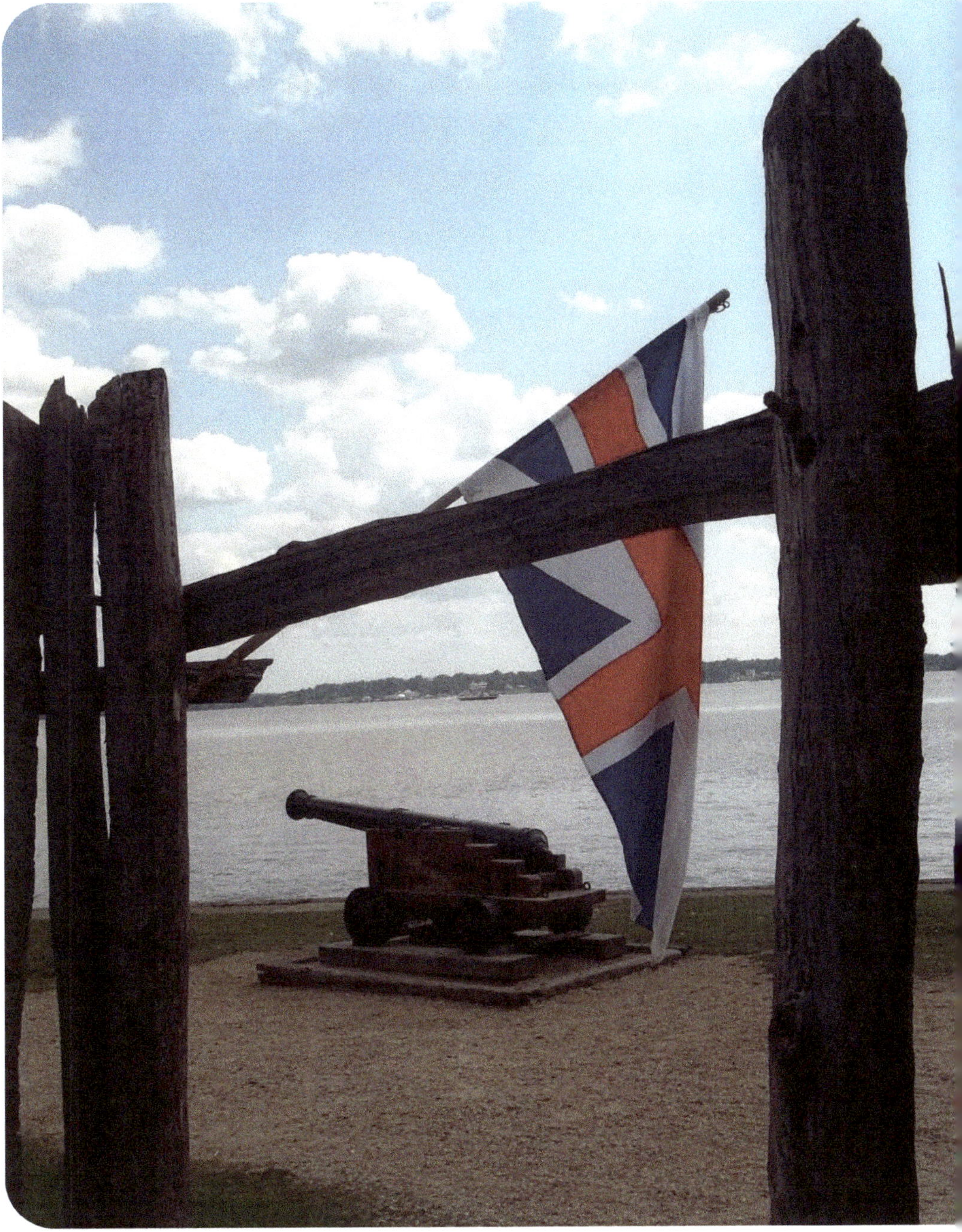

Revisit the defenestration of Prague that triggered the 30 Years' War at the

PRAGUE CASTLE

#68 1618 AD

CZECHIA

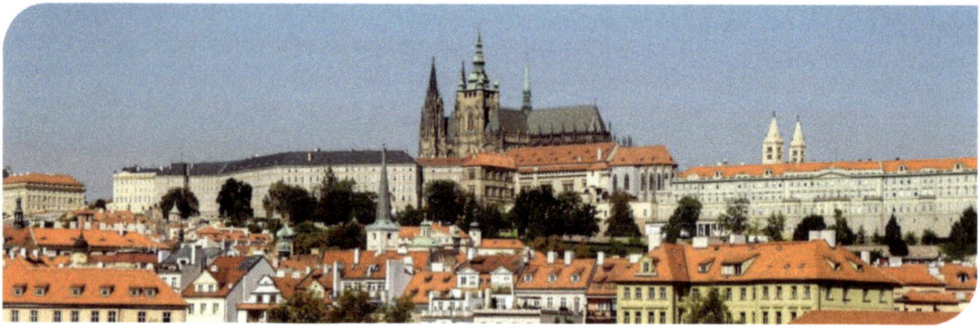

Prague Castle is a must-see for travelers visiting the capital of the Czech Republic. Perched atop a hill overlooking the city, this imposing castle is one of the largest castles in the world and has been the seat of power for Czech kings, Holy Roman Emperors, and presidents of Czechoslovakia and the Czech Republic for over a millennium. The Old Royal Palace, the former residence of Bohemian kings, features impressive Romanesque and Gothic halls and chambers. In addition to its historical significance, Prague Castle is also the official residence of the Czech President and is used for many state ceremonies and events. Wandering through the castle's expansive grounds, visitors can soak in the breathtaking views of the city below and imagine the rich history that has unfolded within these walls over the centuries.

► On May 23, 1618 AD, Protestant nobles led by Count Thurn stormed into the deliberation room of the Hradčany palace governors to protest against the revocation by Emperor Mathias of the Letter of Majesty of 1609 AD, which guaranteed religious freedoms in Bohemia. They also expressed their dissatisfaction with Mathias' decision, to entrust his cousin Ferdinand, Archduke of Styria, with the crown of Bohemia. As Ferdinand was known to be a rigid Catholic, not very concerned with respecting the Peace of Augsburg, this decision was not well received.

Following this intrusion, two governors, Slavata and Martinic, as well as a secretary, Fabricius, were thrown out of the castle windows. Although their fall was cushioned by a pile of manure, they were only slightly injured. However, this event, known as the Defenestration of Prague, had significant consequences, marking the beginning of the rebellion against the authority of Ferdinand II of the Habsburgs in Bohemia. This led to the outbreak of the Thirty Years War.

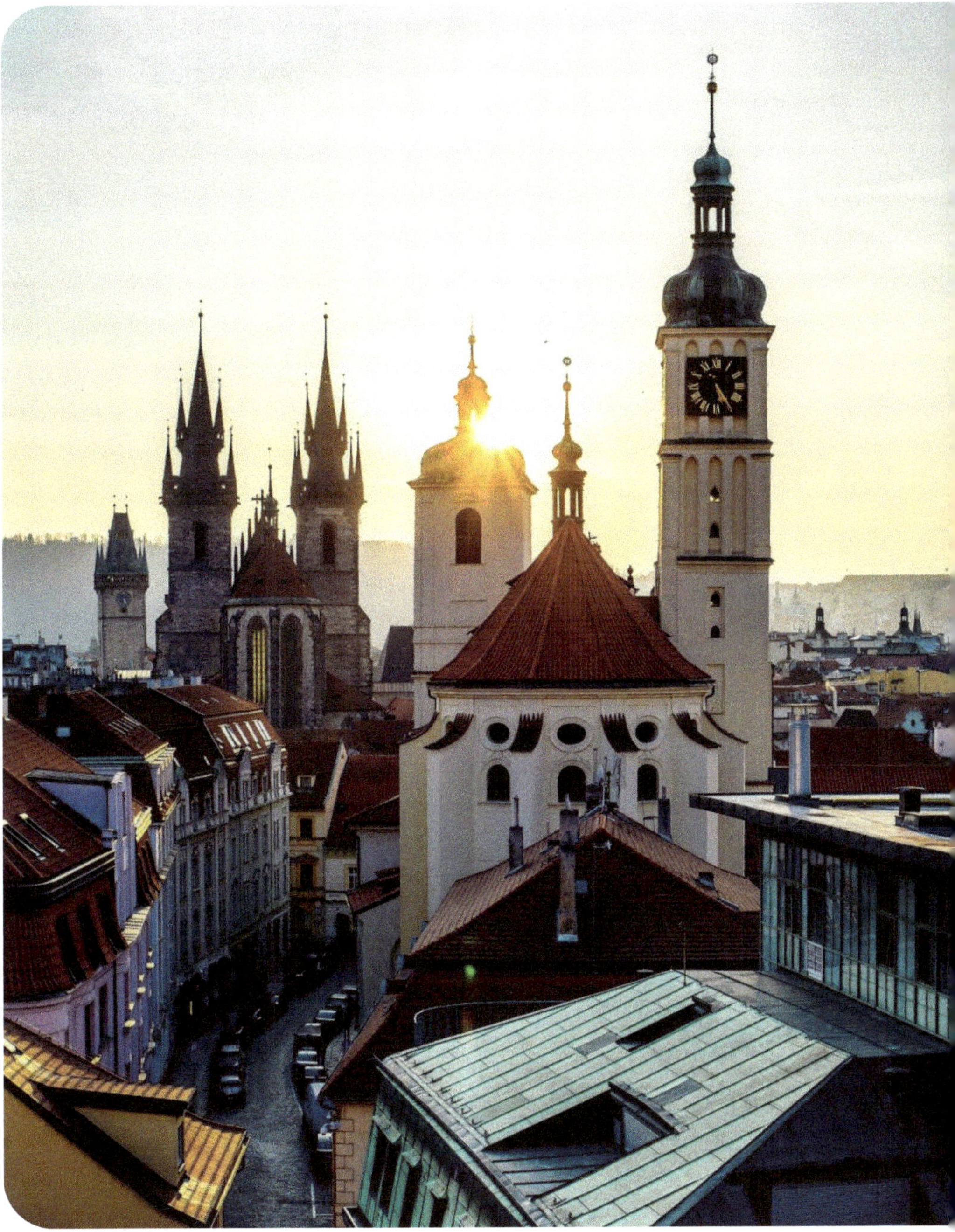

Observe Mughal Emperor Shah Jahan's
architectural masterpiece, the

TAJ MAHAL

#69 ○ **1632 AD**

🗺 **INDIA**

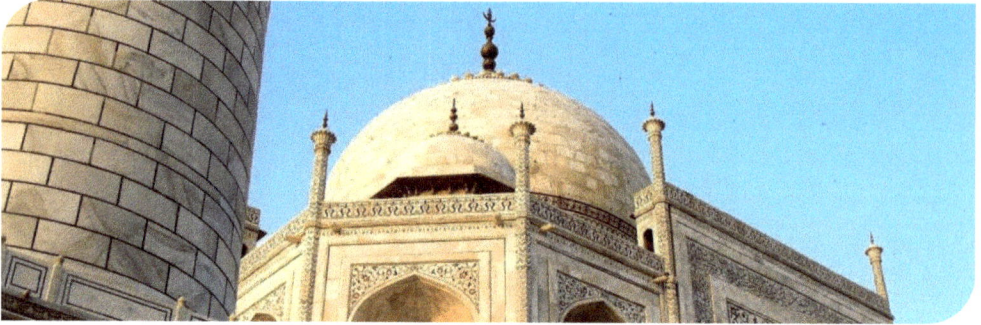

The Taj Mahal is a magnificent mausoleum located in the historic city of Agra, India. Commissioned in the 17th century by the Mughal emperor Shah Jahan, this architectural masterpiece was built as a grand tribute to his beloved wife, Mumtaz Mahal, who passed away in 1631 AD. Considered one of the most iconic and awe-inspiring structures in the world, the Taj Mahal is a true testament to the Mughal empire's architectural prowess and the enduring power of love. Beyond its architectural splendor, the Taj Mahal is also a deeply emotional and symbolic place. It stands as a poignant reminder of the profound love between Shah Jahan and Mumtaz Mahal, and the lengths to which the emperor went to honor her memory.

▶ Babur, a descendant of Tamerlane and Genghis Khan, was driven out of Samarkand after conquering the city in 1497 AD. He became the king of Kabul in 1504 and led expeditions from that region. He crossed the Indus, conquered Punjab, and defeated the Sultan at Panipat in 1526 AD. His grandson Akbar, who took the throne in 1556 AD, continued his work by attacking the Rajput kingdoms and marrying one of their princesses to seal the peace. Shah Jahan succeeded his grandfather and was proclaimed emperor in 1628 AD.

In 1631 AD, Mumtaz Mahal, the wife of Shah Jahan, died giving birth to their 14th child, and he built the Taj Mahal in white marble. At his death, the Mughal Empire was the most powerful India had ever known, but it was divided by succession disputes and in 1857 AD, it disappeared with the creation of the British Indian Empire. The Taj Mahal is a symbol of love and devotion and a masterpiece of architecture and art, with intricate designs of Indian, Persian, and Islamic styles.

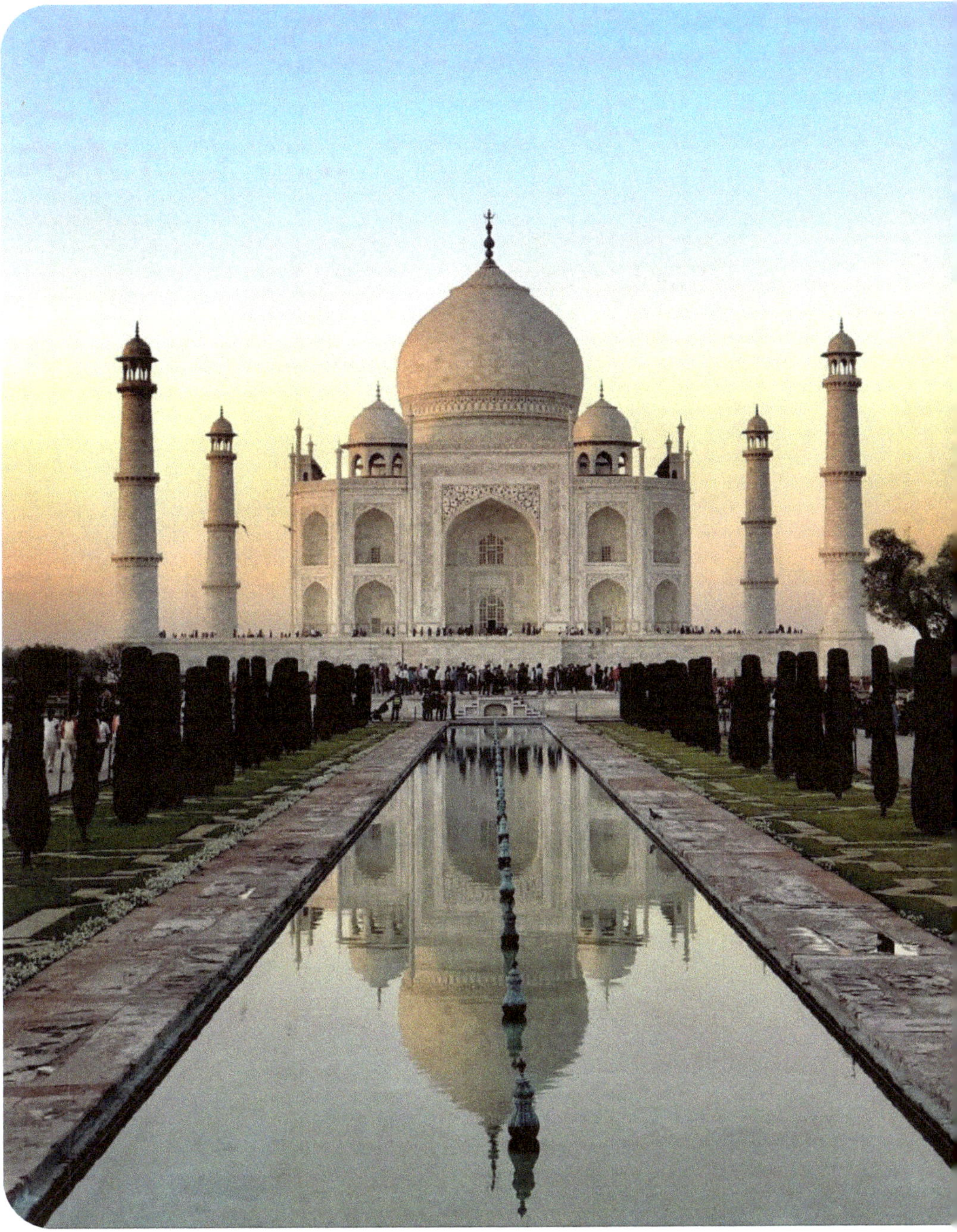

Delve into Galileo's condemnation by the Inquisition at the

GALILEO MUSEUM

#70 1633 AD

ITALY

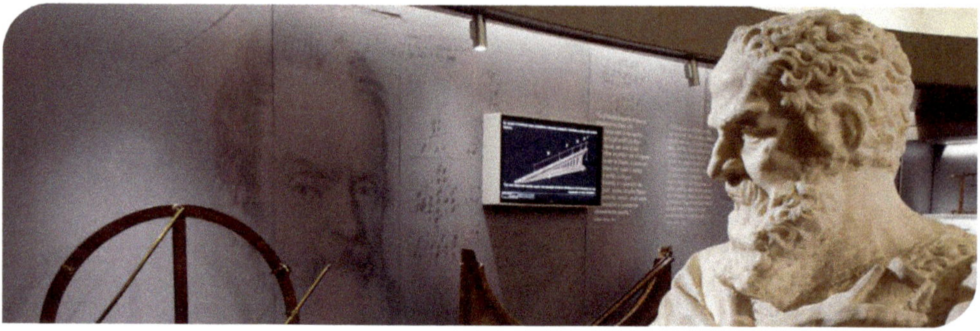

The Galileo Museum is a museum dedicated to the life and work of the Italian astronomer, mathematician and physicist Galileo Galilei. Located in Florence, Italy, this museum is a real treasure for all lovers of the history of science and technology. The museum is divided into several sections, each dedicated to a different aspect of Galileo's life and work. There are many scientific and mathematical instruments used by Galileo during his lifetime, as well as models of his most famous experiments and discoveries. The Galileo Museum is also known for its collection of rare and precious books, including many works by Galileo himself. If you are passionate about the history of science and technology, the Galileo Museum is a must-see on your trip to Florence.

► In the 17th century, groundbreaking discoveries revolutionized the traditional view of the world by showing that the Universe is governed by scientific laws that challenge religious dogmas. The Italian astronomer and physicist Galileo was the one who caused the Church's reaction by using a telescope to observe celestial bodies and discovering that the Earth revolves around the Sun. He published his results in 1632 AD, which led him to be summoned by the Pope and judged by the Inquisition.

Even under the duress of being forced to acknowledge his errors, Galileo famously uttered the defiant words "And yet, it moves!" - a testament to his unwavering belief in the heliocentric model of the solar system, which placed the Sun, rather than the Earth, at the center. Galileo's revolutionary ideas and observations paved the way for a new era of scientific perspectives, earning him the title of the "father of modern science. One of Galileo's most significant contributions was his discovery of the four largest moons of Jupiter, which he named the Medicean Stars in honor of his patron, the Medici family.

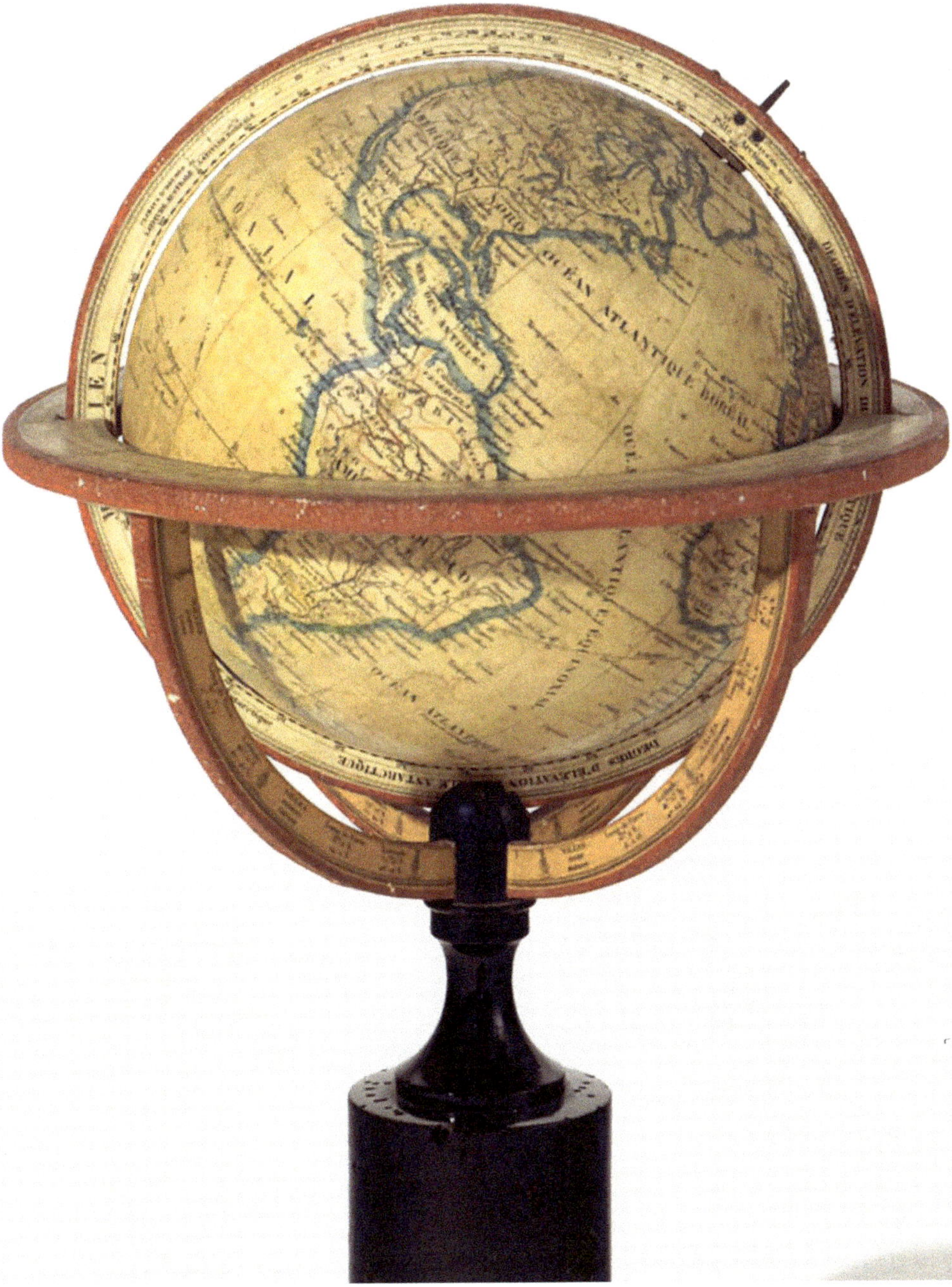
OCÉAN ATLANTIQUE

Visualize the defeat of the Ottoman Turks against the Holy Roman Empire at the

HOFBURG PALACE

#71 1683 AD

AUSTRIA

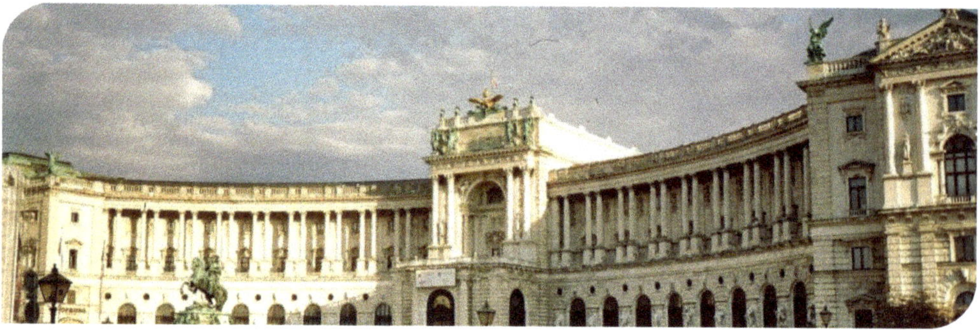

The Hofburg Palace is an imposing palace located in the heart of Vienna, Austria. This historic building was the residence of the Austrian emperors for over 600 years and is now open to the public for tours. The Hofburg is known for its many gardens and sumptuous interiors, including the Imperial Chapel, the Hall of Thrones and the National Library. The palace is also home to several museums, such as the Sisi Museum, which is dedicated to the famous Empress Elisabeth of Austria. It also displays a collection of more than 3,000 ancient musical instruments. If you are a history buff or simply curious to discover an emblematic place in Vienna, a visit to the Hofburg is an experience not to be missed.

► Soliman I, also known as Soliman the Magnificent, was at the head of the Ottoman Empire at its peak. He annexed most of the Middle East during his wars against the Safavids of Iran as well as large parts of North Africa, up to Algiers. Under his rule, the Ottoman navy, led notably by Grand Admiral Barbarossa, dominated the Mediterranean, the Red Sea, and the Persian Gulf. In 1683 AD, the war against the Habsburgs turned, despite the long siege of Vienna, in favor of the Austrians.

This decisive defeat of the Ottomans was the starting point of a military campaign that allowed the Habsburgs to retake the territories of Hungary-Croatia, putting an end to the Ottoman threat in Central Europe. Legend has it that the day after the battle, the Viennese discovered bags filled with coffee beans in an abandoned Ottoman military camp. A fighter transformed the grains into a drink known as coffee accompanied by a croissant. This croissant has the shape of the emblem of the defeated Ottomans, the crescent.

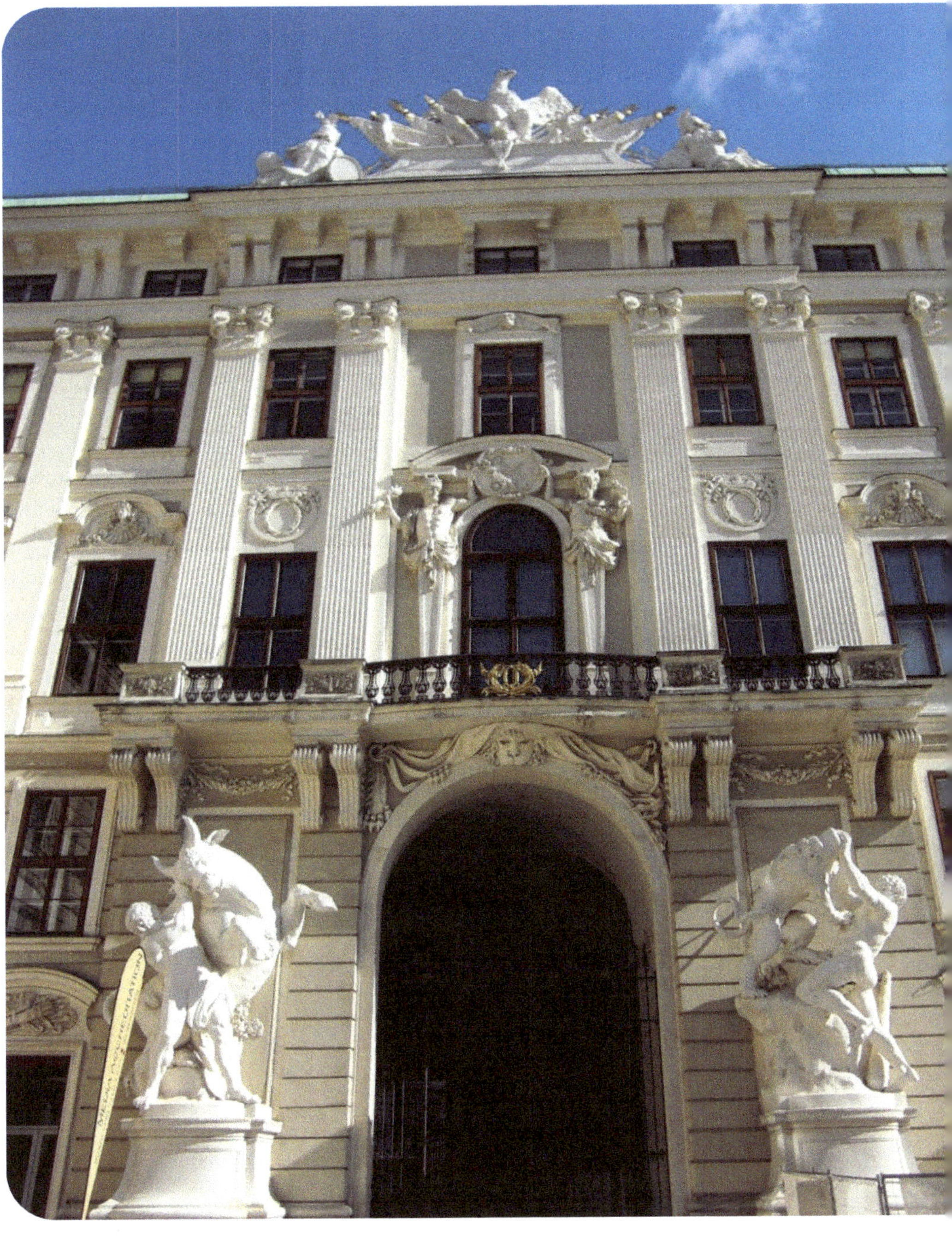

Recall Isaac Newton's explanation of the universal laws of gravitation at the

WESTMINSTER ABBEY

#72 1687 AD

UK

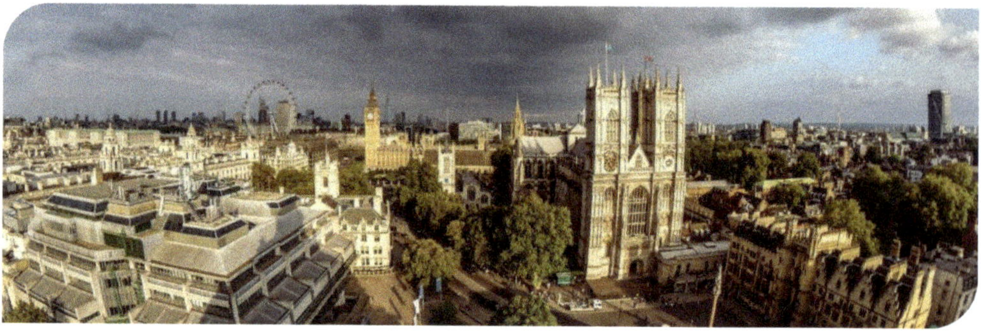

Westminster Abbey is one of London's most iconic and historically significant landmarks. Located right in the heart of the bustling city, this magnificent Gothic abbey has stood as a testament to England's rich royal heritage for centuries. It is famous for being the coronation site of the majority of the country's monarchs since the Middle Ages, with the first recorded coronation taking place in 1066 AD when William the Conqueror was crowned king. In addition to its role in coronation ceremonies, Westminster Abbey also serves as the final resting place for many of England's most revered figures. The abbey's interior is dotted with the tombs and memorials of monarchs, statesmen, poets, and other luminaries, making it a veritable who's who of British history.

► Isaac Newton is a key figure in the history of science. He published his work entitled *Philosophiae naturalis principia mathematica*, in which he synthesized Kepler's laws on planetary orbits and those of Galileo on the fall of bodies in 1687 AD . He developed a physics based on the law of inertia, the fundamental principle of mechanics and the principle of action and reaction. He added the law of gravity to these three principles. This revolutionary mechanic allowed him to explain previously mysterious phenomena, such as the movement of planets, satellites and tides.

The Universal Attraction force was however violently rejected by Cartesians who accused Newton of reintroducing magical explanations into science. Newton acknowledged that this force was incomprehensible and also admitted that he did not know why the stars did not end up clumping together under this attraction. Newton held prestigious positions such as Director of the Mint and President of the Royal Society, a position he held from 1703 AD until his death in 1727 AD.

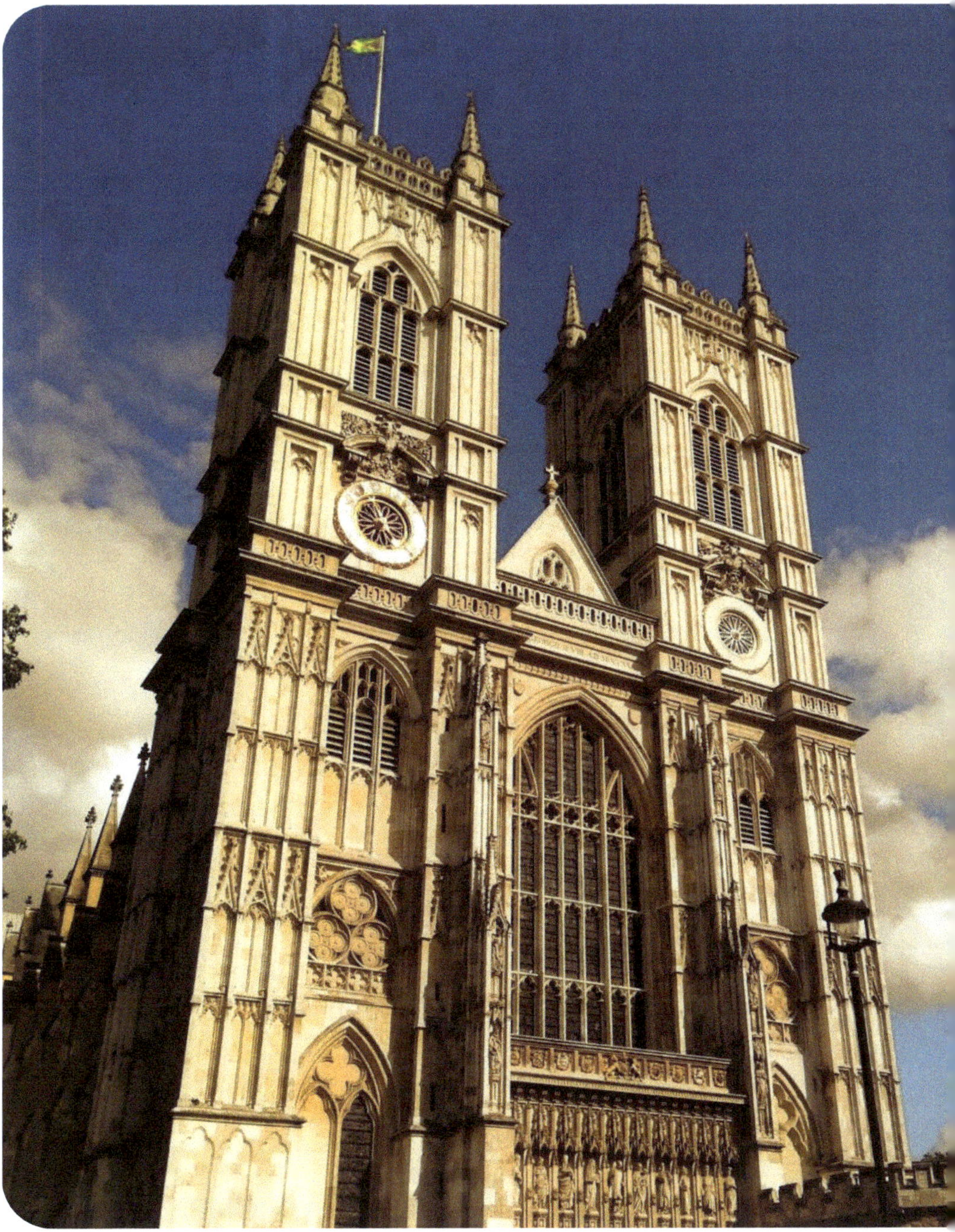

Relive Cook's first voyage to the Pacific at

CAPTAIN COOK'S LANDING PLACE

#73

⏱ **1770 AD**

🗺 **AUSTRALIA**

Captain James Cook first set foot on the Australian continent at Captain Cook's Landing, where a memorial obelisk and plaque commemorate the 200th anniversary of his landing. A number of monuments to Cook and his crew can be found at the site, including a water course believed to be that from which he obtained water, a monument erected in 1822 AD at Inscription Point, an obelisk of 1870 AD, a monument to Forby Sutherland, the first British subject to die in Australia, and monuments to Dr Solander and Joseph Banks. On August 22, 1770 AD, Cook claimed the entire Australian east coast for Great Britain, referring to it as "New South Wales."

▶ The Pacific Ocean was not well known to Europeans until the fifteenth century. Scientists anticipated discovering a sizable continent. Commercial and scientific maritime missions were planned. Although there had already been a number of expeditions there, James Cook was given a mission to explore the South Pacific by the British government. He departed London on the Endeavour on August 26, 1768, bringing with him astronomers and botanists who were in charge of enhancing knowledge of populations, animals, and plants. Cook charted New Zealand on this trip, and in April 1770 AD he found Australia's eastern coast. The first English settlers arrived in Botany Bay in 1788 AD, most of them being convicts. The colony had significant economic growth in the 19th century and population increase at the expense of the Aboriginal people who had inhabited these grounds for 60,000 years. Australia gained its independence in 1901 AD although the King of England is still recognized as the state's head of state, the Australian government is independent.

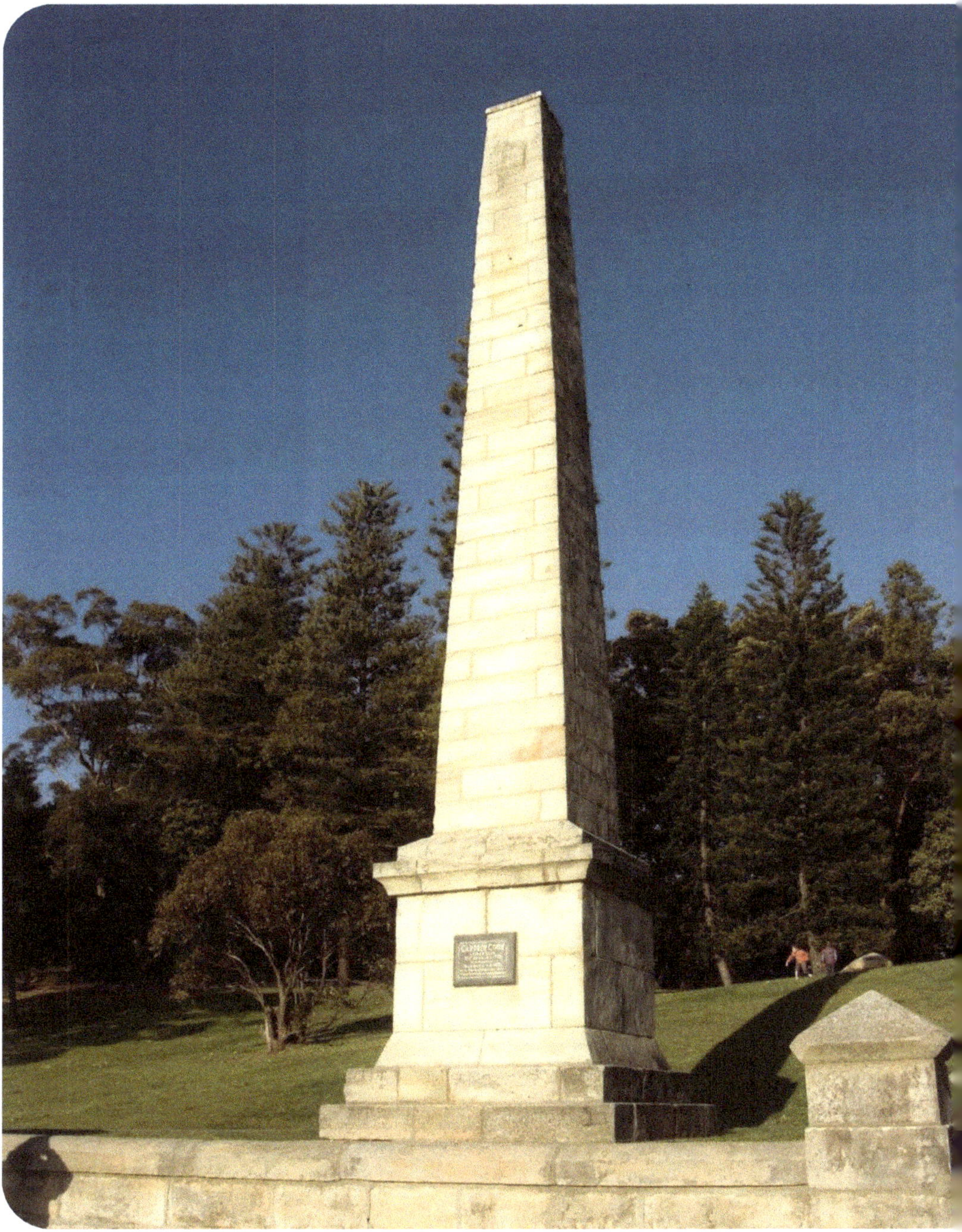

74

Discern the Independence of the United States of America at

THE CAPITOL

🕐 **1776 AD**

🗺 **USA**

The Washington Capitol is one of the most iconic and recognizable symbols of the United States. This grand and imposing building is located in the heart of the nation's capital, Washington, D.C., serving as the meeting place for the U.S. Congress and the seat of the legislative branch of the federal government. Completed in 1800, the Capitol was designed by the renowned architect Charles Bulfinch, whose masterful design has stood the test of time. The building's outstanding neoclassical architecture, featuring a striking white marble exterior and a majestic dome, has made it a beloved landmark and a source of national pride. The Capitol's stunning gardens and landscaping further enhance its grandeur, creating a picturesque setting that attracts visitors from around the world.

▶ In the 18th century, the British colonies in North America thrived due to transatlantic trade. However, in 1764-1765 AD, England imposed many taxes on items such as official documents, sugar and tea, which angered the colonists and sparked a growing desire for independence. In 1773 AD, residents of Boston dressed as Indians dumped 342 crates of tea from London into the sea, and King George III ordered the closure of the port of Boston. The representatives of the colonies met on July 4th, 1776 AD to proclaim the independence of the United States of America, inspired by the ideas of the Enlightenment.

A war then broke out with England, and George Washington rallied American militias to form an army, but he was unable to dislodge the well-established British in New York. Washington's army eventually defeated the British at Yorktown in 1781 AD. The famous phrase no taxation without representation was coined by James Otis in 1765 AD to express the colonists' resistance to the taxes imposed by the British government.

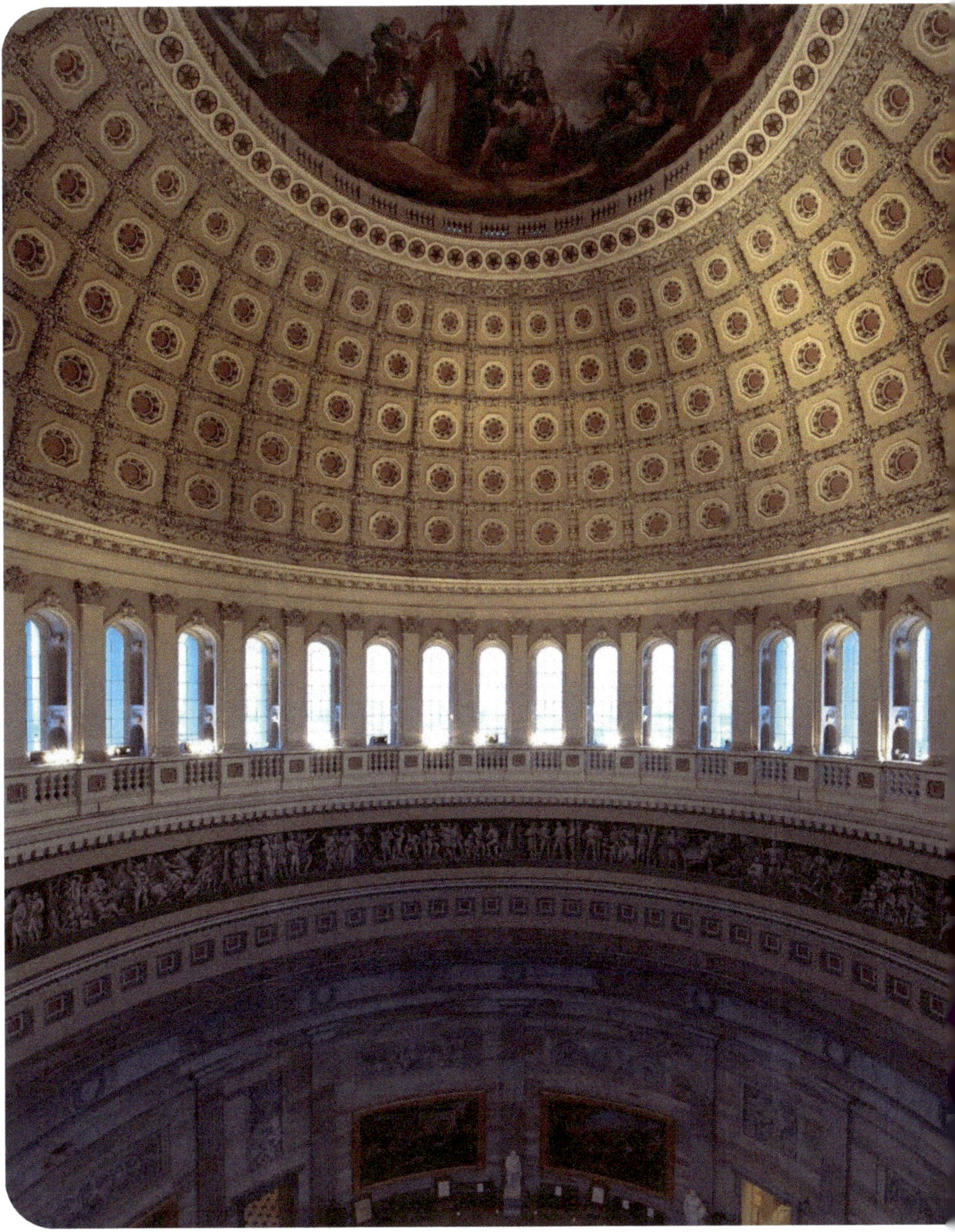

Relive the Coronation of Rama 1st and re-establishment of the Chakri dynasty at the

ROYAL PALACE OF BANGKOK

#75 ⏱ **1782 AD**

🗺 **THAILAND**

The Royal Palace of Bangkok is one of the most famous and visited sites in Thailand. It is located in the heart of the city and is home to several spectacular buildings, such as the Temple of the Emerald Buddha and Wat Phra Kaew. It is also the official residence of the King of Thailand and is used for many official ceremonies and events. Visitors can learn about Thailand's history and culture by visiting the various buildings and admiring the sumptuous gardens and gilded decorations. Arrive early in the morning and take at least a whole day to visit the reclining Buddha and the Grand Palace.

▶ The Chakri dynasty, founded in 1782 AD, succeeded the kings of Ayutthaya who were defeated by the Burmese. Rama I seized power by killing the son of the monarch and was crowned on April 7, 1782 AD. He continued the task of Taksin in saving the country which had just been reunited by recovering the Buddhist texts lost after the sacking of Ayutthaya and building the new capital Bangkok, as well as the temple to house the Emerald Buddha. During the reign of King Bodawpaya, the war against the neighboring kingdom of Burma continued.

Bodawpaya's armies made two attempts to capture the city of Ayutthaya, once in 1785 AD and again in 1808 AD, but were ultimately unsuccessful in their efforts to expand Burmese control over the region. Following the establishment of the Chakri dynasty in 1782 AD, ten successive kings have ascended to the throne of Thailand. The Chakri kings adopted the dynastic name "Rama" after a decision made by King Rama III, who was the third monarch of this royal lineage.

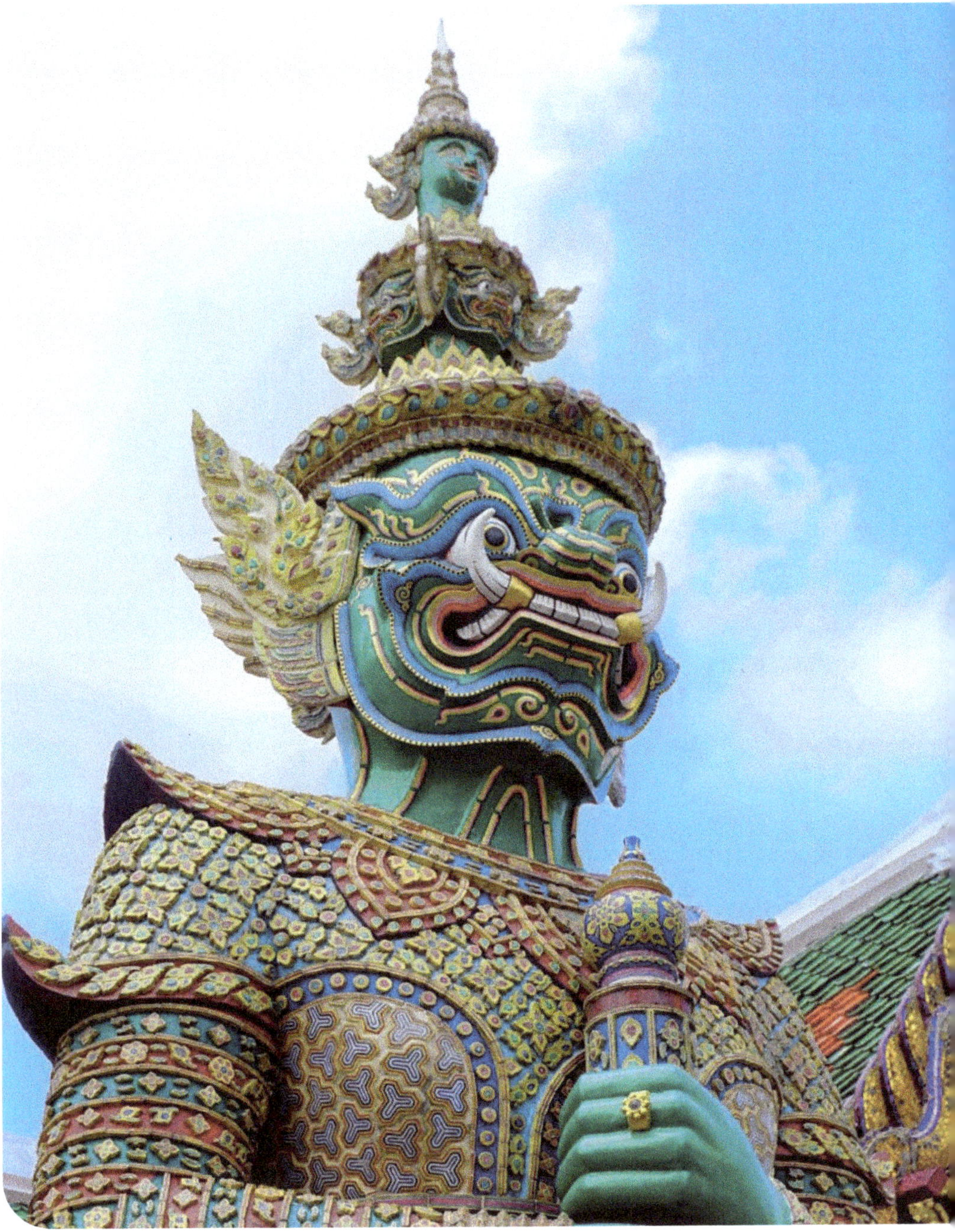

Understand the French Revolution in front of the

REPUBLIC MONUMENT

#76 1789 AD

FRANCE

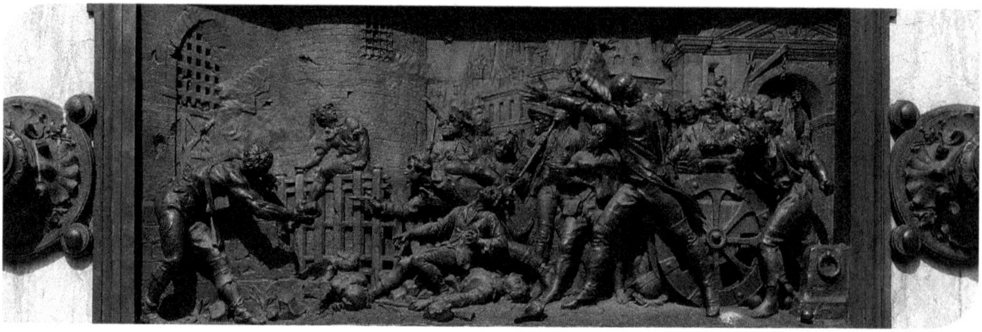

The "Monument de la République" in Paris is made of bronze and measures 9.5 meters high. It represents Marianne, the allegory of the Republic. Marianne is standing, wearing a toga and the Phrygian cap, symbol of liberty. In her right hand, Marianne holds an olive branch, symbolizing peace. Her left-hand rests on a tablet bearing the inscription "Droits de l'Homme "Atop the stone plinth, the statue is surrounded by three other stone statues: Liberté, with a flame, Égalité,brandishing the flag of 1789, Fraternité, seated on a plough. All around the pedestal, bronze reliefs represent the great dates in French republican history.

The Monument de la République is located at the center of the place de la République, where it embodies the fundamental values of the French Republic.

► In 1789 AD, France was facing financial, social, and political crises. King Louis XVI called for the Estates General to vote on revised taxes. On July 14th, 40,000 Parisians took arms and cannons from the Invalides barracks and stormed the Bastille fortress, killing the Marquis de Launay. This dramatic event is regarded as the iconic starting point of the French Revolution, in which a mob of Parisians stormed the hated symbol of royal power and oppression, marked the beginning of the overthrow of the French monarchy and the establishment of a new republican government, based on the Declaration of the Rights of Man, which proclaimed equality of rights for all citizens.

Revolutionary France spread revolutionary ideas throughout Europe and the world, and the Revolutions of the 19th century in Italy, Germany, and South America are claimed to have been derived from them. The storming of the Bastille prison is now celebrated as a national holiday in France, known as the "Bastille Day" or "National Day".

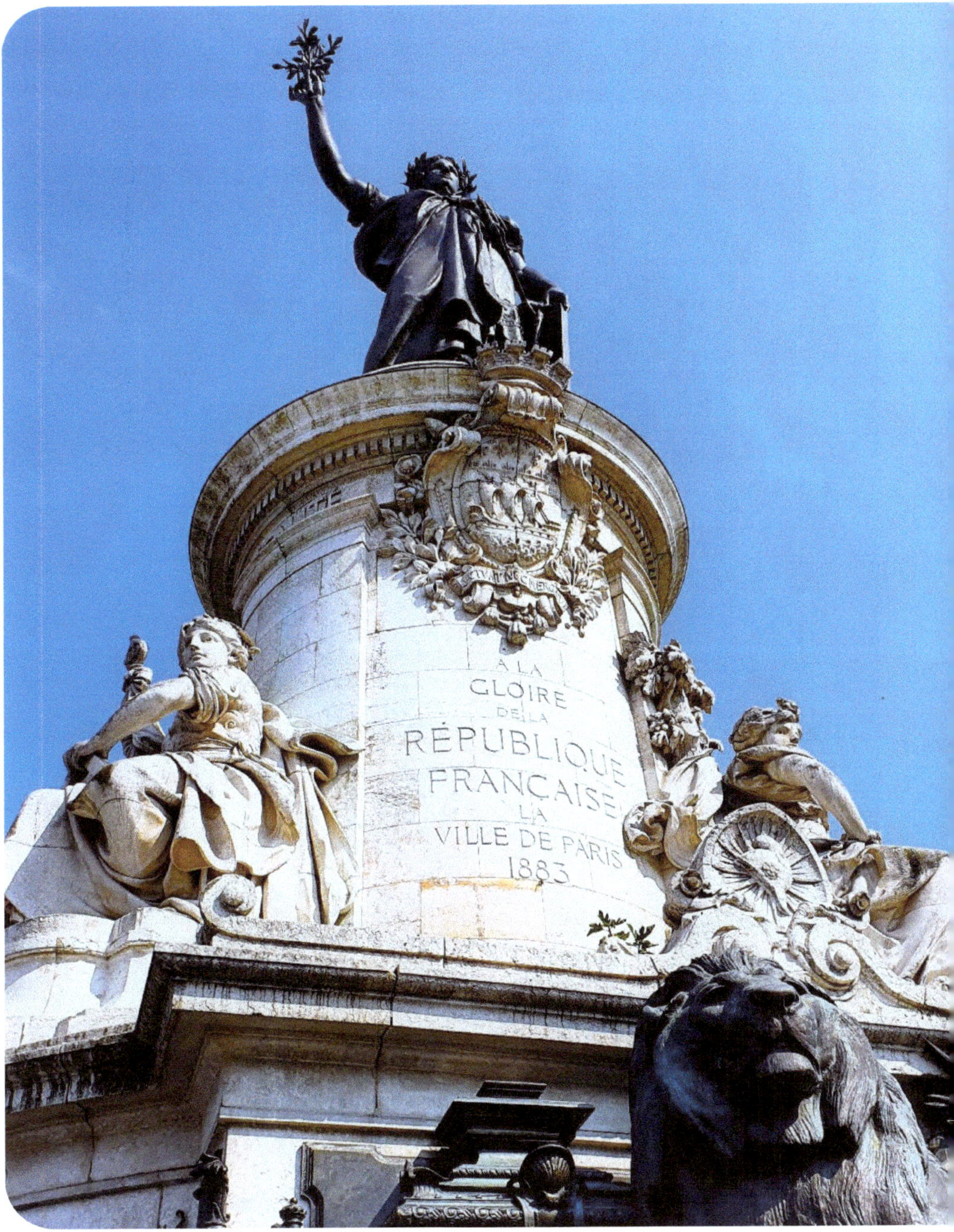
A LA
GLOIRE
DE LA
RÉPUBLIQUE
FRANÇAISE
LA
VILLE DE PARIS
1883

Recollect the Napoleonic Wars in Europe around the

TOMB OF NAPOLEON

#77 1799 AD

FRANCE

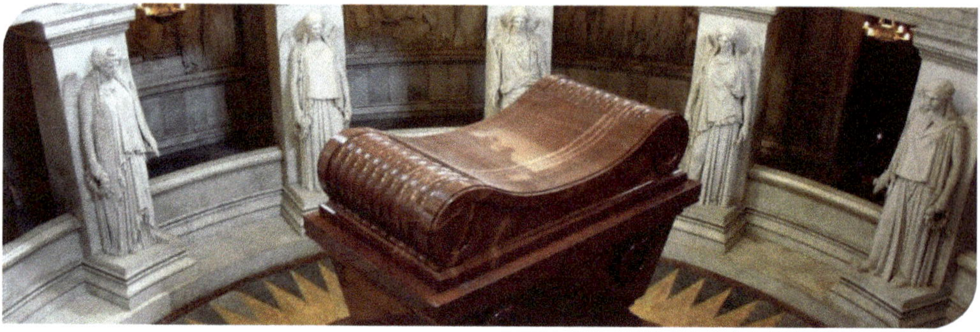

The Tomb of Napoleon at Les Invalides is a place of worship for lovers of French history and culture. It is a true tribute to Napoleon Bonaparte, who ruled the French in the early 19th century. The tomb itself is located in the Chapelle de Saint-Louis des Invalides, which is a monumental church built in the late 17th century. Napoleon's tomb is covered with a tricolor flag and an imperial escutcheon, and is surrounded by statues of soldiers and military decorations. Visitors can also see the chapel itself, which is adorned with frescoes and mosaics in the Baroque style. The Tomb of Napoleon at Les Invalides is a place of memory and reflection for all those interested in the history of France and its empire.

► Napoleon Bonaparte was born on August 15th, 1769 AD in Ajaccio, Corsica and arrived in France in 1799 AD. He seized power through a coup d'état and named himself consul for life in 1802 AD. He promulgated the Civil Code and defended the accomplishments of the Revolution. In May 1804 AD, Napoleon Bonaparte was proclaimed emperor in order to strengthen his power. He meticulously organized his coronation ceremony, which took place on December 2, 1804 AD in Notre-Dame Cathedral in Paris, and succeeded in reconquering the country, but the English, Russians, Prussians, and Austrians united against him and defeated him at the Battle of Waterloo on June 18th, 1815 AD.

He surrendered to the English who exiled him to the island of Saint Helena where he died on May 5th, 1821 AD. His memory endures through the legend that portrays him as a man of the Enlightenment, a son of the French Revolution, and a promoter of European unity, but it is important to remember the 800,000 French people who died during the Napoleonic Wars.

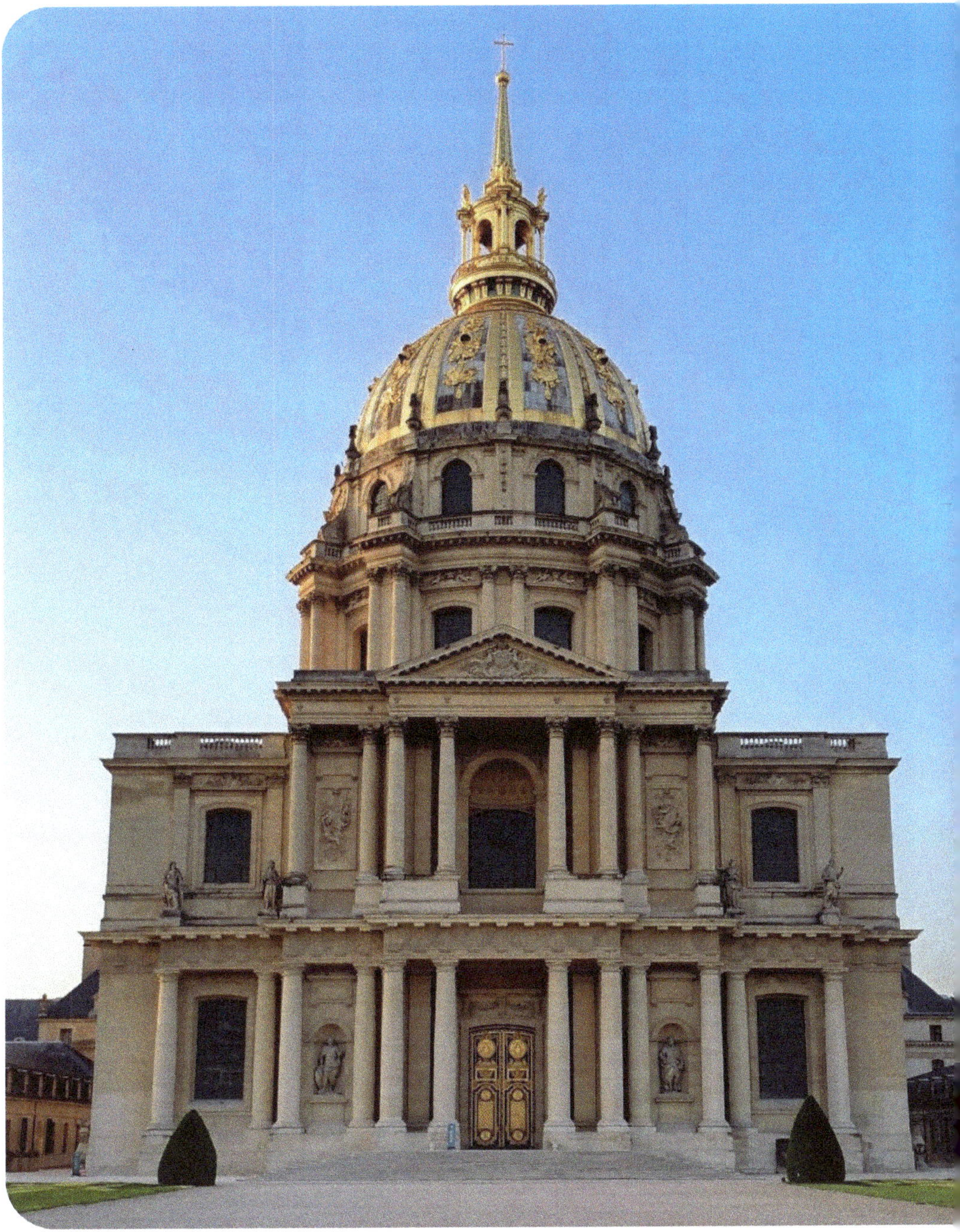

19TH CENTURY

The 19th century was marked by rapid industrialization, major political upheavals, the expansion of European colonialism, and groundbreaking technological and social changes that laid the foundations for the modern world.

Comprehend the abolition of slavery at the

LINCOLN MEMORIAL

#78 1807 USA

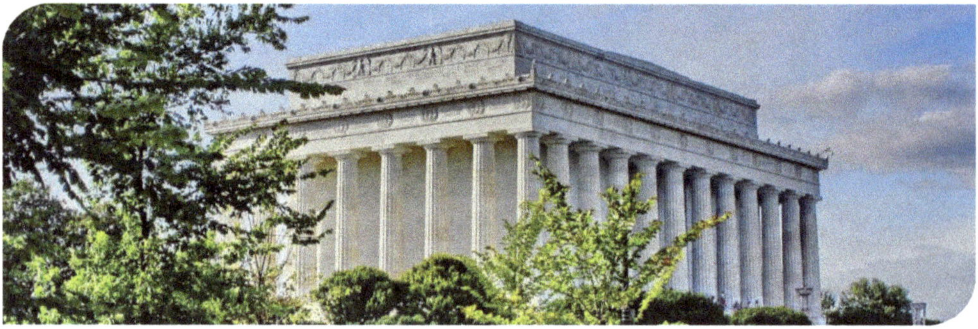

The Lincoln Memorial is a national monument located in Washington D.C. honoring the 16th President of the United States, Abraham Lincoln. Built in 1922, it sits on the banks of the Potomac River and is a place of pilgrimage for many Americans. The monument is designed in the style of Greek antiquity and consists of a white marble temple with an imposing statue of Lincoln within. The Lincoln Memorial is a significant memorial for the United States because it was here that Martin Luther King Jr. gave his famous "I have a dream" speech at the March on Washington for Work and Freedom in 1963. If you're in Washington D.C., the Lincoln Memorial is absolutely a must. Its grandeur and symbolism make it an inspiring and moving place to visit.

► Although critiques of slavery and the transatlantic slave trade began with Enlightenment philosophers, the French Revolution accelerated the process. Despite the Declaration of the Rights of Man and of the Citizen of 1789 and references in the *cahiers de doléances*, the Constituent Assembly did not immediately abolish slavery in the colonies. It wasn't until the Saint-Domingue revolts in 1791 that slavery was abolished in the colonies. It was Denmark that became the first country to officially dismantle the transatlantic slave trade in 1792.

The rest of Europe followed later. It wasn't until the second half of the 19th century that countries such as the Netherlands, Spain, Portugal, and their colonies abolished slavery. In the United States, the abolitionist movement followed the British model starting in 1815. Abraham Lincoln then decreed the abolition of slavery in 1863 during the Civil War. On January 31, 1865, Lincoln finally obtained the two-thirds majority required. A few months after its ratification, the 14th amendment guaranteed Black people the right to vote and equality with whites under the law.

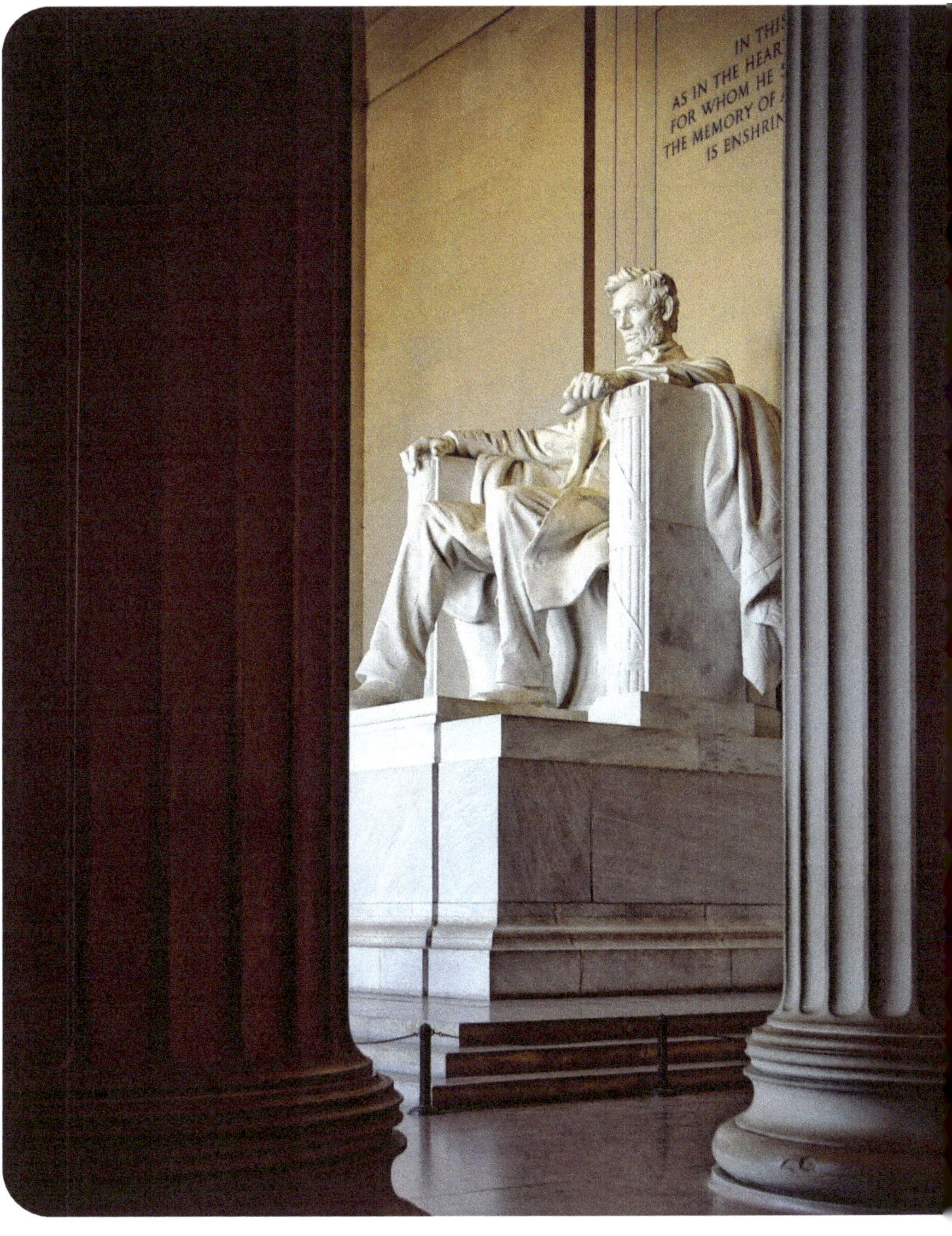
IN
AS IN THE
FOR WHOM HE
THE MEMORY OF
IS

Conceive the independence of the Latin American colonies at the

MAUSOLEUM OF SIMÓN BOLÍVAR

#79 🕐 **1821**
🗺️ **VENEZUELA**

The Mausoleum of the Liberator Simón Bolívar is a monumental structure located in Caracas, Venezuela. It is dedicated to the memory of the South American leader who played a crucial role in the liberation of several Latin American countries from Spanish colonial rule. It is a magnificent architectural masterpiece and is considered to be one of the most important historical landmarks in Venezuela. It contains the remains of Bolívar and his closest collaborators, including Antonio José de Sucre, Francisco de Paula Santander, and Rafael Urdaneta. It is not just a monument, but also a symbol of the struggle for freedom and democracy in South America.

▶ In 1808, Napoleon's armies invaded Spain. The generals took advantage of this to lead the Spanish colonies of South America to independence. The young patriot Bolivar, an aristocrat from Caracas inspired by the philosophers of this era, then led an army to liberate these colonies. He won the Battle of Boyacá in 1819 and triumphantly entered Bogotá, where he proclaimed the Great Colombia in 1821, which brought together present-day Colombia and Venezuela.

With the help of his lieutenant Sucre, he freed Ecuador in 1822 and other South American territories such as Chile in 1818, and Peru with General San Martin. Bolivar's most cherished dream, that of a Federal Republic, was not achieved due to internal problems of the newly formed nations. Simon Bolivar is known as the George Washington of South America as he played a crucial role in leading several countries to independence from Spanish colonial rule.

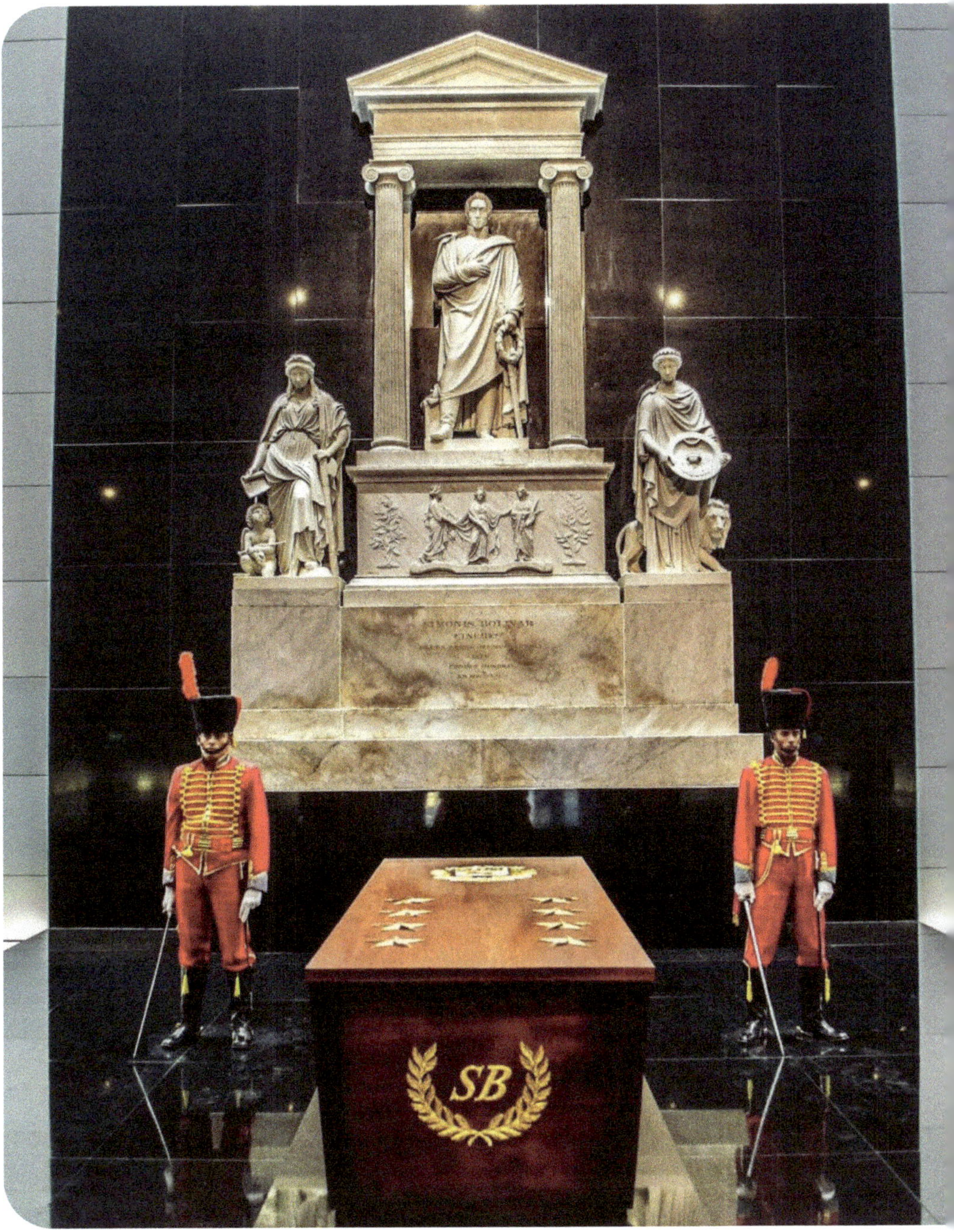
SB

Witness the first passenger train put into circulation at the

SWINDON STEAM RAILWAY MUSEUM

#80 1825 UK

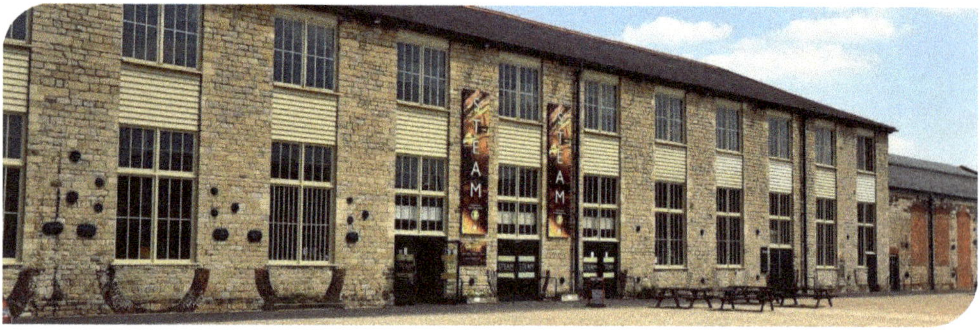

STEAM
STEAM

The Swindon Steam Railway Museum is a must-see for lovers of railways and industrial history. Located in Swindon, England, this museum is dedicated to the history of the region's railway industry and is full of exciting historical treasures. Visitors can discover a collection of steam locomotives, wagons and railway cars dating from the nineteenth and twentieth centuries. The museum also features exhibits on the lives and work of railway workers and the impact of the railway industry on the development of Swindon and the region. In addition to its permanent exhibitions, the Swindon Steam Railway Museum also offers special events such as open days and steam train journeys. If you are interested in railway history, don't miss a visit to this exciting museum.

► During the Middle Ages, the principle of rail and wheel was used for mining extraction. However, it was the demand for raw materials in the late 18th century that led to the improvement of infrastructure and traction. Wooden rails were replaced with iron and steel bars, and the steam engine was used to increase traction power. In 1814, George Stephenson designed the first true steam locomotive and in 1825, his *Locomotion* was the first ever steam train carrying 450 passengers from Darlington to Stockton, on September 27th, 1825. The development of the railway was rapid in countries with coal or able to import it, such as Europe and the United States.

It also helped in the conquest of lands and territories. In Europe, prestigious lines linked London and Paris to the Riviera or the Bosphorus. In North America, the transcontinental railroad completed in 1869 contributed to the legend of the conquest of the West. The first steam railway service in the world started operating in 1804 between Redruth and Chasewater in Cornwall, England.

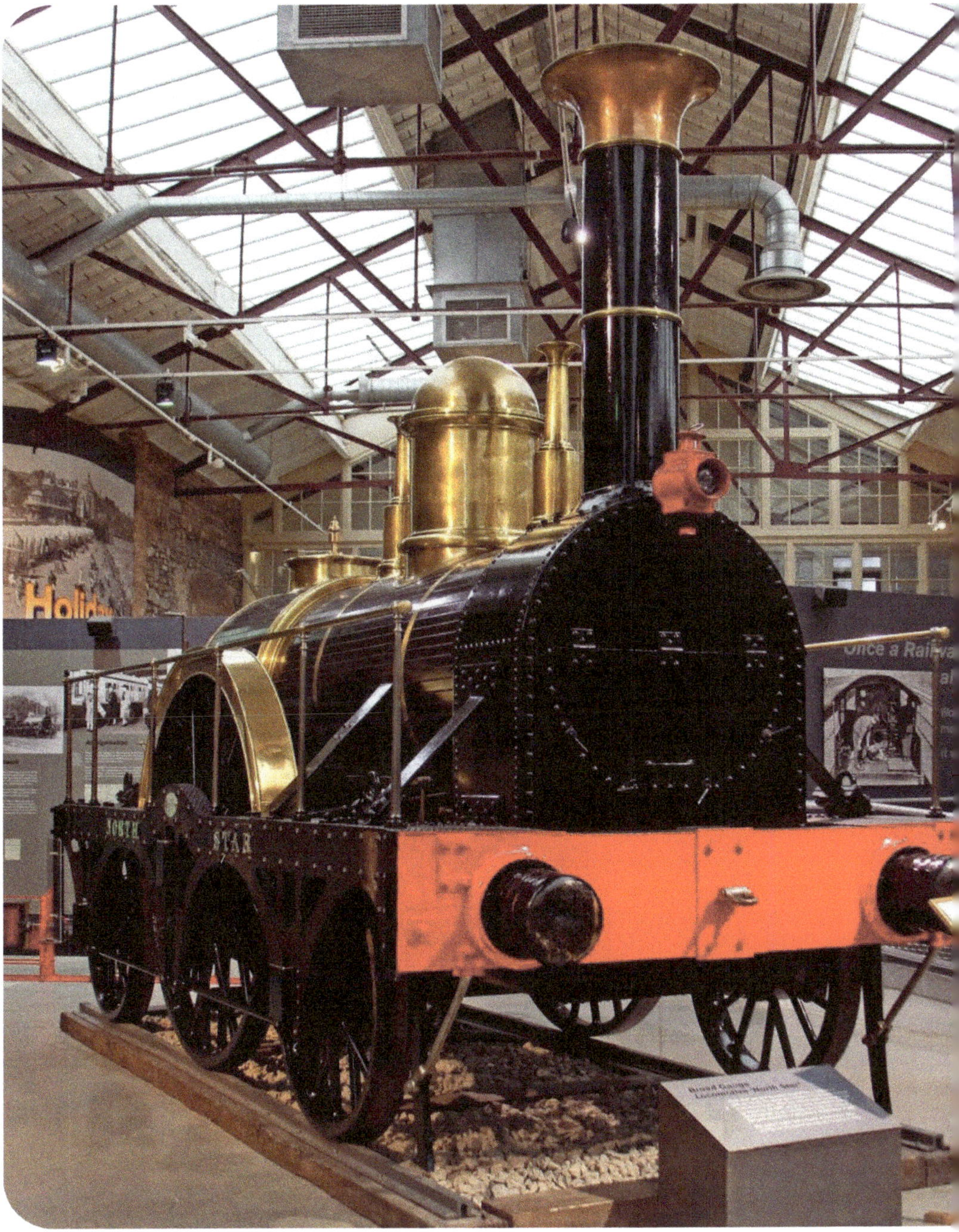
NORTH
STAR

Delve into the Opium War between China and the United Kingdom walking by the

HONG KONG BAY

#81 ⏱ 𝟙𝟠𝟜𝟚

🗺 **HONG KONG**

Victoria Harbor is located between Hong Kong Island and the Kowloon Peninsula and is the first major port in Asia and the third largest port in the world. It is considered "the Pearl of the Orient" and has an excellent reputation as "one of the three natural harbors in the world". The name Victoria derives from Queen Victoria of Great Britain, and the British seized Hong Kong to develop maritime trade in the Far East. Hong Kong Bay is also known for its popular tourist attractions, such as Victoria Peak and the Hong Kong Aquarium. In the evening, the bay lights up with the glow of the lights of the skyscrapers, offering a spectacular view of the city.

▶ The Opium War was the first time that China was defeated by a foreign power, and marked the beginning of the decline of the Qing Dynasty. Since 1773, the United Kingdom has had a monopoly on the sale of opium in China, which was particularly profitable for the British. In 1839, China banned the importation and consumption of opium and destroyed a stock of over 1000 tons in the city of Canton. In retaliation, the British sent a fleet of war ships, but failed to retake Canton.

The war lasted a few more months, but on August 29th, 1842, the Treaty of Nanking officially declared victory for the British, in which the United Kingdom received 99 years' concession of Hong Kong territory and the right to sell opium in China. French, British, American and Japanese companies created many companies in concessions, which are in fact small states outside of Chinese authority. This system will last a century.

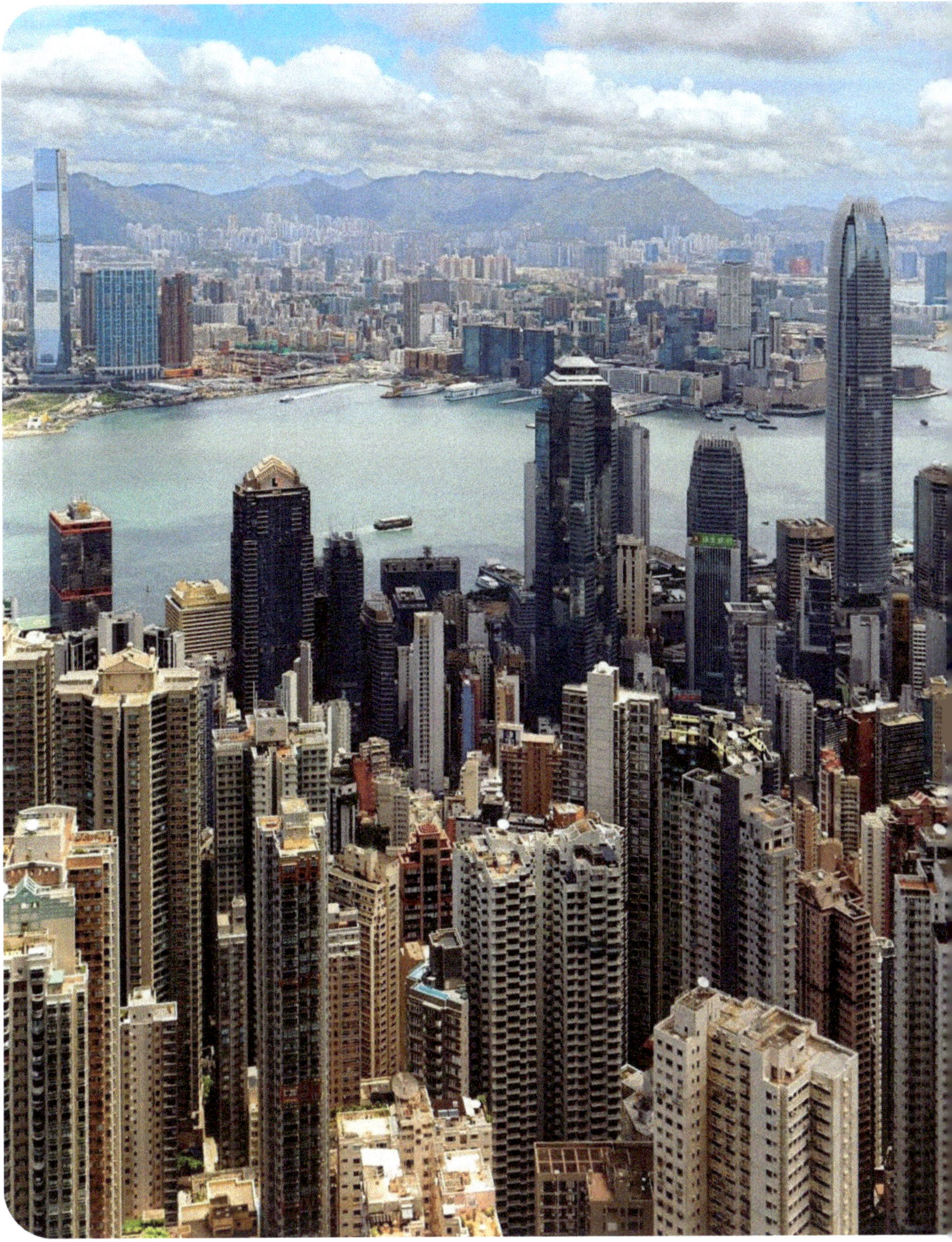

Visualize Charles Darwin writing "On the Origin of Species" in the

GALAPAGOS ISLANDS

#82 1859 GALAPAGOS

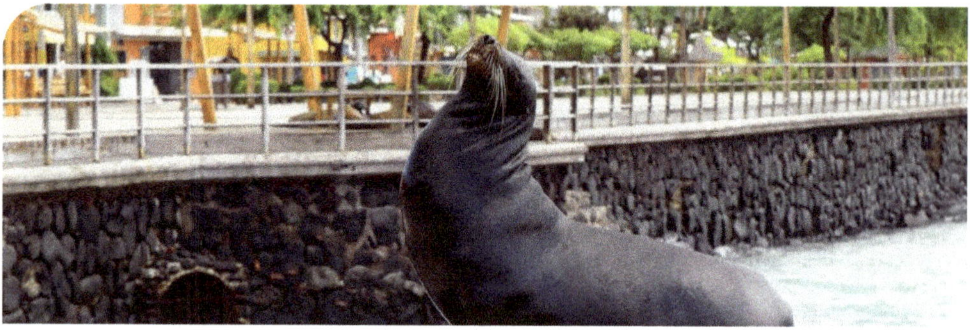

The Galapagos Islands are an archipelago located in the Pacific Ocean, about 1000 kilometers from the equator. This unique place is known for its exceptional fauna and flora, which have been greatly influenced by the isolation of the archipelago. Indeed, the Galapagos Islands have been inhabited by many animal and plant species that have evolved separately from the species on the mainland coast. The archipelago is also known to have been a place of inspiration for the famous naturalist Charles Darwin, who stayed there for five weeks in 1835 and was deeply influenced by his observations of the fauna and flora of the islands. Today, the Galapagos Islands are protected by UNESCO as a World Heritage Site.

► The Galapagos Islands are a group of equatorial islands that were crucial to Charles Darwin's theory of evolution. During his voyage on HMS Beagle in 1835, he studied the differences between bird species on these islands. He discovered that their adaptation to their environment was the source of these differences. He observed, in particular, that although the environmental conditions did not vary much from one island to another, these differences were sufficient to influence the size of the beaks of birds of the same species depending on the types of seeds available in the area.

He concluded that it was possible to find 14 types of birds of the same species on a relatively small territory, these differences being linked to the environment in which they grew. This led to the publication of *The Origin of Species* two decades later, in 1859. Darwin established the principles of natural selection and reproduction, which states that species adapt to their environment to survive and reproduce, and individuals better adapted have more chances of survival and reproduction.

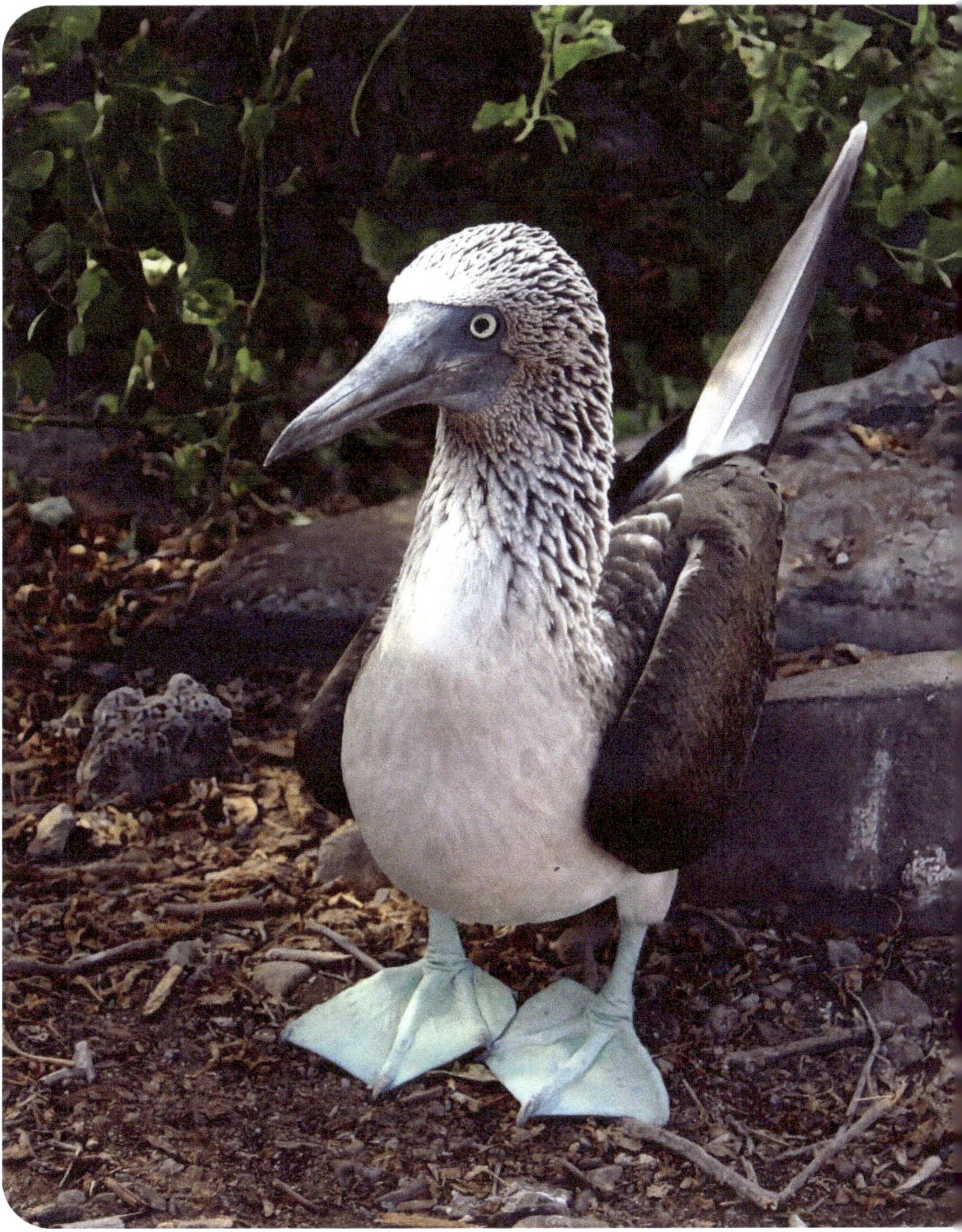

Understand the establishment of the International Committee of the Red Cross at the

RED CROSS MUSEUM

#83 1863 **SWITZERLAND**

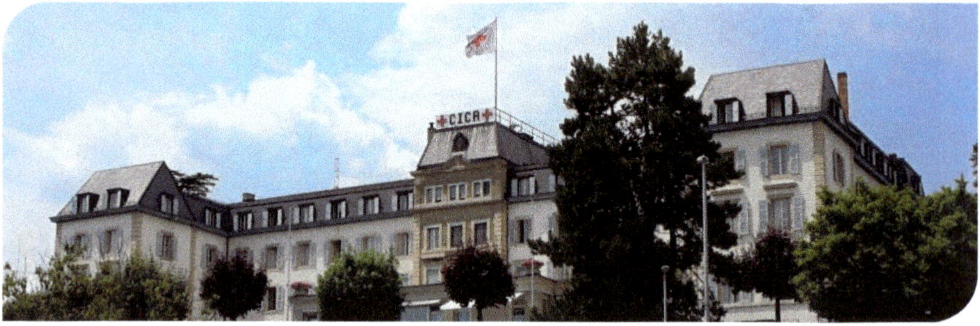
CICR

The Red Cross Museum, located in Geneva, Switzerland, is a place of memory and reflection on the history of the international humanitarian organization. Founded in 1863 by Henri Dunant, the Red Cross' mission is to protect and help vulnerable people, regardless of their country of origin. The museum presents a rich and diverse collection that traces the history of the organization and its actions. It also traces the role it has played in protecting human rights and promoting peace. You can discover historical objects and documents, as well as temporary exhibitions on various themes, such as mental health or volunteering. If you are passionate about history or simply curious about the work of the Red Cross, the Red Cross Museum is a must during your visit to Geneva.

► It was after the Battle of Solferino in 1863, that Swiss citizen Henry Dunant witnessed the horrible conditions of the war wounded. He had the idea to create a humanitarian aid association. On February 17, 1863, Henry Dunant and 4 other citizens from Geneva discussed their common ideas regarding war wounded, describing the conditions in which the Battle of Solferino took place later, these ideas gave birth to a humanitarian aid association.

This association is made up of independent national societies and is responsible for training volunteers when they do not have to intervene on battlefields. The same year, an international conference (Geneva Convention) allowed the creation of national aid societies in 17 countries. Since its creation, the ICRC has had the sole objective of protecting the victims of armed conflicts and providing assistance to them. It acts all over the world, encourages the development of international humanitarian law, and urges governments to respect this law.

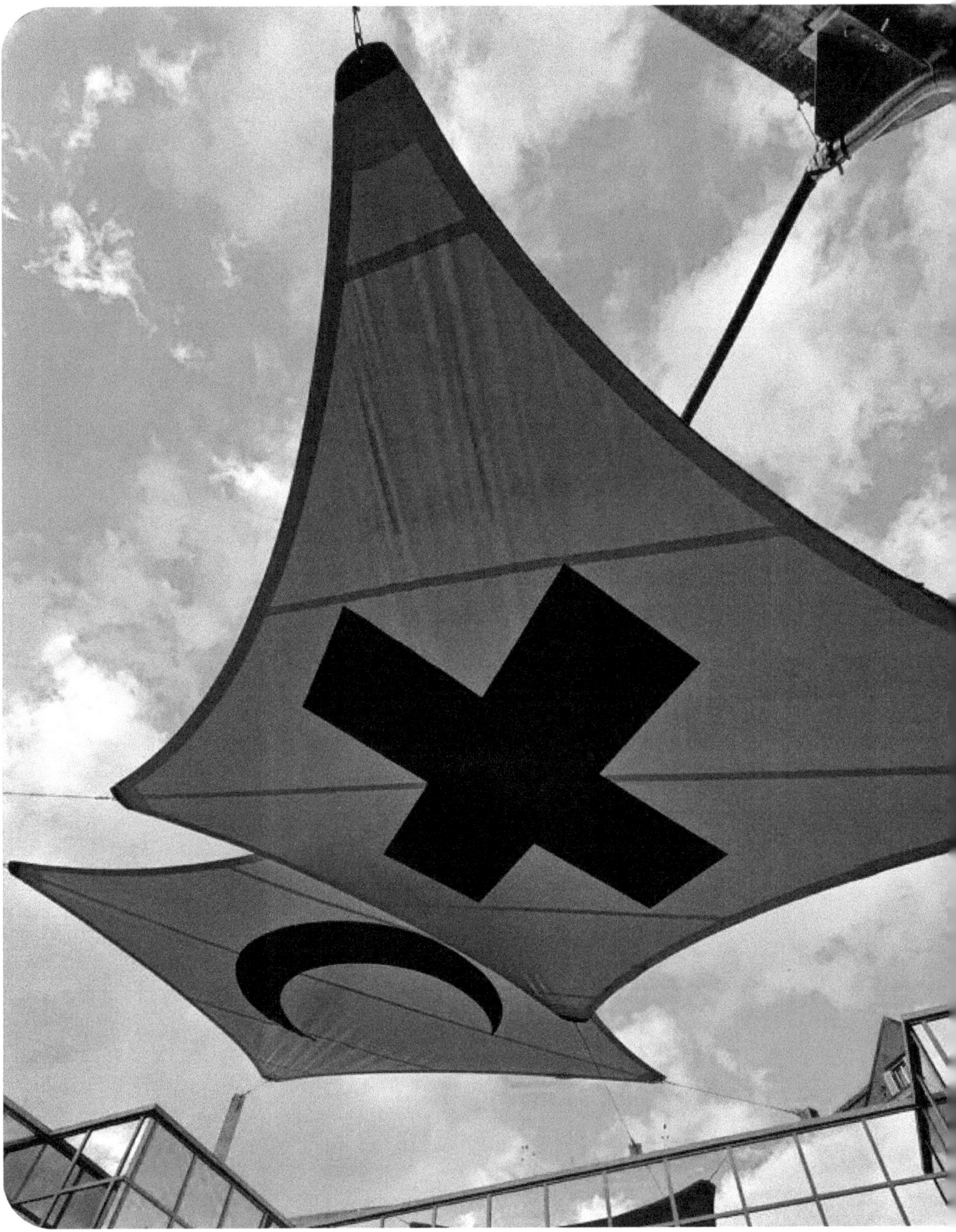

Recall Mutsuhito becoming the Emperor of
Japan, ending the Shogun era at the

HIMEJI CASTLE

#84 🕑 **1867**
🗺 **JAPAN**

Himeji Castle, also known as Himeji-jō, is a castle in Himeji, Japan. It is one of the most picturesque castles in the country and is a UNESCO World Heritage Site. Built in the fourteenth century, Himeji Castle has survived the centuries and has been perfectly preserved, offering visitors a fascinating insight into Japanese history and culture. The structure of the castle is impressive, with its multiple floors and pristine white rooster crest-shaped roofs. The castle garden is also a wonder to behold, with its winding paths and wooden bridges that cross ponds and waterfalls. If you are traveling in Japan, do not miss the opportunity to visit Himeji Castle and discover the fascinating history of this unique place.

▶ In the 19th century, major world powers began to expand their influence in Asia in search of new markets. In 1853, American naval officer Commodore Matthew Perry demanded the opening of Japanese ports to American trade and the Tokugawa Shogunate conceded, opening the ports of Hakodate and Shimoda. Other European powers also gained similar advantages, ending Japan's isolation that had been in place since 1638. The newly appointed emperor, Mutsu Hito, who took power in 1867, abolished the Shogunate and launched the Meiji Era, the policy of enlightenment.

He moved the government to Edo (Tokyo), abolished the feudal system, made education mandatory and brought in European engineers and lawyers to modernize Japan. In 1889, he adopted a Constitution modeled after the Prussian political system and developed a modern industry including railroads, telegraphs and a navy. Japan participated in world expositions to showcase its technical progress and adopted a policy of expansion in East Asia.

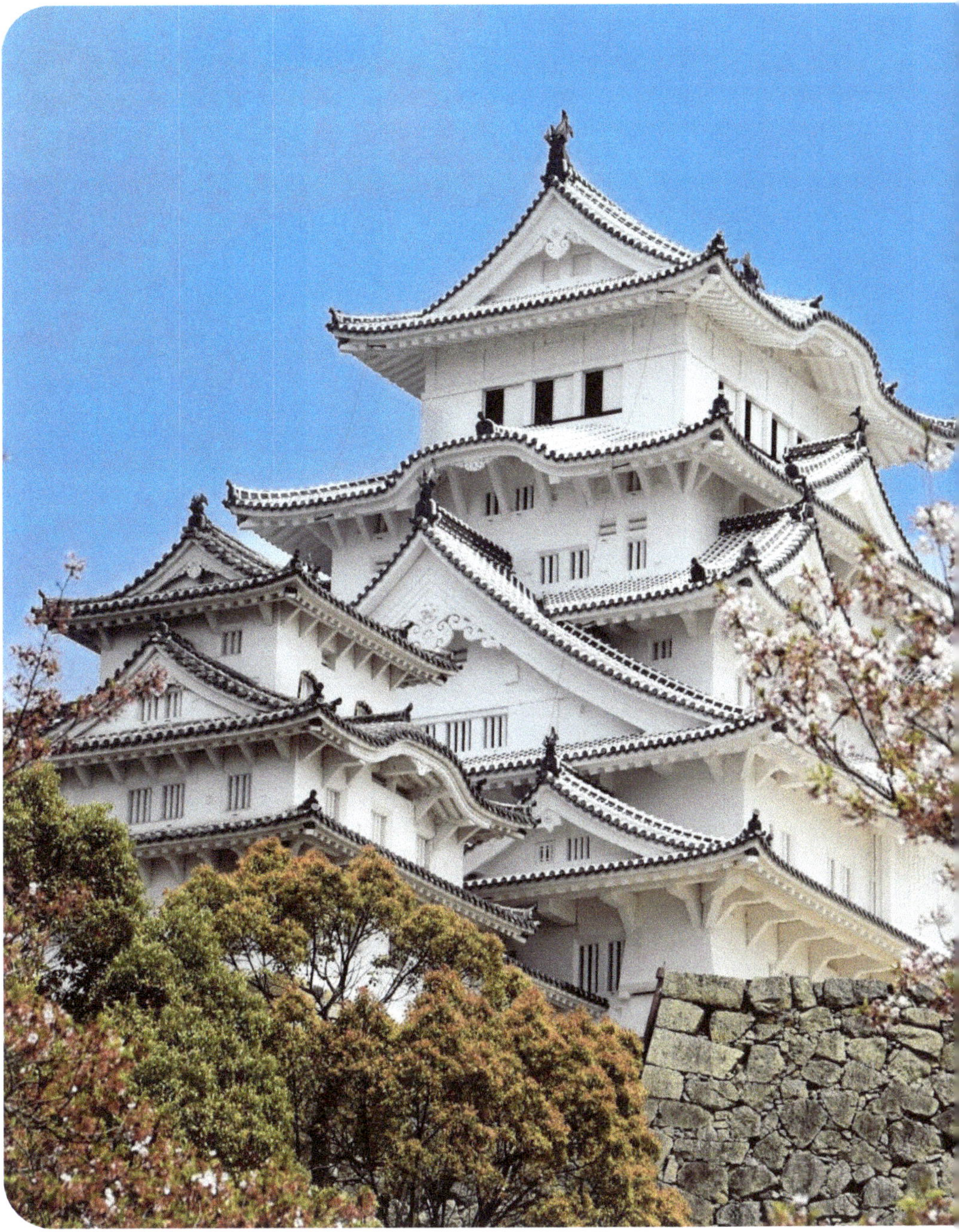

Venture into European colonial expansion in Africa as far as the

VICTORIA FALLS

#85 1884 ZIMBABWE

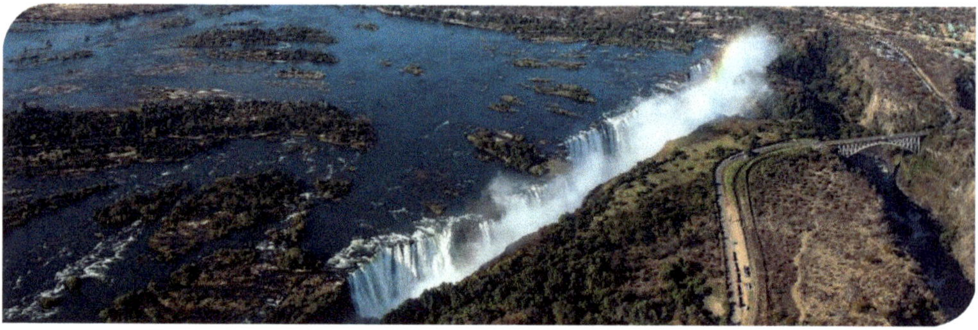

Victoria Falls, also known by its local name Mosi-oa-Tunya, is undoubtedly one of the most awe-inspiring natural wonders in all of Africa. Situated on the border between Zambia and Zimbabwe, this magnificent waterfall stands an impressive 360 feet high and spans a width wider than the iconic Niagara Falls. The sheer power and volume of the Zambezi River as it plunges over the edge is truly breathtaking, creating a deafening roar that can be heard for miles around. Adrenaline junkies can experience the rush of whitewater rafting on the Zambezi, while more serene visitors can opt for a scenic helicopter flight over the falls. For the truly daring, there is even the opportunity to swim in the Devil's Pool, a natural rock pool right at the edge of the precipice.

► During the 19th century, Europeans began to take control of the territories in Africa. In 1880, only a small portion of the continent was under their dominance, but twenty years later, only Ethiopia, Morocco, and Liberia escaped colonization. Western powers agreed at the Berlin Conference of 1884 to divide Africa among themselves. Colonization was encouraged by the technological advancements of the time and by the emerging international economic context. Colonial trading companies, such as the British South Africa Company, organized the trade between African products exported to Europe and European industrial products sold in Africa.

They used a network of trading posts and commercial representatives, as well as transportation and communication means sometimes financed with their own funds. These companies generated substantial profits, often in a monopoly or duopoly position. This is often considered the starting point of the Scramble for Africa and the beginning of the colonization of the continent.

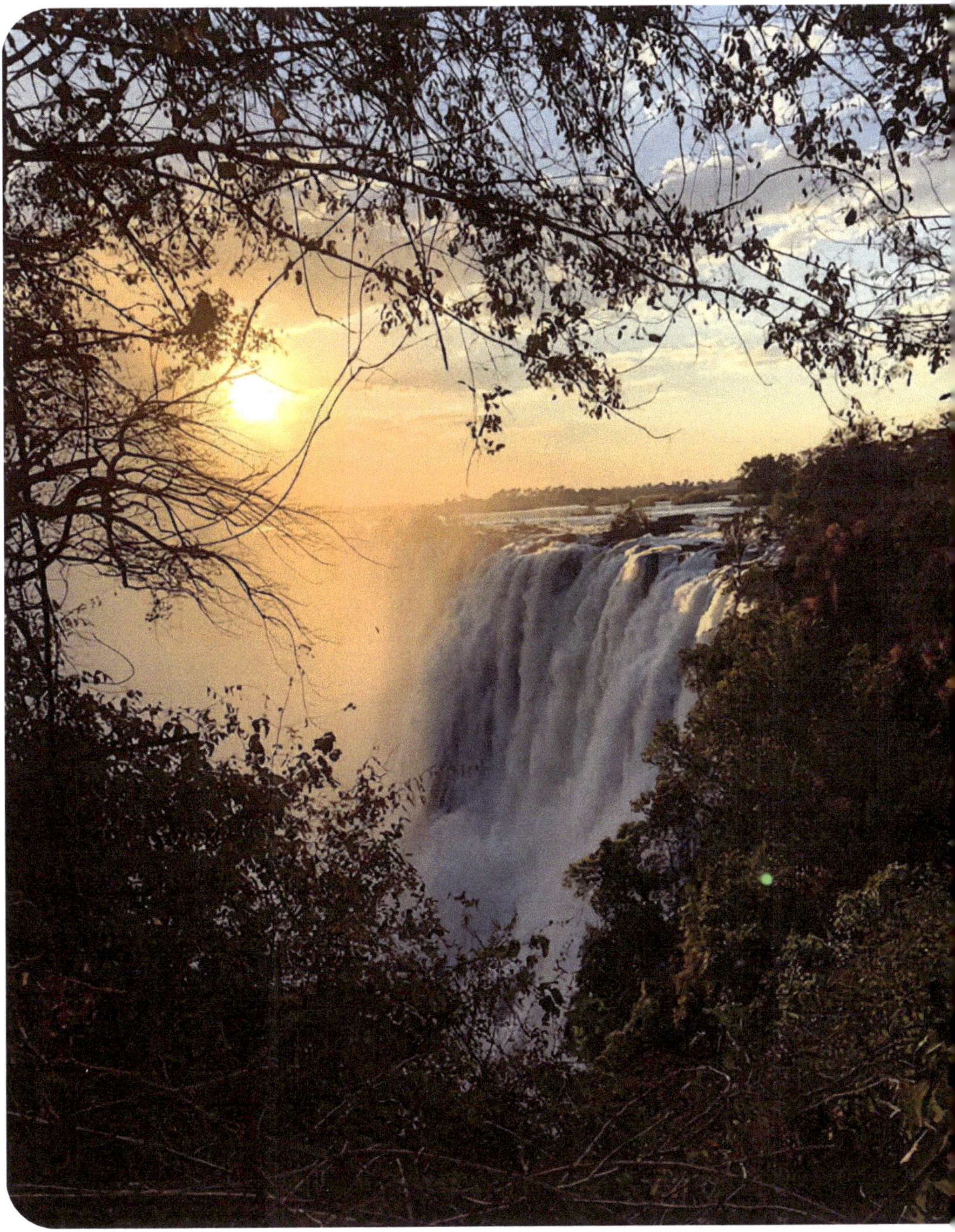

20TH CENTURY

The 20th century was a period of immense global upheaval, technological advancement, and social change, with events like the world wars, the rise and fall of communism, and the space race shaping the modern world.

Picture Blériot crossing the English Channel by plane at the

MUSEUM OF ARTS AND CRAFTS

#86 1909 FRANCE

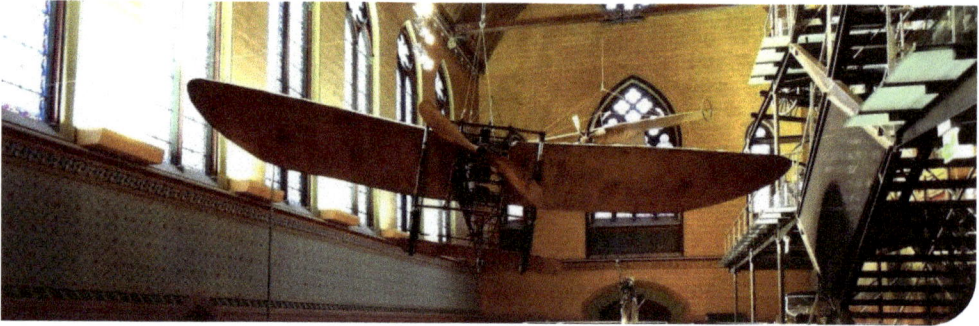

The Museum des arts et métiers de Paris is a captivating destination for all those fascinated by the rich tapestry of science and technology. Located in the heart of the 3rd arrondissement, this renowned museum offers visitors a remarkable journey through the annals of engineering and innovation. The museum boasts an impressive collection of machines, models, and technical drawings that chronicle the evolution of technology over the centuries. From the earliest mechanical devices to cutting-edge modern innovations, the exhibits provide a comprehensive overview of humanity's ingenuity and problem-solving prowess. Its captivating exhibits and breathtaking architecture make it a true gem in the cultural landscape of Paris.

► The crossing of the English Channel by airplane was one of the first remarkable aviation feats that captivated the imagination of people. The British newspaper Daily Mail offered a substantial sum of £1,000 to the first aviator who successfully crossed the Channel by plane. Several French aviators attempted this adventure, among them, Louis Blériot who despite previous failures, was determined to succeed. He used his latest model, the Blériot-XI, to attempt the crossing. He succeeded in covering the distance in 37 minutes, reaching an average speed of 57 km/h, on July 25th, 1909.

His success was greeted by an enormous crowd upon his arrival in Dover, and he became the first aviator to cross the Channel by air. Following his success, he received financial aid to mass-produce his crossing model, which was used for the Aéropostale, air transportation, and even during World War I. Blériot's crossing of the Channel was a key moment in aviation history and paved the way for many other aerial exploits in the following years.

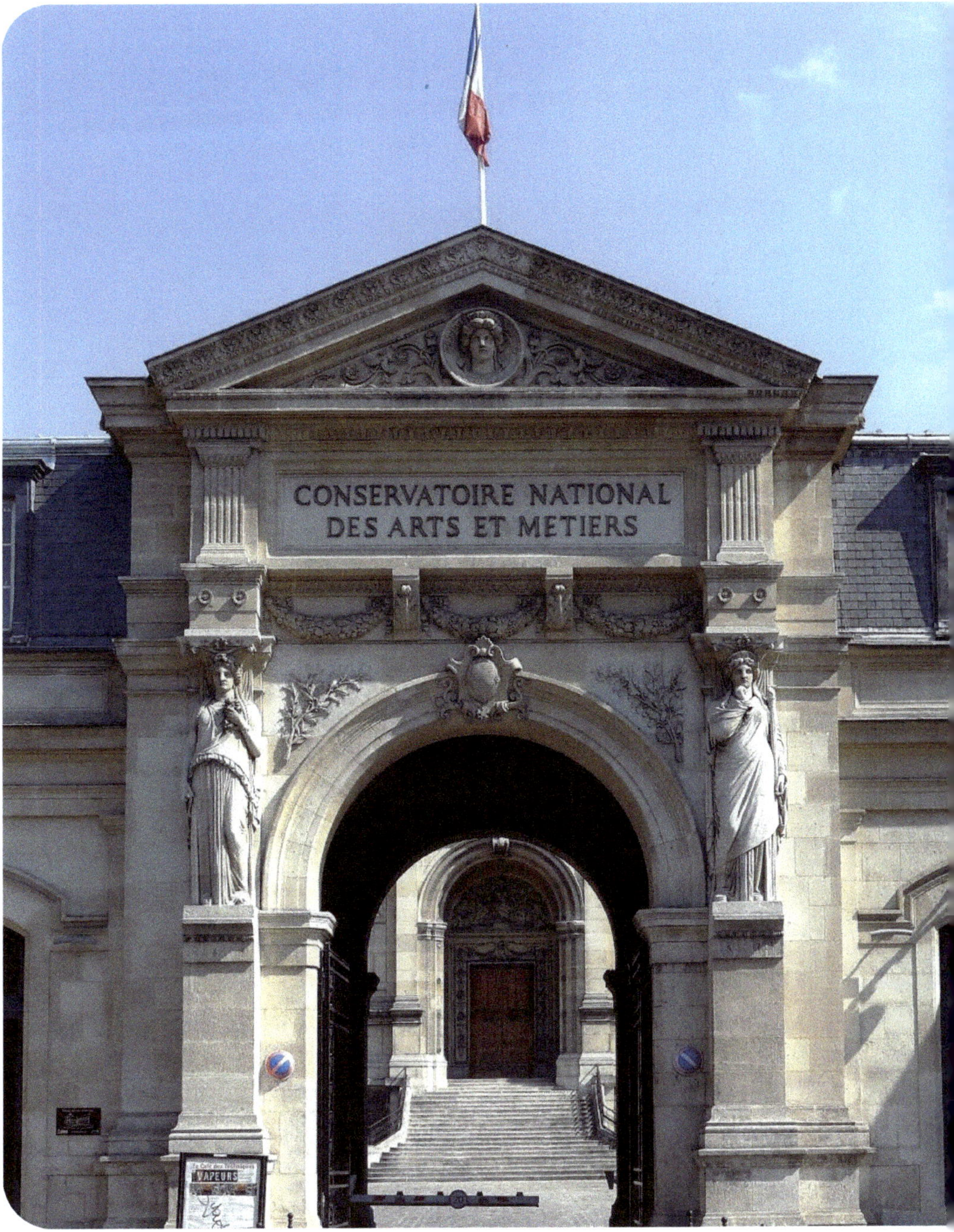
CONSERVATOIRE NATIONAL
DES ARTS ET METIERS
VAPEURS

Visualize Ferdinand's assassination triggering the World War I at the

SARAJEVO MUSEUM 1878–1918

#87 1914 **BOSNIA**

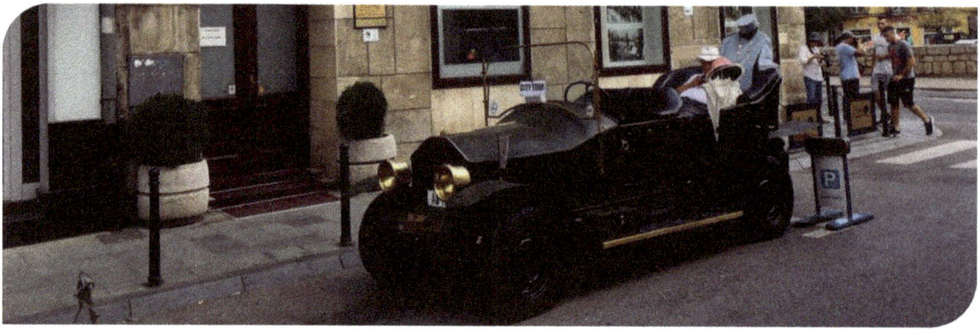
P

The Sarajevo Museum 1878-1918 is an outstanding cultural institution located in the city of Bosnia and Herzegovina. It was established in 1878 by Emperor Franz Joseph of Austria-Hungary and has become one of the most prominent museums in the region. It displays a large collection of objects and artifacts dating from the Ottoman era until the end of World War I, including rare and valuable objects such as weapons and armor, gold and silver objects, as well as manuscripts and historical documents. The museum also has a section dedicated to the daily life of the time, with exhibits on clothing, food, music and entertainment. It offers an unparalleled opportunity to discover the history of the city and the region in an interactive and immersive way.

► The assassination of Archduke Franz Ferdinand and his wife in Sarajevo by Gavrilo Princip, a militant advocating the annexation of Bosnia to Serbia pulled Europe into the First World War due to entangled alliances. The government of Vienna, supported by Germany, declared war on Serbia on July 28th, 1914. This led to the mobilization of Russia and the declaration of war by Germany on Russia and France. The war spread on a global scale due to the colonies of various European countries and lasted for 4 years. Armies dug into trenches and offensives were relatively short-lived.

The United States joined the conflict in 1917 and sent two million soldiers to the French front. Germany eventually surrendered and signed the armistice on November 11th, 1918. The war led to the collapse of four empires: the Russian, German, Austro-Hungarian and Ottoman empires, and marked the end of the First World War.

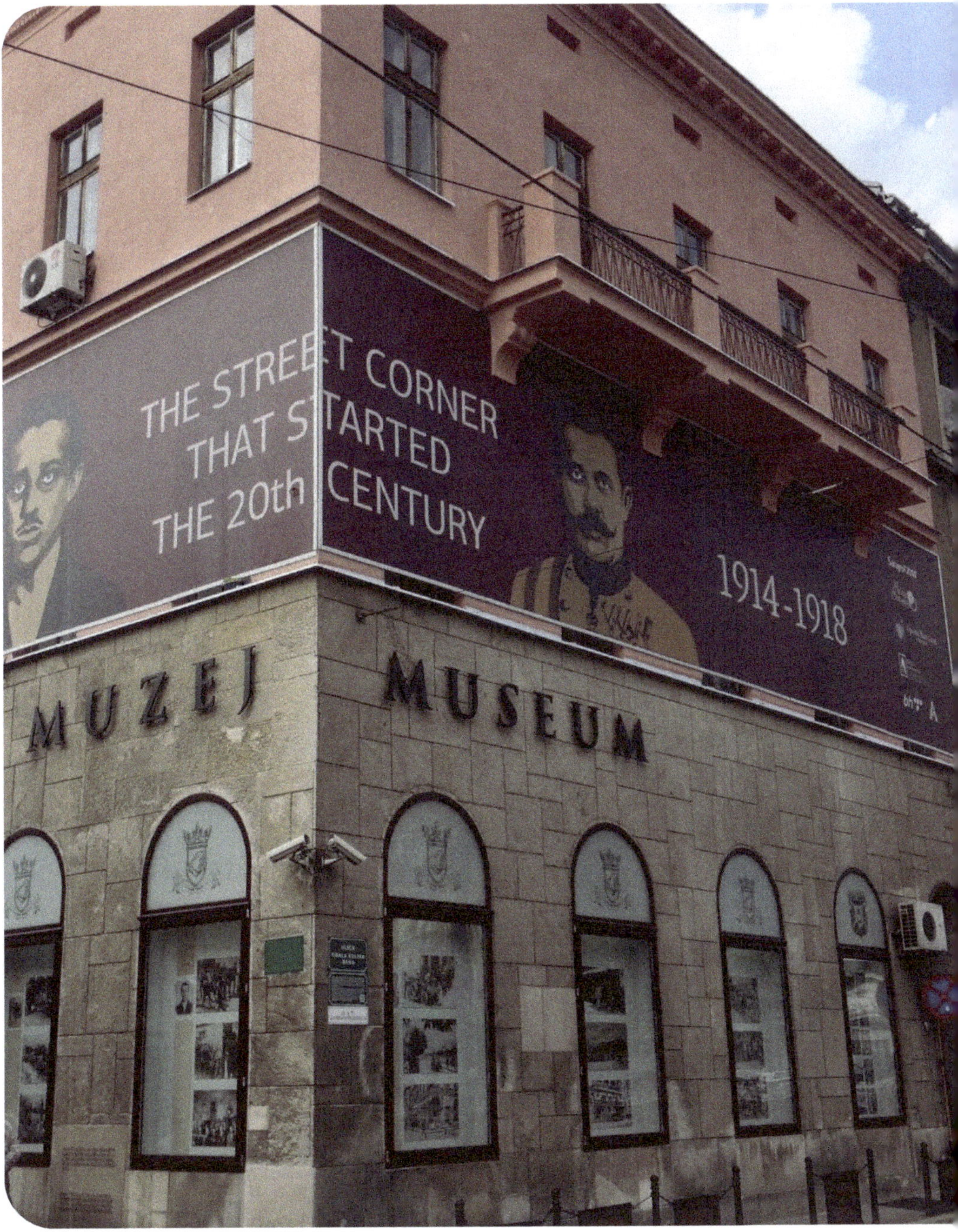
THE STREET CORNER
THAT STARTED
THE 20th CENTURY
1914-1918
MUZEJ
MUSEUM

Comprehend the beginning of the Russian Revolution at the

LENIN MAUSOLEUM

#88

1917

RUSSIA

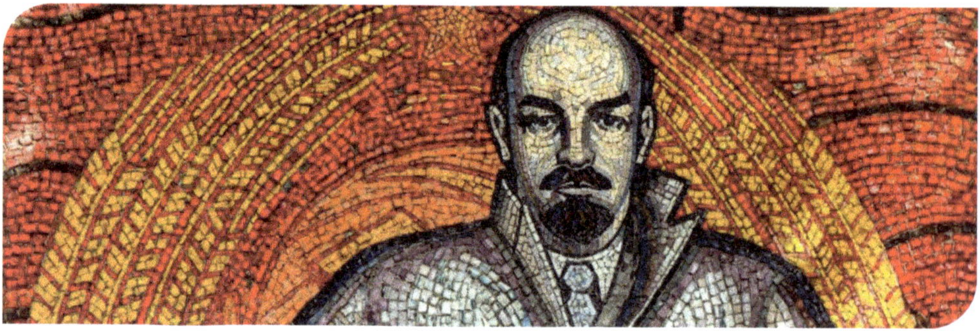

The Lenin Mausoleum is an iconic and significant monument located in the heart of Moscow, on the famous Red Square. Constructed in the 1920s, this neoclassical structure was built to house the embalmed remains of Vladimir Lenin, the first leader of the Soviet Union and a pivotal figure in the Russian Revolution. Despite the passage of time and the dissolution of the Soviet Union, the Lenin Mausoleum remains an integral part of Moscow's cultural and historical landscape. It continues to draw visitors from around the world, who come to learn about Russia's communist past and to pay their respects to one of the most influential figures in modern history. However, access to the mausoleum is strictly regulated, with visitors required to follow specific protocols and dress codes to ensure the sanctity of the site.

► During World War I, a new era opened in Russia with the February Revolution of 1917 which led to the abdication of Tsar Nicholas II. The Bolsheviks, led by Lenin, called for a revolution to create a republic of soviets, that is, groups of workers and peasants. The Bolsheviks seized power in Petrograd (formerly Saint Petersburg) on October 24th and 25th, 1917, and forced the government to resign. Lenin abolished private property of land, gave the Russians equality and independence, established an 8-hour workday and prepared for peace with Germany. This October Revolution established the first communist regime in history. This regime quickly became a dictatorship, with the suspension of press freedom and the repression of opponents by the secret police. Only the Bolshevik party, which became the Communist Party, was allowed. In 1922, after a long civil war between the Red Army and supporters of the Tsar, the Union of Soviet Socialist Republics (USSR) was founded. Vladimir Lenin's body was embalmed and placed on permanent public display in Moscow's Red Square, where it remains to this day.

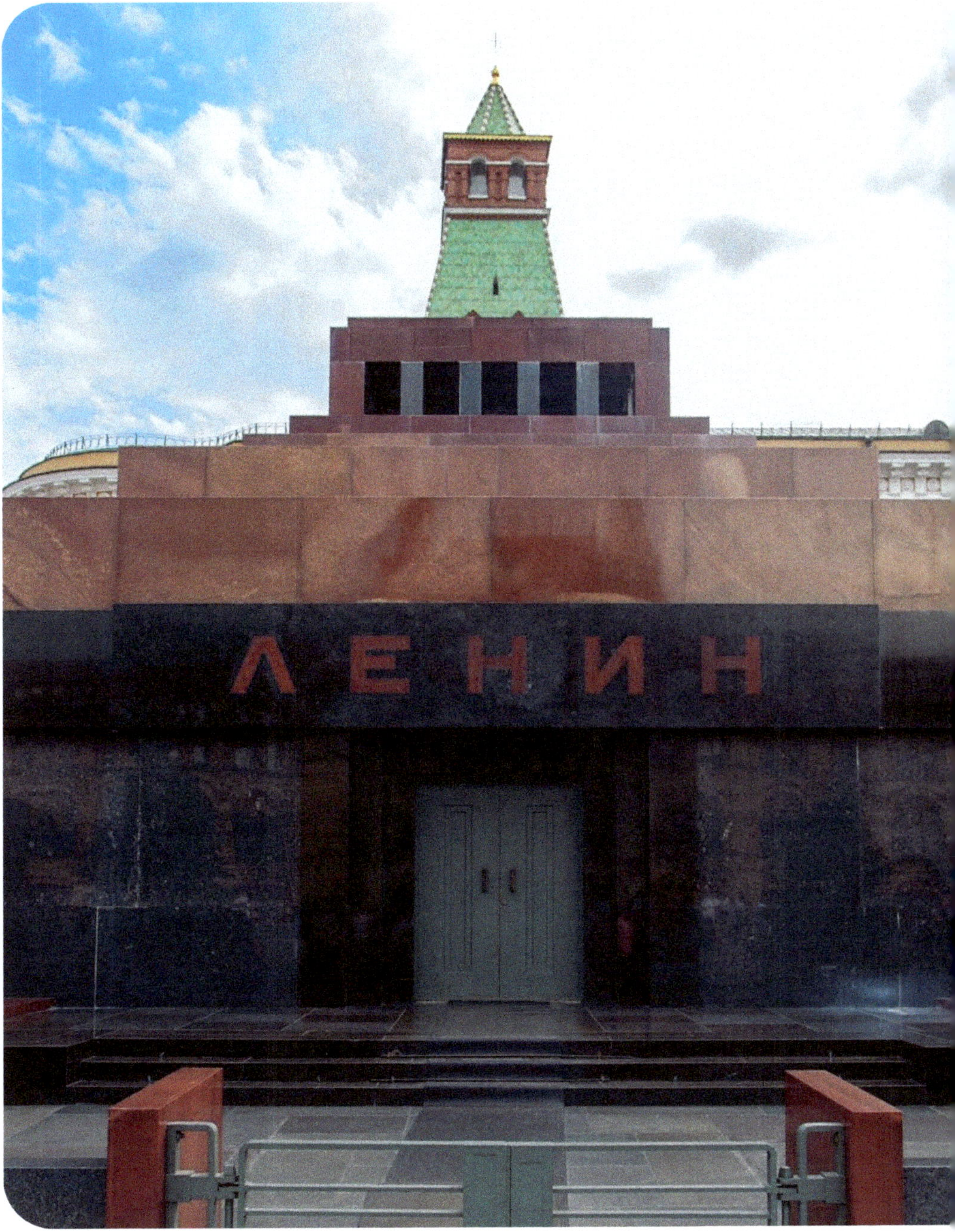
ЛЕНИН

Imagine the signature of the Treaty of Versailles at the

PALACE OF VERSAILLES

#89 1919 **FRANCE**

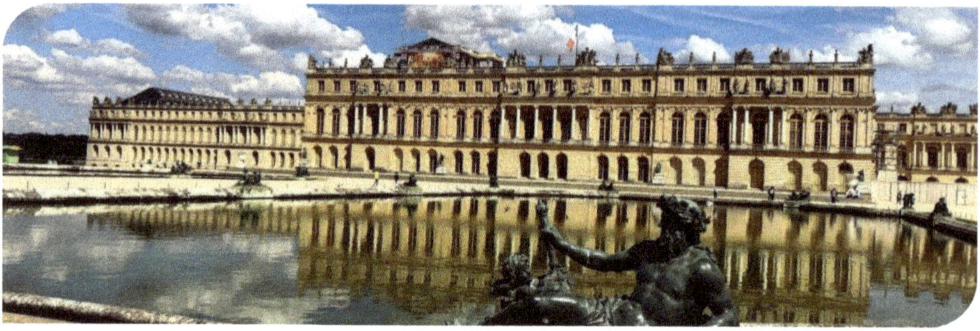

The Palace of Versailles is a must-see destination for all lovers of history and cultural heritage. This magnificent royal castle, located in the suburbs of Paris, was constructed in the seventeenth century by the renowned French monarch, Louis XIV, to serve as the official residence of the royal family. The palace's construction and design were a testament to the Sun King's ambition and desire to project the power and prestige of the French monarchy. Beyond its architectural splendor, the Palace of Versailles holds immense historical significance. It was within these grand halls and gardens that some of the most pivotal events in European history unfolded. The palace was the setting for the signing of the peace treaties that marked the end of both the First and Second World Wars.

► The First World War ended in 1919 at Versailles after four years of conflict. The peace treaty was considered a dictate by some and contained the causes of a second conflict that would break out twenty years later. Decisions were made by the four main victors: France, Great Britain, the United States, and Italy. American President Woodrow Wilson wanted to treat Germany with leniency, while French Prime Minister Georges Clemenceau wanted to crush it. The treaty, signed on June 28, 1919, was a compromise that no one was satisfied with. It is humiliating for Germany, who is held solely responsible for the conflict.

Germany must pay war reparations, loses its fleet and colonies, its army is reduced to 100,000 men, and its territory loses Alsace and Moselle, which return to France. Its ally, the Austro-Hungarian Empire, is divided into several states. The Treaty of Versailles also affirms the right of peoples to self-determination and establishes an international institution, the League of Nations, to prevent or resolve conflicts.

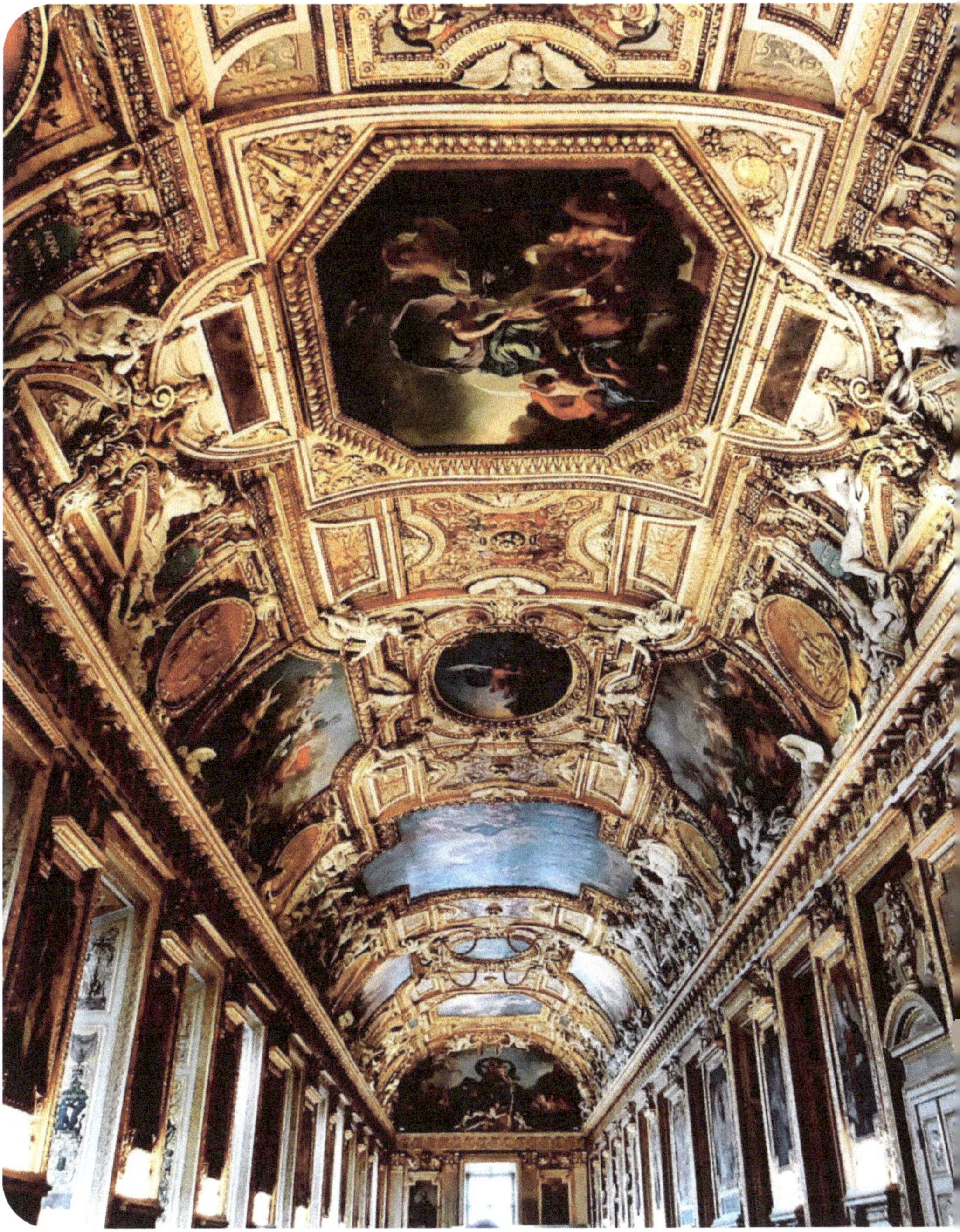

Recollect the Black Thursday at the

WALL STREET STOCK EXCHANGE

#90 ⏱ **1929**

📍 **USA**

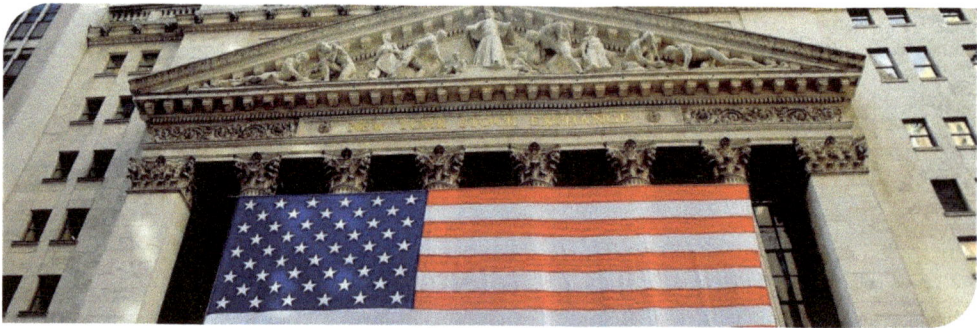

The Wall Street Stock Exchange is one of the most famous and influential places in the world. Located in New York City, this exchange is where companies and investors come to buy and sell stocks and bonds. The Wall Street Stock Exchange is considered one of the most critical barometers of the global economy, as it reflects the health of companies and industries around the world. Since its inception in 1792, the Wall Street Stock Exchange has experienced many ups and downs, but it remains a crucial place for investors and companies around the world. If you're interested in the world of finance, a visit to the Wall Street Stock Exchange is a must-do experience.

▶ In the 1920s, the United States experienced a period of economic prosperity. Many people borrowed money to buy stocks on Wall Street, with the hope of becoming rich quickly. However, in the summer of 1929, the reality of the industry proved less favorable, and on Thursday, October 24th, a stock market crash shook the United States. On Tuesday, October 29th, thousands of stocks were sold, causing a collapse in stock prices.

Thousands of small investors were ruined and hundreds of thousands of companies and banks went bankrupt. Unemployment increased to reach 12 million workers in 1933, and European economies were also affected by the crisis. The economic turmoil paved the way for the rise of authoritarian, far-right political movements. In Germany and Italy, for example, the desperation and instability created by the Depression helped fuel the ascent of fascist leaders. The term Black Tuesday was used to refer to the stock market crash on October 29th, 1929.

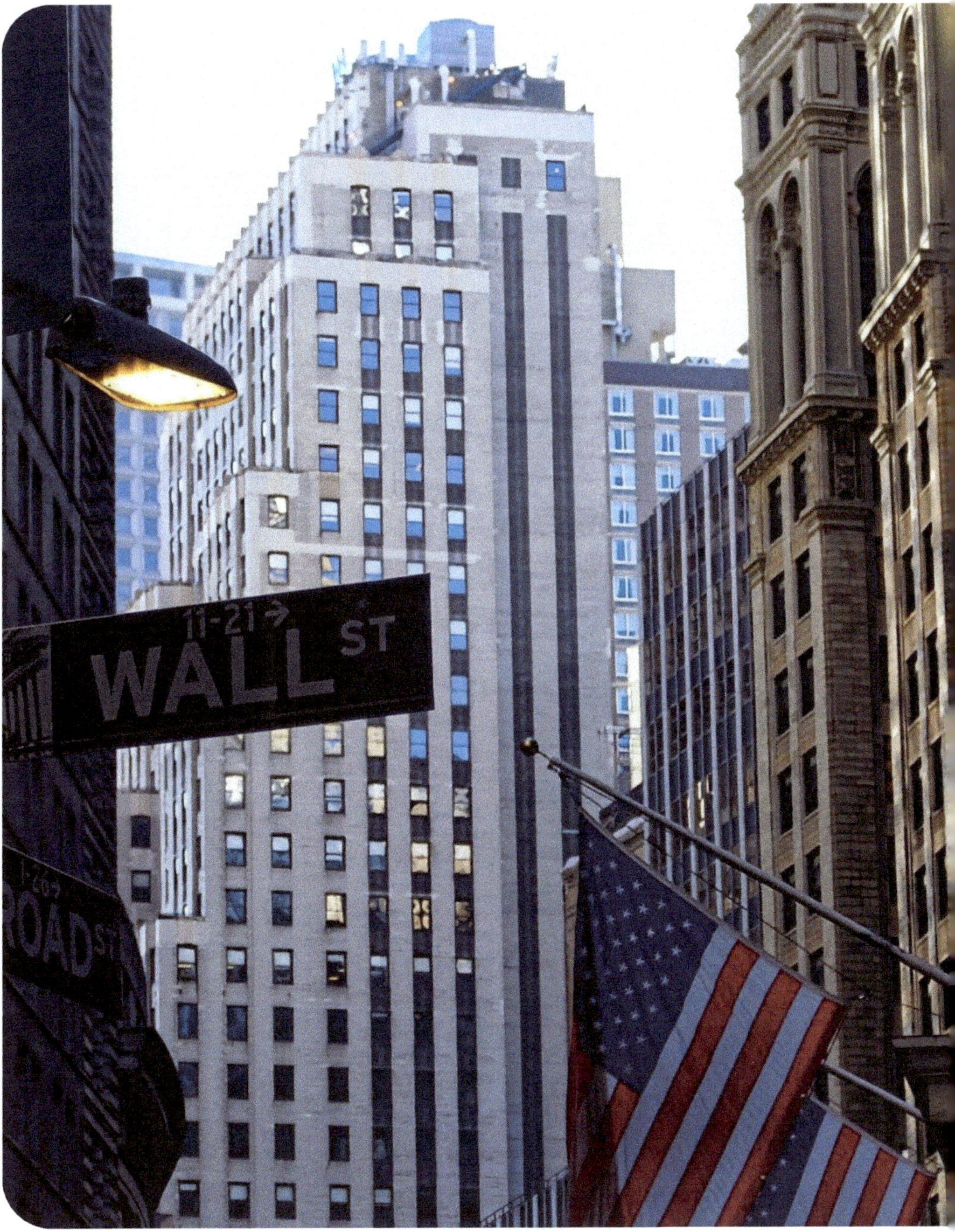
11-21
WALL ST
ROAD ST

Apprehend Germany's invasion of Poland at the

MUZEUM II WOJNY ŚWIATOWEJ W GDAŃSKU

#91   ⏱ **1933**
🗺 **POLAND**

The World War II Museum of Gdansk is a must-visit destination for history enthusiasts traveling to Poland. Opened in 2017, this impressive museum offers a comprehensive and immersive exploration of the events of World War II from the unique perspective of Poland and its people. One of the museum's most impactful sections is dedicated to the Holocaust. This sobering and comprehensive exhibit provides visitors with a profound and moving look at the devastating impact of the war on Poland's Jewish population. By sharing personal narratives and historical evidence, the museum ensures that the horrors of the Holocaust are never forgotten, while also inspiring reflection on the importance of human rights and social justice.

▶ After World War I, Adolf Hitler, the leader of the Nazi Party, quickly established a totalitarian regime in Germany. He believed that Germany's defeat in 1918 was due to the Weimar Republic, which he claimed was supported by Jews, Communists and Democrats. Hitler promoted the exclusion of these groups in favor of the Aryan race in order to restore the strength and greatness of Germany.

The economic crisis that began in 1929 made Germans more receptive to these racist theories. In the November 1932 legislative elections, the Nazi Party came in first place. On March 23rd, he obtained full power and on July 14th, the Nazi Party was declared the only party in Germany. Hitler then pursued an aggressive expansionist policy in Europe, annexing Austria and part of Czechoslovakia in 1938 and invading Poland on September 1st, 1939. On September 3rd, 1939, Great Britain and France declared war on the Third Reich.

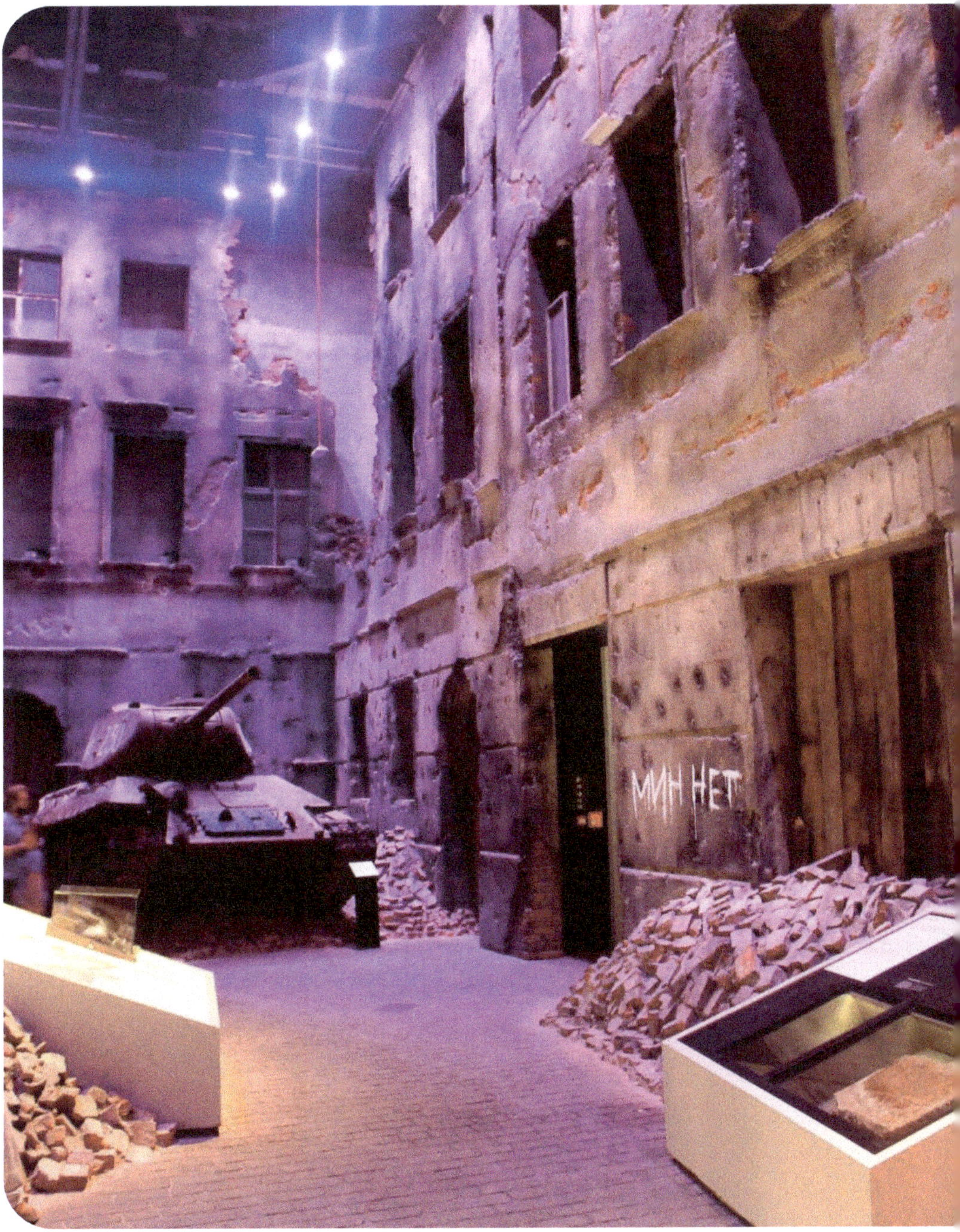
МИН НЕТ

Visualize the allied landing in

NORMANDY CEMETERY

#92

1944

FRANCE

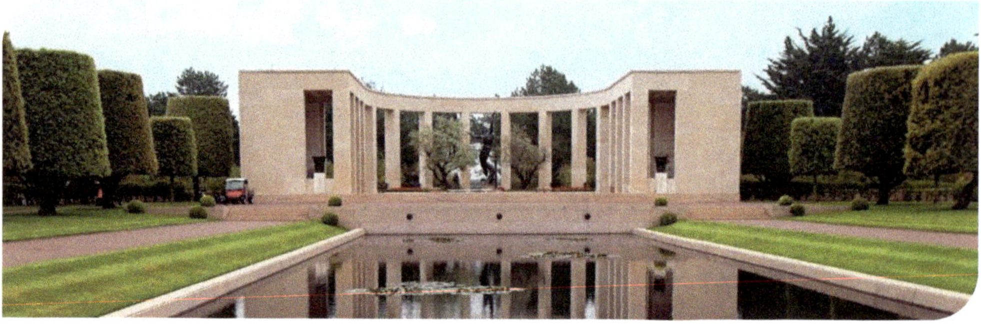

Normandy Cemetery, located in France, is a place steeped in history and significance. It was created after World War II to honor the American soldiers who gave their lives in the Battle of Normandy in 1944. The cemetery is located on the heights of Colleville-sur-Mer and is accessible to the public. It is maintained by the American Battle Monuments Commission and is considered one of the most famous and moving American military cemeteries in the world. Most of the soldiers buried here were killed during the Normandy landings in June 1944 and they came from all over the United States. The cemetery is a peaceful and moving place that commemorates the sacrifice of these soldiers and allows visitors to reflect and pay tribute to their memory.

▶ During the Tehran Conference in 1943, Allies Franklin Delano Roosevelt, Winston Churchill and Joseph Stalin decided to open an additional front in the west. This was to aid the Soviets in the east. After considering options between Normandy and Calais, they ultimately chose to launch a military landing on the coasts of Calvados and the English Channel. Under the command of American General Dwight Eisenhower, the Allies launched an assault on the Normandy coastline. On the night of June 5th to 6th, 1944, bombers pounded German fortifications and several hundred paratroopers were dropped to slow down enemy counterattacks. At the same time, ships set off from England heading towards France on the morning of June 6th and over 130,000 men landed on five beaches.

Despite 10,000 allied soldiers being injured or killed, the operation was a huge success. In two months, two million men, three million tons of equipment, and 430,000 vehicles were transported, allowing for the progressive liberation of France and Western Europe.

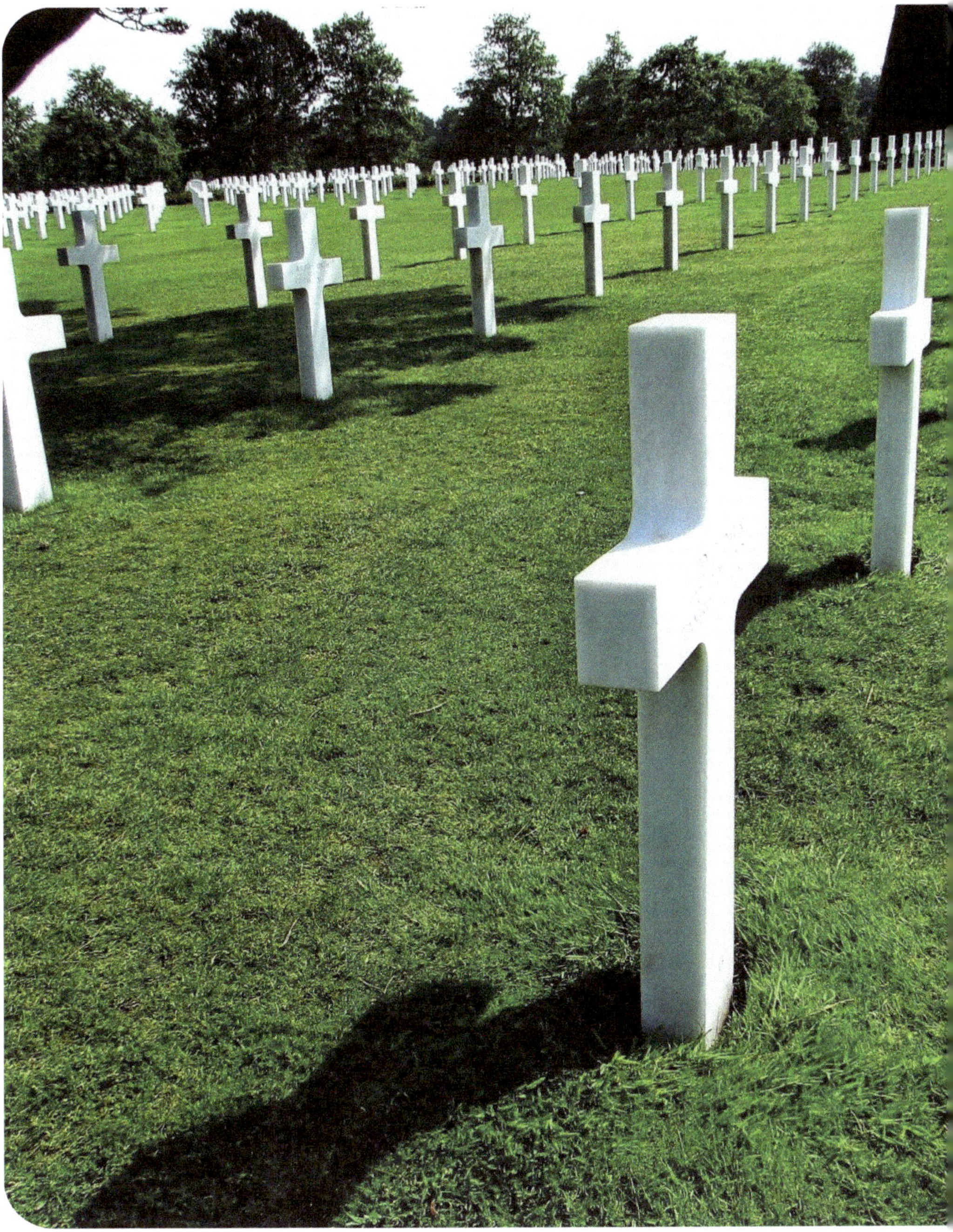

Witness the establishment of the United Nations Organization at the

PALACE OF NATIONS

#93

1945

SWITZERLAND

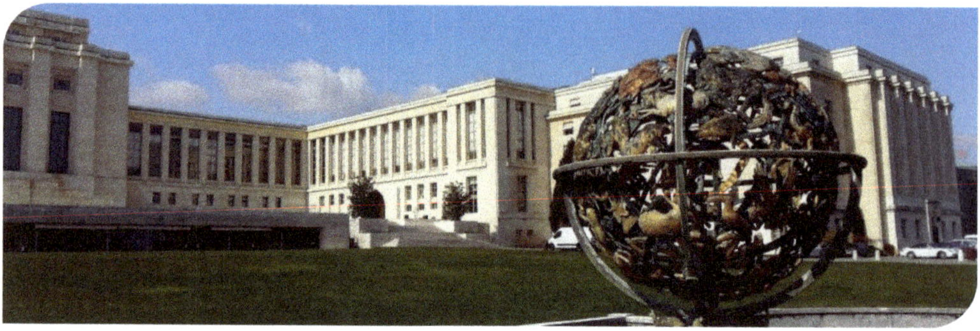

The Palais des Nations in Geneva is a must for history and architecture lovers. It was built in the 1930s to house the League of Nations, the precursor to the United Nations. Located on the Ariana hill, it owes its origins to John D. Rockefeller, who offered the League a library impossible to fit on the plots planned by the lake. During your visit, you can explore its many meeting rooms and discover the different organizations that work there. The building itself is a true architectural marvel, with its grand columns, intricate details, and impeccably manicured gardens. The sheer scale and grandeur of the Palais des Nations are a testament to the ambition and vision of its creators, who sought to establish a center for international cooperation and diplomacy.

► In 1945, during the Yalta and Potsdam conferences, the main allies, Great Britain, the United States, and the Soviet Union, established the foundations of the post-war world by deciding to disarm Germany, to divide it into three occupation zones, and to prosecute war criminals. A special tribunal was created in Nuremberg to try the main Nazi leaders. The United States did the same for the Japanese war leaders. Japan lost all the territories it had conquered in the last 50 years.

To ensure peace in this reconstructed world, the victors created the United Nations (UN) to replace the ineffective League of Nations (LoN). However, the Soviet Union and the United States had very different visions of the future world. They soon opposed each other, announcing the coming conflict between the East and the West, the Cold War. The term cold war was coined by the British statesman and writer George Orwell in his essay You and the Atomic Bomb in 1945. He used it to describe the uneasy relationship between the US and the Soviet Union in the aftermath of WWII.

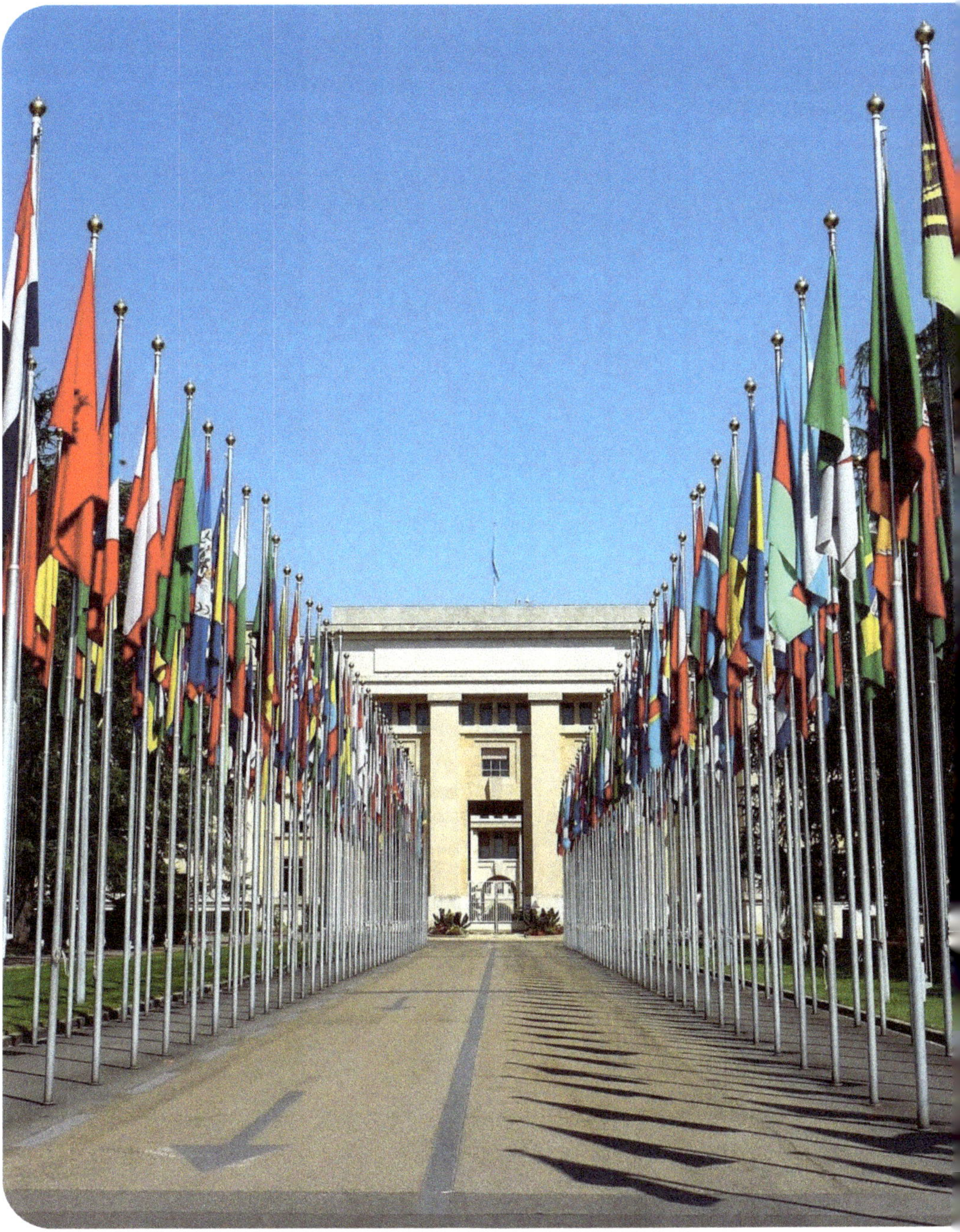

Picture Mao Zedong's establishment of the People's Republic of China inside the

FORBIDDEN CITY

#94 1949 CHINA

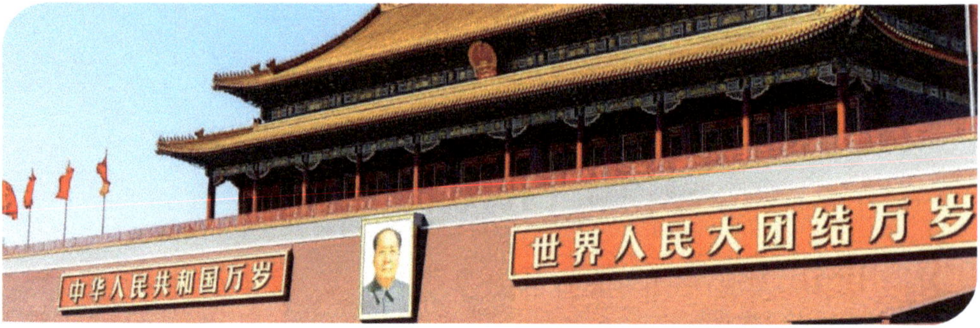
中华人民共和国万岁
世界人民大团结万岁

The Forbidden City is the palace of the Chinese emperors of the Ming and Qing Dynasties, which ruled China from the fifteenth century to the early twentieth century. It was built between 1406 and 1420 and served 24 Chinese emperors until 1911. It is now a museum presenting artistic and cultural treasures and is considered one of the five greatest palaces in the world. It was classified by UNESCO as a World Cultural Heritage Site in 1987 and is one of the most famous and visited sites in China. The Gate of Heavenly Peace is the main entrance to the Forbidden City in Beijing, China and is a symbol of Chinese imperial power. It was built during the Ming Dynasty in 1420 and is adorned with intricate carvings and inscriptions.

► In 1949, the Chinese communists led by Mao Zedong won the power struggle that had opposed them to the nationalists led by Chiang Kai-shek since 1927. The nationalists were sent out to Taiwan. On October 1st, 1949, Mao Zedong proclaimed the People's Republic of China from the balcony of the Gate of Heavenly Peace, in front of the entrance of the Forbidden City overlooking Tiananmen Square.

Thanks to the fame he had acquired during the struggle against the Japanese occupation (1937-1945) and the support of the peasant population, the Chinese Communist Party (CCP) then dominated the country's political life. From the moment he came to power, Mao's opponents were persecuted and sent to labor reeducation camps. In 1958, the Great Leap Forward program forced family-run peasant farms to group together in collective structures that had to carry out both agricultural and industrial work. This restructuring disrupted production and led to a terrible famine that caused more than 30 million deaths.

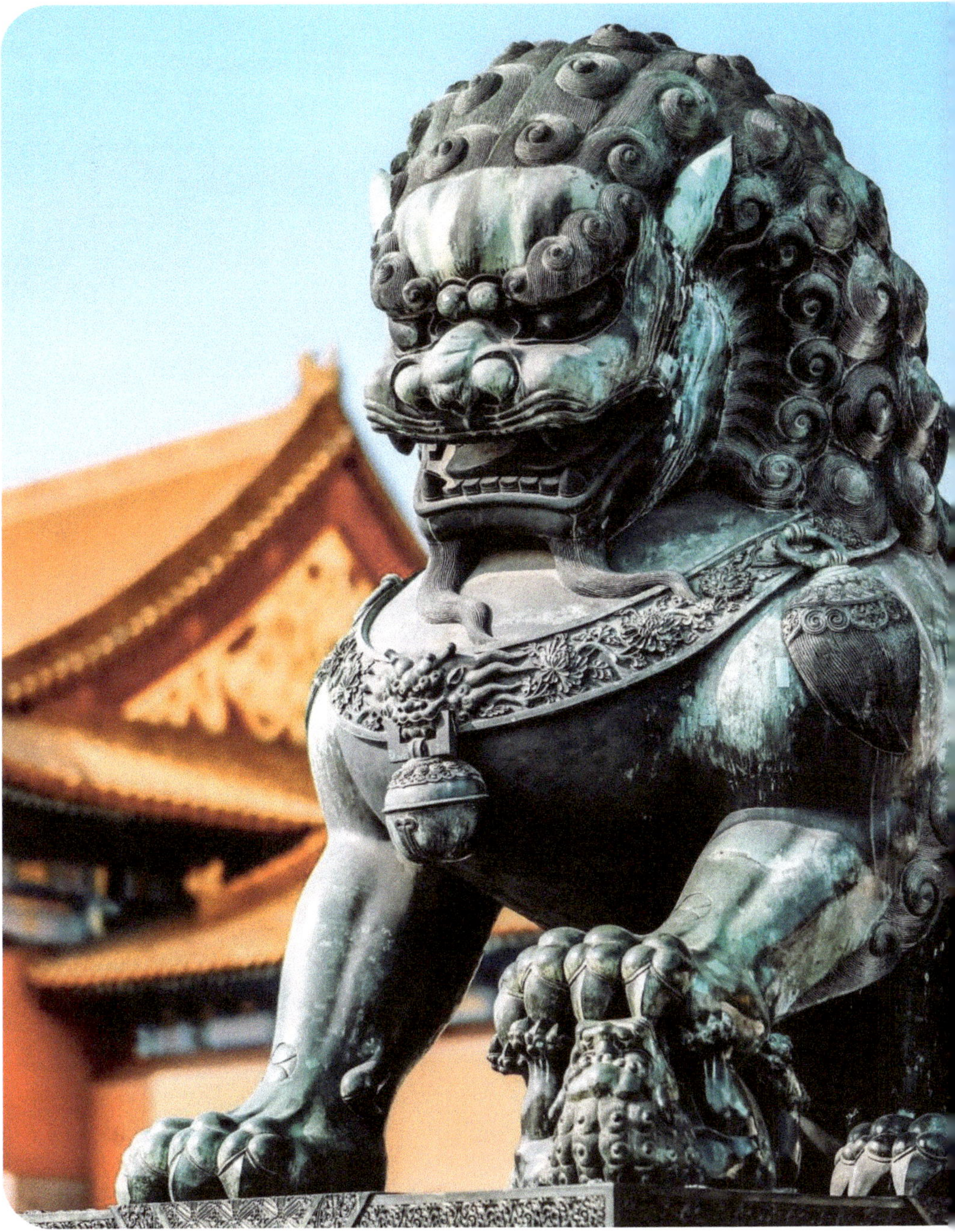

Relive the Vietnam War through the

CU CHI TUNNELS

#95 1955 VIET NAM

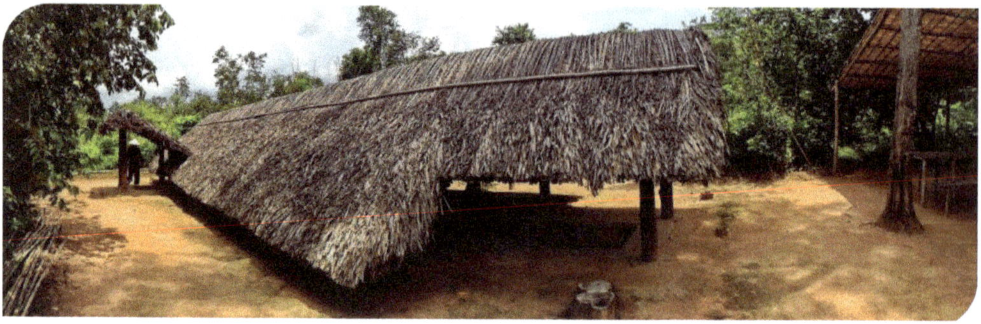

The Ho Chi Minh Tunnels are a network of underground tunnels that were used during the Vietnam War to move and hide. They were dug by the Viet Cong and their name comes from the famous Vietnamese leader Ho Chi Minh. The tunnels are located about 60 km north of Saigon and stretch for more than 250 km. They were used to move safely, to store food, water and weapons, and to hide from American bombing. Today, the Ho Chi Minh Tunnels have become a popular tourist site, where visitors can explore the tunnels and learn about the history of the Vietnam War. If you are interested in the history of war or looking for an unforgettable experience, a trip to the Ho-Chi Minh Tunnels is definitely something to add to your list of things to do.

► The Vietnam War was a crucial moment in the Cold War between the United States and the communist bloc led by the Soviet Union, China, and many national resistance movements. On January 30th, 1968, the National Front for the Liberation of South Vietnam (NLF) took advantage of the Tet holiday to launch a general offensive and simultaneously assault a hundred cities with thousands of fighters. Commandos attempted to seize the presidential palace in Saigon, now Ho Chi Minh City.

This offensive was a turning point in the war, as the United States began to lose ground in Vietnam and American public opinion turned against the war. This event was the first domino that led to the defeat of the United States, considered invincible. The Tet Offensive was actually a military failure for the NLF, but it had a significant impact on American public opinion and media coverage of the war. It marked a turning point in the war, as it revealed the true scale and brutality of the conflict. This led to a decline in support for the war among the American people.

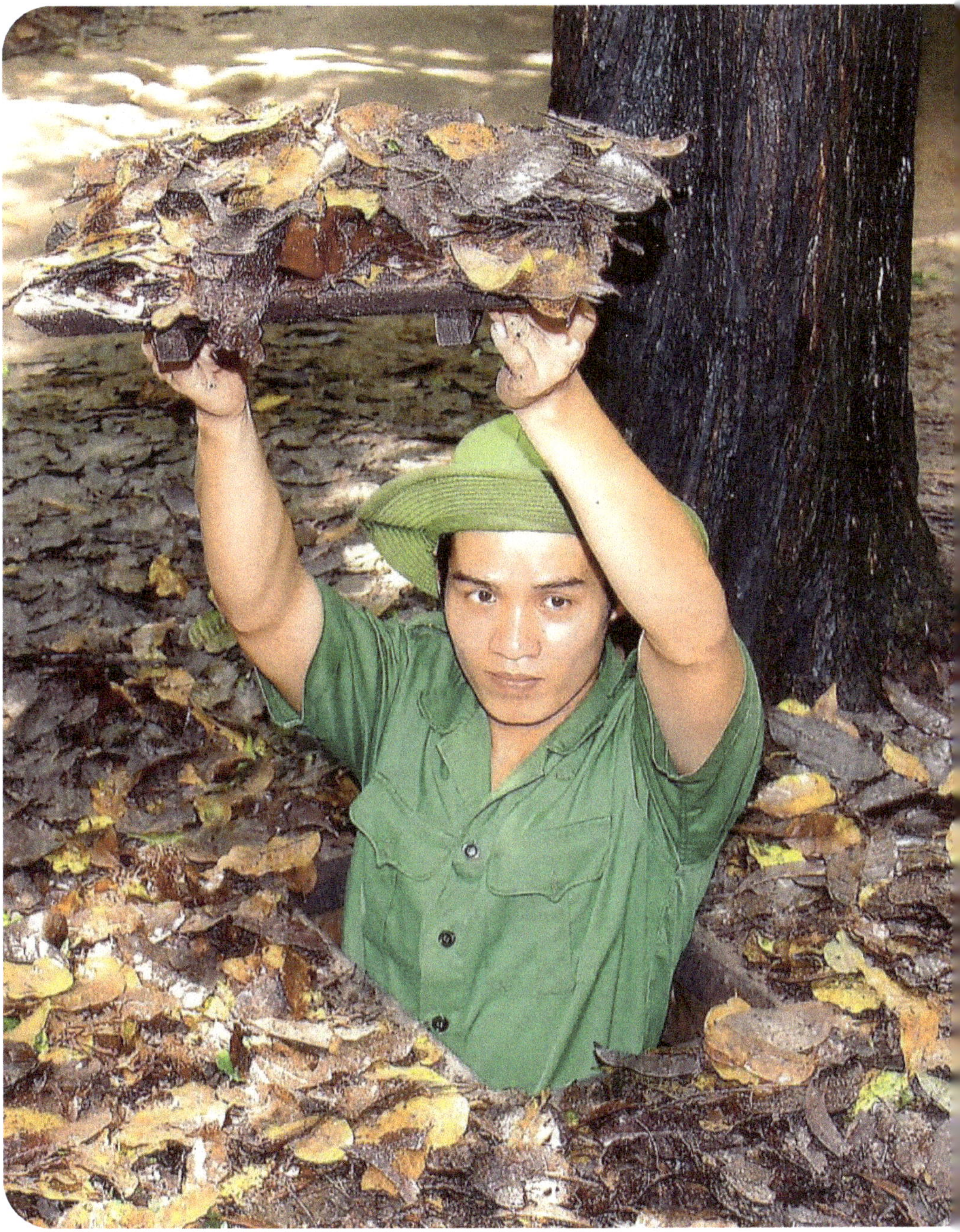

Visualize the first man to fly into space at the

AERONAUTICAL MUSEUM

#96 1961 RUSSIA

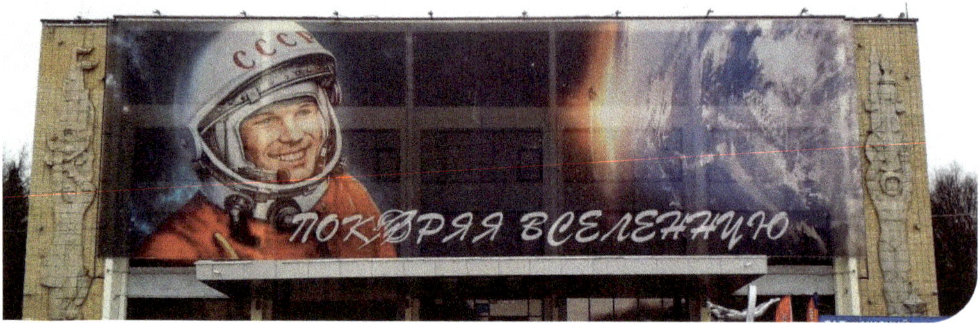
CCCP
ПОКОРЯЯ ВСЕЛЕННУЮ

The Moscow Aeronautical Museum is a true gem for enthusiasts of aviation and space history. Located within the expansive National Economy Achievements Exhibition Park, this museum is easily accessible via the metro, making it a convenient destination for visitors to the Russian capital. The museum's collection is nothing short of astounding, boasting over 150,000 objects and historical documents related to the fields of aviation and aeronautics. From historic aircraft and model rockets to the actual uniforms worn by Soviet space pioneers, the museum offers a comprehensive and immersive experience for its guests. Visitors can delve into the fascinating world of aviation and space exploration through the museum's interactive exhibits and captivating films.

▶ On April 21, 1961, the unimaginable became reality: the Soviet Union succeeded in sending a man into space. Iouri Gagarin, measuring 1.58m, was chosen among the candidates for the Soviet space program for his exemplary physical and mental condition, as well as for his modest background. This made him an ideal example of Soviet equality. The launch took place at the Baikonur Cosmodrome, after numerous unmanned tests.

However, the risk was still high as only 8 out of 16 previously launched rockets had succeeded in taking off. At 9:07, Vostok 1 left Earth and the Soviet team was exalting. Gagarin spent 1 hour and 48 minutes in orbit around the planet and was welcomed as a hero upon his return. However, Vostok 1 was his only and last flight in space, as he died in a plane crash at the age of 34, on March 27, 1968. Gagarin became the first human to journey into outer space. His historic flight paved the way for future space missions and inspired generations of scientists, engineers, and adventurers to push the boundaries of what is possible.

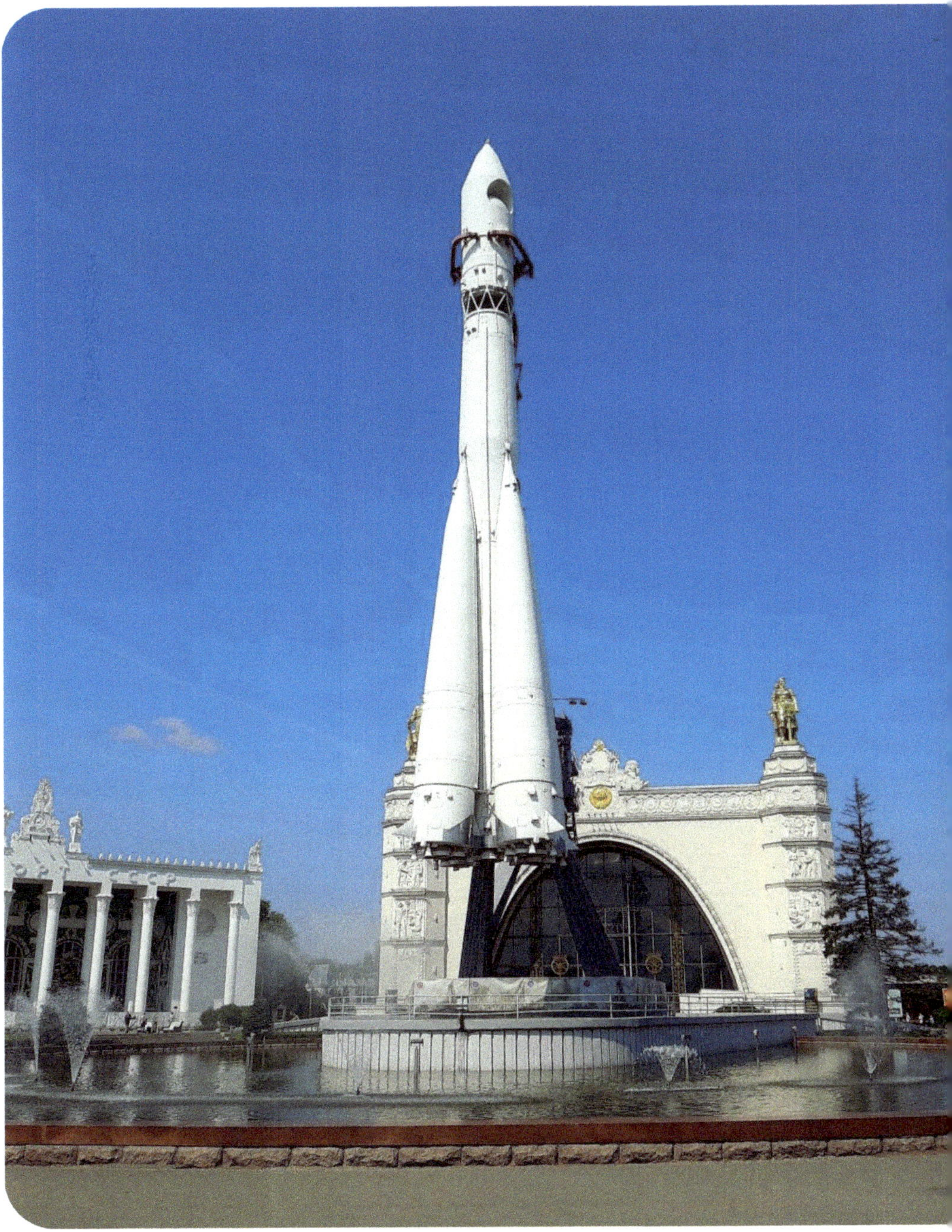

Witness Nelson Mandela's imprisonment and fight against the apartheid at the

ROBBEN ISLAND MUSEUM

#97 ⏱ 1962

🗺 **SOUTH AFRICA**

Off the coast of Cape Town, South Africa, is the historic site known as Robben Island. Nelson Mandela notably spent 18 years there while being held as a political prison during the apartheid era. The museum now serves as a poignant reminder of South Africa's turbulent past and democratic struggle. On a guided tour of the island, visitors may see the jail cells, the limestone quarry where convicts toiled, and discover the island's history. The museum also has displays about the anti-apartheid movement and the difficulties South Africans experienced at the time. Visiting the Robben Island Museum is a moving experience and provides an opportunity to learn about the struggle for justice and equality in South Africa.

▶ Founded in South Africa in 1948, the racial apartheid state is contested by the African National Congress (ANC), the leading black defense organization. In 1962, Nelson Mandela, one of its most prominent leaders, is put behind bars. Several ethnic groups lived apart from one another throughout apartheid. Indians, Coloreds, and Blacks resided in congested ghettos on the periphery, while Whites, who made up the majority, lived in privileged inner-city neighborhoods. Radical change resulted upon Frederik de Klerk's ascension to power in 1989.

Nelson Mandela was released from prison on February 11, 1990, at the age of 72, with his fist raised and prepared to carry on the fight for equality. Once de Klerk ended apartheid in 1991, all citizens, whether white or black, were granted the right to vote. On December 10, 1993, Nelson Mandela and Frederik de Klerk received the Nobel Peace Prize together in Oslo for their work in putting an end to apartheid and laying the groundwork for democracy in South Africa.

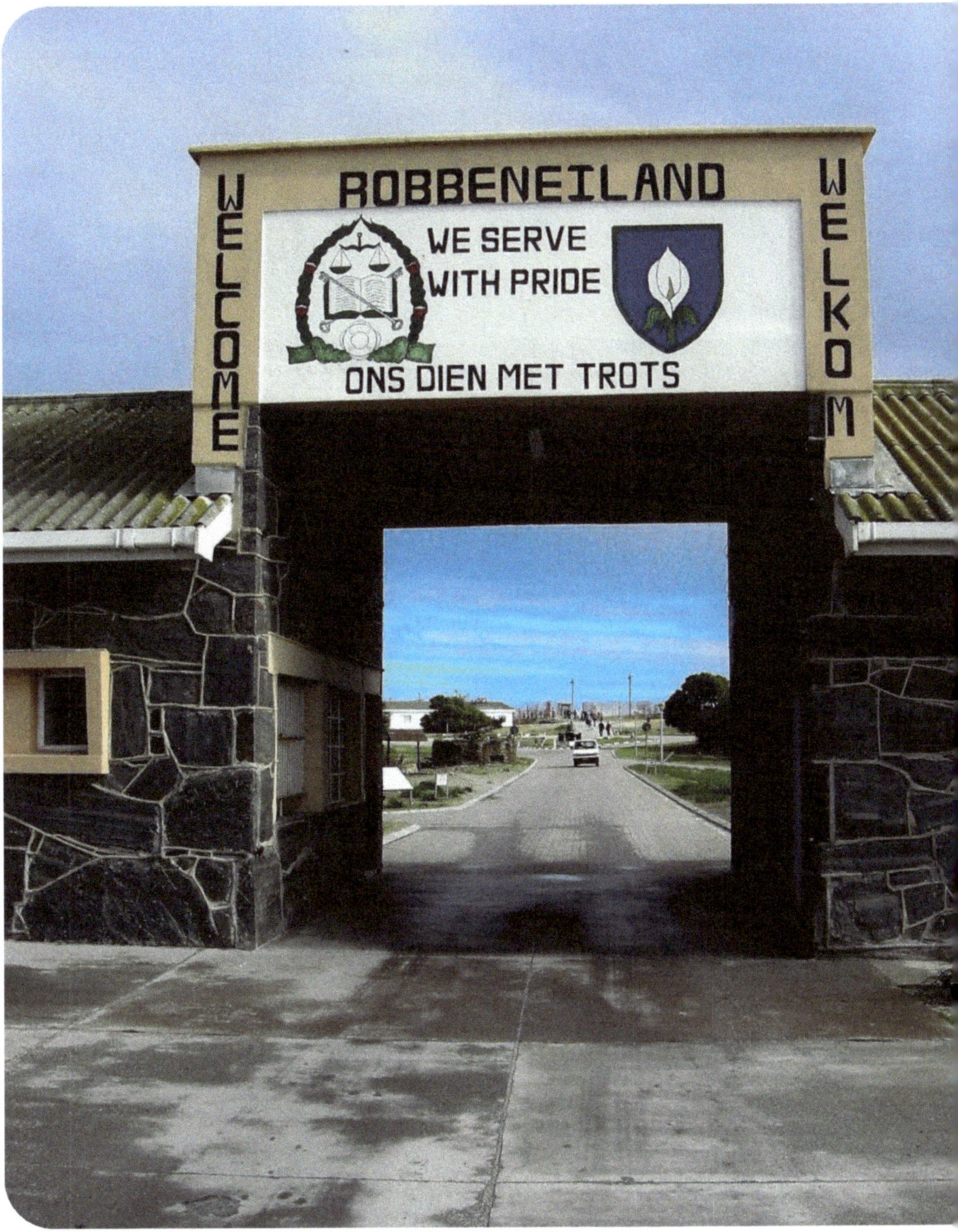
ROBBENEILAND
WELCOME
WELKOM
WE SERVE
WITH PRIDE
ONS DIEN MET TROTS

Conceive the first man on the moon at the

NEIL ARMSTRONG MUSEUM OF AIR AND SPACE

#98 🕐 1969
🗺 USA

The Neil Armstrong Air and Space Museum is a must-see for lovers of aeronautical and space history. Located in Wapakoneta, Ohio, this museum pays tribute to one of the most famous astronauts of all time, Neil Armstrong. The museum is full of interactive exhibits and models of spaceships that will appeal to young and old alike. You can also discover the history of aeronautics through the ages, from the first flight to the conquest of space. The museum also has a movie theater where films about space and space missions are shown. If you are looking for an exciting and informative activity, the Neil Armstrong Museum of Air and Space is the place to be.

▶ During the Cold War, another type of competition emerged, that of space. This is how the Apollo program was launched on May 25, 1961 by President John Fitzgerald Kennedy, aiming for a landing on the Moon. After the first man was launched into space, Yuri Gagarin in March 1962, the United States had to react quickly. After many years of research and many launches, NASA successfully sent, on July 16, 1969, aboard the Apollo 11 spacecraft, the first team to land on the Moon. The two people who walked on the Moon, Neil Armstrong and Buzz Aldrin, were accompanied by a man who was often forgotten, Michael Collins, who remained in the spacecraft.

Millions of people around the globe tuned in to witness the live broadcast as Neil Armstrong placed his boot onto the powdery gray regolith, and uttered the now-iconic words: "That's one small step for man, one giant leap for mankind."

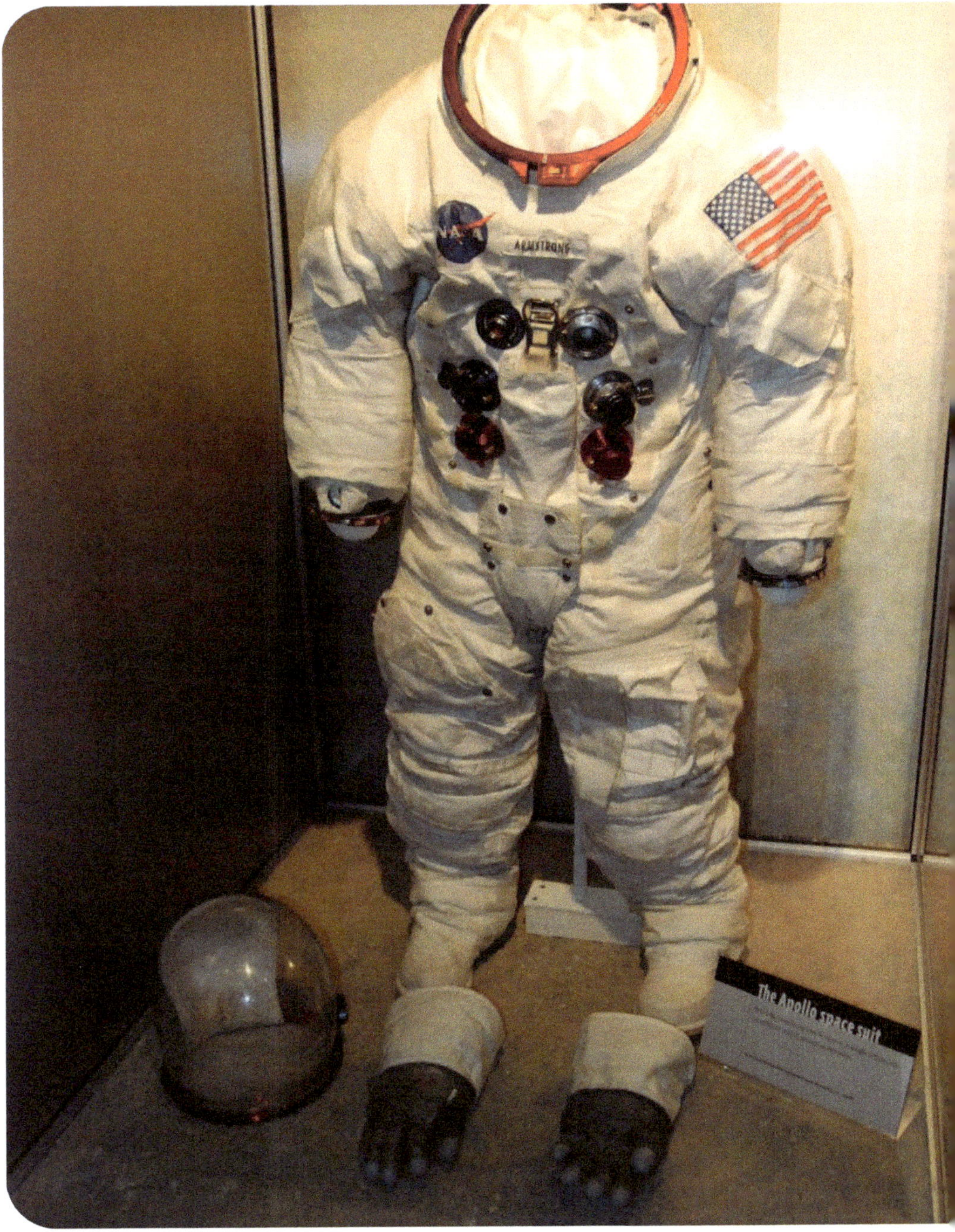
ARMSTRONG
The Apollo space suit

Experience the fall of the Berlin Wall and end of the Cold War at the

CHECKPOINT CHARLIE

#99 1989 **GERMANY**

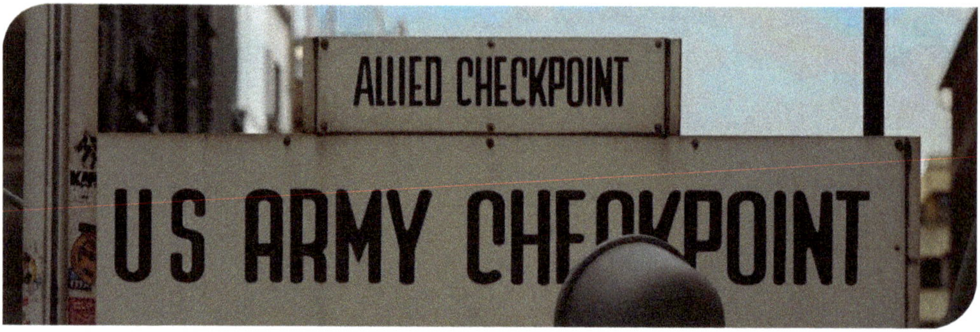
ALLIED CHECKPOINT
US ARMY CHE

Checkpoint Charlie was one of the most iconic crossing points between West and East Berlin during the tumultuous years of the Cold War. It served as the sole authorized transit point where Westerners could enter the Soviet-controlled sector of the divided city, and vice versa. The checkpoint gained global notoriety during the tense standoff of the Cuban Missile Crisis in 1962, when the United States and the Soviet Union came dangerously close to engaging in open warfare, heightening the already palpable tensions at this strategic border crossing. For those with an interest in the history and geopolitics of the 20th century, a visit to Checkpoint Charlie is a must-do experience. The site serves as a poignant reminder of the sacrifices, struggles, and triumphs that defined a turbulent period in European and global history.

► On August 12th, 1961, East Germany accused the powers of NATO of sabotaging the East German economy by inciting unstable elements of the population to leave their homes. This was done using lies, corruption, and blackmail. In response, East Germany decided to restore order by closing all communication routes except for twelve and dividing Berlin in two with barbed wire coils. Western Berliners waited in vain for confirmation that the Americans would come to their aid as they had done in 1948. Meanwhile, the East Germans cut postal and telephone connections and announced that Western cars would no longer be able to drive in East Berlin.

The Western powers finally decided to react by organizing an air bridge to supply West Berlin with food and fuel. The Berlin airlift, known as Operation Vittles, was the largest humanitarian airlift in history, delivering over 2.3 million tons of supplies to the people of West Berlin between June 1948 and May 1949.

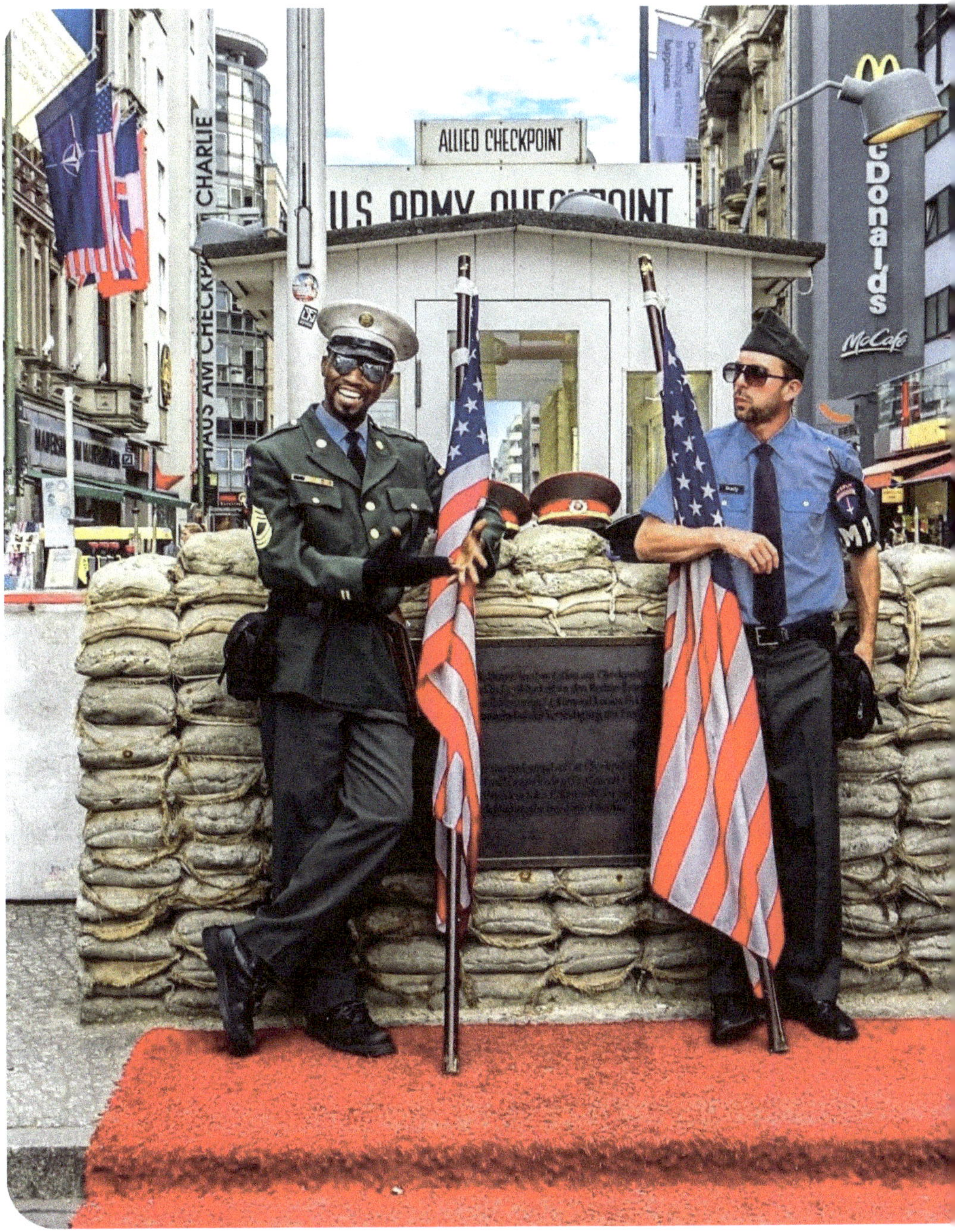
ALLIED CHECKPOINT
CHARLIE
McCafé

Witness the birth of the Internet at CERN's

SCIENCE GATEWAY

#100 ⏱ 1995

🗺 SWITZERLAND

The CERN Science Gateway is an exciting new visitor and education center that will allow the public, including school groups, to experience the world of particle physics and scientific research at CERN. Designed to ignite curiosity and inspire the next generation of scientists, this state-of-the-art facility will feature a wide array of hands-on education labs, captivating multimedia exhibits, and dynamic science shows that bring the mysteries of the universe to life. The Science Gateway features hands-on education labs, immersive multimedia exhibits, and science shows that bring the mysteries of the universe to life. Visitors can to see a real particle accelerator in action and learn about the big bang and the quantum world.

▶ At the end of 1989, Tim Berners-Lee, a British physicist working at the European Organization for Nuclear Research (CERN), wrote the first proposal for the creation of an online information sharing system, called the World Wide Web (WWW). He then collaborated with Belgian engineer Robert Cailliau to improve the project. In November 1990, they developed a formal version of their proposal that described the fundamental concepts and key terms related to the web. Their goal was to allow scientists working in universities and institutes worldwide to share information in real-time.

In 1991, they developed prototype software for a basic web system, with an interface to encourage adoption and applied it to the CERN computer center's documentation center. This is how Tim Berners-Lee launched his first WWW software, which included an online mode browser, software for the web server and a library for developers. The first website ever created by Tim Berners-Lee is still online and can be accessed at *info.cern.ch/hypertext/WWW/TheProject.html.*

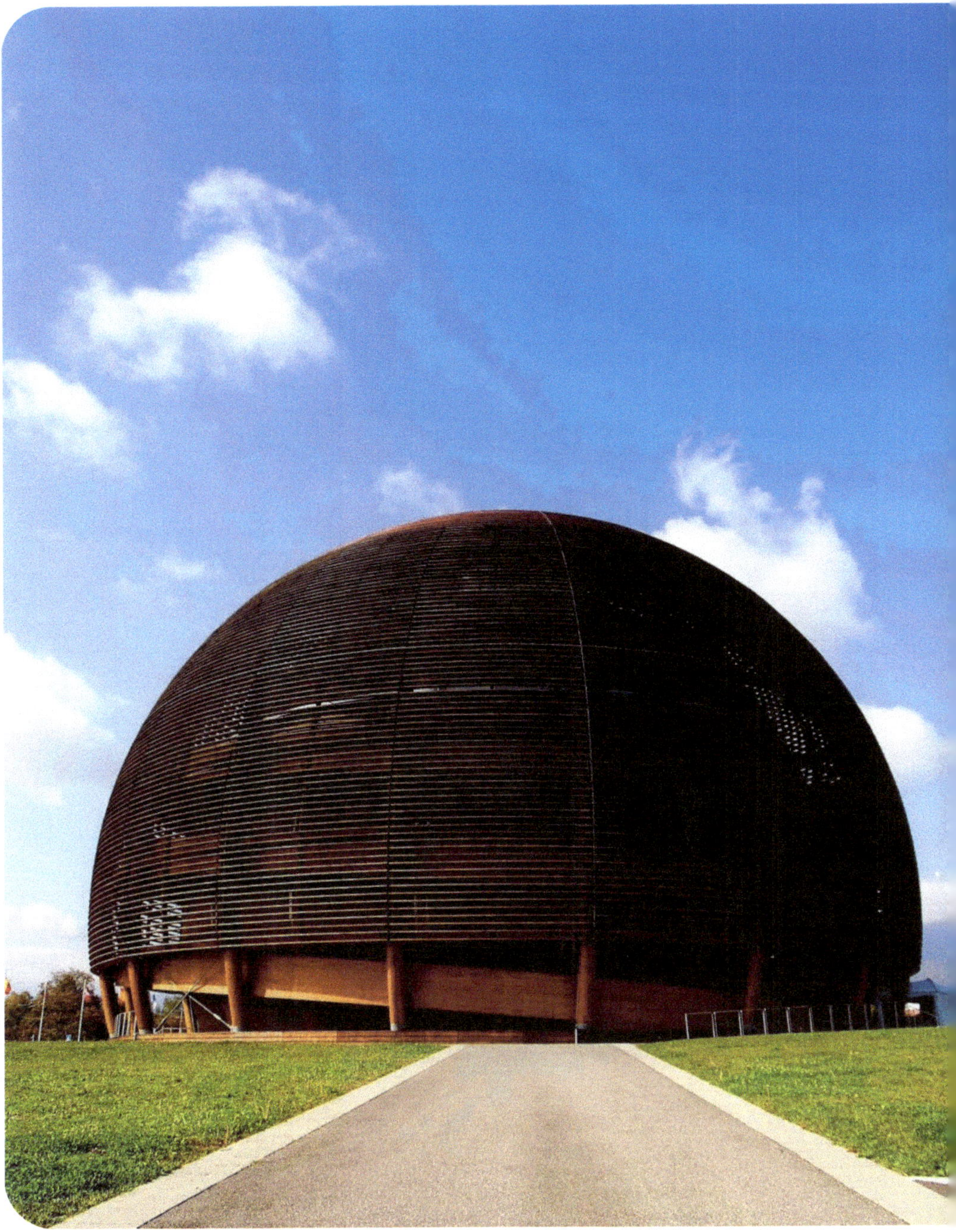

CREDITS

The copyright is indicated with the page number on which the work is reproduced. If, despite all our care, an error or omission has occurred, we apologize in advance and will be happy to make the necessary correction(s) in a future edition.

p.12 Romainbehar, CC0, via Wikimedia Commons; **p.13** Harp, CC BY-SA 3.0, via Wikimedia Commons; **p.15** Melizabethi123, CC BY-SA 3.0, via Wikimedia Commons; **p.16** O.Mustafin, CC0, via Wikimedia Commons; **p.17** Neanderthal-Museum, Mettmann, CC BY-SA 4.0, via Wikimedia Commons; **p.18** JanManu, CC BY-SA 4.0, via Wikimedia Commons; **p.19** JoJan, CC BY 4.0, via Wikimedia Commons; **p.22** Tla2006 sur Wikipédia anglais, Public domain, via Wikimedia Commons; **p.23** Kaufingdude, CC BY-SA 3.0, via Wikimedia Commons; **p.24** henryleester, CC0, via pixabay; **p.25** Abdelrhman Allam, CC0, via Unsplash; **p.26** Lapplaender, CC BY-SA 3.0 DE, via Wikimedia Commons; **p.27** Leonhard_Niederwimmer, CC0, via pixabay; **p.28** Girl with red hat, CC0, via Unsplash; **p.29** MohammadHuzam, CC BY-SA 4.0, via Wikimedia Commons; **p.30** brianneises, CC0, via pixabay; **p.31** Sharon Hahn Darlin, CC BY 2.0, via Wikimedia Commons; **p.32** Pier B., CC BY-SA 3.0, via Wikimedia Commons; **p.33** Vadim Zhivotovsky, CC BY 3.0, via Wikimedia Commons; **p.34** Safa.daneshvar, CC BY-SA 4.0, via Wikimedia Commons; **p.35** Solider 16IQ, CC BY-SA 4.0, via Wikimedia Commons; **p.37** Bpilgrim, CC BY-SA 2.5, via Wikimedia Commons; **p.38** Vmenkov, CC BY-SA 3.0, via Wikimedia Commons; **p.39** Vmenkov, CC BY-SA 3.0 , via Wikimedia Commons; **p.40** Diego Delso, CC BY-SA 4.0, via Wikimedia Commons; **p.41** Amirabbas Fanaei, CC0, via Unsplash; **p.42** George Fournaris, CC BY-SA 4.0, via Wikimedia Commons; **p.44** Jim Niakaris, CC0, via Unsplash; **p.45** free public domain CC0, via rawpixel; **p.46** dimitrisvetsikas1969, CC0, via pixabay; **p.47** berndmalle, CC0, via pixabay; **p.48** Jamie Street, CC0, via Unsplash; **p.49** MemoryCatcher, CC0, via pixabay; **p.50** Максим Улитин, CC BY 3.0, via Wikimedia Commons; **p.51** Benreis, CC BY-SA 3.0, via Wikimedia Commons; **p.52** Abio Fistarol, CC0, via Unsplash; **p.53** Katie Kalmykova, CC0, via Unsplash; **p.54** Fabio Fistarol, CC0, via Unsplash; **p.55** Juanma Clemente Alloz, CC0, via Unsplash **p.56** MumblerJamie, CC BY-SA 2.0, via Wikimedia Commons; **p.57** Clemens Van Lay, CC0, via Unsplash; **p.58** guertzen, CC0, via pixabay; **p.59** Che_co, CC0, via pixabay; **p.60** Anton Mislawsky, CC0, via Unsplash; **p.61** Shraga Kopstein, CC0, via Unsplash; **p.62** bogles, CC0, via pixabay; **p.63** Mathilde Ro, CC0, via Unsplash; **p.64** Barosaurus Lentus, CC BY 3.0, via Wikimedia Commons; **p.65** Helen Simonsson, CC BY-SA 3.0, via Wikimedia Commons; **p.66** mana5280, CC0, via Unsplash; **p.67** dancepool, CC0, via pixabay; **p.68** Bollweevil, CC BY-SA 3.0, via Wikimedia Commons; **p.69** Dmitry A. Mottl, CC BY-SA 4.0, via Wikimedia Commons; **p.70** Mick Night, CC0, via Unsplash; **p.71** Rafaella Ferraro, CC0, via Unsplash; **p.74** Dylan Shaw, CC0, via Unsplash; **p.75** Jannes Jacobs, CC0, via Unsplash; **p.76** DEZALB, CC0, via pixabay; **p.77** Michelle Williams, CC0, via Unsplash; **p.78** Ri_Ya, CC0, via pixabay; **p.79** Dan Gold, CC0, via Unsplash; **p.80** DEZALB, CC0, via pixabay; **p.81** MrChris89, CC0, via pixabay; **p.82** Julo, CC0, via Wikimedia Commons; **p.83** Radosław Botev, CC BY 3.0 PL, via Wikimedia Commons; **p.84** waldomiguez, CC0, via pixabay; **p.85** Girl with red hat, CC0, via Unsplash; **p.86** Geolina163, CC BY-SA 3.0, via Wikimedia Commons; **p.87** Alex Riechert, CC BY-SA 3.0, via Wikimedia Commons; **p.89** Elenarts, CC0, via pixabay; **p.90** Leon Petrosyan, CC BY-SA 3.0, via Wikimedia Commons; **p.91** Neitram, CC BY-SA 4.0, via Wikimedia Commons; **p.92** Pawel Ryszawa, CC BY 3.0, via Wikimedia Commons; **p.93** Girl with red hat, CC0, via Unsplash; **p.94** CC0, via rawpixel; **p.95** Raimond Klavins, CC0, via Unsplash; **p.96** Joe Planas, CC0, via Unsplash; **p.97** Iyad, CC0, via pixabay; **p.98** pen_ash, CC0, via pixabay; **p.99** Sushuti, CC0, via pixabay; **p.100** Zairon, CC BY-SA 4.0, via Wikimedia Commons; **p.101** Tsuyoshi chiba, CC BY-SA 4.0, via Wikimedia Commons; **p.102** Patrick Schneider, CC0, via Unsplash; **p.103** Tolunay Karavar, CC0, via Unsplash; **p.104** Axp-photography, CC0, via Unsplash; **p.105** Catherine Zaidova, CC0, via Unsplash; **p.107** Parpan05, CC BY-SA 4.0, via Wikimedia Commons; **p.109** albertocalzari, CC0, via pixabay; **p.110** Mousssa NIAKATE, CC BY-SA 4.0, via Wikimedia Commons; **p.111** Francesco Bandarin, CC BY-SA 4.0, via Wikimedia Commons; **p.112** David Klein, CC0, via Unsplash; **p.113** Martin Falbisoner, CC BY-SA 4.0, via Wikimedia Commons; **p.114** Axp-photography, CC0, via Unsplash; **p.115** Axp-photography, CC0, via Unsplash; **p.116** Nick Fewings, CC0, via Unsplash; **p.117** Giuseppe Mondi, CC0, via Unsplash; **p.118** Pedelecs, CC BY-SA 3.0, via Wikimedia Commons; **p.120** A.Savin, FAL, CC0, via Wikimedia Commons; **p.121** Carole Raddato, CC BY-SA 2.0, via

Wikimedia Commons; **p.122** Jebulon, CC0, via Wikimedia Commons; **p.123** Karabo_Spain, CC0, via pixabay; **p.126** Anual, CC BY 3.0, via Wikimedia Commons; **p.127** Hispalois, CC BY-SA 3.0, via Wikimedia Commons; **p.129** jemafg, CC0, via pixabay; **p.130** joeblack564, CC0, via pixabay; **p.131** Jörg Bittner Unna, CC BY 3.0, via Wikimedia Commons; **p.132** Dorian Mongel, CC0, via Unsplash; **p.133** DJMT, CC0, via pixabay; **p.134** TomTyler, CC0, via pixabay; **p.135** MHM55, CC BY-SA 4.0, via Wikimedia Commons; **p.136** Ljuan99, CC BY-SA 4.0, via Wikimedia Commons; **p.137** sheomdesign, CC0, via pixabay; **p.138** Wolfgang Fricke, CC BY 3.0, via Wikimedia Commons; **p.139** Magallanes1, CC0, via Wikimedia Commons; **p.140** Pedro Lastra, CC0, via Unsplash; **p.141** Wells Baum, CC0, via Unsplash; **p.142** Allie Caulfield, CC BY 2.0, via Wikimedia Commons; **p.146** Bellina 09, CC BY-SA 4.0, via Wikimedia Commons; **p.147** Marie-Lan Nguyen, CC BY-SA 4.0, via Wikimedia Commons; **p.148** BeursvanBerlage, CC BY-SA 4.0, via Wikimedia Commons; **p.150** Pi3.124, CC BY-SA 4.0, via Wikimedia Commons; **p.152** Duernsteiner, CC0, via pixabay; **p.153** Fredy Martinez, CC0, via Unsplash; **p.154** Vyacheslav Argenberg, CC BY 4.0, via Wikimedia Commons; **p.155** Sanin-sn, CC0, via Unsplash; **p.158** Jorg Bauer, CC0, via Unsplash; **p.159** jensjunge, CC0, via pixabay; **p.160** Colin, CC0, via Wikimedia Commons; **p.161** Jdforrester, CC BY-SA 3.0, via Wikimedia Commons; **p.162** Maksym Kozlenko, CC BY-SA 3.0, via Wikimedia Commons; **p.165** USCapitol, Public domain, via Wikimedia Commons; **p.166** foursummers, CC0, via pixabay; **p.167** foursummers, CC0, via pixabay; **p.170** 139904, CC0, via pixabay; **p.171** waldomiguez, CC0, via pixabay; **p.174** AnnDixon, CC0, via pixabay; **p.175** 12019, CC0, via pixabay; **p.176** EneasMx, CC BY-SA 4.0, via Wikimedia Commons; **p.177** Daniel A. Acosta R., CC BY-SA 3.0, via Wikimedia Commons; **p.179** Tony Hisgett, CC BY 2.0, via Wikimedia Commons; **p.182** wasi1370, CC0, via pixabay; **p.183** xat-ch, CC0, via pixabay; **p.184** Henry Mühlpfordt, CC BY-SA 3.0, via Wikimedia Commons; **p.186** Martin Falbisoner, CC BY-SA 4.0, via Wikimedia Commons; **p.188** Diego Delso, CC BY-SA 4.0, via Wikimedia Commons; **p.189** Lasermanmcgee, CC BY-SA 4.0, via Wikimedia Commons; **p.192** Rilba, CC BY-SA 3.0, via Wikimedia Commons; **p.193** Mbzt, CC BY 3.0, via Wikimedia Commons; **p.195** Mastrchf91, CC BY 4.0, via Wikimedia Commons; **p.196** soviet-artefacts, CC0, via Unsplash; **p.197** Don-vip, CC BY-SA 4.0, via Wikimedia Commons; **p.198** Tiffany Cade, CC0, via Unsplash; **p.199** 12857833, CC0, via pixabay; **p.200** bones64, CC0, via pixabay; **p.203** Andrzej Otrębski, CC BY-SA 4.0, via Wikimedia Commons; **p.205** csharker, CC0, via pixabay; **p.207** Cayla, CC BY-SA 3.0, via Wikimedia Commons; **p.208** viarami, CC0, via pixabay; **p.209** wong zihoo, CC0, via Unsplash; **p.210** trungydang, CC BY 3.0, via Wikimedia Commons; **p.211** Wong Zihoo, CC0, via Unsplash; **p.212** Sergey Sebelev, CC BY-SA 4.0, via Wikimedia Commons; **p.214** South African Tourism from South Africa, CC BY 2.0, via Wikimedia Commons; **p.215** Francesco Bandarin, CC BY-SA 3.0, via Wikimedia Commons; **p.216** Tysto, Public domain, via Wikimedia Commons; **p.218** Gzen92, CC BY-SA 4.0, via Wikimedia Commons; **p.219** pcjvdwiel, CC0, via pixabay; **p.221** Tryfon Kar, CC BY-SA 3.0, via Wikimedia Commons;

INDEX PER COUNTRY

AUSTRALIA
Captain Cook's Landing Place, *162*

AUSTRIA
Hofburg Palace, *158*

BOSNIA
Sarajevo Museum 1878–1918, *194*

BRAZIL
Christ the Redeemer, *58*

CAMBODIA
Angkor Wat, *98*

CHILE
Nao Victoria Museum, *138*

CHINA
Temple and cemetery of Confucius, *38*
Great Wall of China, *48*
The Forbidden City, *208*

CROATIA
Diocletian's Palace, *66*

CZECH REPUBLIC
Prague Castle, *152*

ECUADOR
Galapagos Islands, *182*

EGYPT
Great Pyramid of Giza, *24*

ETHIOPIA
National Museum of Ethiopia, *16*

FRANCE
Lascaux Caves, *18*
Basilica of Saint-Remi, *76*
Palace of the Popes, *108*
Chambord Castle, *132*
Republic Monument, *168*
Tomb of Napoleon., *170*
Museum of Arts and Crafts, *192*
Palace of Versailles, *198*
Normandy Cemetery, *204*

GERMANY
Aachen Cathedral, *86*
Gutenberg Museum, *118*
Checkpoint Charlie, *218*

GIBRALTAR
Pillars of Hercules, *82*

GREECE
Minoan Palace of Knossos, *26*
Marathon Mound, *42*
The Acropolis, *44*
Church of Saints Cyril and Methodius, *88*

HONG KONG
Hong Kong Bay, *180*

ICELAND
Viking World Museum, *90*

INDIA
Temple of Mahabodhi, *36*
Taj Mahal, *154*

IRAN
Persepolis, *40*
Sheikh Lotfollah Mosque, *92*

IRAQ
Ziggurat of Ur, *22*
Ishtar Gate, *28*
Winged bulls of Khorsabad, *34*

ISRAEL
Western Wall, *60*

ITALY
The Capitoline Wolf, *32*
Temple of Caesar, *52*
Mausoleum of Augustus, *56*
Ruins of Pompei, *62*
Column of Marcus Aurelius, *64*
Colosseum, *70*
Florence Cathedral, *116*
Galileo Museum, *156*

JAPAN
Kenchō-ji, *100*
Kinkaku-ji, *112*
Himeji Castle, *186*

JORDAN
Petra, *54*

MALI
Timbuktu, *110*

MALTA
Fort St. Elmo, *146*

MEXICO
Chichén Itzá, *80*
Teotihuacan, *136*

MONGOLIA
Equestrian statue of Genghis
Kahn, *102*

NETHERLANDS
Amsterdam Stock Exchange,
148

NORTH MACEDONIA
Statue of the warrior on
horseback, *46*

PALESTINE
The Dome of the Rock, *78*

PERU
Machu Picchu, *140*

POLAND
Collegium Maius, *142*
Muzeum II Wojny
Światowej w Gdańsku, *202*

PORTUGAL
Belem Tower, *128*

RUSSIA
St. Basil's Cathedral, *144*
Lenin Mausoleum, *196*
Aeronautical Museum, *212*

SOUTH AFRICA
Robben Island Museum, *214*

SPAIN
Great Mosque of Cordoba,
84
The Alhambra, *122*
Archives of India, *126*

SRI LANKA
Sigiriya Rock, *74*

SWITZERLAND
Large Hadron
Collider, *12,*
Grütli meadow, *106*
Wall of Reformers, *134*
Red Cross Museum, *184*
Palace of Nations, *206*
Science Gateway, *220*

SYRIA
Krak des Chevaliers, *96*

THAILAND
Royal Palace of Bangkok,
166

TUNISIA
Archaeological site of
Carthage, *50*

TURKEY
Trojan horse, *30*
Column of Constantine, *68*
Hagia Sophia Cathedral, *94*
Wall of Constantinople, *120*

UNITED KINGDOM
Westminster Abbey, *160*
Swindon Steam Railway
Museum, *178*

UNITED STATES
Smithsonian Museum Of
Natural History, *14*
Jamestown Settlement, *150*
The Capitol, *164*
Lincoln Memorial, *174*
Wall Street Stock Exchange.
200
Neil Armstrong Museum of
Air and Space, *216*

UZBEKISTAN
Registan Square, *104*
Go'ri Amir Mausoleum, *114*

VATICAN
Sistine Chapel, *130*

VENEZUELA
Mausoleum of Simón
Bolívar, *176*

VIETNAM
Cu Chi tunnels, *210*

ZIMBABWE
Victoria Falls, *188*

THEMATIC INDEX

NEW 7 WONDERS

Great Wall of China, 48
Petra, 54
Christ the Redeemer, 58
Colosseum, 70
Chichén Itzá, 80
Machu Picchu, 140
Taj Mahal, 154

ARCHEOLO-GICAL SITES

The Acropolis, 44
Angkor Wat, 98
Great Pyramid of Giza, 24
Ishtar Gate, 28
Krak des Chevaliers, 96
Winged bulls of Khorsabad, 34
Lascaux Caves, 18
Persepolis, 40
Ruins of Pompei, 62
Sigiriya Rock, 74
Temple of Caesar, 52
Teotihuacan, 136
Timbuktu, 110
Ziggurat of Ur, 22

CASTLES & PALACES

The Alhambra, 122
Belem Tower, 128
Chambord Castle, 132
The Capitol, 164
Diocletian's Palace, 66
Forbidden City, 208
Fort St. Elmo, 146
Himeji Castle, 186
Hofburg Palace, 158
Palace of Nations, 206
Minoan Palace of Knossos, 26
Palace of the Popes, 108
Palace of Versailles, 198
Prague Castle, 152
Registan Square, 104
Royal Palace of Bangkok, 166

MUSEUMS

Aeronautical Museum, 212
Archives of India, 126
Collegium Maius, 142
Galileo Museum, 156
Gutenberg Museum, 118
Museum of Arts and Crafts, 192
Muzeum II Wojny
Światowej w Gdańsku, 202
Nao Victoria Museum, 138
National Museum of
Ethiopia, 16
Neil Armstrong Museum of
Air and Space, 216
Red Cross Museum, 184
Robben Island Museum, 214
Sarajevo Museum 1878–1918, 194
Smithsonian Museum Of
Natural History, 14
Swindon Steam Railway
Museum, 178
Viking World Museum, 90

RELIGIOUS SITES

Aachen Cathedral, 86
Basilica of Saint-Remi, 76
Church of Saints Cyril and
Methodius, 88
Dome of the Rock, 78
Florence Cathedral, 116
Great Mosque of Cordoba, 84
Hagia Sophia Cathedral, 94
Kenchō-ji, 100
Kinkaku-ji, 112
Sheikh Lotfollah Mosque, 92
Sistine Chapel, 130
St. Basil's Cathedral, 144
Temple and cemetery of
Confucius, 38
Temple of Mahabodhi, 36
Western Wall, 60
Westminster Abbey, 160

STATUES, COLUMNS & MAUSOLEUMS

Column of Constantine, 68
Column of Marcus Aurelius, 64
Equestrian statue of Genghis
Kahn, 102
Go'ri Amir Mausoleum, 114
Lincoln Memorial, 174
Mausoleum of Augustus, 56
Mausoleum of Lenin, 196
Mausoleum of Simón
Bolívar, 176
Pillars of Hercules, 82
Republic Monument, 168
The Capitoline Wolf, 32
Statue of the warrior on
horseback, 46
Tomb of Napoleon, 170
Wall of Reformers, 134

NATURAL SITES

Captain Cook's Landing
Place, 162
Galapagos Islands, 182
Grütli meadow, 106
Hong Kong Bay, 180
Jamestown Settlement, 150
Victoria Falls, 188

WAR FIELDS

Archaeological site of
Carthage, 50
Checkpoint Charlie, 218
Marathon Mound, 42
Normandy Cemetery, 204
Trojan horse, 30
Cu Chi tunnels, 210
Wall of Constantinople, 120

MODERN SITES

Amsterdam Stock Ex., 148
Large Hadron Collider, 12
Science Gateway, 220
Wall Street Stock Ex., 200

www.ingramcontent.com/pod-product-compliance
Ingram Content Group UK Ltd.
Pitfield, Milton Keynes, MK11 3LW, UK
UKHW050909210525
6012UKWH00026B/293

9 781445 786551